Leading, Managing and Developing People

5th edition

Gary Rees and Ray French

The Chartered Institute of Personnel and Development is the leading publisher of books and reports for personnel and training professionals, students, and all those concerned with the effective management and development of people at work. For details of all our titles, please contact the publishing department:

tel: 020 8612 6204

email: publishing@cipd.co.uk

The catalogue of all CIPD titles can be viewed on the CIPD website:

www.cipd.co.uk/bookstore

An e-book version is also available for purchase from:

www.ebooks.cipd.co.uk

Leading, Managing and Developing People

5th edition

Gary Rees and Ray French

Chartered Institute of Personnel and Development

Published by the Chartered Institute of Personnel and Development
151 The Broadway, London SW19 1JQ

This edition first published 2016

Designed and typeset by Exeter Premedia Services, India

Printed in Great Britain by Ashford Colour Press Ltd

British Library Cataloguing in Publication Data

A catalogue of this publication is available from the British Library

ISBN 9781843984122
eBook ISBN 9781843984375

Chartered Institute of Personnel and Development

151 The Broadway, London SW19 1JQ
Tel: 020 8612 6200
Email: cipd@cipd.co.uk
Website: www.cipd.co.uk
Incorporated by Royal Charter.
Registered Charity No. 1079797

Shelfie

A **bundled** eBook edition is available with the purchase of this print book.

CLEARLY PRINT YOUR NAME ABOVE IN UPPER CASE

Instructions to claim your eBook edition:
1. Download the Shelfie app for Android or iOS
2. Write your name in **UPPER CASE** above
3. Use the Shelfie app to submit a photo
4. Download your eBook to any device

Contents

List of figures and tables

Acknowledgements

Leading, Managing and Developing People is underpinned by some classical insights and findings developed over many years, but at the same time it is a fast-moving area, strongly influenced by the wider economic and social context. This fifth edition contains new research findings, case studies and other examples to reflect topicality and enhance relevance for readers. We would like to thank the previous contributors from the fourth edition chapters and welcome our new contributors, Dr Matthew Anderson, De Wenjin Dai and Dr Peter Scott. Thanks are also due to Keri Dickens at CIPD Publishing for keeping us on track in an efficient and always pleasant way. We wish to thank, finally, reviewers of draft chapters for their constructive feedback and trust that we have responded to their observations in this fifth edition of our textbook.

Gary Rees
Ray French
University of Portsmouth Business School
April 2016

List of contributors

Matthew Anderson
Wenjin Dai
Ray French
David Hall
Liza Howe-Walsh
Margaret Mackay
Charlotte Rayner
Gary Rees
Sally Rumbles
Peter Scott
Alex Tymon

All the contributors work at the University of Portsmouth Business School, Portsmouth UK.

CIPD qualifications map

Leading, Managing and Developing People

The content of this CIPD module is covered as follows:

Leading, Managing and Developing People learning outcomes	Leading, Managing and Developing People chapters
1. Review and critically evaluate major contemporary research and debates in the fields of HRM and HRD.	Chapter 1: Introduction Chapter 2: The Scope and Nature of Human Resource Management and Human Resource Development Chapter 3: HRM Contributions in Different Settings Chapter 13: Summary Themes and Future Trends
2. Evaluate major theories relating to motivation, commitment and engagement at work and how these are put into practice by organisations.	Chapter 5: Leadership and Leader Development Chapter 7: Flexibility and the Psychological Contract Chapter 11: Managing the Employment Relationship Chapter 12: Performance Management, Motivation and Reward
3. Debate and critically evaluate the characteristics of effective leadership and the methods used to develop leaders in organisations.	Chapter 5: Leadership and Leader Development
4. Contribute to the promotion of flexible working and effective change management in organisations.	Chapter 6: Managing Change Chapter 7: Flexibility and the Psychological Contract Chapter 8: Organisational and Job Design Chapter 9: Recruitment and Selection
5. Critically discuss the aims and objectives of the HR function in organisations and how these are met in practice.	Chapter 8: Organisational and Job Design Chapter 9: Recruitment and Selection Chapter 10: Developing Employees Chapter 11: Managing the Employment Relationship Chapter 12: Performance Management, Motivation and Reward
6. Assess the contribution made by HRM and HRD specialists in different types of organisation.	Chapter 8: Organisational and Job Design Chapter 9: Recruitment and Selection Chapter 10: Developing Employees Chapter 11: Managing the Employment Relationship Chapter 12: Performance Management, Motivation and Reward

Leading, Managing and Developing People learning outcomes	Leading, Managing and Developing People chapters
7. Promote professionalism and an ethical approach to HRM and HRD practice in organisations.	Chapter 4: Professionalism and Ethics in Managing People Chapter 11: Managing the Employment Relationship Chapter 13: Summary Themes and Future Trends

Walkthrough of textbook features and online resources

LEARNING OUTCOMES

After reading this chapter, you should be able to:

- identify important themes within the area of leading, managing and developing people through an analysis of three case studies
- complete case study exercises which explore generic leading, managing and developing people issues
- familiarise yourself with the learning features within this book
- understand the structure of the book in relation to the CIPD Leading, Managing and Developing People unit (7002)

LEARNING OUTCOMES

At the beginning of each chapter a bulleted set of learning outcomes summarises what you can expect to learn from the chapter, helping you to track your learning.

 AGILENT TECHNOLOGIES

CASE STUDY 3.2

The move to reduce costs has seen a decline in the number of long-term assignments, with organisations utilising short-term assignments instead. Collecting data in this area holds many challenges and long-term case studies are rare.

knew expatriates were expensive but did not realise the extent. The challenge of tracking expatriates is echoed by many MNEs (see Doherty and Dickmann 2012).

CASE STUDIES

A number of case studies from different sectors and countries will help you place the concepts discussed into a real-life context.

REVIEW QUESTIONS

1. To what extent can there be a 'perfect shape' to an HR function in an organisation? Consider the arguments both for and against this proposition.

2. Does the HR business partner role sit most comfortably within private, public or third sector organisations? Support your answer with practical benefits.

3. How can the HR/HRD function build relationships with line managers so as to put improved working practices into effect?

4. What is meant by 'strategic HRD'? Evaluate the major components of strategic HRD.

REVIEW QUESTIONS

These questions are aimed at reinforcing what you have learnt in the chapter.

 REFLECTIVE ACTIVITY 2.2

To what extent can an organisation exercise duty of care to all its employees and at the same time drive towards the highest level of cost-efficiency? How can HR balance these potentially conflicting goals?

REFLECTIVE ACTIVITIES

Questions and activities throughout the text encourage you to reflect on what you have learnt and to apply your knowledge and skills in practice.

1   The HR department or function has changed considerably in the last 40 years, and currently tends to adopt a managerialist (corporate) position.

2   HR needs to take time to evaluate and justify itself as a function or face attack or possibly outsourcing or replacement.

3   Where HR sits within corporate planning is pivotal to its involvement with strategic and mainstream business activities.

4   HRD and strategic HRD play an important function in the development of employees to adding to business success.

5   The HR business partner model carries with it a series of potential benefits and limitations, and should therefore be adapted according to the organisation and context, and possibly face up to the fact that it simply won't work as a model.

KEY LEARNING POINTS

At the end of each chapter, key learning points consolidate your learning.

Aston Centre for Human Resources (2008) *Strategic Human Resource Management: Building research-based practice*. London: CIPD.

Boxall, P. and Purcell, J. (2008) *Strategic and Human Resource Management*. 2nd edition. Basingstoke: Palgrave Macmillan. This textbook is strong on theory surrounding strategic HR.

Caldwell, R. (2008) HR business partner competency models: recontextualising effectiveness. *Human Resource Management Journal*. Vol 18, No 3. pp275–294. This article provides useful arguments around the business partner model.

Rees, G. and Smith, P. (2014) (eds) *Strategic Human Resource Management: An international perspective*. London: Sage Publications.

EXPLORE FURTHER

Explore further boxes contain suggestions for further reading, encouraging you to delve further into areas of particular interest.

ONLINE RESOURCES FOR STUDENTS

- Glossary to support understanding of terminology
- Annotated web links
- Case studies
- Example essay/exam questions

Visit **www.cipd.co.uk/sss**

ONLINE RESOURCES FOR TUTORS

- PowerPoint slides – design your programme around these ready-made lectures.
- Lecturer's guide – including guidance on the activities and questions in the text.
- Case studies
- Example essay/exam questions

Visit **www.cipd.co.uk/tss**

EBOOK BUNDLING

CIPD have partnered with Shelfie to offer print and eBook bundling. Shelfie has built a free eBook bundling app for iOS and Android that allows you to get a discounted eBook if you own the print edition.

Visit **www.bitlit.com/how-it-works/**

LEADING, MANAGING AND DEVELOPING PEOPLE: AN OVERVIEW

CHAPTER 1

Introduction

GARY REES AND RAY FRENCH

LEARNING OUTCOMES

After reading this chapter, you should be able to:

- identify important themes within the area of leading, managing and developing people through an analysis of three case studies
- complete case study exercises which explore generic leading, managing and developing people issues
- familiarise yourself with the learning features within this book
- understand the structure of the book in relation to the CIPD Leading, Managing and Developing People unit (7002)
- locate or map the Leading, Managing and Developing People unit (7002) learning outcomes to particular chapters in the text.

1.1 OVERVIEW

Leading, managing and developing people forms a key part of everyday life in work organisations. While topics and issues covered in this book may fall within the formal remit of a specialist human resource management (HRM) function, there is equally a strong sense in which leading and managing employees infuses all aspects of working life.

In the previous edition of this book we focused upon recession and post-recession aspects of HRM and how these were manifested in practice. Whilst it is impossible to foresee the future and include every key aspect of leading and managing people, we start with a summary of the key findings of the CIPD Outlook Survey 2014/15:

1. Current and future priorities for HR functions include employee engagement (27%); managing change and cultural transformation (24%) (particularly public sector HR professionals); and leadership development and capability (21%) (the public sector citing this as a future priority).

2. How HR contributes to business performance, with 76% of HR professionals stating that they understand how business practices work, with the majority of both public and private sector professionals stating that 'HR ensured the organisation has the right people capability' (CIPD 2015a, p5).

3. Developing HR capability, by driving change, combining HR and commercial expertise.

4   HR's use of data and metrics to demonstrate impact, with 63% of respondents agreeing that HR data informs business decision-making, and the majority agreeing that HR draws insight from data to stimulate change and organisational improvement.

5   The profile of HR departments, with reported stagnation in the size of HR departments, and downsizing of the HR function more likely in the public than private sector. Half of the HR departments stated that they had undergone structural change in the last two years, with cost reductions quoted for just over a third of these organisations.

6   Routes into the profession and career paths, with the rise of internships cited by a quarter of respondents, but the majority of HR professionals reported that their organisation did not offer specific routes into HR for young people.

There is little doubt that the future challenges facing HR professionals will be substantial, with the demands of leading and managing people (both upward and downward) in organisations becoming even more demanding and complex.

We hope that insights contained within this book will help you both to manage people effectively and support other managers with people responsibilities.

Individual chapters within this book identify and discuss the core topics that make up the study and practice of leading, managing and developing people. We have organised the chapters into discrete areas – for example leadership, managing the employment relationship and performance management. However, managing people is a broad area of work and day-to-day events and challenges are best understood and acted on by taking an overview which goes beyond any one subdivision of HR work. This can be seen in Case Study 1.1 below, which deals with a single theme, but one that has broader ramifications in leading, managing and developing people.

 TREAD CAREFULLY BEFORE SAYING 'BAH! HUMBUG!'

CASE STUDY 1.1

As Christmas approaches, thoughts turn to the annual office bash. But given the tough economic climate, it is not surprising that many organisations look to cut costs. We consider whether an organisation that has always paid for a staff Christmas party, covering the cost of the venue, meal, entertainment and bar, can suddenly forego paying for this and instead ask employees to make an individual contribution.

If the employees of an organisation have received a fully subsidised Christmas party for many years, then it could be argued that it has become an implied form of the contract of employment (see Chapters 7 and 11) through custom and practice. Although it might seem a rather strange thing to become an implied term, many employees will see the Christmas party as a valuable benefit, particularly given their own outgoings at this time of year.

In this situation, the organisation may wish to consult with employees about ways of reducing Christmas party costs, for example by using a less expensive menu or some other cost-saving measures.

When the organisation really cannot afford to pay for it at all, it will need to consult with employees as this will be a variation of contract. Such a variation can only be achieved through mutual agreement. Employers should also be aware that imposing the change without agreement might lead to an employee resigning and then claiming constructive dismissal (where a worker resigns due to perceived breaches of contract). This scenario is unlikely and any claim may not succeed, but is possible nonetheless.

Source: HR-inform (2012)

A survey conducted on Christmas and New Year working arrangements in 2012/

13 identified other implications of special events at that time of year.

These included the following questions:

- Do you have a behaviour policy for the work Christmas party?
- Do you give advice on getting home after the Christmas party?
- Did any problems arise at the last work party/meal and, if so, what were the consequences of these?
- Can employees opt out of arranged celebrations if they do not celebrate Christmas?
- Can members of non-Christian faiths mark their own religious festival in the workplace?

Source: XpertHR (2012b)

We see here how Christmas parties can legitimately be viewed as a people management issue. As a result it may be that work organisations decide to devise a robust policy covering such events. Even if there is such a policy managers will need to exercise discretion and there are unlikely to be many 'right' answers. Managers should be prepared to be subtle and creative in seeking solutions: managing people is rarely viewed as a hard science. In this book we will show that in many areas of HR, one size definitely does not fit all. At the same time, there is a need to be fair and equitable, and policies can act as a useful way of working towards these aims.

Finally, HR managers wish to nurture their talented or key workers (whether we believe this term applies to everyone who makes a contribution, or just to a named subgroup of workers). Employees will often seek to work for a 'good employer' and being treated shabbily – at least in their own perception – might adversely affect their psychological contract; this is a term we go on to explore in Chapter 7, but is essentially the mental picture a worker has of how their input in an organisation relates to what they receive from it. If employees experience negative feelings (in this case about Christmas parties) they may come to see this as a sign that they do not, after all, work for a good employer, with all the consequences that such a feeling can lead to.

Questions

1   Summarise arguments for and against holding work Christmas parties in the context of people management. On balance, would you recommend they take place? Give reasons for your conclusion.

2   How would you seek to avoid talented workers of non-Christian faiths becoming disaffected by Christmas work celebrations?

1.2 INTRODUCTION

This chapter introduces the purpose, content and structure of the book. This fifth edition has been adapted to meet the requirements of the Leading, Managing and Developing People unit (7002). We have updated the book to include new research and survey report findings and have also devised newly relevant and topical reflective activities and case studies.

A consistent rubric has been developed for each chapter which includes the following key features:

- a set of learning outcomes
- an overview
- an introduction
- short reflective activities
- critical reflection
- a conclusion

- case studies
- key learning points
- review questions
- explore further (suggested further reading and references).

The text introduces a balance of theory and practice, drawing upon major research work, including theoretical and conceptual models through to major survey research findings. A combination of learning activities, including reflective activities, case studies, vignettes and links to relevant articles, are intended to bring the subjects to life and offer you scope for self-reflection. See 1.3 'The structure of the book' for more details.

Leading, managing and developing people is fundamentally a topical area and can draw debates and actions from every possible aspect of a business environment, from strategic decision-making to the number of car parking spaces that are available to staff and customers. Case Study 1.1 addressed the potentially light-hearted issue of the Christmas party, but the unintended consequences of such a singular event could be considerable, and employers need to consider their duty of care to employees. Case Study 1.2 continues the theme of employers managing well-being (and exercising duty of care) by addressing resilience in the workplace.

Constant and relentless change within an organisation can have a profound impact on employees, ranging from a reduction in motivation and engagement through to well-being, burnout and tragically suicide. Case Study 1.2 examines the notion of resilience, a possible mediator for both employee engagement and well-being.

 RESILIENCE AT WORKGURU

CASE STUDY 1.2

Workguru began trading in 2013 as an online service that aims to help build employee resilience at work. It uses interactive self-help material, messaging support from job coaches and offering more intensive support through one-to-one coaching delivered over the telephone.

Workguru's service is built on research by Dutch academics. In 2012, Suzanne Lagerveld – building on research by Blonk et al (2006) – published her findings comparing traditional cognitive behavioural therapy (CBT) with work-focused CBT, both delivered by therapists. She found that work-focused CBT achieved on average a full return to work 65 days earlier, with an estimated saving to the employer of $5,275, compared with the traditional CBT group.

Both the 2006 and the 2012 research used a specific work-focused brief CBT protocol that was assigned to those groups that achieved the faster return to work. Workguru contacted the academics and worked with them to translate the protocol into English, and then developed it for a digital market.

The team at WorkGuru includes clinical and work psychologists, a CBT specialist, a mindfulness practitioner and a team of job coaches. These specialists work together to combine work-focused CBT with other interventions that research has shown to work, including positive psychology, mindfulness and job coaching. Their approach integrates all the factors that enhance resilience: positive emotions, cognitive flexibility, meaning, social support and active coping styles.

'Resilience' describes our ability to adapt and function in the face of stress or trauma – it is our ability to 'bounce back'. Researchers have identified a number of psychosocial factors associated with resilience to stress. These include: positive emotions (including optimism and humour); cognitive flexibility (including positive explanatory style, positive reappraisal and acceptance); meaning (including religion, spirituality and altruism); social support (including role models); and active coping style (including exercise and training) (Southwick et al 2005).

We see that Workguru aim to put the concept of resilience into action by developing an infrastructure comprising specialists, who help ideas such as 'positive emotions' take effect in an actual work situation.

The overarching philosophy behind Workguru is that individuals cannot control everything, but we can change how we think about and respond to situations.

Sources: XpertHR (2014a), Lagerveld et al (2012), Southwick et al (2005)

Questions

1   How can the HR function adopt the approach proposed by Workguru in order to enhance resilience in the workplace?

2   To what extent is WorkGuru's evidence-based approach both preventative and cost-effective?

REFLECTIVE ACTIVITY 1.1

'All present and correct, Ma'am'

A recent CIPD *Absence Management* annual survey report (2015b) identified two opposing challenges: presenteeism and illegitimate absence. The survey reports that notably more organisations included 'illegitimate' absence within their top causes of absence for non-manual workers. Perhaps some of these reasons may be employees 'pulling sickies' due to conflicting demands of work and home.

Conversely, this report highlighted that a third of organisations reported an increase in employees coming to work in the past 12 months. Presenteeism is therefore more likely to have increased where long working hours are seen to be the norm, and where personal demands take precedence over employee well-being. Not surprising was the association of increases in presenteeism in organisations nearly twice as likely to report an increase in stress-related absence (and increase in mental health problems). More worryingly, 56% of organisations who noticed an increase in presenteeism have not taken any steps to discourage it.

1   How can HR professionals take steps to manage this contradiction?

2   What sort of advice can HR professionals provide line managers with in order to improve this particular situation?

Whilst presenteeism may be seen as a positive factor by some line managers, the need for the correct work–life balance remains significant in more turbulent work environments and further work intensification.

Our final case study focuses upon a context familiar to many post-recession organisations, where austerity simply has not disappeared and there is a need to manage the potential paradox of motivating and engaging staff whilst simultaneously operating a lean philosophy and approach.

LEAN AND MOTIVATED IN MEDTRONIC, GALWAY

Founded in 1949, Medtronic is the world's largest medical technology company, currently employing around 45,000 staff globally. With a mission to alleviate pain and restore patients to full health, the company is composed of six main business units developing and producing medical equipment and therapies to treat chronic diseases such as heart failure, diabetes, Parkinson's disease, urinary incontinence, chronic pain and spinal disorders. The company is increasingly engaging in training activities for healthcare practitioners. The US-based company operates across a number of countries, including Ireland. The medical devices industry forms an important part of Ireland's economy. With 24,000 workers employed in this sector, Ireland has the highest number of people per capita working in this area and is the second-largest European exporter of medical devices (European Foundation for the Improvement of Living and Working Conditions 2013a).

Medtronic in Galway

The company has been operating in Ireland since 1999, based both in Dublin and Galway. It employs around 2,000 employees at its Galway site, which makes this plant the company's largest in Europe. In Galway, Medtronic manufactures and has research and development responsibilities for a range of products for the company's Vascular Division, which include stents, stent delivery systems, angioplasty balloons and ancillary products for the treatment of coronary artery disease. Moreover, this site has become a centre of excellence for cardiac rhythm management, developing leading devices used for treating heart failure.

Out of the 2,000 employees in Galway, 1,300 fall into the category of semi-skilled process workers, who are organised by the Irish Services, Industrial, Professional and Technical Union (SIPTU). SIPTU represents the company's workforce at plant and sector level.

Once a worker's contract is made permanent, trade union membership becomes obligatory in a 'closed shop' model. However, trade union membership only covers the company's production staff; higher positions (for example, supervisor roles) are not included. Medtronic's Irish subsidiary and a smaller subsidiary in Brescia, Italy are currently company sites where a trade union is recognised.

The company is working in an industry in which both quality and innovation in products and procedures are crucial for business success. Since its establishment, Medtronic has introduced a series of product innovations, which has helped the company to secure its market position. The company is keen on increasing its efficiency by streamlining its production processes and cutting down on inefficiencies. Moreover, the company's Galway plant has a strategic interest in sustaining its production operations within the parent multinational firm where, compared to alternative production sites, it is subject to relatively high labour costs. For this purpose, Medtronic runs a Lean Six Sigma department in Galway.

Medtronic's business development has been affected by the financial crisis, and in this respect the company has recently experienced a decrease in the demand for its products. This fall in demand is mainly a result of the overall fall in sales volumes in the industry caused to a large extent by streamlining measures and reductions in public health budgets, with less expensive devices increasingly substituting for premium products (Roche and Teague 2012). Moreover, since 2008 the company's stock value has dropped significantly. In light of falling sales figures negatively affecting the company's growth and profit developments, the US parent company has since initiated a series of restructuring measures including redundancies and pay freezes.

Due to Medtronic Galway's position within the multinational company structure, an increase in pressure on the high-cost production site in the west of Ireland (in part due to relatively high labour costs) has been reported. Aware that competition for investment within the company was likely to rise, Medtronic Galway, together with the trade union, has put in place restructuring measures in the form of a pay freeze. However, some improvements to terms and conditions were also negotiated, including employees on fixed-term contracts gaining permanent employment contracts.

Despite the current economic climate, the company seems to have good relationships with both its staff and trade union representatives. While it has been reported that Medtronic has been experiencing considerable pressure during the most recent financial and economic crisis, there are no plans for downsizing the company's current workforce.

The workplace innovation at the centre of this case study was first introduced in 2011. In a search for greater efficiency and productivity as well as a reduction of waste, Medtronic Galway started redesigning its work organisation as the company's production partly shifted from line production to cellular manufacturing with lean practices. This process was launched to modernise the previous system of work organisation, which largely corresponded to typical line production.

This shift resulted in new work organisation and introduced teamwork involving small teams of staff (typically seven worker) working standing up in a u-shaped 'cell'. In contrast to more traditional line production, this set-up allows a team of workers to work on one product at a time. Moreover, the shift

also resulted in two important changes from the perspective of workers: firstly, all team members were trained in order to carry out each work task; secondly, a new role of team leader was created.

The cross-skilling of employees has since proven beneficial for both employees and the company: if a worker is absent, another team member can easily step in so production is not interrupted; the work is now less monotonous as workers are able to perform different work steps; and the workplace has become more interactive and engaging. The newly created position of team leader offers new career opportunities for experienced workers.

Introducing lean practices

For a number of years, Medtronic Galway had been investigating systems for streamlining its production. The company wanted to become market leader in its area and take a leading role in innovation within the company structure, and knew that a change in the production process was needed. It was expected that most improvements could take place in the company's production area, where workers carry out the same processes about 300 times per day. This was the first company department where innovative processes were introduced; subsequently new practices were also implemented in the company's support service area.

While finding that the amount of information on improvement tools was huge and nearly unmanageable, the company identified two major systems for increasing its efficiency. The first approach was Six Sigma, where improvement is largely based on statistics leading to process improvements. The second approach was Lean, which is largely based on learning by doing, leading to smaller but faster improvements. Lean management is based largely on trial and error from the experiences of the Japanese car producer Toyota. Medtronic Galway involved an expert from Toyota in the introduction of lean processes at the Galway site. Today, Medtronic Galway is making use of both approaches after adopting a Lean Six Sigma approach, which involves both strategic management for direction and bottom-up input.

Hoping to improve efficiency and reduce waste, the company first introduced an 'improvement engine', which, although initially seen as a success, was soon felt to have reached its limits. This improvement engine, in use between 2004 and 2008, was based on a lean methodology where several lean leadership roles were identified. Although this project generated considerable savings, which in turn made space for a new project, its methodology was felt to be too limited as not all the staff could be involved in the improvement process. Medtronic, however, had a keen interest in involving all workers in the improvement processes. As a next step, the company introduced pilots for lean processes in 2008, with the positive results of these pilots exceeding the company's expectations. According to Medtronic, the newly introduced lean processes unleashed great potential

among its workers, leading to an overall 5–10% increase in production.

However, the company has found that in order to maintain these positive results, a great deal of motivation to improve processes has become necessary. Nevertheless, the company is largely satisfied with the results stemming from the introduction of lean processes. Today, largely through the involvement of all of its workers, the company manages to engage its workforce and with their help finds solutions to problems that would otherwise be difficult for it to identify and address.

Source: European Foundation for the Improvement of Living and Working Conditions (2013a)

Question

Considering the changes that took place, how do you think that the following parties would feel about the changes:

- employees
- managers
- trade union?

1.3 THE STRUCTURE OF THE BOOK

The learning outcomes and content for the Leading, Managing and Developing People unit can be subdivided into three particular areas: contextual factors; core themes; and effective practice. As we have already stressed, readers need to appreciate the context within which HR operates and how HR can directly or indirectly affect the leadership, management and development of employees. Three core themes of leadership, change and flexibility assist in understanding how the HR function can add value to organisations, whilst the effective practice section of this book addresses how functional aspects of HR can make a direct impact upon organisations and organisational performance.

The text is therefore presented in five parts (see Figure 1.1):

- **Part 1** provides the introduction and setting the scene of the text.
- **Part 2** addresses the contextual factors which have shaped the nature of HR, and considers the aims, objectives and contribution of HRM across the public, private, third sectors and across small, medium, large and multinational organisations.
- **Part 3** addresses the core themes that run through the process of leading, managing and developing people. Leadership, managing change and flexibility form the bulk of these core themes.

- **Part 4** considers how HR practitioners and managers can turn relevant and valid theory into practice and use research findings to add value in terms of worker and organisational performance.
- **Part 5** comprises the conclusion to the book and makes suggestions about the future of HR by drawing upon various research findings and reports.

Chapters 1 and 13 introduce and conclude each topic through the use of integrated arguments, case study illustrations and contemporary thinking and research.

Figure 1.1 The structure of the text

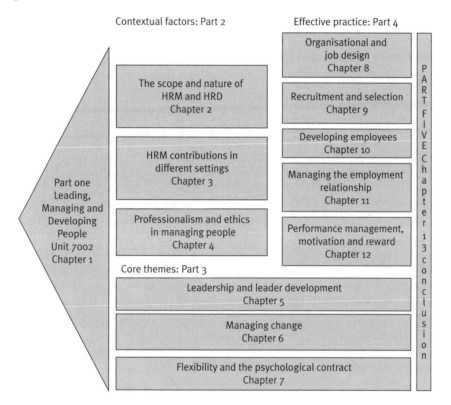

1.4 CONCLUSION

The nature of leading, managing and developing people makes this is a highly challenging and integrative area, but also a very rewarding one. Having a good grounding in leading, managing and developing people is core knowledge for those working in HR. We trust that you find the following chapters informative, thought-provoking and a useful framework for understanding leading, managing and developing people.

At this point it is appropriate to introduce brief clarification on terminology. As we will see in Chapter 2, tasks involving leading, managing and developing people often fall to specialist HR managers within work organisations. In an important sense, however, general or line managers need to be involved in managing people too in their day-to-day work. The term 'HR manager' therefore denotes anyone who takes a role in leading, managing and developing people. In some cases HR work is outsourced to specialist providers. In view of this complex picture some writers use the term 'human resource practitioner' to encompass anyone whose work touches our subject area. For our purposes, though, the terms 'human resource manager' and 'human resource practitioner' are sufficiently close for both to be used interchangeably and you will find examples of both terms throughout the book.

THE AIMS, OBJECTIVES AND CONTRIBUTION OF HRM

The Scope and Nature of Human Resource Management and Human Resource Development

GARY REES

LEARNING OUTCOMES

After reading this chapter, you should be able to:

- have an appreciation of the role and function of HRM and HRD
- explore approaches to, and models of, HRM and HRD
- be aware of and evaluate models of strategic HRM and HRD
- consider the links between organisational strategy and HR strategy
- understand the interrelationship between line management and HRM/HRD
- identify recent research findings about how HR equates into practice
- assess the value and contribution of HRM and HRD.

2.1 OVERVIEW

In Part 2 of this book, we examine some of the factors influencing the nature of human resource management (HRM) and human resource development (HRD). The aim is to lay the groundwork for subsequent sections in which we firstly identify core themes in leading, managing and developing people (Chapters 5–7), and then go on to examine effective practice in selected areas (Chapters 8–12). In Chapter 3, we will highlight the ways in which leading, managing and developing people may vary across different types of organisational settings. In this chapter we will discuss some even more fundamental questions, including how HRM and HRD are defined, who does – and who should – take responsibility for leading, managing and developing people, and whether HRM and HRD can be regarded as strategic activities. Underlying these questions is the concept of HR practitioners adding value, possibly by taking on the role of business partner.

It is useful at this stage to clarify the relationship between the two terms HRM and HRD. They could be considered as separate aspects of an overall HR function, while one of these sub-functions may take precedence over the other at any one point. Within academic models, HRD is typically subsumed within HRM when functional aspects are taken into consideration. In this chapter we will explore the HR function in terms of

HRM and HRD, without making judgements as to how these two areas converge or separate themselves. Dependent upon the context, some organisations may combine the HRM and HRD functions into an HR function, while other organisations may have a predominance of HRM within the HR function.

HR requires the collaboration of line and senior management. We attempt to pinpoint the value of HR and, within the overall aims of our book, look at key research findings from recent research, which inform current debates.

2.2 INTRODUCTION

Robert Townsend, former CEO of Avis (1981), likened the HR function ('personnel' as it was typically known then) to a malignant growth. Townsend claimed that if personnel people were left unchecked, they would multiply and ultimately take over the company. His controversial and, we can assume, provocative analogy is that of serious and possibly terminal disease. Personnel is therefore by definition abnormal and pathological, thus requiring treatment. One important task of an organisation, according to Townsend, is to stem the growth of the personnel function and, if necessary, cut it out altogether.

Denigrating Townsend's notion of personnel should be an easy task, and we might also question whether such an unpleasant and, for many of us, distressing analogy is appropriate at all. It does shine a light, though, on the negative reputation that HR or personnel has sometimes had, and points to the need for HR practitioners to demonstrate clear valued contributions to an organisation.

 REFLECTIVE ACTIVITY 2.1

Despite the change of name from 'Personnel' to 'HR', it could be argued that the HR function is still suffering from a lack of status and, like Cinderella, does not get invited to the ball (or top table). Why is it that HR, on the whole, lacks the reputation to make strategic contributions to organisations and establish a strong reputation for itself?

We will argue that the role and function of HR has transformed itself over the last 40 years or so. However, there will no doubt be examples of the full span of traditional personnel and modern HR in contemporary UK organisations. To what extent can HR be pigeonholed into structural or functional compartments, thereby limiting its scope and impact?

Ulrich, quoted by Brockett (2010, p11), stated that, 'I think that HR people should see themselves as a professional services group within their own organisation, being a key account manager for the most important clients. Their job is to assess the resources available and use their knowledge to determine how best to transfer those resources to client productivity.'

However, before we look at contemporary HR roles, some historical perspective is useful, and it is important to consider the transition from personnel management to HR, and to address definitions in order to make appropriate contrasts.

2.3 DEFINITIONS OF PERSONNEL MANAGEMENT, HUMAN RESOURCE MANAGEMENT AND HUMAN RESOURCE DEVELOPMENT

2.3.1 PERSONNEL MANAGEMENT

We begin by considering a widely used definition of 'personnel management' from several decades ago: 'Personnel management aims to achieve both efficiency and justice, neither of which can be pursued successfully without the other. It seeks to bring together and develop into an effective organisation the men and women who make up an enterprise, enabling each to make his/her own best contribution to its success both as an individual and as a member of a working group. It seeks to provide fair terms and conditions of employment, and satisfying work for those employed' (IPM, quoted in Hendry 1995, p10).

As we can see here, personnel management is perceived as occupying a neutral position, placed between employers (in the form of management), and other rank and file employees. Its role was reinforced by the development of policies and procedures indicating professional independence and objectivity. An emphasis upon standardisation and equal treatment would often underlie such policies.

2.3.2 HUMAN RESOURCE MANAGEMENT AND HUMAN RESOURCE DEVELOPMENT

Any brief consideration of definitions of HRM elicits a set of definitions which differentiate HR from personnel, in academic terms at least. Storey (1995, p5) defines HRM as: 'a distinctive approach to employment management which seeks to achieve competitive advantage through the strategic development of a highly committed and capable workforce, using an integrated array of cultural, structural and personnel techniques'.

However, definitions of HRM are by no means identical, or even especially similar. Boxall and Purcell (2000, p184) argue that 'HRM includes anything and everything associated with the management of the employment relationship in the firm. We do not associate HRM solely with a high commitment model of labour management or with any particular ideology or style of management.'

Whilst a universal and generally accepted definition of HRM is lacking, the same could be said for defining HRD. HRD has been defined by Stewart and McGoldrick (1996, p1) as follows: 'Human resource development encompasses activities and processes which are intended to have impact on organisational and individual learning. The term assumes that organisations can be constructively conceived of as learning entities, and that the learning processes of both organisations and individuals are capable of influence and direction through deliberate and planned interventions. Thus, HRD is constituted by planned interventions in organisational and individual processes.'

Whilst defining HRM and HRD may prove to be a tricky task, the nature, scope and objectives of HRM and HRD may change considerably in differing contexts. The historical background, senior management philosophy and practice, external forces and internal forces may shape different outcomes as far as what HRM/HRD actually does within the organisation.

In terms of what HR typically 'does', we could include the following as typical: HR planning, job and organisational design (see Chapter 8); recruitment, selection and induction (see Chapter 9); training and development (see Chapter 10); managing the employment relationship (see Chapter 11); pay, reward and performance management (see Chapter 12); ethical treatment of people including equal opportunities and diversity management (see Chapters 4 and 11); health and safety; knowledge management; mentoring; and disciplinary and grievance-handling, to name just some.

2.4 THE SCOPE AND NATURE OF HRM AND HRD

In understanding what HR does in an organisation it can be useful to take a historical perspective. Who actually started the HRM process in an organisation (eg a CEO deciding that due to growth of the organisation, an HR function and HR manager needed to be brought in) can provide a starting point from which to trace its subsequent development. The question of why the HR function was started (perhaps with specific goals in mind, such as identifying training gaps, dealing with increased specialist recruitment, etc) is also highly relevant. Following this, identifying key milestones in the history of the HR function may provide further understanding of how HR has evolved (eg the introduction of a performance management system). Whilst each organisation evolves in its own inimitable fashion, generic models of the goals of HRM can, nonetheless, be considered.

2.5 HRM GOALS

Whilst the academic debate surrounding the defining of HRM goals continues, Boxall and Purcell (2008, p20) suggest that there are four underpinning motives in HRM:

- *Cost-effectiveness* – maintaining stakeholder loyalty and trust is essential here, and this may mean running the business within budgetary constraints or maximising profits.
- *Legitimacy* – in essence, the allocation of moral legitimacy and ethical standing in society (see Chapter 4).
- *Flexibility* – in order to cope with change, organisational flexibility is vital for survival. It incorporates both short-term responsiveness and long-term agility (see Chapter 7).
- *Autonomy* – particularly managerial autonomy and the power to act. The political context may bring about change in managerial behaviour which may need some regulation in terms of corporate social responsibility.

The goals of HRD could be defined simply as developing and improving the performance of individuals and organisations, and we might also include team performance at this point.

In addition to this, 'the most obvious role HR has to play is as the expert on ethical employment practices (which is a core strand of corporate responsibility)' (CIPD 2013a, p5).

Whilst the various goals of HR may differ across private, public and not-for-profit sectors (see Chapter 3), there will also be some similarities. Current UK public sector HR goals may tie in with strategic initiatives linked to the Gershon Efficiency Review (2004) and any other key governmental initiatives; for example, Agenda for Change, commissioning, private finance initiatives and best-value-type initiatives. Ultimately, efficiencies (savings) are sought, with the stated goal of maintaining, or even increasing, service-level quality, which means that employees will ultimately have to work harder or, more euphemistically, to work 'smarter'.

Managers in the private sector will already be familiar with the imperative for efficiency gains and, as we will note in the next chapter, the third (or not-for-profit) sector is also facing pressures in this regard.

 REFLECTIVE ACTIVITY 2.2

To what extent can an organisation exercise duty of care to all its employees and at the same time drive towards the highest level of cost-efficiency? How can HR balance these potentially conflicting goals?

In order to move HR from a mere internal function, we need to analyse the broader strategic context within which it operates to consider whether HR can be strategic in its intent, actions and contribution.

2.6 STRATEGY AND HR

Strategy in its most basic sense is a plan of where the organisation would like to go. Although a strategy may take the form of a statement, it is also likely to be supported by strategic plans and imperatives that make up the building blocks required to meet its planned destination. A strategy should not be envisaged as an end in itself, as there may be a requirement to change course, or to embark on several journeys. One metaphor for business strategy is that of travel. So your strategy might be to travel in a northerly direction. At some points in time people might observe you travelling toward the south. However, your long-term strategic intent is still to move northwards and your apparent change of direction might be a short-term retreat or tactical manoeuvre.

De Wit and Meyer (2004, p50) define strategy as 'a course of action for achieving an organisation's purpose'. Taken in its broadest sense, this may not automatically mean profit generation and maximisation, or market domination. Strategy could be determined from more of a bottom-up approach, for example in a workers' collective, than a purely top-down approach; or alternatively a range of key stakeholders/shareholders can be involved in making strategic decisions.

There may also be a vision or mission statement to accompany a strategy. The vision is sometimes a means of providing employees with a notion of where the organisation is heading and the values associated with it. The mission statement should reinforce to employees where the company is intending to go, but is often directed at shareholders or customers.

Possessing an organisational strategy and HR strategy is not enough. Strategic fit between HR strategy, HR practices and organisational strategy is paramount (Wang and Shyu 2008). So how is such strategic fit accomplished? One method is to consider the vertical and horizontal integration of HR policies and procedures. The vertical fit is important in terms of achieving organisational goals through ensuring the alignment of HR activities to strategy. Horizontal fit plays an essential role in making use of these resources. Horizontal integration of HR activities includes aligning different HR activities such as recruitment and selection, performance management and reward so that each activity supports (rather than contradicts/interferes with) other HR activities. Vertical integration includes the way in which these activities fit into and support overall organisational activities, including the organisational vision, mission, etc.

In order to assess the extent to which HR as a function can be strategic in its thinking and actions, we need to consider the various approaches/models of HR and the extent to which these align with strategic intent.

2.7 MODELS OF HRM AND STRATEGIC RM

Hall (in Gilmore and Williams 2009, p144) defines strategic HRM as 'not any one particular HR strategy, but is a framework for shaping a number of people management strategies'.

While the analysis of the employment relationship and context is important, Beardwell and Claydon (2010) argue that two other issues affect the definition of HRM. First, the significance of HRM is variable, sometimes with emphasis upon people, strategy, employment relationships, etc. Secondly, HRM is derived from a range of antecedents, and depends on the stance and philosophy of the analyst.

Figure 2.1 The hard model of HRM

Source: Fombrun et al (1984, p35)

These definitions also ally themselves to the hard and soft models of HRM (Fombrun et al 1984, Beer et al 1984). Hard models emphasise using employees to gain competitive advantage and focus on business and employment strategies by linking HR to business systems. Soft models, contrastingly, emphasise employee commitment and engagement, and attempt to align the interests of employees and management (see also Chapter 11). Devanna et al (1984) suggest that within the organisation there needs to be an alignment of mission/strategy, the organisational structure and HRM. External to the organisation are forces (eg political, cultural and economic) impacting upon the organisation. This approach assumes that HR emerges from the other factors, with strategy as the primary driver, and that HR needs to seek a 'best fit' within this context.

Another approach found within the field of HRM is the resource-based view of the firm; namely one 'that focuses on the resources and capabilities controlled by a firm as sources of competitive advantage' (Barney and Hesterly 2008, p74).

Another approach used in HR is that of the 'best practice' model, often referred to as 'high commitment' or 'high involvement' HRM, in which managers consider how bundles of effective HR practice merge together.

Beer et al. (1984) incorporates human resource flow, rewards and the work system within a soft model of HRM. Pivotal to these three concepts is employee influence. The interchange of these four concepts help us understand the role and function of HR within organisations.

2.7.1 CRITIQUE OF BEST FIT AND BEST PRACTICE MODELS

A major criticism of the best fit model is that it may ignore employee interests, and be ignorant of some of the important aspects of the psychological contract (see Chapter 7). The focus of the best fit model may be the pursuit of economic performance to the detriment of everything else. There may also be academic criticisms when addressing the measurement of various HR practices. How do we assess the validity of best fit practices?

The transient nature of strategy and the need for constant change also makes alignment of current and future needs difficult. When considering the best practice model, it is difficult to argue that HRM can apply across all organisational settings at all times. To what extent do HR practices transfer from the United States to Eastern Europe or the Indian subcontinent, for example? Another central concern is the extent to which organisations can adopt a long-term approach in reality.

In order to assess whether the 'fit' has been appropriate, it may be necessary to gauge this against some sort of measure. One possible approach may be to consider the balanced scorecard.

2.7.2 BALANCED SCORECARD

Another model that helps to assess the contribution that HR makes to a business is that of the balanced scorecard. The CIPD *Human Capital* reporting survey (2004a) argues that the central focus in this model is upon vision and strategy, with four key supporting elements that require targets and measure taken, namely:

- *Learning and growth* – relating to how we sustain our ability to change and improve (see also Chapters 6 and 12).
- *Customer* – how we should appear to our customer (see also Chapter 4).
- *Financial* – how we should appear to our shareholders.
- *Internal business processes* – to satisfy shareholders and customers, what business processes must we excel at?

This model assumes planned and effective communication (internally and externally) to be a key imperative. The question arises then as to what level HR can become involved in developing and measuring the balanced scorecard.

Whilst the scorecard takes into account important aspects such as customers, contextual factors may be omitted. The Bath model may be useful in providing an understanding of such factors.

2.8 THE BATH MODEL OF HRM AND INNOVATION

The concepts of human, social and organisational capital are not new. The Bath model adds extra understanding by providing contextual issues such as: climate, trust and culture as the platform from which innovative outputs can then emerge. Where traditional human capital approaches have addressed inputs and outputs, the context is often overlooked. There is now an appreciation that employees work within teams and contexts, relying upon successful working relationships in order to add value to the organisation, with less emphasis upon the measurement of an individual's performance (CIPD 2012a).

2.9 HRD AND STRATEGIC HRD

However, as we noted at the start of this chapter, 'mainline' HR may not necessarily include HRD and strategic HRD. HRD may be considered to be a sub-set of HR, and strategic HRD a sub-set of strategic HR. But the field of HRD has grown rapidly in the last 30 years and 'development' as a theme cuts through many traditional HR areas. The current heightened interest in talent management (see Pilbeam and Corbridge 2010) includes a great deal of debate and research around talent development; see also Martin (2012).

The definition of development carries with it a series of different connotations and meanings. Thomas (2001, p184) defines it as 'a process of competency attainment and of self-differentiation in the sense of progressively distinguishing oneself from the environment and from other people in order to create a unique self-identity'.

Gubbins and Garavan (2009) argue that the primary responsibility of HRD professionals traditionally focused on identifying, selecting and evaluating training programmes. In effect this equates to transactional HR. However, Gubbins and Garavan contend that the role of HRD includes the consideration of environmental forces, and how the development of employees can add to competitive advantage.

Beer and Spector (1989, p25) define strategic HRD as 'a proactive, system-wide intervention, linked to strategic planning and cultural change. This contrasts with the traditional view of training and development as consisting of reactive, piecemeal interventions in response to specific problems.'

Perhaps the question of where HRD sits as a discipline is a moot point. On a micro level, can HRD be aligned to adult learning and associated psychological theories? On the other hand, at a macro level, where national policy and HRD will be linked, the influence of educational policy and societal impact should be investigated. Wang and Sun (2009) argue that economics, psychology and system theory constitute foundations of HRD.

McCracken and Wallace (2000) devised a model depicting nine key characteristics of strategic HRD. Underpinning these characteristics are a strong learning culture, strategic change focus and a highly mature organisation in HRD terms. These nine characteristics bear similarity with the strategic HR theory outlined above. The first characteristic that McCracken and Wallace identify is that of shaping organisational missions and goals.

Secondly, there is top management leadership (including support). Thirdly, the environmental scanning by senior management is in HRD terms. Fourthly, there are HRD strategies, plans and policies in place. Fifthly, strategic partnerships exist with line management. Following that, there are strategic partnerships with HRM. The seventh key characteristic is that trainers act as organisational change consultants. The penultimate characteristic is the ability to influence corporate culture. Lastly, there is emphasis upon cost-effectiveness evaluation.

To what extent are skills, knowledge and core competencies the drivers of innovation and the key sources of competitive advantage (Gratton 2000)? If core competence leads to organisational capability and competitiveness, then developing employee competence will be a strategic priority.

The CIPD *Learning and Development* survey 2015 included some useful insights and conclusions on various learning and development (L&D) issues:

Role and purpose of L&D

1   Learning and development is usually incorporated within the HR department – in over two-fifths of organisations L&D is a specialist function/role within the HR department and in one-fifth it is part of generalist HR activities.

2   L&D strategy is extremely aligned with the needs of the business in a quarter of organisations and a further two-fifths report that they are broadly aligned, with some discrepancies. Just 6% report no alignment.

3   Respondents are evenly split regarding whether they have experienced barriers in achieving business alignment. The most common barriers are L&D practitioners' lack of clarity regarding the business strategy and lack of resources, but also lack of interest or understanding of the purpose and capability of L&D from business leaders.

Trends in L&D

1   On-the-job training, in-house development programmes and coaching by line managers or peers remain the most popular development methods.

2   Learning technologies are more common in larger organisations.

3   Three-quarters of organisations currently offer coaching or mentoring and an additional 13% plan to offer it in the next year. Most expect to increase their use of coaching.

4   Most L&D content is developed from scratch.

5   Approximately two-thirds of organisations offer training to non-employee groups, most commonly students, clients or volunteers, depending on sector.

6   The most common organisational changes that will affect L&D over the next two years are closer alignment with the business strategy and more emphasis on monitoring and evaluation. Devolving responsibility to learners and line managers is also anticipated to be among the top changes.

Learning technologies

Three-quarters of organisations use learning technologies, but to varying effect, and many lack confidence in their ability to harness technologies in increasing of L&D interventions.

Leadership development

Most organisations plan to conduct leadership development in the next 12 months, focusing on equipping line managers to improve staff performance, changing/enhancing organisational culture and improving leadership skills, particularly with a strategic focus.

Talent management

Nearly three-fifths undertake talent management activities, through high potential in-house development schemes, mentoring and buddying schemes.

Developing L&D professionals

Focusing on business and commercial awareness and the ability to work collaboratively are key success factors in L&D. A quarter of organisations integrate findings from social/behavioural science into practice.

Assessing the impact of L&D activity

One-seventh of companies don't evaluate their L&D initiatives, and one-third rely upon 'happy sheet' satisfaction scores. Learner and manager reflection feedback are the most commonly used method to assess the effectiveness of L&D interventions. More than half of companies always share their results internally, with a fifth doing so externally.

Economic situation and training spend

More than half of the public sector report their L&D budget has decreased over the last year, whereas the private sector report that a quarter has increased and a quarter decreased in budget. A similar picture reflects the L&D headcount figures increasing in the private and decreasing in the public sector.

 REFLECTIVE ACTIVITY 2.3

Think of an organisation, and consider the following questions:

1   What makes this organisation distinct?

2   What precisely is the organisation good at doing (ie what are its core competences)?

3   What has led to the organisation being successful?

4   How has any HRD intervention assisted its current competitive position?

5   To what extent is the HRD/L&D function operating like organisations described within the CIPD 2015 *Learning and Development* survey?

The HRD function can play an important part in developing an organisation's culture to learn and its aspiration to be a 'learning organisation'. However, caution needs to be adopted here, in that we need to continually strive to link learning with performance (Henderson 1997).

The interplay of HRD and HRM will continue to prove challenging to organisations. In some cases there are obvious structural divides in organisations; for example, HRM and HRD departments that don't particularly work well together and deliberately separate out the functional aspects. In other cases, there is a strong synergy of activities that seamlessly integrate with organisational practices, and add value, and are seen to be adding value.

2.10 THE SHAPE OF HR

Harrison (2009, p297) provides a useful framework when deciding the shape of the L&D function, which can then be extended to HR more generally. First, there is the line-managed function, where line managers are handed the main responsibility for HRD/HRM. Secondly, the HR and HRD function could be outsourced.

Thirdly, there is the three-legged stool model proposed by Ulrich (1997). Within the line-managed function, there is very much a devolved approach, handing over the majority of responsibility to line managers. The outsourced model may work well for specific aspects of HR and HRD; for example, assessment centres and competence development. Some of the key determinants in deciding whether to outsource include cost-efficiency, added value, control and partnership.

Previous work by Harrison (2005) cited three other shapes that HRM/HRD could adopt: as a cost or profit centre; as a consultancy; or the traditional centralised function. Operating as a profit centre may prove more attractive to an organisation than viewing HR as a cost centre, which does not necessarily generate its own revenue and therefore is a drain on corporate budgets. The argument of accountability may be less profound if a profit centre is generating sufficient funds. It could be argued that an HR function that can 'sell' its services successfully exhibits a level of professionalism within the market. However, the converse argument could also be true. HR operating as a consultancy service may bring into question the internal/external fit, and to what extent the 'consultancy' aligns with corporate culture and values.

In a CIPD survey (2013b), just over half of HR professionals reported that their departments outsource some activities. This recent trend offers another perspective on the shape of HR and shows again the importance of contextual factors, eg developments in technology which enable activities to be outsourced, possibly to another country.

2.10.1 HR BUSINESS PARTNER MODEL

Perhaps one of the more talked-about current models is that of the HR business partner.

Ulrich's original work in 1997 emphasised four key roles that HR need to adopt:

- strategic partners
- administrative experts (shared services)
- employee champions
- change agents.

If HR adopts a more business-focused approach, as advocated by Ulrich et al (2008), then the emphasis upon customer focus, cost efficiencies, innovation and the ability to respond quickly to changes is highly important. Business partnership describes the relationship between HR managers (partner) and line/functional managers within an organisation, with an emphasis upon outputs and performance measures, and a view to increasing effectiveness and efficiency of the organisation as a whole.

A research report produced by the CIPD (2007a) found that less than 30% of respondents had introduced the model in full, with another 30% having partially introduced the Ulrich model.

Perhaps larger organisations are more likely to adopt the Ulrich model, commonly known as the 'three-legged stool', whereby three functional areas of HR include (CIPD 2010a):

- Shared services handling transactional services, such as absence monitoring, payroll, etc. The emphasis here is upon low-cost and effective HR administration.
- Centres of excellence, consisting of small teams of HR experts with specialised knowledge of leading-edge HR solutions. Competitive advantage is sought through HR innovations, such as reward, learning, engagement and talent management.
- Strategic business partners working with business leaders to influence strategy formulation and strategy implementation. Some activities include organisational and people capability building, resource and talent planning, intelligence gathering, etc.

A report from Henley Business School looked at the factors behind successful HR departments and asked how others could do better. The Henley report found that the majority of non-HR professionals believed that getting the operational side of HR right was more important than the function understanding business strategy; and while chief executives and board-level colleagues valued strategic skills more than operational, this was never as much as HR did. It also suggested that: 'Some functions operate in victim mode, which isn't conducive to securing investment or confidence in the function' (*Personnel Today* 2012).

2.10.2 BUSINESS PARTNERING: THE COUNTER ARGUMENTS

Pitcher (2008) argues that the business partner model had not resulted in strategic thinking, and was primarily only a change in title. He cites the example of Elizabeth Arden, where the HR director, Gabriele Arend, disagreed with any model that split HR professionals into recruiting, training and employee relations experts. Her company is moving towards a traditional structure, where HR employees are trained to develop generalist knowledge.

A CIPD factsheet (2015b) recommended exercising caution when adopting the business partner model and suggests that there is a danger of creating silos when the HR function is segmented because one size does not fit all.

Perhaps the key question comes down to credibility and contribution, summed up succinctly in a Deloitte report (2009, p8): 'The business partners' greatest failing has been their inability to convince senior managers that they have the necessary business acumen to contribute to the strategic debate.' The CIPD factsheet (2015b) supports this argument by stating that the HR function needs to focus on both short-term financial goals and maintaining longer-term objectives, such as organisational health and long-term people performance issues. In addition to this, the HR function must support the organisational strategy and maintain credibility, particularly from board-level members.

Ways of strengthening partnering

The CIPD (2015b) argue that the HR business partnering relationship should be regularly reviewed and strengthened by:

- adopting an analytical approach to business performance measures through people metrics
- ensuring that business partners are involved from the outset in the planning process, are prepared, and also spend time exploring the broader aspects of the business context
- being able to communicate through business language, particularly through HR metrics and their links to business performance

- setting personal objectives for strategic HR partners aligned to those of managers who share their business area
- using tools to obtain a broad-ranging view of the HR function, including business partners, to see the extent to which they are fulfilling their role.

CASE STUDY 2.1

BUSINESS PARTNERING AT THE AA

The Automobile Association has undergone significant change since 2004, having passed between three different owners. The overriding strategic imperative of these changes was to increase profitability. The HR function developed a strategy and HR business partner model to support the new business targets and help drive commercial success. In order for Hazel Lee, the HR manager, to grow profits from £100m in 2005 to £300m in 2008, she had to dovetail HR and business strategy.

HR business partners were appointed and made responsible for planning the people strategies for the AA's business units. Three senior business partner roles were set up to cover the following:

- corporate, policy and reward
- insurance, driving school, publishing and signs
- road operations.

In addition to this, a communications section was set up to integrate the different functions, which all reported to the HR director.

A new competency framework identifying key behaviours and experience requirements to operate at business partner level, including commerciality, influencing, operational decision-making and facilitating change, was introduced.

The new-look HR function was a leaner department, now operating with 60 employees rather than the previous 85.

The strategic business themes were:

- business focus (more profitable business)
- operational efficiency (lower operating costs with industry-best quality of service)

- brand differentiation and scale (by leverage of strategic advantage driving sales and market share).

The HR department looked at how it could deliver value to the business in each of these three areas.

In practice, this meant that Lee and her fellow business partners were automatically invited to operational management team meetings within their specialist area. In effect, emphasis was given to the proactive capabilities of HR, which led to expectations from the operational team that HR would make a continuous contribution. The learning curve for all HR business partners was a steep one.

HR's expertise with managing human capital meant that the types of roles and competencies required to meet the business strategies could be created by HR.

According to Lee, some of the critical success factors included:

- HR seizing the business strategy quickly through buy-in
- strong leadership within HR
- business partners having sound commercial knowledge and focus on the right organisational issues
- HR strategy developing alongside business strategy
- performance measures to demonstrate the tangible benefits of having business partners
- some quick wins, and the ability to deliver with speed, then focus on longer-term projects
- a seat on the board for the HR director.

Source: Suff (2008)

www.XpertHR.co.uk

Question

1   Despite the AA being a highly
    unionised organisation, why did

the HR business partner model
appear to be an appropriate
choice in terms of improving the
value of HR?

REFLECTIVE ACTIVITY 2.4

The changing nature of HRM

Using the analogy of management of the transformational process, four key themes emerged from the CIPD research report, *Landing Transformational Change: Closing the gap between theory and practice (CIPD 2015d)*.

1   Relational leadership – transforming change achieved through relationships and social interactions with organisational members rather than authority and control.

2   Building trust – delivering the enabling conditions in which significant change can thrive.

3   Voice, dialogue and rethinking resistance, where labels of resistance are replaced with understanding of employee voice as legitimate and enabled through dialogue.

4   Emotion, energy and momentum, by managing the change process by maintaining levels of energy and momentum within the change process.

If we turn the emphasis away from change management and focus this approach to the HR function, how could HR operate within the spirit of the change process? How could HR operate in the way described under these four principles?

2.11 CAPABILITY BUILDING BY THE HR FUNCTION

Another view is presented by Deloitte Consulting LLP and Bersin in their report 'Global human capital trends 2014: Engaging the 21st-century workforce', which identifies three key areas of capability for business-orientated HR professionals. These are:

- HR and talent skills, including: technical HR skills such as training, recruitment, employee relations and compensation strategies, which need to be refreshed each year as new technologies and strategies emerge; a deep understanding of the labour market in the area and sector in which their organisation operates; the ability to manage a service operation; and high-level skills across multiple technologies and with data, statistics and analytics.
- Business, industry and global skills, including a deep understanding of their organisation's business, sector and global reach, covering, for example, how their organisation makes money, what drives long-term competitive advantage, new product development and how to drive innovation.
- Leadership, management and change implementation skills, including the ability to achieve practical results through change management.

Their research found that less than 8% of the HR leaders who responded to the global survey thought that their HR team had the skills needed to meet the challenges of the global environment and consistently deliver innovative programmes driving business impact. While 27% of business leaders responding to the survey rated HR as excellent or good in delivering

HR and talent management, 42% believed that their HR team was underperforming or just getting by. This survey indicates that improving HR capabilities and skills may be desirable for many organisations, and can be both an objective for HR transformation where the required skills are lacking and a means of transforming the HR function in practice.

For further discussion regarding the future implications for HR, see Chapter 13. The shape of the HR/HRD function may evolve through historical developments, or may be deliberately changed to meet the needs of key decision-makers. Perhaps the important factor here is how HR can constantly adapt its HRM and HRD activities, services and interventions to suit critical needs in that particular situation. Flexibility, adaptability and survival of HR remain the key determinants of HR's ability to transform itself to differing contexts. HR does not operate in isolation and requires management support – sometimes senior management support, but more often, line management support and engagement.

2.12 HR SHOWING ADDED VALUE

For HR to maintain its credibility, it not only has to be seen to be adding value, but needs to provide evidence through appropriate measurements that it is. The use of HR metrics and other indices like human capital management measures continue to be an aspect of HR. Warech and Tracey (2004) believe that HR is far more than a cost centre, and that being able to communicate assertively affects HR's collective impact on the company's bottom line.

The role of the line manager cannot be overplayed, and both HR and HRD specialists need to engage with line managers in order to establish and maintain a successful business partnership. Cantrell and Benton (2007, p360) state that their research 'shows that the more involved managers are in employee development, learning and performance appraisals, the better the financial performance of the organisation'. These authors also emphasise the important role that line managers have in active involvement with selection and development of employees.

If we consider the results of the IRS survey (2010, p5) on HR roles and responsibilities, 'most employers measure the effectiveness of their HR functions, with 72 per cent rating their HR function as very effective or above average based upon their evaluation'. Here HR has contributed towards managing cost-cutting exercises, an increased role in developing strategy (with senior managers) and reorganising and restructuring work (in order to save costs).

When it comes to creating a learning culture in organisations, where will this emanate from? Who will be the custodian of knowledge management (including knowledge creation and share)?

With regard to HRD showing added value, there is some similarity of arguments presented from HR material earlier. In a study of Indian companies, Rao and Varghese (2008, p33) found that:

- HRD managers need to recognise stakeholder expectations and understand the overall business and strategic context of their function.
- The HRD function should focus on intellectual capital generation activities and ensure good return on investment on training and other interventions.
- HRD practitioners need to equip themselves with capacity and competencies needed to build the HRD function, and become proactive strategic partners.
- HRD practitioners need to strengthen their partnership and credibility among stakeholders through involvement with policy-making.

Ulrich and Smallwood (2004) argue that HRD can create value through building organisational capabilities such as talent, speed of change, shared mindset, accountability, collaboration, learning and leadership.

CASE STUDY 2.2

GLASSECO

Introduction

GlassEco was established in 2005 and is located in Crawley, West Sussex. The company is a small enterprise with 20 employees (at times rising to 30), including between four and five people working as administrative staff. The major economic activity of GlassEco is the manufacture of solid surface worktops for bathrooms, kitchens, reception desks and other surfaces, made entirely from recycled materials, primarily post-use consumer glass. The company sources and processes its own aggregate. The resulting products have unusual design features, are stain-resistant and have tried-and-tested internal strength. The company is not engaged in any secondary activities.

The sub-sector of manufacturing worktops and other related products from recycled glass is very small in Europe. GlassEco names as its direct competitors only one other UK company producing on a much smaller scale, and the Spanish facility of a large international worktop producer. The company's primary competition comes from more traditional materials, ie granite and marble along with other types of stone.

The company has been selected as an interesting example of a unique and innovative start-up green company with its own green technology. The experiences of the company give a valuable perspective on how small innovative green businesses develop their HR solutions, in particular a skills development model that involves the creation of a core team of internal experts who provide blue-collar workers with skills and advice as needed.

Drivers and motivations

In common with many other green start-up companies, the desire of the founders to create a business which would be both profitable and environmentally responsible was the key motivation in starting GlassEco. As the founders came from the recycling industry, they decided to develop a technology in which the 'where possible' approach taken by other manufacturers would be replaced by sourcing the vast majority of raw materials from recycling processes.

The key driver was the invention in 2003 of the technology the company now uses. It is quite basic, but its particularities have been protected as an intellectual property.

Also in common with other green start-ups, there was no pressure on the company from customers, the community or regulatory frameworks since this was a new business rather than an old one being restructured. The practice was developed entirely as a search for market opportunities for a new product with a low environmental footprint and exceptional, flexible design.

The fact that the raw materials are cheaper than those used by competitors does not create any significant cost advantages because of the higher costs of production.

The economic and financial crisis has made the company search for new markets, shifting its focus from Europe to the Americas, but the management of the company is optimistic about its future performance.

Green business practices

The idea to engage in this type of business was proposed by the current director of the company, who is also one of the owners. As mentioned above, the development of the technology was gradual. The founders of the company experimented to develop the best way to produce utility worktops made of as much recycled material as possible.

The various types of waste glass, ranging from bottles and jars to cathode ray tube glass from old television sets and computer monitors, are collected by the company in the UK and preferably in London, to minimise transportation costs and the carbon footprint of the final product. It is then transformed through a series of steps into worktops used for various domestic and commercial applications.

The waste glass is first of all crushed into small particles, which are then bound together in a solvent-free epoxy resin to create a surface similar in appearance and behaviour to granite. The mixture of glass and resin is moulded into frames to produce differently shaped sheets and surfaces may also be bent to produce curves. Finally, the product is calibrated and polished.

The final products may consist of as much as 93% of recycled materials, while having favourable performance in terms of durability, staining and heat-resistance compared to non-recycled alternatives.

The products of GlassEco have a virtually non-existent carbon footprint. The company has won a National Recycling Award for its commitment to sustainability.

A square metre of the product contains the equivalent of 190 glass bottles. Various other waste, including discarded shells (from seafood restaurants), waste stone and broken ceramics, may be added later to achieve different finishes. The peculiar design feature which separates a range of GlassEco's products from traditional surfaces is the possibility of under-lighting them.

In 2012, GlassEco was offered the opportunity to provide worktops for bathrooms in the London Olympic Village. The offer came through an external company which had used GlassEco's services previously. Other past clients include the BBC, Deutsche Bank, Transport for London and other well-known national and international organisations.

The company also has other environmentally sustainable practices in place, such as water recycling (the same water is used up to three times), minimum energy use, a waste policy and the heating of its premises by biomass.

Anticipation and management of the impact of green change on quantity and quality of jobs

Impact on quantity of jobs

Initially the company was started with four employees, who were heavily involved in the development of the recycling technology and establishment of the enterprise itself. These first employees became experts in the working methods of the company and have built an in-depth knowledge of its functioning, including the manufacturing process, the sales process, management of human resources and overall situation in the market.

In recent years, the number of workers employed by the company has fluctuated between 20 and 30. At the moment, there are 20 employees in total in the company, including the director, administrator, sales managers, designer, templaters (responsible for visiting the homes of clients, taking measurements and preparing blueprints) and a range of blue-collar workers (responsible for different phases of the manufacture process, such as crushing the glass, constructing moulding frames, moulding, polishing).

The recruitment process is done in the usual way for small enterprises, mainly through advertisements and personal recommendations. The company employs new staff *ad hoc*, based on its immediate labour force needs. Long-term skill needs are hard to predict and the company does not use sophisticated methods to anticipate demand for new employees.

Impact on quality of jobs

As the company's type of activity is very rare in the UK and Europe, the company has difficulty finding staff with suitable skills. The company's approach is therefore to train new employees through its own internal training process.

For the same reason (the uniqueness of the activities and the fact that the technology has been developed by this one company) it isn't possible to create external training courses. The best possible know-how is already available within the company and it cannot be matched by external experts.

There are two key approaches to internal skills development. In cases where additional workers are needed for jobs already being done, or where departing employees are to be replaced by others, training is provided by established and trained employees. Where this is not possible, training is done by core staff who have overall knowledge of the manufacturing process.

This cluster of core experts is also responsible for supplementing the skills of blue-collar workers with continuing support on any issues that arise.

As already explained, there are many types of employees in GlassEco, and the workers of every type need to learn different skills before they start their daily work.

- Designers and sales managers need detailed knowledge of the technology applied by the company, and its limitations, so that potential clients can be offered both the best solutions and also the most feasible.
- Templaters need in-depth knowledge of what has to be taken into account while taking measurements, and must be skilled in developing and making blueprints.
- Manufacturers of moulding frames need the ability to read the blueprint (the blueprints show the frames upside-down) and manufacture the frames accordingly.
- Crushers of glass need knowledge about the tools and machinery which can be used to crush different types of collected glass – the technology differs for crushing thin or thick glass and bottles.

- Moulders calculate the volumes of resin and glass needed and need to understand moulding techniques.
- Polishers need knowledge about the machinery, settings, speeds and types of abrasives to be used at different stages of the process.

One worker, who has been with the company for about half a year and is responsible for the moulding process, confirmed that her training in how to calculate the volume of the moulded mass and the amount of the resin and the glass to be used was given to her by an employee who has now left the company. She reports that she was fully ready to take over the work within about two weeks of starting her job. Further tasks allotted to her required only minimal additional learning – the set of skills she needs has not changed significantly.

There were no reported influences of green business practice on the other working conditions of the employees, such as career and employment security, health and well-being, and work–life balance. The standards set by national legislation are observed and there are no significant additional issues.

Collaboration in anticipating and managing green change

Being a unique company, GlassEco does not collaborate with social partners and/ or public authorities on issues such as the anticipation and management of green change, or its impact on the skills and other working conditions of employees.

While the lack of collaboration with trade unions and employer organisations is understandable due to the small size of the company, the management expressed disappointment at the lack of collaborative opportunities with public actors. In their opinion, national and European public authorities could do more in supporting green change in business by offering 'green' companies such as theirs assistance with additional funding, perhaps through provision of direct financing measures or offering guidance on opportunities to support green products. Tax breaks for customers buying sustainable products could also be offered, and public institutions could be encouraged to procure green products.

The key problem in anticipating the skills needs of the company is the difficulty in predicting production demand. The recent economic and financial crisis has harmed the company's performance and motivated it to start widening the geographical focus of its marketing beyond Europe.

Conclusions and recommendations

GlassEco is a small green start-up enterprise with a unique technology developed by its founders. A number of conclusions and recommendations can be drawn from GlassEco's experience:

- Unique green companies with their own technology may experience difficulties in obtaining employees with the necessary skills, since there is no supply of such skills on the labour market.
- The solution to this issue is to provide internal training to newly hired employees. This training may be provided either by other employees doing the same function at the same level or by highly skilled employees who are experts in the manufacturing process.
- It is beneficial for a company to have a core team of experts who have in-depth knowledge about the overall production process, sales, HRM and

the situation in the market. Such experts may assist workers at any time when they have questions or meet difficulties or skill shortages in doing their tasks.

- While it is important for small companies to secure the support of public authorities, this should not be counted on, as such support may prove to be very limited.
- The skills needed in small companies are always highly dependent on the performance of the company. The anticipation of such skills may prove to be difficult given the changing demand for the company's products, especially in the times of economic hardship. The search for new markets (geographically) may be one solution to the problem of these fluctuations and in the numbers of staff needed. In the meanwhile, the development of transferable skills among the employees could help the companies increase the adaptability of their workforce to ever-changing economic and working conditions.

Source: European Foundation for the Improvement of Living and Working Conditions (2013b)

Question

As the newly appointed HR business partner at GlassEco, what initial advice would you provide to the management in terms of

- HR issues
- HRD issues

so as to improve upon the current business objectives?

2.13 LINE MANAGERS AND HR: EVIDENCE FROM RESEARCH FINDINGS

The question of how much line managers are expected to contribute towards implementing people management activities and practices is a moot one. What is the level of intervention from HR's perspective when they spot errors and mistakes in the way in which line managers operate? If HR is purely acting in an 'advisory' capacity, whereby managers can ignore advice, then by definition, does this not spell the denigration of the HR function?

In an IRS survey (2009), it was found that in some cases HR took the lead (eg specialist knowledge or expertise surrounding a tribunal claim). In contrast, policies that needed to be applied across every individual employee in the workforce involve greater focus on the role of the line managers (eg performance appraisal reviews). The survey found that in 87.3% of tribunal claims, HR took the main responsibility compared to 5.5% who reported a shared responsibility between line managers and HR. The other two areas where HR took on a significant role were equal opportunities and employee relations (see also Chapters 4 and 11). It may be presumptuous to assume that the three key areas avoided by line managers could be considered to be 'dirty work', ie tricky areas that can be drawn out, complex and potentially damaging to the reputation of the individuals concerned. In the IRS 2008 survey on line managers' roles in people management, the key findings included:

- Line managers are increasingly expected to implement people management policies, with duties ranging from managing flexible working requests to handling disciplinary and grievance procedures.
- HR practitioners are not always impressed with the way that line managers carry out these responsibilities, and assess their performance as poor in some areas. Line managers are judged ineffective in training and development, absence management and maintaining personnel records.
- HR practitioners believe that training for line managers should be compulsory, and that levels of training and support on offer are inadequate.
- Two-thirds of organisations predict the role of line managers to change further in the next three years, and this means taking on more HR functions.

Despite the IRS survey finding that HR use a number of techniques to support line managers in their people management role, such as coaching, meetings advice and support, training and posting information on various channels, the attitude that line managers possess can sometimes inhibit outputs. Some of the problems here may be quite simple, eg the line manager is taking on too much, which may detract from what they perceive as their core function or contribution.

REFLECTIVE ACTIVITY 2.5

Consider how a formal arrangement can be made so as to secure a strong working relationship between HR managers and line managers. What key aspects would this arrangement include and how could they be evaluated?

2.14 STRATEGIC HRM AND HUMAN CAPITAL MANAGEMENT (HCM)

Human capital management (HCM) can be defined as the collective knowledge, skills, abilities and capacity to develop and innovate through company employees. At the core of HCM is an integrative and strategic approach to the management of people. The CIPD 2015 factsheet states that HCM strengthens strategic HRM by:

- drawing attention to the significance of 'management through measurement', so as to provide objective linkages between HR interventions and organisational success
- providing guidance on what to measure, how to measure and how to report on the outcomes of measurement
- proving that superior people management is delivering superior results and indicating where HR should proceed

- reinforcing attention on the need to base HRM strategies and processes on the requirement to create value through people and achieve organisational goals
- defining the link between HRM and business strategy
- strengthening the HRM belief that people are assets rather than costs
- emphasising the role of HR specialists as business partners.

Whilst operating strategically, an organisation will typically undergo several change initiatives in order to meet these objectives. The concept of HR transformation helps organisations to progress both the organisation and the function itself.

Organisations need to decide their objectives for HR transformation. The most common reasons for organisations to embark on HR transformation are to:

- meet a business goal, such as cost reductions, or refocusing on changed priorities, for example improving the organisation's capacity to recruit and retain the right people
- respond to cost-reduction pressures in a strategic rather than an incremental or piecemeal way
- align HR more closely with the organisation's business strategy in relation to people management
- improve the match between the skills and competencies of the HR team and the future needs of the organisation
- increase the effectiveness and efficiency of operational processes
- focus on a business-critical people issue such as a recruitment, skills or performance challenge
- change the balance of ownership of/responsibility for people issues across the organisation in relation to the HR function, senior managers, line managers and employees.

(www.xperthr.co.uk/good-practice-manual/hr-transformation/155200/?)

CASE STUDY 2.3

INNOVATIVE WAYS OF WORKING AND HR PRACTICES IN NEW FORMS OF ORGANISATION

Although many of us still work for a single employer, we increasingly experience work in a much more networked way than in the past (Marchington et al 2009, Swart et al 2007, Kinnie et al 2006). Think about the last project team in which you were involved: the chances are the members were drawn from both inside and outside your organisation. Despite this, we know very little about the management of human capital in a cross-boundary, or networked, context.

Indeed, we might go further and say that much of current HR thinking, strategy, structure and practice is predicated on and reflects more traditional hierarchical structures. We therefore need to develop our understanding of these contemporary ways of working and how organisations use innovative forms of organising to manage human capital across boundaries.

A prominent way of working across organisational boundaries is to organise work in projects. Such arrangements are widespread, both within and between firms, in sectors such as pharmaceuticals, car manufacture, advertising, marketing and media and consulting. Complex, so-called 'mega-projects' or integrated project teams (IPTs) are the principal way in which large-scale major construction projects, such as Terminal 5 at London Heathrow Airport and the London Olympic Park, and IT integration projects, such as the change to online self-assessment tax returns for HMRC, are designed, developed and then operationalised.

These changes reveal an interesting paradox: potentially fragmenting changes, which could mean that organisations may not be able to maximise the value from their human capital, are taking place at the same time as greater emphasis is placed on the central role of human capital in organisational success (Takeuchi et al 2011).

Increasingly, we are faced with the task of managing employees across organisational boundaries. In more traditional organisations we tend to equate employees with the people whom we directly manage; but more and more we are finding disconnect between those whom we employ and manage. We may, for example, employ people but not manage them on a face-to-face basis because they may be providing outsourced services on a client's site, as in the recruitment process outsourcer Alexander Mann Solutions (AMS). Alternatively, the clients of AMS find they are interacting on a daily basis with staff who are not their employees but are central to their success. Indeed, Paul Fielden, Associate Partner in IBM, said in a recent interview for our research, 'I can draw on over 150 IBM people to staff projects for my clients, but I only directly manage three of them.'

These innovative forms of organising have multiple benefits because they allow firms to leverage the knowledge, skills and experience of staff they do not employ, but there are also various challenges. The financial services firm which outsources its call centre operations to India achieves both cost and expertise advantages, but it knows these call centre workers are perceived by their customers as the public voice of their organisation. These innovative ways of working in 'adhodcratic', project-centred, knowledge-intensive networks (see also Chapter 8) throw up challenges for achieving the traditional HR aims of integration, alignment and consistency (Marchington et al 2011).

The consultant will have to display commitment not only to her employer, but also to her client, team and her own professional development. Indeed, many of these HR practices sit more comfortably in an environment where there is a single focus of commitment rather than the potentially multiple foci of commitment found in the networked way of working where employees are habitually working across organisational boundaries (Kinnie et al 2012).

We need to consider the consequences for HR if the source of competitive advantage shifts from the single firm to the complex network involving literally thousands of firms. This means that the classic HR practices for recruitment, talent development and retention are no longer solely the property of an individual firm.

Source: Kinnie et al (2012).

Questions

1   What are the potential benefits of these innovative, networked ways of working?

2   What are the potential conflicts and tensions in HR terms?

2.15 CONCLUSION

HR needs to operate effectively at strategic, tactical and operational levels. Rees and McBain (2004, p25) argue that in order for HR to maintain its importance, it needs to:

- participate in strategic decision-making, demonstrate added value, and act as a business partner
- move from assuming full responsibility for all HR managers and engage with line managers (and develop the capability of line managers)

- shift the focus from internal to external, including benchmarking against other organisations, and collecting data on competitors. This includes keeping in touch with business trends and how these impact upon people management practices within the organisation
- become more anchored in, and central to, the contribution to business, thereby building commitment from employees
- move away from reactive supporter to proactive strategic adviser, anticipating required changes.

This model echoes the principles of business partnership, but is less concerned with structural issues and focuses upon the role and contribution of HR more. This 'internality' argument on meeting customer needs is explored by Jenner and Taylor (2007, p8), where HR views employees (and potential employees) as internal customers, and 'anticipating, identifying and satisfying customer requirements'.

Perhaps the final word needs to come from Boxall and Purcell (2015, p275):

Strategic HRM should help researchers and practitioners to recognise models of HRM, to understand how they have evolved and the strategic tensions that characterise them, help them to measure their impacts and develop ways for how they might be improved.

The HR function will continue to evolve with the onset of increased globalisation, technological enhancements, etc. Perhaps the focus should not be on whether it is 'strategic enough' (post-Ulrich), but more on its practical value added, with an eye upon continuous improvement and customer focus.

KEY LEARNING POINTS

1   The HR department or function has changed considerably in the last 40 years, and currently tends to adopt a managerialist (corporate) position.

2   HR needs to take time to evaluate and justify itself as a function or face attack or possibly outsourcing or replacement.

3   Where HR sits within corporate planning is pivotal to its involvement with strategic and mainstream business activities.

4   HRD and strategic HRD play an important function in the development of employees to adding to business success.

5   The HR business partner model carries with it a series of potential benefits and limitations, and should therefore be adapted according to the organisation and context, and possibly face up to the fact that it simply won't work as a model.

6   Despite the theory, there is a great deal of evidence to suggest that HR does receive the attention and support that it requires as a key function within organisations. The interplay between line management and HR is crucial in obtaining the right business outcomes.

REVIEW QUESTIONS

?

1   To what extent can there be a 'perfect shape' to an HR function in an organisation? Consider the arguments both for and against this proposition.

2   Does the HR business partner role sit most comfortably within private, public or third sector organisations? Support your answer with practical benefits.

3   How can the HR/HRD function build relationships with line managers so as to put improved working practices into effect?

4   What is meant by 'strategic HRD'? Evaluate the major components of strategic HRD.

EXPLORE FURTHER

Aston Centre for Human Resources (2008) *Strategic Human Resource Management: Building research-based practice*. London: CIPD.

Boxall, P. and Purcell, J. (2008) *Strategic and Human Resource Management*. 2nd edition. Basingstoke: Palgrave Macmillan. This textbook is strong on theory surrounding strategic HR.

Caldwell, R. (2008) HR business partner competency models: recontextualising effectiveness. *Human Resource Management Journal*. Vol 18, No 3. pp275–294. This article provides useful arguments around the business partner model.

Rees, G. and Smith, P. (2014) (eds) *Strategic Human Resource Management: An international perspective*. London: Sage Publications.

HRM Contributions in Different Settings

Charlotte Rayner and Liza Howe-Walsh

LEARNING OUTCOMES

After reading this chapter, you should be able to:

- appreciate how HR practices may differ across sector types: private, public and third sector
- recognise that delivering HR services in smaller organisations differs from those in larger organisations
- consider the ways in which the HR function may change as an organisation grows in size
- understand the concept of global HRM and its implications for practice in terms of policy and practice for localisation and control from head office
- explore the notion of strategic international HRM and the variegations in practice for staffing overseas.

3.1 OVERVIEW

This chapter takes theory from Chapter 2 and applies it to the working lives of HR practitioners (HRPs). In particular we will look at how, while the function of managing HR is similar in most organisations, the work of the HRPs themselves varies between different organisational contexts; this is partly dependent on size, and also whether the organisation is profit or not-for-profit. Without doubt the needs of an organisation change as it grows, and although all have to be compliant with the law, often small businesses only seek involvement by HR to ensure such compliance, commonly using external consultants. Following growth, generalist internal HR managers are typically appointed and, with further success and growth, specialists, policy designers and strategists broaden the input from HR. Their continued tenure means they are perceived as adding value to the organisation – although naturally the nature of value-added varies between roles.

Public sector and third sector (not-for-profit) HR practitioners can sometimes feel undervalued in academic research, which typically focuses on those organisations seeking profit. In this chapter we argue that all HR managers 'add value', and we will explore this notion in depth with examples.

Taking the concept of context further, we explore international and global HRM, presenting the practical issues of locus of control (how far the organisation controls from head office or allows localisation), and the movement of staff overseas by the use of expatriates and other forms of staffing (Reichel and Lazarova 2013). Some expensive techniques are used by organisations for staffing overseas, often with little understanding of the benefits accruing to the organisation. Throughout this chapter, the relationship of HR practice and the interface between line managers and specialist HRPs is discussed, as we regard this link as a highly salient issue for the management and leadership of people in all types of organisation.

3.2 INTRODUCTION

Chapters 1 and 2 outlined the main influences on HRM and HRD with regard to managing and leading people. In this chapter we will seek to change the focus in several ways. First we will concentrate on how HR adds value, initially examining what it is to add value. Quite often it is perceived that value is only added by the introduction of high-quality products and services. Value can be added in many other ways too. We examine the original concept of 'value-added', which demonstrates that cost-cutting, efficiencies and simply resolving value-losing conflicts can add to the offering of the organisation. HRPs may not have headline visibility in these achievements very often, but are usually important players in the success of initiatives as part of their daily work (Boxall and Purcell 2015). Hence we will explore the notion of adding value through a narrowing of focus to specific types of organisation and also using examples, and illustrate how the nature of the challenge within HR can vary enormously depending on the context in which one is working.

In the second section of the chapter we will broaden our scope to an international focus in order to examine the management and leadership of people in multi-country organisations (Stahl et al 2012). It is not only when operating from sites in other countries that international understanding is needed. When one is sending employees abroad to work on assignments, or using staff employed by organisations based in countries offshore, there is a need to understand the HR implications of increasing geographic scope. With the success of Internet-based selling and recruitment, the need for international HRM (IHRM) is now not just the province of large multinationals, but a real possibility for many smaller organisations and the third sector. Hence practitioners' competence in international and global HR becomes more prevalent than unusual.

3.3 HR IN DIFFERENT CONTEXTS

It is essential that all staff contribute to the organisational effort. The work output of some staff such as those in sales is highly tangible and their contribution to the organisation's goals obvious. But what of HR practitioners? As a service function, one needs to be explicit in order to identify the organisational benefit from their work (Messersmith et al 2011). HRM as a profession is connected to employees and their outputs regarding the organisation (Huselid 1995). Our understanding of how employees contribute is largely driven by the Resource-Based View (see Boxall and Purcell 2015 for a full description) where the value of the organisation is created from resources, of which one is employees, and HR practitioners are intricately involved in delivering such value (Glover and Butler 2012). Glover and Butler undertook a four-year study to gain a deeper understanding of HRPs' role within the organisation. Alongside HR's role at a strategic level, contributing to the business, the study highlights the contribution of HR behind the scenes. Such work includes amendments to policy and practices and negotiating with line managers. As this work is not immediately visible there is a danger that the HR function is not credited with any resulting benefit, putting into question how it adds value (Glover and Butler 2012, p212).

The notion of 'value' in contemporary strategic thinking was developed by the strategist Michael Porter, who saw those in the organisation adding value in a cumulative 'value chain' (1985). As an economist he saw 'value' being related through performance of resources (including staff) to profits. This view is reflected in a CIPD *Employee Outlook* survey (CIPD 2015a). The survey for Spring 2015 indicates that regardless of whether the organisation is private, voluntary or public, the importance of managing performance is of paramount focus to employees, a purpose linked directly to enhancing profits. Porter suggests that value is added in two ways: either by reducing costs (hence leading to a higher profit margin); or by adding features and benefits which clients and customers value and are willing to pay for and, although they cost more to deliver, can be charged for at a premium, hence adding to the profit margin.

Applying Porter's guidance to the HR context of managing and leading people reveals a multitude of ways in which added value can be achieved.

Although public sector and third sector organisations do not usually seek to make profits, they are immensely budget-conscious, especially in the strictures of austerity measures implemented by government. Hence we need to pay attention to how they can use Porter's fundamentals of adding value. Being publicly funded, such organisations have to take care with all expenditure. Given that many public sector institutions carry a staff cost of at least 50% of their overall budget as they are usually in a service capacity, the role of HR should be fundamental (see Knies et al 2015 for a review). Value can be added by a reduction in overall expenditure after savings are made in an area or doing more with the same staff, or by developing staff so that the service they provide outweighs the cost of the development.

Let us consider the public sector. Given that wages are such a major cost, HR can influence added value by contributing to projects which reduce staff costs. This might be through helping line managers reorganise work or job roles so that the same can be done with less. For example, local councils conduct much business using IT contact with their residents – meaning initial investment in website design, equipment and training existing staff, but eventual savings as automation takes effect. Paying for parking tickets online rather than sending in a cheque (to be processed by staff and incurring bank charges) or visiting council offices (with the accompanying costs of being met and dealt with in-person) are two examples. The Ordinance Survey office moved to a much smaller building after recruiting and training staff (over a long period) competent in technologically based mapping, reducing the need for a paper-based library of maps and bulky equipment. The organisation leveraged developments in mapping that, combined with HR practices, delivered a sustainably lower-cost platform job design meaning that this generation of staff can do more with less space. Value has been added through reducing costs.

Truss and Gill (2009) investigated the process that HR delivered in the UK public sector, exploring the issues of social capital, perceived added value and HR process through in-depth interviews at two NHS hospitals and two local councils. Their study found both value-adding and value-reducing examples. Value is reduced when extra costs are incurred that cannot be passed onto the customer, thus lowering effectiveness. Perceptions of value reduction in their study included poor union–employer relationships, which led to stagnation and blocks to change. Poor time boundaries within recruitment were an example where line managers saw HR as reducing value through the loss of good candidates (p679), and inconsistency in HR personnel in providing their internal services was always seen negatively (p680).

One can see how this would add to costs as line managers and senior staff sought to use the HR department members they trusted and who had a reputation for delivering processes, whilst avoiding those less reliable. Timely responding by the HR department in the delivery of processes was perceived as value-adding by non-HR managers in all areas.

It appeared that a visible and proactive HR leader was highly influential on how HR was perceived. In most cases the HR strategic contributions were acknowledged as solid; it was in the detail of more day-to-day process where value was not positive, and also through inconsistency of personnel. Their study included HRPs where they correlated stronger performances with a strong sense of identity and purpose such that even if HRPs were working at a level of isolation, they knew the HR strategy and understood their contribution. HR departments which were led less well and had a poor sense of identity and cohesion amongst members were perceived less well. These lessons are likely to be useful in non-public-sector contexts too as an underperforming staff affects the function's image in a disproportionate way and places extra burden on staff trusted to deliver.

The CIPD carries out biennial reviews of the HR profession, the last being in the winter of 2014/15, which showed stark contrasts in the public and private sectors following the imposition of austerity measures by government after the 2008 financial crisis.

What comes across in the 2014/15 CIPD *HR Outlook* research is the embeddedness of HR departments in the 'business' of their organisations and implementing change. As such, HR initiatives appear to be rarely undertaken; instead the organisation (or a segment of it) has a change project which involves HR as organisational development consultants or involved in delivering changes connected to the new direction. Hence the notion of HR being strategic had become embedded, especially in larger organisations. A study demonstrated such changes in 2010 where Surrey Police HR undertook a strategy allowing local managers more discretion, reaching into all parts of the operation. HR policies were reviewed, reduced and rewritten 'with broad principles rather than detailed dictat' (Sears 2010, p9). Hence sometimes financial constraints can lead to invoking better HR-related practice.

REFLECTIVE ACTIVITY 3.1

Consider the example of Surrey Police provided above.

1   In what ways do you think the relationship between line managers and HR may have changed as a result of the new approach?

2   How would staff in your HR department react to enabling more managerial discretion?

3   Discuss the strengths and weaknesses of devolving power to the line manager in the public sector.

Turning now to the private sector, several large studies have examined the link between HR strategy and business strategy (Wang and Shyu 2008) and these are based on private sector organisations, often taking 'top performing' organisations in a financial sense and then asking about HR practices. It is becoming clear that although researchers do find positive relationships between HR alignment with business strategy and performance, the causal direction is less clear (Biron et al 2011). Are the better financial performers just more organised and integrated, or is there something special about the alignment of HR? With regard to costs, the need to be assured that the benefits from spending are optimal raises the issue of whether HR have the analytic skills to be able to undertake such analysis, which is inherently difficult in a constantly changing environment (Woodall et al 2009). The 2014/15 feedback from HR professionals in *HR Outlook* showed that this is a key area for focus in the future development of HR skills. Analysing performance at the individual level is one thing; analysing the business effects of any specific change is arguably more complex, but much needed.

An aspect which emerged for the private sector in particular in the recent CIPD research (CIPD 2015d, Sears 2010) was the need for HR to challenge all types of managers. Naturally one has to already have a culture where challenging the status quo (and also those with status) does not carry a penalty. However, HR is uniquely positioned to add value as it reaches into all corners of the organisation. The ongoing debate regarding senior staff remuneration packages is a good example. Senior staff use skills (bringing together market knowledge from a range of sources), experience and professional judgement, contributing a key set of competencies that are central to the organisation's strategic success. A highly complex set of (often incomplete) data means the skill of senior staff in decision-making is at a premium. For any organisation in times of austerity there is an argument in favour of paying more for skilled people who will create wealth (value) far beyond the cost of remuneration. This balance has to be weighed carefully and is one in which HR plays a role, bringing its own skills in knowledge and understanding of the implications on all parts of the business.

HRD can be the lynchpin for the achievement of strategies where job redesign is an aspect of implemented business strategies. Job redesign is often at the centre of cost-saving, for example when new technology is implemented (such as picking systems to reduce the number of warehouse staff), and staff cuts where roles need to be reshaped to achieve a lower staff footprint: cost-efficiency and using high-performance working practices fundamentally add value (Katou and Budhwar 2009). Such changes are strategic in nature and result in redeployed staff undertaking altered roles, having been retrained and probably under new terms and conditions of service. HR is involved in achieving strategic change, and although it may never serve a customer directly, adds value (Ulrich et al 2008) through implementing business strategy.

The differences between the public and private sectors may not be great in many instances. All are about empowerment, learning and training so that responsibilities can be flattened in the hierarchy with cost savings. The value added might be spent in different ways; the hospital may do more with the same number of staff, the distribution firm might expand using the savings from their strategy or pay higher dividends to shareholders. But the strategy was the same, and HR has played a key role, even though the spending of the value added might be very different.

The final sector we consider is the third sector, that is, charitable and voluntary organisations, which often operate in fragile environments, vulnerable to changes in funder behaviour. Most have needed to turn their activities towards different streams of funding and meant they have had to be as nimble as any commercial organisation, but are constrained in ways not experienced by for-profit companies.

The sector has expanded as government has retracted from providing direct services, such as in elderly care with provision being delivered by private and third sector organisations (Wainwright et al 2006). There is a blurring between public, private and third sector (Rodwell et al 2008) with far more private sector organisations working within third sector constraints. We now turn to the challenges for HR to add value in the third sector context.

Without doubt, issues to do with recruitment can be especially tough in this sector. Many charities engage volunteers, and HR has an important role in ensuring these individuals are treated well outside of the parameters of the traditional employment contract, and that value is added (Ridder et al 2012). It is usually the case that third sector pay at all levels, being open to scrutiny by funders and the public alike, is low (Cunningham 2008). How does one attract and retain talent in such contexts? How does one fund training and other learning opportunities in order to develop staff when budgets are commonly connected in discrete ways to deliverable projects? How far can 'rewarding work' be used or abused? The sector is poorly researched from an HR perspective, although with the development of the non-profit sector, a trickle of research is now being published (Selden and Sowa 2015).

Central to issues around funding and reward of employees is the relationship between the third sector group and other agencies with which it partners. In elderly care the partner might be a local council; in education, a government department; in research it may be the NHS or specific benefactors. It is common that funders impose terms and conditions on those agencies which deliver services (Marchington et al 2005a), thus leaving the third sector provider little room for movement in some HR policy. In addition, competitive tendering for third sector contracts may mean those involved with negotiating contracts have to be very lean with their highest cost factor, that is, employees (Cunningham 2008). As funding is based on contracts typically lasting one to two years, substantial long-term investment or investment in potential new areas of work through HRD can be difficult to resource.

REFLECTIVE ACTIVITY 3.2

Funding HRD activities in the third sector can be problematic, especially providing learning events for the many staff who are on low wages. The Children's Society takes advantage of a strong link with the trade union UNITE. In several instances, the charity enabled a few employees (who are often workplace trade union representatives) to attend UNITE training, who then cascaded the knowledge and skills through the Society at far lower cost than external providers, but to exacting standards.

The Children's Society is quite a large charity. How might a small charity enable learning and development to be funded or delivered at low cost?

Some areas of HR add value directly in any organisation; for example, in the provision or overseeing of administrative tasks connected to people, for example wage systems, pensions, employment records, benefits and rewards systems. These are fundamental to the functioning of all organisations. However, they are often seen as 'hygiene factors' and so not necessarily valued when everything goes well, but heavily criticised when they fail to perform. Few employees are grateful for being paid on time, but most would be unhappy if wages arrived late! Their effectiveness provides value and ineffectiveness causes cost, thus reducing value.

Without doubt HR adds value through some of the roles described by Ulrich and Brockbank (2005). It is always valued for its contribution in keeping the organisation in compliance with legal requirements (the HR expert), and HR specialists have developed into providing policy advice and implementation at a strategic level (HR strategists).

The data for the performance value (financial and otherwise) created by HR professionals is difficult to study with certainty (Paauwe 2009) as if one uses broad-brush measures (such as return on capital employed) many non-employee components are involved, thus making a 'straight line' between HR involvement and organisation-level performance measures to be impossible to measure with certainty or at least to be treated with extreme caution (Wright and Haggerty 2005). Many HR initiatives concern longer-term development where an outcome (such as learning) might take many years to impact directly (Anderson 2007) and hence shorter-term value might be perceived in more fluid terms as a function of 'return on expectations' by senior and line managers (ibid). On the other hand, HR-based initiatives which are well communicated as aligned with strategy (for example, Nijssen and Paauwe 2012) can make the case through clear articulation alone. It is therefore a positive reflection on the maturing of our profession that there is concern in *HR Outlook* (CIPD 2015a) from HRPs for more training in evaluating complex programmes.

REFLECTIVE ACTIVITY 3.3

Consider a recent major change in your organisation.

1   Could this have been undertaken without HR input?

2   What was the nature of that input (with regard to that specific type of organisation) and did it add value through reducing costs further or achieving the change more efficiently or effectively?

3.4 HR ROLES AS THE ORGANISATION GROWS: SMEs

The function of HR is needed in all organisations beyond the simple formation of a partnership between two or more individuals. Many small organisations do not see the need to employ an HR specialist and, forever cost-conscious, tend not to directly employ HR assistance until it is really needed – perhaps as a result of hygiene factors not being met. Instead, HR might be outsourced to an HR consultant retained for policy and administrative tasks with their legal expertise enabling the small organisation to adhere to regulations. The small business is highly reliant on the skills and knowledge of such consultants, and is dependent on the provider being effective. Many HR consultants do excellent work with small businesses, often beginning with a limited and legalistically geared brief and patiently expanding their role into organisational development, HRD and other facets of delivery as the organisation is successful. Indeed, contact with HR consultants is sometimes the only space when owner-managers of small businesses take time away from their operational focus to consider their staff in a systematic and future-oriented manner.

The next evolutionary step is to hire an HR generalist to service the small firm, and logically occurs when it is cost-effective to do so. A small business generalist needs by default to be a jack of all trades (perhaps with the exception of legal support) and undertake (or at least co-ordinate) all HR roles. HR generalists may not be providing very sophisticated services, but it is likely they will be closely aligned with the business as their day-to-day activities are immersed with those connected to clients, suppliers and the product/service to be delivered. Short lines of communication and close contact with seniors should mean fast delivery of change. Naturally, the agenda will be limited in scope and subject to tight funding, but the capacity to add value focused on the business is very high.

Greiner (1972) suggests that as organisations grow they pass through a series of crises. Almost like a squeeze-box movement, the locus of control is central. Most small business-owners like to have control, but this can become more difficult as the organisation grows, failing to deliver optimal effectiveness as the owner-manager becomes a bottleneck of decisions and checking employees' work. In some senses many small businesses reflect the 'hard HR' model (see Boselie et al (2009) for a review of the Michigan Approach). A resolution of this early Greiner crisis for small business sees a middle line of managers having more autonomy to enable growth.

It is possible at this time to move into more staff development as typified by the 'soft HR' Harvard school (Boselie et al 2009), although hard HR may predominate. But greater autonomy risks fragmentation as the organisation may grow in different ways under the direction of a team of sub-unit leaders, leading to a crisis of control. Greiner's next crisis is therefore a need to pull things back into a more coherent whole again. Even at this stage, as often SMEs do not devolve much decision-making, the HR generalist has only a few key managers to deal with. Unitarism is assumed, and the atmosphere is often still patriarchal (Legge 2005), especially if the owner-manager is still in charge. If a full-time HR professional has not been hired before now, it is likely this crisis sets the scene to do so whether the organisation is for-profit or not (see Ridder et al 2012 for a review).

In what way can the generalist HR practitioner provide value for the SME? Boxall and Purcell (2015) are clear that beyond the standard HR administration, the focus of any HR activity, if it is to be aligned into the organisation strategy, needs to focus on areas rich in human capital. Hence, HR can provide insight on focusing effort to those who create the value which is essential for strategic success. Thus an importer geared to growth through extending market share can focus on rewards connected to performance targets with appraisal and feedback to those sourcing and selling products as the nexus of HRM strategy. A professional firm of knowledge workers may have a different focus such as that of HRD opportunities and an emphasis on work–life balance as a means to recruit, retain and foster performance in the professionals key to delivering the organisational offering.

In the medium-sized organisation, HR professionals thinking through these 'bundles' (Selden and Sowa 2015) for the organisation can add great value. But as the firm grows, it is likely that so too will the number of HR professionals, with evolution into the better defined roles (as described by Ulrich). However, as the medium-sized organisation works its way through the growth cycles, the final stage Greiner suggests is a 'crisis of red tape' as bureaucracy has been used to co-ordinate the organisation – a complaint which will not surprise any seasoned HR practitioner, and resonates with Reflective Activity 3.1 on Surrey Police. Recent work suggests that commensurate changes in HR practice occur in larger non-profit organisations and for-profit organisations (Guo et al 2011).

QUICKSILVER'S HR CHALLENGES

CASE STUDY 3.1

Quicksilver has 200 employees and is a worldwide leader in yacht insurance worldwide, based in Cowes on the Isle of Wight. Careful stewardship through the early years, and the retraction of mainstream insurers from the niche, has allowed steady growth. Internet and magazine advertising links customers to the call centre (100 staff), which also deals with initial claims.

Each staff area has a board director. There is an underwriting and claims group (40 staff), the marketing department works with IT (15 staff), and the finance department (18 staff) is under the direct control of the CEO, who is a qualified accountant.

Quicksilver has a differentiated strategy – not the cheapest in the market, but reliable for reasonable claims.

The firm employs three HR practitioners who also oversee the building and non-IT facilities. One looks after recruitment – with call centre staff being a main headache – one deals with HR administration and facility issues, and the third, Sylvia Norris, is the HR director dealing with policy and strategic issues, and also helps out her line-reports. Call centre staff are trained by an external provider.

The financial crisis affected the company's financial standing at first, but with the return of corporate stability the retention of established customers has been excellent, and in 2015 there has only been a 20% drop through customers giving up their expensive hobby. But new customers are looking for cheaper deals and 'dodgy claims' are increasing from this cadre. These dynamics have led to stagnation in sales, and internal tensions are rising in the firm as non-payment of claims has affected the company's reputation in the close-knit boating community.

Sylvia has been challenged that the once-positively regarded 'professional' practices in HR (for example, clear job description, target-setting and performance appraisal systems) are tying everyone down far too much as 'belts need to be tightened'.

Questions

1   How can Sylvia respond to these pressures?

2   In what other ways can she and her team add value at this time of stagnation?

The larger organisation holds different challenges for HR. Diversification may mean different strategies in different sub-units and human capital investment may vary across the organisation (Boxall and Purcell 2011). The drive for efficiencies through standardisation of processes and policies may mean over-bureaucratisation in some cases and insufficient support in others (ibid); in larger organisations there are many decision-makers, and co-ordination within the HR department may become paramount to gather issues and focus effort. No doubt supported by trends connected to austerity, there is a growing set of commentary and research supporting the notion that HR is in danger of short-term opportunistic practices rather than adopting a long-term sustainable contribution to the organisation (Marchington 2015, Sears 2010, Sparrow 2012). As the distance between key areas for attention and HR increases, so gaps may appear. It is perhaps not surprising that the seam of 'critical HR' research (which includes examination of dysfunction between HR effort and what is valued) is undertaken almost always in large organisations (Truss and Gill 2009, De Vos and Meganck 2009) and there is a gap in systematic research knowledge of what goes on in the smaller set-up. One might see that co-ordination activities within HR costs salaries, but the effect a synergistic team can provide can make a real difference (Becker and Huselid 2006).

There has been a trend over the last decade away from vertical integration (where one owns all aspects of the organisation) towards outsourcing and supply-chain management. A common technique in large organisations, but how far can HR be outsourced? The strategy literature suggests that when outsourcing, it is only those aspects of the organisation that do not contribute to strategic success which should be considered – otherwise one has competitive competency owned by others. Many CIPD surveys show that payroll administration is commonly outsourced by organisations of all sizes – a specialist firm can often provide payroll cheaper than in-house. Other aspects of HR are far more contentious. How far should training and other learning events be outsourced? If knowledge is central to the product or service being offered, surely HRD must be provided in-house? Opinions differ, and there are bold examples of outsourcing, such as at Hampshire County Council, where the whole HR department was outsourced.

 REFLECTIVE ACTIVITY 3.4

Visit the CIPD website at www.cipd.co.uk. Look through the collection of surveys and related articles on outsourcing there. Pick one function of HR that is contentious in terms of being outsourced and show how it is controversial. At this point you may wish to look at Chapter 4 and the discussion there on professionalism and ethics in HR.

1   Are the factors to be considered the same for private, public and third sector organisations?

2   Can HR ever be entirely outsourced and, if not, which aspects of HR should always remain in-house?

Give reasons for your conclusions.

Outsourcing in HR is a debate that will no doubt continue (Butler and Callahan 2014, Glaister 2014). An interesting set of data is shown by Wahrenburg et al (2006), displaying variation across the portfolio of HR activities, and is explicitly echoed in the very recent practitioner survey *HR Outlook* (CIPD 2015a). As one would expect, clerical functions are far more likely to be outsourced than top management advice. They found variation between industries, with some commonality within industry (they examined finance in particular). We would argue that if the whole of HR is outsourced it is seen as a commodity, adding no strategic value, then in some senses the profession could fail. However Reichel and Lazarova (2013) offer some useful insights in their attempt to investigate the effects of outsourcing and development of the strategic position of HR departments. One must recognise that some strategic advice will come from consultants who have broadened activities from being auditors and advising on finance to helping with cost and value-added. If HR is entirely outsourced, clearly the message from the architects of the organisation is that HR as a function is not seen as central to the management and leadership of people in providing competitive advantage; however, the latest data presented in *HR Outlook* (CIPD 2015a) suggests outsourcing is perhaps not growing as strongly as it has in the past.

The shift into and out of outsourcing has provided a highly variegated situation for HR practitioners and those seeking a career in HR. Opportunities for roles exist within all sectors, either fully employed by an organisation or acting as a consultant independently or as part of an outsourced agency. In the end the HR function is delivered. But how the value is created and by whom varies. Any internal HR function relies on the interaction with the business and ensuring thus HR practitioners have to ensure they have the skills to interact with the business (CIPD 2012b).

REFLECTIVE ACTIVITY 3.5

A small law firm is having difficulty attracting and retaining lawyers in a provincial office overseas. It currently has no in-house HR function. The partner in charge has decided to introduce flexible benefits in line with the larger competitors.

1   Brief the management team on how the benefits could be introduced and managed.

2   How could they utilise HR input to assist with their goal?

3.5 EXPANDING OUR BORDERS: THE GROWTH OF INTERNATIONALISATION

The Internet has created in the twenty-first century a connected, international framework that has changed the scope for recruitment, working and operations at a fundamental level. Such advances mean that national borders are being crossed by even small organisations who now find foreign markets offer the staff they need, or customers who might want their organisations' products and services. Thus the portfolio of skills needed in managing and leading people is becoming an international arena, and one for which the HR professional needs to be prepared. It is to the international context that our attention now turns.

Why do we need to explore global strategy in HRM? HR as part of the strategic component delivering organisational strategy is increasingly breaking national borders (Evans et al 2012). With wider globalisation, HR is under pressure to deliver policies and practices that will support the business objectives of the organisation and demonstrate results in an increasingly competitive economic environment. Working alongside the other business functions such as finance, operations and corporate departments, HR have to understand how they can help to deliver the vision to the business in an international context.

Changes to demographics (Kulik et al 2014), such as an ageing workforce and the emergence of developing countries, mean that looking towards future staffing may require an international approach. We see more organisations requiring staff to be internationally mobile. Organisations compete for talent across the globe as individuals broaden their search for the best employment opportunities, globalising recruitment markets. Those organisations with sites overseas require an understanding of the complexities involved with managing staff internationally and the impact this has upon the global HR strategy.

Global staffing can play a key role in shaping the competitive position of multinational enterprises (MNEs), via individuals' transfer of knowledge across the organisation, which is often cited as one of the main reasons to undertake an international assignment. Additionally, the widely accepted reasons for transferring staff from one country to another include developing the individuals' management or leadership skills, knowledge of markets or products or to strengthen the organisation's international competencies (Caligiuri and Tarique 2012).

Much of the research in IHRM focuses upon the management of staff within MNEs and involves the study of expatriates, but can also apply to small and medium-sized enterprises (SMEs) and a broader definition of international staff.

3.6 STRATEGIC INTERNATIONAL HRM

The trend over the last few years has been to attempt to link IHRM to the strategy of the organisation in line with fulfilling the company's global objectives (SIHRM) (Stahl et al 2012).

REFLECTIVE ACTIVITY 3.6

HSBC defines itself as 'The World's Local Bank' in its marketing. Visit its websites and examine their corporate messages.

1   What effect does this international branding have on HR in the UK?

2   Given its messages, how would you approach someone in a London office of the firm to undertake an overseas assignment in a subsidiary in Detroit for two years?

3.6.1 DEFINING STRATEGIC INTERNATIONAL HRM

In order to highlight the context of SIHRM, a definition is needed. Schuler et al define SIHRM as:

> human resource management issues, functions, and policies and practices that result from the strategic activities of multinational enterprises and that impact the international concerns and goals of those enterprises. (1993, p422)

The definition brings together a number of factors that includes literature from international business and management, as well as IHRM: 'In essence, MNEs are firms that need to be global and local (multi-domestic) at the same time' (Schuler et al 1993, p421).

Schuler et al (1993) explore this notion through the development of an integrative framework to further our understanding of SIHRM. The development of a framework leads to including three major components: issues; functions; and policies and practices, which in turn are influenced by MNEs' strategic activities. These are discussed below.

SIHRM issues

The organisation needs to decide how much control it allows the local business whilst considering that this may vary depending on the local environment. Cultural differences play a part in the decision as to which approach the organisation will pursue. HRM plays an important role within the organisation in terms of integrated or differentiating practices.

SIHRM functions

The function relates to human resource orientation; the time, energy and financial resources operating the human resource organisation; and the locations of the resources. There are several ways that the company may choose to manage its human resources. For example, all HR policy and practice activities are handed down from the headquarters of the MNE. In contrast, local divisions are able to tailor HR practices that are more locally accepted, such as promotion criteria.

SIHRM policies and practices

Policies and practices involve developing general guidelines on how individuals will be managed and developed within the organisation. For example, the HR policy may outline the reward structure and instruct all sites to pay the local median for certain grades of employees. However, it may be part of the company's overall strategy to take into consideration the nuances within a particular environment. For example, providing specific practices that are appropriate to the local market such as incentivised pay schemes or specific talent sectors. Indeed, there may be particular local requirements that will impact upon HR policy and practices in terms of legislation such as a minimum wage, etc. Therefore a single policy acts as a guide whilst consideration is provided as to local terms and culture.

It can be seen that one thread throughout the issues, functions and policies described above is that of the degree of localisation allowed by the parent office. Organisations vary enormously as to how far this is granted, and it may not be standard across the whole organisation (Farndale et al 2010a). But how does international or global HRM differ from domestic HRM? As HR practices are complicated by the practicality of applying internationally understanding IHRM's development is useful. There are different types of employees to consider, such as host-country nationals (HCNs), parent-country nationals (PCNS) and third-country nationals (TCNs).

Let us use the illustration of IBM, where the parent organisation is based in the USA. It has offices in the UK, where British employees would be seen as HCNs. It might also have staff from the USA (PCNs), and employ specialist staff from anywhere in the world who are neither British nor American nationals (TCNs). The international context introduces different ways in which these employees are employed, such as: expatriates (the USA manager takes a two-year job in the UK, but is still employed by the parent office); inpatriates (coming from a subsidiary into headquarters – in our example a UK manager taking a two-year contract to work in IBM in the USA but still employed through the British office); hybrid arrangements or on local conditions, where a foreign national decides to be employed directly by the local organisation.

REFLECTIVE ACTIVITY 3.7

Your organisation, a UK-based telecoms company employing 100 people, wants to expand its market share in South Africa, and opens a dedicated office in Johannesburg as part of its long-term strategy. The office will provide the hub for future training of local employees. Advise the organisation on which strategy would achieve its aims to introduce the headquarters culture and ethos in terms of work practices to the new office. The current HR function is served by one consultant with part-time administration support. Which of the following approaches would you advise and why?

- Use a two-year long-term assignment, traditional expatriate package.
- Use a short-term assignment.
- Hire someone locally and provide them with some headquarters training.
- Employ someone from the headquarters on local terms and conditions.

It is useful at this point to highlight the various staffing strategies that global organisations utilise. Influences towards staffing strategies were first addressed by Perlmutter (1969) and later extended to provide the following approaches to global staffing (Heenan and Perlmutter 1979):

- *Ethnocentric* – strategic decisions are made by the headquarters by PCN expatriates. Therefore it is accepted that all policies and practices emanate from the headquarters. Arguably, the advantage is that qualified managers are available from the home country (precluding any local labour shortage). However, this approach does limit the opportunity to promote HCNs to senior managerial positions, thus risking the loss of staff with this potentially short-term view.
- *Polycentric* – generally the operations would be managed by HCNs with the intention that they remain in the host country, precluding the use of expensive expatriates from the parent company. There are disadvantages to this approach in the limiting of assignments by home or host, reducing knowledge transfer and management.
- *Geocentric* – this approach seeks to resource the best person for the position regardless of their nationality.
- *Regiocentric* – some autonomy is reflected in this approach towards decision-making.

This approach is likely to facilitate more local responsiveness towards operation and form regional boundaries according to geographic location, such as Eastern Europe, the Mediterranean, the USA, etc. Both polycentric and regiocentric approaches allow for more local responsiveness, with less corporate integration. However, the danger is that there is knowledge being built in subsidiaries by HCNs which the parent does not benefit from, at a risk of losing competitive edge.

Many of these strategies ask people to work overseas. The term 'expatriate' refers to someone who is temporarily assigned to an overseas location from their home organisation. Some organisations refer to such individuals as 'international assignees'.

Traditionally, expatriate assignments are considered to fall into either long-term assignments over 12 months to a maximum of four years; short-term assignments lasting three to 12 months; or business trips typically lasting no longer than three months.

Long-term assignments are considered to be over 12 months in duration and offer a full compensation package whereby the expatriate is provided host housing, living allowances, removal services, etc. Often in long-term assignments a partner and children will be included in arrangements. In terms of cost it is generally accepted that an assignment will cost the organisation three to four times the expatriate's salary.

PricewaterhouseCoopers (2014) predict that there will be a further 50% growth in international assignments by 2020. Their research highlights that the use of short-term assignments has become the norm, rather than the expensive traditional long-term assignments.

 REFLECTIVE ACTIVITY 3.8

If the costs for the use of expatriates are so high, what arguments are there for such assignments to be used by organisations?

The rationale for an overseas assignment should always be considered. MNEs often favour a long-term assignment when the objective is to commence business operation in an overseas location. However, a smaller organisation may not have the resources to utilise a long-term assignment as that individual is intrinsic to the home company. Therefore the strategy of staffing may well differ depending on the size of the organisation.

 AGILENT TECHNOLOGIES

CASE STUDY 3.2

The move to reduce costs has seen a decline in the number of long-term assignments, with organisations utilising short-term assignments instead. Collecting data in this area holds many challenges and long-term case studies are rare.

In order to understand the cost involved in its expatriate programme, Agilent outsourced the administration of its expatriates. In 2000 Agilent had approximately 1,000 expatriates, costing $72 million. Over the next three years, the company reduced the number of expatriates to around 300 expatriates. In order to achieve this large reduction in headcount Agilent looked at alternative ways of resourcing positions, favouring the local market. In addition, a review of its policy and expatriate package has seen large-scale reduction in benefits offered, to reduce costs by 70% to $23 million.

Agilent's example raises some interesting points. Until the company decided to outsource its expatriate programme it had not considered the actual costs; it knew expatriates were expensive but did not realise the extent. The challenge of tracking expatriates is echoed by many MNEs (see Doherty and Dickmann 2012).

Questions

1. How would you recommend Agilent assess the success of its programme, other than the reduction of cost for its expatriate programme?

2. What do you think the effect of reducing the number of expatriate opportunities could have been at Agilent head office?

3. How would you be able to track such effects?

4. What effect might you want to look for in the various subsidiaries?

5. How might you measure the impact?

3.6.2 SHORT-TERM ASSIGNMENTS

The move towards cost reduction has contributed towards the increase in short-term assignments. Instead of providing an expatriate package that allows the employee to take their immediate family on assignment, the organisation supports only the assignee. Costs are saved by precluding education costs as well as reduced housing costs (as the expatriate is not accompanied by their family) and further allowances associated with a long-term assignment such as family healthcare insurance. Thus the employee is sent overseas with minimal support and cost.

REFLECTIVE ACTIVITY 3.9

Consider this description: GreenTech Inc, a provider of reusable energy systems to large industrial corporations, has started sending more employees on short-term assignments. Assignments are with producers of equipment sold by GreenTech and to install equipment systems into purchasers' sites. Typically assignments last for six months and are managed as a business trip. The employee stays in a hotel and is reimbursed for meals and trips home every other month, eliminating the need to pay costly housing allowances and costs related to moving the employee's family.

The previous system placed the employee on two-year assignments accompanied by their family. The assignee would have had several projects running in this time.

1   What effect would this change have had on the type of applicants for the job?

2   What effect would the change have had on recipients of the services of these assignees in the host country?

3   Would any of these changes worry you from an HR perspective?

4   How would you advise GreenTech to proceed?

3.6.3 THIRD-COUNTRY NATIONALS

A TCN is an individual who works for an international organisation and whose nationality is different from that of the company, and of the country, in which the organisation operates. For example, a UK manager working for a Spanish subsidiary of an American company. The advantages of TCNs from the company's point of view are that they require the provision of very limited additional assistance, such as housing, and education tax, and only for a restricted period.

3.6.4 LOCALISATION

Another alternative to an expatriate assignment is the use of localisation. This is where expatriates move permanently to local terms and conditions, and it has seen an increase over the last decade (Harry and Collings 2012). This could be at the end of a long- or short-term assignment at the choice of the individual, or that an individual was sent on assignment with the expectation that they would localise with minimal support from the company. The move towards recruiting expatriates on the basis that they will localise from the beginning is not new, especially within the 20-year-old-plus market. However, what has changed is the push to hire employees locally and not use expatriates at all – here the local employer might take on someone who lives only miles from the parent company but who is never employed by the parent. The benefit to the organisation is the significant saving in expatriate terms and conditions, especially education and housing costs. An emerging trend of hybrid packages allows expatriates access to some of the expatriate package initially to set them up in the new country and then gradually remove the benefits during the year, such as help with rented accommodation.

3.6.5 SELF-INITIATED EXPATRIATES

A relatively underexplored area is the increase in self-initiated expatriates (Howe-Walsh and Schyns 2010, Doherty 2013). A self-initiated expatriate (SIE) independently moves to another country for employment. As such, an SIE does not receive any additional support from their home country employer. However, there are opportunities to manage this growing pool of resources more effectively. Research has shown that self-initiated expatriates themselves note several combined reasons for pursuing an overseas appointment: career development; location of vacancy; no family ties; dissatisfaction with current lifestyle; timing (Fitzgerald and Howe-Walsh 2008).Who manages these types of staffing arrangements can often become blurred. Whilst the self-initiated expatriate will be treated as an ordinary new joiner, other support mechanisms can be put in place to support their initial move. There are additional considerations to explore regarding the level of support the HR function can offer during the recruitment phase. In a traditional expatriate assignment services such as cultural training would be offered prior to the assignment.

Howe-Walsh and Schyns (2010) show how different types of adjustment require the use of differing HR practices. In order to make the most of self-initiated expatriates, consideration of how the organisation can aid their initial adjustment can provide a strategic advantage over companies that do not provide support by attracting good candidates. The points below are highlighted as areas to explore in order to improve the process of recruitment and retaining self-initiated expatriates:

Recruitment strategy

Developing the reputation of the organisation as an employer of choice attracts candidates, thus assisting with recruitment of talent (Vaiman et al 2015). Selecting the right candidates poses challenges for any organisation. Self-initiated expatriates offer additional benefits to the organisation during the early stages of their employment as they are already receptive to working in an overseas location. In addition, they have chosen the organisation and the position offered, rather than 'being sent' on an assignment. Women are particularly open to becoming an SIE as a means to enhance their career (Andersen et al 2015). This is part due to lack of career progression in their current country of work.

Training and mentoring

Whilst new joiners are often provided with some sort of induction training it is unlikely that an SIE will be offered any cultural training for the reasons outlined above. However, the benefits of mentoring should be considered. One area in which a mentor can provide assistance is in helping the self-initiated expatriate to gain a greater working knowledge of the organisation, again akin to the services offered to any new joiner.

Non-work support

The types of activities that HR would traditionally support for an expatriate should also be considered in terms of self-initiated expatriates. Finding accommodation can be one of the most stressful parts of relocation. HR can provide support in terms of facilitating the search for properties as well as assistance with tenancy agreements. Other forms of support include: opening bank accounts; social security and residence registration; communication connections; and expatriate social groups. When facilitated, these types of support enable the SIE to start work faster and add value to the organisation.

3.6.6 GLOBAL/INTERNATIONAL HMR AND THE SME

The discussion so far has revolved around MNEs. Arguably, however, much business conducted today is undertaken by SMEs, many of whom have a global dimension, often levered through technology, but with implications for the HR function. As IHRM literature is mainly focused upon MNEs, there is an argument that transferability of HRM practices from MNEs to SMEs is limited (Festing et al 2013). Drawing upon the research of MNE organisations, SMEs pose different challenges (ibid). SMEs are more dependent upon environmental situations in different countries.

- The importance of the founder/owner influences the development of HRM strategy of the organisation (Garavan et al 2015). Within any organisation there are links to how the organisation is perceived and their leader (Bernhard and O'Driscoll 2011). Within an SME the owners' entrepreneurial style and the way they conduct business can be part of the attraction of working for the organisation.
- Recruitment, selection and retention within an SME is likely to be managed without the assistance of an HR function as much more informal processes are utilised with the owner/CEO often responsible for recruitment and selection (Festing et al 2013).

The most striking difference between MNEs and SMEs is that the SMEs do not have the same HRD infrastructure capability, as mentioned above. Therefore, sending managers overseas to open or start new business ventures is not supported by an HR function locally or any specialists at the parent organisation. Being able to construct value-adding arguments for managing a limited number of staff overseas becomes more difficult in such circumstances (Garavan et al 2015).

3.6.7 WHO IS RESPONSIBLE FOR INTERNATIONAL HR POLICY?

Traditionally within MNEs, IHR policy and practice is undertaken by specialists, either as part of the HR team or partially or fully outsourced, as outlined in Case Study 3.2. The decision of what policies the company chooses to adopt towards its international workforce ultimately rests with the organisation's overall strategy. Nearly two-thirds of companies (64%) have no specific procedures in place to measure the success of their expatriate benefit programmes (Mercer 2008/09). Thus from the outset there are issues with retention and monitoring the expatriate's career path.

3.6.8 DEVOLUTION TO LINE MANAGERS

With increased devolution to line managers it is important to consider the perceptions of more than one stakeholder. We have already noted that HR delivery of international services may be internal to the HR function, a separate specialised function or outsourced. It is increasingly becoming the norm with MNEs that HR policy and practice delivery is undertaken by the line manager (Reichel and Lazarova 2013). In an international context, the likelihood within an MNE is that there will be a duplication of stakeholders within the home country and host country. The multiple stakeholders involved in managing individuals across more than one country add another dimension to managing people. A greater understanding of the stakeholders highlights the necessity for clear and transparent strategy supported by HR policy and practice.

3.7 CONCLUSION

In concluding this chapter, one can see that approaches for delivering support for managing and leading people are becoming more complex as the organisation expands in terms of the number of employees, the scope of the organisation, and its geographical reach. We have examined how the emphasis on what an HR practitioner actually does varies with the size, stage in development and sector of the organisation being served.

Adding value from HR is possible in all circumstances. Although much is made of HR aligning with the strategy of the organisation (Buller and McEvoy 2012), this becomes more difficult as the organisation grows and the physical and psychological distance between HR and decision-makers increases. No doubt an area for development in research is the political skills HR practitioners need to develop in order to influence and ensure that their value-adding ideas are tried by the organisation (Verbrigghe and Buyens 2015, Olson 2014), and that their work receives sufficient profile to make sure it is perceived as value-adding (Sears 2010).

We have seen that cutting costs through outsourcing is a common trend, and likely to continue as vertical integration is lessened. HR is not immune from these trends, but if it is to remain a strategic component of success, aspects of HR need to be kept in-house (Woodall et al 2009). The level of outsourcing provides many varied career opportunities for HR practitioners working in providers of services. There is a danger, though, that career paths in these directions may be limited to 'being efficient' only in cost-effective terms rather than adding value in more subtle ways.

International issues are no longer the prerogative solely of large multinationals. Globalised job markets, as well as the opportunities that the Internet provides for selling products and services abroad, means that complexity can arrive sooner rather than later for many in the HR function.

KEY LEARNING POINTS

- The HR function adds value to the organisation in a number of ways through delivering business strategy.
- The HR function adds value, but how it does so, and who is perceived as adding value, is complex and sometimes a function of internal politics and the perceptions of line managers.
- The way in which HR adds value changes as the organisation grows, and also between sectors.
- Outsourcing aspects of HR is common, but needs to be done carefully to ensure the organisation does not lose competitive edge.
- Internationalisation is a current issue for those who recruit, and for those involved in mobilising staff between countries.
- The degree of control from the parent company in the area of international HR presents a challenge which needs to be balanced depending on the context.

CASE STUDY 3.3

INTERCONTINENTAL HOTELS GROUP

Asia is a rapidly developing continent and the ubiquitous 'war for talent' is accentuated for Intercontinental Hotels Group (IHG), with rival hotels from China constantly approaching staff with job offers. HR's biggest challenge, according to Ricky Wong, HR director, IHG Hong Kong, is finding and keeping the right people in such an aggressive labour market.

'I'm really concerned that our staff will be poached by competitors,' Wong says. 'Managers from hotels in Macau come to our hotel and sit in the lobby to check out the staff they want to poach. The particular hotel I'm talking about has 3,000 rooms and they need experienced managers.'

So where will they find them? 'They'll find them at the five-star hotels in Hong Kong – hotels like ours,' says Wong. As a result of such measures, he takes career development very seriously.

Many of IHG Hong Kong's employees have been at the company for several years, and while he cannot promise promotions, on-the-job learning with greater participation in management decisions is a must to keep staff engaged.

'Many employees are looking for personal development. They can suggest how to do the job better, and we encourage that. They can disagree with managers – and that's not easy in the traditionally hierarchical culture of Asia. We "allow" them to disagree and to have a sense of involvement,' says Wong. This mature approach to managing employees

seems to be working. IHG's staff turnover is at 12%, a hefty 8% lower than that of its main Hong Kong competitor (another five-star hotel), according to Wong.

Source: XpertHR (2008)

Questions

1   Identify and appraise the attitudes and approaches adopted in this excerpt.

2   What other tactics might be employed to further enhance the achievement at IHG?

3   In what ways is the HR strategy adding value to the organisation?

REVIEW QUESTIONS

1   Do you think HR professionals at all levels can demonstrate value-added, or is this an issue only for people at the top?

2   What would you see as the challenges of someone changing job from being an HR business partner in the private sector to one in the public sector? How would you suggest such an individual prepares for their new role?

3   Assuming there are financial gains for providing an outsourced HR service, what other parameters would you consider when evaluating this issue?

4   Why is adding an international dimension to one's operation so challenging for HR? Use the example of a UK organisation setting up a sales office in Canada to illustrate your ideas. In this operation some local Canadian staff would be employed, but need head office assistance during the set-up period.

EXPLORE FURTHER

Boselie, P., Brewster, C. and Paauwe, J. (2009) In search of balance – managing the dualities of HRM. *Personnel Review*. Vol 38, No 5. pp461–471. This paper provides an excellent overview of strategic HR issues and constructs in contemporary thinking with an excellent reading base for further exploration. This can be compared to the CIPD-sponsored research (Sears 2010), which is drawn from large organisations where the notion that practice outstrips thinking and academic work is put forward.

CIPD (2015) *HR Outlook* survey. This survey is undertaken every other year to a large body of UK HRPs and is key reading for all UK-based HRPs. Well designed and well-reported, the analysis is undertaken for profit/non-profit and large/smaller organisations.

Doherty, N. (2013) Understanding the self-initiated expatriate: a review and directions for future research. *International Journal of Management Reviews*. Vol 15, No 4. pp447–469.

Howe-Walsh, L.J. and Schyns, B. (2010) Self-Initiated Expatriates: implications for HRM. *International Journal of Human Resource Management*. Vol 21, No 2. pp260–273. This contribution gives useful insights into the developing area of self-initiated expatriates – a field which is likely to become more important for recruiters in all organisations and one which is not often studied.

Marchington, M. (2015) Human resource management (HRM): too busy looking up to see where it is going longer term? *Human Resource Management Review*. Vol 25, No 2. pp176–187. This is a challenging paper and represents some critical HR thinking. Certainly as a thought-provoking stimulus it is well worth reading for discussion with other HR colleagues, although the response to the challenge of short-termism is hardly easy.

Reichel, A. and Lazarova, M. (2013) The effects of outsourcing and devolvement on the strategic position of HR departments. *Human Resource Management*. Vol 52, No 6. pp 923–946. This article provides a very good literature review of outsourcing HR and a fascinating study of practice in contemporary UK-based organisations. Tracking through their references, readers will find key evidence regarding the need for HR to not only undertake an effective role, but also to be seen to do so.

Sparrow, P.R. (2012) Globalising the international mobility function: the role of emerging markets, flexibility and strategic delivery models. *International Journal of Human Resource Management*. Vol 23, No 12. pp2404–2427. This paper reports on the international HR function and how IHR supports globalisation and is a good overview.

CHAPTER 4

Professionalism and Ethics in Managing People

MATTHEW ANDERSON AND CHARLOTTE RAYNER

LEARNING OUTCOMES

After reading this chapter, you should be able to:

- understand the foundations of the 'professions'
- understand the role of professional associations
- appreciate the role of ethical codes of conduct
- understand the concept of business ethics
- explain the difference between the duties, consequences and virtues approaches to ethics
- comprehend what is meant by an 'ethical dimension' to the management and leadership of meeting corporate social responsibility (CSR) targets
- discuss the implications for professional leadership in HRM.

4.1 OVERVIEW

Is HRM a profession? What does it mean to be a professional? In this chapter we begin by examining what is understood as constituting a profession together with the role of professional bodies such as the CIPD. We show that professionalism implies certain ethical standards of behaviour, which, together with systems of training, form a quality assurance system for users of the profession. This insight forms the basis of our link to a more general discussion on ethics.

Ethics must be understood at the conceptual level, but these principles only have meaning if they can be applied. In this chapter we introduce the main conceptual components of ethics and use a variety of examples including an illustration of equal opportunities and the potential for positive discrimination – a debate no doubt set to run for some time. As shown, ethical decisions are rarely about choosing between right and wrong, but rather between different pathways none of which are perfect. It is crucial that we all grasp the basics of ethics so that we are aware of our actions and the choices we are making.

4.2 INTRODUCTION

We need to first examine what a profession is. While the notion of 'profession' goes back many centuries to the social establishment of medical and legal practitioners, we focus here on present-day meanings. Professionals and professionalism are described by Evetts

(2013) as implying the involvement of trust which she sees as applying to many occupations: plumbers and electricians as well as lawyers and doctors. Trust may include the handling of sensitive or confidential information, employing expertise and/or expert judgement. Professionals have to be worthy of that trust by acting in the best interests of their clients, not abusing the trust, and maintaining confidentiality. Evetts summarises that 'professions are regarded as essentially the knowledge-based category of service occupations which usually follow a period of tertiary education and vocational training and experience' (Evetts 2013, p781) and imply minimum standards of practice and behaviour. As such, professionalism is a process of quality assurance whereby the professionals adhere to standards and their clients are willing to trust them. The emphasis on education and training means that a whole mechanism needs to be in place to establish appropriate standards, communicate these standards, validate and test members of the profession and provide updating – as well as setting up and monitoring processes for complaints and remedial action. Traditional professions such as engineering, medicine and the law require practice as well as academic validation such as providing evidence through practice diaries to demonstrate the application of knowledge. This emphasises that it is not just the knowledge base that is important: the application of knowledge is equally critical. The traditional professions often have differentiated branches as their knowledge base has grown too large to be managed simply, as HR practitioners who employ these groups will know.

Professions 'create and maintain distinct professional values or moral obligations . . . (by) encouraging co-operation as well as practitioner pride and satisfaction in work performance' (Evetts 2013, p785). Hence professionalism is not just about knowledge; it is also about professional attitude and ethics. Crucially, the relevant behavioural and moral standards are set by the professionals themselves, usually working under the umbrella of a professional association adding legitimacy as a body independent from employers. The professional association has grown over years to be an organisation that sets, tests and maintains standards and regulates its own membership as autonomous from the employer. Nevertheless, it is essential the association engages employers and 'customers' to ensure that its work is relevant to need.

Professional associations continue to perform the role of providing credibility to their members through the control of membership (Farndale and Brewster 2005), although this a difficult path to tread as the associations are funded by their members. Hence strong leadership is needed to ensure conflicts of interest do not impede effective decisions. In the end, a strong professional association is respected by consumers, and members of a strong association are proud of their membership and careful to not compromise its reputation. The strength of affiliation felt by members to their professional association will of course vary (Pritchard and Symon 2011). For some, being 'a professional' will be central to their identity and they will want to be involved as much as possible, attending events and sitting on committees; for others this will be less so (Brown 2015, Alvesson and Willmott 2002). Some associations require evidence of involvement with the professional association to retain or continue their membership, others require professional updating evidence, whilst other associations grade membership so that member can choose an appropriate level of commitment.

Let us now turn to HRM as our exemplar. Looking through UK advertisements for HRPs it is clear that CIPD qualifications are required for the majority of posts, and in this sense the CIPD has an enviable reputation in the UK for excellent and relevant qualifications. Extensive engagement with practitioner members is part of curriculum planning for the CIPD where variegation (levels of membership) is linked to the passing of exams and evidence of practice. Administration of exams and provision of support for students entails a complex, effectively run infrastructure. A network of branches ensures that continuing professional development (CPD) is available to UK members. In the USA the Society of Human Resource Management (SHRM, pronounced 'sherm') is known better for CPD and the co-ordination of large updating events than for its qualification structure, and has been far more assertive regarding global spread in years past.

 REFLECTIVE ACTIVITY 4.1

Take some time to explore the CIPD website to examine the committee structure and overall organisation of CIPD staff and roles. Examine the different membership categories, and reflect on how 'being a professional' includes being part of one's professional association.

1   Can one call oneself an HR professional without having CIPD qualifications?

2   Suppose a CIPD member never engages with local branch or national events – would you consider them less 'professional' than someone who does?

3   Explore the CIPD Code of Professional Conduct and comment on how this might affect your work.

Being a member of the CIPD and 'acting as a professional' entails far more than passing exams, as indicated in the CIPD Code of Professional Conduct (2015). It requires a commitment to update professional knowledge, uphold legal thresholds and behave with integrity at all times. In addition, CIPD members are required to 'challenge others if they suspect unlawful or unethical conduct or behaviour' (para 4.2). It is clear the CIPD permits no exceptions to positive professional behaviour in all aspects of working life. Those embracing such standards may use them as a frame for professional identity, where the standards become part of their working self (Brown 2015). For other stakeholders, a published code of conduct signals to everyone the standards of behaviour required by members of the profession. From the point of view of ethical theories, codes of conduct contain principles or duties to be respected by members, abuse of which may mean the loss of professional status. A well-written code of conduct can be highly valuable to members as it is difficult to forecast exactly which course of action is going to be in the best interests of the stakeholders even for individuals who are strongly committed to acting in an ethical way (Foote 2001). The continuing debate of live ethical situations is enormously helpful to everyone. Recently, VW's emission scandal was well-discussed by the CIPD in terms of HR roles and responsibilities in a highly accessible blog (Zheltoukhova 2015). More and more organisations are developing their own ethics committees. Traditional in some industries such as pharmacology and other medical-related areas, some professionals will have not only their professional body's code of ethical conduct, but also their own organisation's ethical code. It is crucial that any organisation's ethical code has clear and direct links to its disciplinary procedure. With widening responsibilities, organisation ethical codes are becoming more common.

The more zealous ethical champions amongst us will point out that, as an internal service function, HRM has a great opportunity to influence behaviour through role-modelling, helping on culture shifts, and in daily discussions with line managers. If the HR practitioner can advise on and model ethical behaviour, then they can contribute to raising the standards of practice in all managers. This approach does not come without caveats. Given the recent push towards enabling line managers to undertake some functions, one might argue that the HR profession has diluted its direct effect. One must also bear in mind that many of those practising at board and other senior levels do not have CIPD qualifications or indeed membership (Caldwell 2008, Wiley 2000, Wright 2008) and may have little background in ethics.

Some research has been conducted into HR and ethical practices, and it is to the research evidence that we now turn. How well is HR doing? Following the 2008 financial crisis there has been a growing set of studies analysing the delivery of ethical practice in organisations. The HR role services many stakeholders and we have always known this can present challenges (Legge 2000) and the possibility of split allegiances for HRPs (Guest and Woodrow 2012). Is there necessarily a tension between the roles of HRPs in serving strategic organisational needs, working with line managers and ensuring that employees are treated properly? Some recent publications have examined the practice of HRPs and looked at the ethical implications of their work.

Van Buren et al (2011) studied Australian HRPs and their involvement in ethically related decisions. As in any other managerial role, tasks had to be prioritised, and the study suggested that strategic and managerial issues were often accorded a higher priority than those of staff coming to them for assistance. Given the nature of the HR remit, many will not be surprised by this, but if an HR department positions itself as the ethical guardian of employees, then there is clearly some scope for scepticism on the part of the workforce (Searle and Skinner 2011).

Based on employee reports of very poor attention from HR when handling complaints about bullying, Harrington et al (2012) sought the views of HRPs on the issue. Qualitative data from a British sample found that HRPs knew that staff were not always properly supported, but the reasons for this were complex. It appeared that HRPs' dependence on line managers for their power could influence their judgement, almost always meaning that the HRP denied a situation was bullying in order to avoid challenging line managers. Several HRPs reported that even raising the accusation of bullying with line managers would be destructive to that relationship; a relationship central to their day-to-day work. The researchers concluded that while the HRPs' actions were entirely understandable, it left employees unsupported. Their findings helped to explain the cynicism of those who felt bullied, and their anger towards HR and its claim to be the guardian of the anti-bullying policy. It provides a warning for HR to only 'own' policies they can support – as perceived neglect can be contagious to others' judgements of HR's trustworthiness (and general professionalism).

Another study (De Gama et al 2012) examined the competing priorities for HRPs in a time of economic difficulty and downward pressure on employment. Drawing on a Canadian sample, this study found that HR managers' tendency to depersonalise staff and think of them as 'resources' resulted in an attitude which the authors argued was dehumanising to staff. However, there is also recognition that HR practitioners and managers are frequently conflicted by the decisions that they are required to take, and a suggestion that a holistic re-evaluation of professional practice may offer possibilities for an alternative, ethical approach to HRM.

The authors of this chapter found evidence that HRPs are very involved in ethical decision-making both as a profession and as practitioners. We found no systematic studies where simple conclusions could be drawn, but in reports where the research is simply framed, HR does not appear to be well thought of by others. This may be because of weak methodologies, reflect poor image management by HR (Rayner et al 2014), or reflect actual poor practice by HRPs. It is a complex field to research and well worth us exploring the conceptual side further to enable better analysis.

4.3 BUSINESS ETHICS

Business ethics is relevant to both the conduct of individuals and to the operations of an organisation as a whole. In the UK, the Institute of Business Ethics (IBE) provides support and guidance for business ethics practitioners through a range of training workshops and education programmes. The IBE website states that business ethics applies to 'any and all aspects of business conduct, from boardroom strategies and how companies treat their employees and suppliers to sales techniques and accounting practices' (IBE 2016). Importantly, ethics goes beyond the legal requirements for a company and therefore is about discretionary decisions and behaviour guided by values. Put simply, business ethics is the application of ethical values to business behaviour (IBE 2016).

From an academic perspective the subject of business ethics can be defined as, 'the study of business situations, activities, and decisions where issues of right and wrong are addressed' (Crane and Matten 2016, p5). Often business ethics is about the 'grey areas' of business where values are in conflict (Trevino and Nelson 2014). Moral rules exist in all societies and recognising the existence of different values and norms of behaviour is an important dimension in understanding the business environment. Morrison (2015, p11) usefully summarises this approach to business ethics and highlights the significance of, 'identifying, understanding and respecting the divergences, while being able to identify the right ethical approach which transcends cultural barriers'. It is important to remember that business decision-making does not take place in a value-free vacuum.

It has become increasingly common for organisations to articulate a set of values that aim to guide staff about the culture of the organisation and 'the way things are done'. Some companies provide employees with ethical tests to help them to make decisions in line with those values. These might involve a series of questions to ask, such as: Is it legal? Is it consistent with the company's code of business ethics? What would my mother think? How would I feel about it being on the front page of tomorrow's newspapers? (IBE 2016). In the next section we will look in more detail at the ethical concepts and frameworks that underpin these ethical tests.

4.4 APPROACHES TO ETHICS

The study of ethics seeks a systematic and defensible understanding of good and bad. In Western philosophy, this is usually considered to have resulted in three main perspectives on ethics:

- *Ethics seen as duties*: things that should be done or refrained from, because they are good or bad in their own right.
- *Ethics seen as consequences*: good acts are those that lead to good results, and bad acts are those that lead to bad results.
- *Ethics as virtues*: the desirable qualities or character traits that are possessed by good people.

Strong arguments have been made to support each of these main outlooks and academics have long debated the role that each plays in day-to-day ethical reasoning. However, the question of what is good and bad in human behaviour remains complex and challenging, with the possibility of contradictory answers from the different perspectives (Crane and Matten 2016).

Duty-based views of ethics (known as 'deontological' ethics) see goodness or badness as inherent in the act itself, rather than in the consequences. If lying is bad, for example, it is because the act of deliberately saying something that the speaker knows to be false is bad *in itself*, plain and simple. Deontological ethical frameworks offer a set of duties or principles which must be respected, irrespective of the consequences. The German philosopher Immanuel Kant (1724–1804) has been one of the leading voices in duty-based ethics. In his view, ethics are based on the duties that we owe each other as fellow members of a rational species. For example, we should only act in ways that could reasonably be adopted by anyone in similar circumstances (which is close in meaning to the golden rule: 'do as you would be done by'). Keeping promises, for example, is required, because not to do so would render the idea of a promise absurd. Also, people should always be treated as being of value in themselves, rather than simply used as a means to achieving someone else's goals. In other words, people should be treated with respect for their equal status as moral beings and not subjected to degrading or humiliating treatment, coercion or abuse.

However, problems with an exclusively duties-based view of ethics include:

- *excessive rigidity*: this can result from taking no account of possible consequences of following a principle or duty
- *complexity*: if principles are made more detailed in an attempt to deal with the wide range of real-life situations, then the resulting algorithms can become very unwieldy
- *priority*: which principles should take precedence over which others (and what is the new principle that governs this precedence)?

 MODERN SLAVERY ACT 2015

CASE STUDY 4.1

In March 2015 the UK Government introduced the Modern Slavery Act 2015. The new law requires businesses with a turnover of £36m or more to prepare an annual slavery and human trafficking statement that outlines the steps they have taken to ensure their business and supply chains are slavery-free.

Responsible business is increasingly seen as part of a licence to operate – what society expects as the norm and more than just a risk-management exercise. Eradicating modern slavery is a complex challenge that will involve multi-country and multi-industry alliances. At the moment HR directors have been criticised for defining their role narrowly, with a focus on compliance with the letter of the law, rather than enacting the spirit of the

law. Norman Pickavance, partner and board member at Grant Thornton and author of *The Reconnected Leader*, has stated that, 'we have to bring this back to our fundamental views of dignity and respect that anyone should be entitled to whatever their relationship with our firms. If we do not champion this cause then what does it say of our basic humanity?'

Source: *HR Magazine* (2015)

1   Consider this new Act. What duties and responsibilities does an HR manager have towards their organisation's workforce?

2   What are the implications for the responsibility of companies with global supply chains?

Those who see ethics only in terms of consequences look for good or bad in the results of the act, rather than in the act itself. A deliberate untruth, for example, is neither good nor bad in itself – it depends on the consequences. From this point of view, the ethics of stealing, or even killing, can be judged only by asking what happens as a result of the particular act. One familiar form of consequentialism is utilitarianism, which looks for the greatest good for the greatest number. In its original form, utilitarianism tries to assess the change in happiness for everyone affected by a proposed act (later forms sought to consider the consequences for those affected if the proposed action were to become commonplace). There are two main types of difficulty in an exclusively utilitarian view of ethics:

- *Methodology*: while measuring changes to happiness may sound like a good idea, it is extraordinarily difficult to do so with any precision or consistency. Recent studies have made progress on measuring happiness (for example the UK now has a Happiness Index), but there are still significant methodological challenges with this data measurement and collection.
- *Justice*: as Mackie (1977) points out, the problem with this approach is that it can allow undeserved negative consequences for one group to be offset by positive consequences for another group, as long as the net change in happiness is positive. This can be potentially very bad news for minorities in particular.

 REFLECTIVE ACTIVITY 4.2

Utilitarian thinking

Recent reports suggest that the trend for outsourcing looks set to continue, particularly in sectors such as IT (Deloitte 2014). Despite the potential risks of outsourcing, a survey by Deloitte found that only 16% of respondents had taken the decision to move work back to their home country (ibid). India has been a preferred site, and with relatively low labour costs and growing IT expertise it remains a primary outsourcing location.

This phenomenon provides an opportunity to explore the utilitarian approach to ethics. Imagine a hypothetical case of a large UK-based supermarket that is proposing to outsource its IT applications management software from a medium-sized town in the north of England to Bangalore, India. The UK centre is to be closed and there will be 400 redundancies.

Source: Deloitte (2014)

Make a list of the groups of people who will be affected by this initiative and then:

- describe the likely nature of the effects for each group
- estimate the likely size of each group.

1   How useful is this approach in illuminating the ethical implications of the proposal?

2   Is it possible to judge the 'greatest good for the greatest number'?

3   What difficulties would arise in trying to make this analysis more detailed and precise?

4   Putting these methodological difficulties to one side, how satisfactory does the utilitarian approach seem to be as a way of assessing good and bad in this case? If it seems to be unsatisfactory or incomplete, what is missing?

The contrasting views of duty-based and consequences-based ethics are reflected in the quote ascribed to Machiavelli: 'The end justifies the means'. 'Ends' are results and 'means' are principles or methods, and the debate between the two views has been running for centuries.

CASE STUDY 4.2

£1M EXPENSES FRAUD

In August 2013, the Birmingham Crown Court heard the case of a civil servant and her taxi driver partner who cheated the Crown Prosecution Service (CPS) out of £1m in an elaborate expenses fraud.

Lisa Burrows, a CPS area manager, and Tahir Mahmood pocketed £4,000 a week over five years by lodging claims for non-existent taxi journeys. The pair admitted cheating the CPS out of £1,021,475 by producing invoices for a fictitious cab firm purporting to offer transport for witnesses.

Passing sentence, Judge William Davis QC, described the fraud as a gross abuse of a position of trust:

'It is difficult to imagine a more serious fraud of its type. It was you, Burrows, who created and then authorised the payment of the bogus invoices. You knew how the system worked. Over the course of five years, you, Burrows, paid into your bank account over £320,000 in cash, all of which must have been the proceeds of the fraud. That money went on high living – expensive holidays in Dubai and New York, designer clothing, jewellery.

The fact that the fraud involved the CPS and was committed by a senior member of that service – the body responsible for bringing criminals to justice – will have affected and eroded public confidence.

The pair were each sentenced to six years in prison.

Source: *Guardian* (2013)

Questions

Consider this case and the judge's sentencing remarks with reference to both the duty-based and consequential approaches to ethics.

1   Was it the scale of the fraud that was shocking or the action itself?

2   Would it have made a difference if they had not spent the money on luxuries? For instance, if they had to support their family or pay for medical bills?

3   While this case is perhaps unusual, think about how employees might try to justify their actions if caught inflating their expenses claims.

Virtue ethics is a separate way of thinking about good and bad. Virtues are desirable character traits, exhibited by good people. For Aristotle (384–322 BC), human virtues are those qualities that allow us to fulfil our highest purpose as humans. These qualities lie between undesirable extremes (as courage lies between cowardice and foolhardiness) and wisdom is required to recognise the virtuous approach.

In the duty-based view of ethics the main question to consider was, 'How should I act in this situation?' By contrast, virtue ethics offers a more holistic approach that asks, 'How should I live my life?', and 'What kind of person should I be?' Virtue ethics argues that right and wrong cannot simply be resolved by applying a specific rule or principle. Instead individuals and organisations need to develop knowledge and judgement on ethical matters over time through a process of active learning (Nielsen 2006).

If we consider the characteristics of a good manager, or 'true professional', Dobson (2007) argues that a critical feature is, 'the adherence to certain "virtues" of character, such as honesty, fairness, prudence, and courage'. A virtue ethics approach is about how people should live their lives, in order to realise their highest potential. This takes time and experience. Rather than proposing a series of rules or principles, the main way of becoming virtuous is to study the lives of good people and learn to imitate them.

REFLECTIVE ACTIVITY 4.3

Yahoo CEO Marissa Mayer – A new corporate culture?

Marissa Mayer, former vice president of Google Product Search, joined Yahoo as the new CEO in July 2012. Challenged with turning around the troubled Internet company, Mayer made resetting the culture at Yahoo a top priority.

Within months of taking up the post of CEO, Mayer was faced with criticism for ending the company's popular work-from-home policy. The come-to-work order was first reported when a leaked memo from Yahoo's HR director was published by a technology blog in February 2013.

Mayer defended the new policy arguing that people are more collaborative and innovative when they're together in the same office. However, some reports suggested that this policy was actually aimed at terminating employment contracts of underperforming staff.

In September 2015, Mayer was again in the news following a post on her Tumblr blog announcing that she was pregnant with twins. In the blog post Mayer stated that she would only be taking limited time away and would be 'working throughout'. Most business commentators saw this as a personal decision for Mayer and her family, but for some this announcement raised questions about the corporate culture at Yahoo.

Source: *Fortune magazine* (2013)

1   To what extent do you think that Marissa Mayer's leadership approach is unusual?

2   In this case, what are the ethical factors that need to be considered?

3   What should HR do in such circumstances?

4.5 ETHICS IN THE WORKPLACE

How useful are these ethical perspectives when thinking about the ethics of managing people at work? It is feasible that all three approaches have some relevance:

- Most would agree that there are some ways of treating employees that are just plain wrong, whether or not they are also illegal. Bullying and intimidation, for example, are plainly unacceptable. Duties-based thinking also underlies the establishment of employees' rights (and corresponding duties on employers).
- Similarly, an organisation must consider the consequences of proposed actions for the organisation, employees and for third parties.
- Discussions of leadership often consider what are, in effect, virtues. Yukl (2012) describes the 'qualities' or 'traits' approach to understanding leadership and lists characteristics such as self-confidence, initiative and self-belief – see also Chapter 5. These qualities are very like the idea of virtues – each could be seen as a desirable point between undesirable extremes, for example.

Rather than searching for one theory that offers the best or true view of a moral dilemma, Crane and Matten (2010) advocate a pluralist approach whereby ethical theories act as a prism that throws light from different angles on the same problem. Used in a pragmatic way, ethical theories should complement an intelligent and considered response to real business challenges.

4.6 THE PURPOSE OF AN EMPLOYING ORGANISATION

An important additional factor to consider when thinking about the ethics of HRM is that of the aims and purpose of the employing organisation (Ellesworth 2002). Organisational purpose relates directly to ethics in HRM because organisations can be taken to employ people in order to pursue that particular purpose.

One school of thought defines the business purpose as that of maximising owner (shareholder) wealth, on the basis that this is the aim of shareholders in investing their money. Perhaps the most well-known advocate of shareholder primacy was the Chicago School economist Milton Friedman. Friedman believed that making as much money as possible is a company's only legitimate goal, subject to the basic rules of society and legal constraints (Friedman 1970). From the 1970s, shareholder primacy and profit maximisation became established as the dominant view concerning the purpose of business.

Chicago School economists went further and argued that the goal of profit maximisation was not only legitimate, but was in fact a legal responsibility for company executives. This belief in the legal obligation to shareholders appeared consistent with the dominant economic paradigm and as such was accepted uncritically in both academic and business circles (Morrison 2015). Increasingly, academic studies have challenged this belief in the legal obligations to shareholders (Stout 2012). It is argued that while legal duties are owed to the company itself, this does not necessarily imply legal obligations to individual shareholders or to shareholders as a whole (Stout 2012).

Many academics now define the purpose of business much more broadly, suggesting that a business has a wider responsibility to the society in which it operates and that the task of a manager must recognise additional duties associated with the needs and claims of various stakeholder groups. Donaldson and Preston (1995) discuss the various ways in which businesses can respond to stakeholder groups, pointing out that a company may decide to engage with stakeholder groups because it is a more effective way of making money for shareholders.

Alternatively, a 'normative' approach to stakeholder theory recognises duties towards stakeholders that must be discharged even if those actions are not clearly consistent with maximising owner wealth. One example of the latter might be a company's involvement in local community projects, in which the expenditure cannot be shown to be maximising owner wealth. This is not to say that there will be no commercial benefits from this type of expenditure – customers may approve of the venture, for example, and so switch more of their purchases to the sponsoring company – but it may be very difficult to convert those benefits into forecast cash flows. In a normative view of stakeholder theory, an organisation will acknowledge duties to get involved in this way, even if the commercial benefits are partly unclear.

In 2010, the Society for Business Ethics recognised the work of R. Edward Freeman with its 'Outstanding Contribution to Scholarship Award'. Freeman is perhaps best known for his influential book *Strategic Management: A Stakeholder Approach* (1984) which now has more than 19,000 citations. Freeman makes the case for businesses to build their strategy around their relationships with key stakeholders, but also argues that a deeper understanding of stakeholders can lead to a re-evaluation of business purpose: 'When people forget that value creation is the core purpose of business, this leads to the mistaken notion that we can somehow separate "business" from "ethics" or "society". We argue for an understanding of business and capitalism that puts creating value for all stakeholders in the center' (Freeman et al 2010).

It should also be remembered that employees are an important stakeholder group. Greenwood and Freeman (2011) argue that stakeholder theory offers the potential to open up an analysis of HRM to a more pluralistic and pragmatic approach to ethics. The stakeholder lens may provide a more comprehensive account of the employment relationship that begins to address the tendency of HRM practices to depersonalise interactions with employees. Greenwood and Freeman outline an ethical perspective of HRM that is both employee-centred and explicitly normative – where employees are treated as moral persons with 'names and faces'.

4.7 CORPORATE SUSTAINABILITY AND RESPONSIBILITY

CSR in its broader sense is now accepted business strategy. For as long as customers expect the firms they buy from to give an account of their effects on society and the environment, then prudent companies will be likely to comply (Porter and Kramer 2006). But there are criticisms from those who believe voluntary CSR has largely failed to deliver on its promise of sustainable business and purpose-inspired capitalism (Visser 2012). In a detailed study of international CSR practices, Visser identifies what he calls the 'triple curse of modern CSR' (Visser 2012, p225). Visser outlines three factors that have limited the success and impact of CSR:

- it has remained largely peripheral to business operations
- improvements made have only been incremental
- programmes are frequently uneconomic.

What is now required, according to Visser, is CSR 2.0, or corporate sustainability and responsibility. For this shift to CSR 2.0 to be effective it needs sustainability practices to be embedded and integrated into the core operations of companies. Overall, Visser is optimistic about organisational ability to respond to this challenge and forecasts that by 2022 more employees will have the knowledge of how to integrate CSR issues into their functional areas of the business, meaning that separate sustainable business departments will no longer be required.

CASE STUDY 4.3

SAINSBURY'S 20X20 SUSTAINABILITY PLAN

In 2011, Sainsbury's outlined 20 sustainability commitments to be delivered by 2020. These commitments are brought together by means of five core values:

- best for food and health
- sourcing with integrity
- respect for our environment
- making a positive difference to our community
- a great place to work.

Chief executive, Mike Coupe, has stated the importance of commitments that don't just focus on price. Sainsbury's has promised to deliver, 'value and values for customers, suppliers, colleagues and stakeholders'. Values are seen as part of Sainsbury's long-term strategy for growth – they make good business sense and offer a competitive advantage.

Sainsbury's has committed to decoupling environmental impact from business growth; for instance, by reducing energy usage despite increasing retail floor space. Sainsbury's Cannock store became the first UK retail outlet to come off the National Grid and be powered by food waste alone. The ambitions of the sustainability plan also reach beyond the direct activities of the business: 'Our scale means we can make a massive difference by embedding respect for our environment in our decision-making. We aim to be the UK's greenest grocer, not only by reducing our impact on the environment but by engaging our suppliers and others to do the same.'

Sustainability expertise and accountabilities are embedded in over 30 teams across the business, within a culture that sees the delivery of values as something in which everyone plays a part. Sainsbury's commitment to making it 'a great place to work' are shown in the range of programmes and training to engage and develop its 161,000 employees. The 20x20 plan articulates a strategic approach to sustainable staff development: 'We are committed to providing an inclusive workplace where people have the opportunity to succeed in a safe, healthy, respectful environment. We help people balance family and work commitments, investing in training and development across the business.'

Source: J. Sainsbury's (2014)

Download the latest version of Sainsbury's 20x20 Sustainability Plan

Update and consider the progress made over the last year.

Questions

1   How do Sainsbury's make 'the business case' for sustainability?

2   In which areas of the business can HR help to deliver these sustainability commitments?

As discussed earlier in the chapter, the academic literature on HRM has highlighted the ambiguities, paradoxes and dilemmas of HRM practice particularly when addressing questions of efficiency, employee well-being and sustainability. Recent academic studies have looked to understand the connections between CSR and HRM as one way of exploring these competing tensions and perceptions about the role of HR professionals (HRPs) (Parkes and Davis 2013, Voegtlin and Greenwood 2013, Ehnert 2014, Jamali et al 2015).

In a review of the academic literature, Kramar (2014) asks: 'Does the sustainable HRM literature represent a new approach to the management of people?' While studies of sustainable HRM do not yet represent a coherent body knowledge, Kramar's review suggests that academic work in this field has begun to provide a new focus on the purpose of HRM practices with a wider consideration of a variety of outcomes, not just economic outcomes (Kramar 2014). Paradoxical choices and tensions in relation to organisational efficiency and the corresponding social, individual and ecological outcomes need to be actively addressed and professionally managed. This approach offers the potential for a dynamic CSR–HRM co-creation model (Jamali et al 2015). Aligning sustainability to HRM thinking allows for new solutions to HR problems, such as HR shortages, employee health or HR development, and extends the understanding of HRM performance in relation to sustainable business organisations (Ehnert 2014).

4.8 EQUAL OPPORTUNITIES AND ETHICS

In this section we seek to apply the concepts from our previous discussion into a specific area that is difficult to implement. We have chosen equal opportunities. Originally to discriminate meant distinguishing one thing from another. Strictly speaking, therefore, the word 'discrimination' is ethically neutral. However, discrimination has recently acquired a pejorative sense, alluding to the exercise of prejudice, which is clearly unethical, and often illegal. In this sense of the word, it is 'unfair' or 'irrelevant' discrimination that is objectionable: the introduction into the process of factors that have no connection with the work to be done. Discriminating against lazy or dishonest people is thus acceptable, but discriminating on the basis of gender, ethnic origin or age is unethical.

The principle of equal opportunity (EO) requires that people should be recruited on the basis of their ability to do the job, with no other factors intruding into the decision (Noon in Beardwell and Thompson 2014). In what ways can this be said to be ethically desirable (that is, whether or not it is also legally obligatory)? In this case, both duty-based and consequentialist ethical arguments can be made to support the principle of equal opportunities. The duty-based ethics point is clear: to treat employees on some basis other than EO (for example, to allow ageist or homophobic sentiments to enter into decisions about them) is to fail to show respect for their equal status as fellow members of the moral community. As discussed by Boatright (2000), prejudice also treats people only as members of groups, rather than affording them the individual treatment that they should reasonably expect. Making recruitment, promotion or redundancy decisions on the basis of prejudice is therefore manifestly unjust to those who are disadvantaged.

From the employer's point of view, a strong consequences-based case in favour of EO can also be made. Organisations that rule out candidates from a whole group on the basis of prejudice are depriving themselves of a significant pool of talent in the labour market, and this failure to engage with diverse groups is likely to lead to non-optimal performance (Von Bergen et al 2005, Hunt 2007). Organisations may be damaged by the exercise of prejudice irrespective of any legal penalties to which they may be exposed.

However, anti-discrimination legislation is commonplace in modern economies, which suggests that the market-driven response to prejudice has been found to be inadequate. This may be because in real life, some employers might perceive enough scope to exercise their prejudices without significant disadvantage, unless legal penalties were also in prospect. It would be wrong, however, to infer from these arguments that equal opportunities is the sole – or even the pre-eminent – ethical principle at play in contemporary HRM. In large numbers of businesses around the world, the owners or managers may regard it as perfectly normal to prefer to recruit or promote an acceptably competent member of the same family over a better-qualified stranger. This is not the place to debate the relative merits of the two principles, but rather to suggest that EO is often not the sole governing principle in HRM, however strong the deontological and consequence-based arguments in its favour.

CASE STUDY 4.4

FAIRTRADE IN SOUTH AFRICA

Fairtrade has been operating in South Africa since 2003, certifying wine and fruit products. Many of the early plantations were large commercial, white-owned farms. It was argued that Fairtrade certification of these farms could undermine the objectives of the newly introduced Broad-Based Black Economic Empowerment (B-BBEE) Act 2003.

The aim of B-BBEE was to legally promote economic empowerment throughout the country's black populations. The Act was designed to transform the economy in post-apartheid South Africa so that black people benefited from better access to employment opportunities and greater inclusion in the economy. In particular, the objective was to readjust the racial composition of business ownership, management and skilled occupations.

Following a consultation with South African producers and NGOs, Fairtrade International developed a new set of standards specific to South Africa. In line

with B-BBEE, the new standards included a 25% minimum worker shareholding in farms and agricultural enterprises. Fairtrade standards now also use the B-BBEE codes to measure the level of worker empowerment – with a focus on four specific dimensions related to worker empowerment: ownership, management control, employment equity and skills development.

Source: Anderson (2015)

Questions

1   What are the challenges of introducing EO policies such as broad-based black economic empowerment?

2   What is the role of HR in this context?

3   How far can standards such as Fairtrade guarantee equal opportunities for all workers?

Arguments about positive discrimination have been in evidence for several decades. We review them briefly here because they provide an example of the complexity of ethical arguments in practice, and also because their practice in some European countries may impact other countries. For example, the Norwegian Government introduced legislation that 40% of main board seats in public companies should be held by women from 1 January 2008. This ruling, first announced in 2003, was virtually achieved by the deadline. In contrast, in 2013 men dominated FTSE 100 boards, Davies (2013) reported that there were 18 female (compared to 292 male) executive directors in the FTSE 100, and 32 female executive directors in the FTSE 250 (558 males), which he used to illustrate the talent pipeline being constrained providing stark comparison to the Norwegian situation. The Norwegian ruling has won popularity with campaigners across Europe and the rest of the world.

4.9 ETHICS IN BUSINESS – THE ROLE OF HR

Given the importance of ethical conduct in business, what contribution can or should an HRP make to an organisation's ethical policy? There is no doubt that much of the work of HRPs involves ethical issues. All HRP roles provide opportunities for extensive ethical impact. By creating and embedding policies in areas of recruitment, selection, job evaluation linked to pay, and performance management for example, HRPs have been highly influential in achieving equality for staff in hiring, reward and censure. HR business partners working with line managers are ideally placed at the front line to highlight areas of practice for attention and give informed advice and guidelines to operational staff and managers – see also Chapters 2 and 13. As such they can achieve an 'ethical guardian' role for the organisation (Lowry 2006).

As suggested above, there is much that HRPs can do to brief, train and communicate in the area of ethical conduct, but there are a number of reasons why an organisation's ethical policy will work best if it is accepted as the responsibility and part of the identity of every employee. If corporate ethics is allowed to become the concern of a few specialists, rather than the responsibility of all, then the risk of major problems will remain high.

There are limits to what HR can effect. By HR (co-)creating policies and working with other staff to set up systems that are ethically positive, their impact has already been seen to be excellent. The apparent move for CSR targets to be within the HR remit is an interesting endorsement of the influence of HR. However, the research reviewed above suggests that, for understandable reasons, asking HR to 'police' their own systems may be too much. Some organisations have compliance sections (for example, in finance), and others internal ombudsman services (for example, the military) so that complaints and investigations can be undertaken away from HR by colleagues independent to those more closely involved with day-to-day operations.

A recent report by the Institute of Business Ethics (IBE) highlights the need for collaboration in order to embed ethical values into organisation culture (IBE 2014). The IBE report focused both on the roles of HR and the ethics function, and recommended a number of areas for improved collaboration. Key areas identified included: developing and updating a Code of Ethics; recruitment and induction; training and performance management; staff survey and 'speak up' channels; ethics ambassadors and internal communications; joint presentations and reporting to the board. Despite potential challenges, the overall findings from the IBE report show that many companies already have good relations between the ethics team and HR, and demonstrate a wider recognition that working effectively together helps embed a values-led culture across the organisation.

4.10 CONCLUSION

Professionalism sits at the core of good HRM practice. Professionalism has trust as a central tenet, and any effective professional body (such as the CIPD) is involved in setting standards and enabling CPD so that their members can remain aligned to good practice. Ethics are central to the judgements we make about what good practice is. Demonstrating good ethical practice means thinking decisions through in a careful manner and developing one's own moral compass. One common problem is that managers fail to perceive the ethical implications of a decision or action at the start. In this area HRPs can contribute uniquely across the organisation. By setting ethically screened policies, they can contribute to providing a framework within which managers can operate that precludes some unethical choices. By working with partner line managers, they can bring an independent view to bear on decisions where the manager might not have considered the ethical implications fully. Embedding ethical principles in training and learning events, the HRD specialist can prompt all employees to be more aware of the nature of their professionalism and the role of ethics within it.

Evidence is beginning to be gathered on ethical behaviour, and HR is among the professions to be studied. The dynamics are complex, and remain to be fully understood, but in the process we may see further developments in ethical approaches within the profession. Evidence suggests that HRPs, like all other professionals, need to be constantly vigilant of their own judgement.

KEY LEARNING POINTS

1   HR and line managers have an important role to play in influencing the level and type of integrity observed beyond the law and thence adopted by others.

2   The CIPD plays an important role in the HR profession. Regardless of one's specialism, membership of the CIPD involves needing to abide by its Code of Professional Conduct.

3   In this chapter we have outlined areas that are becoming increasingly urgent in the HR field and which relate to ethical practice generally and professionalism specifically. These are not easy topics, and possibly require all staff to reflect at a deeper level than previously.

4   There are a variety of approaches to analysing situations from an ethical point of view. Sometimes these can lead to very different logic and actions.

5   Often employees do not analyse the ethical principles they employ.

6   There is a strong case that good ethics makes sustainable business sense.

7   Some issues (such as equal opportunities) are enshrined in law and regardless of one's personal feelings, one must facilitate the adherence to these rights, promoting them and leading the organisation through changing policies and practice.

1   Think about an organisation with which you are familiar. Provide practical examples of ways in which it is operating ethically. Can you relate these examples to the duty, consequences or virtue perspectives on ethics?

2   Discuss the view that an organisation that is providing good value products or services to its customers, paying its bills and treating its staff decently over a long period of time is acting as ethically as anyone can reasonably expect.

3   How do HR decisions become conflicted in an ethical sense? Consider situations where you have felt professionally 'torn' between courses of action, and analyse your response using ethical frameworks.

4   Can one be an 'HR professional' in the UK without being a member of the CIPD?

EXPLORE FURTHER

Crane, A. and Matten, D. (2016) *Business Ethics: Managing corporate citizenship and sustainability in the age of globalization*. 4th ed. Oxford: Oxford University Press. Written by two of the leading academics working on business ethics and corporate responsibility, this new edition includes extended coverage of SMEs and social enterprises and a wider range of global perspectives on ethical debates and dilemmas.

Visser, W. (2012) *The Quest for Sustainable Business: An epic journey in search of corporate responsibility*. Sheffield: Greenleaf Publishing. This book is based on a journey undertaken by Dr Wayne Visser as he set out to explore the many varieties of global approaches to sustainable business practices first-hand and to share some of the most innovative global examples.

LEADING, MANAGING AND DEVELOPING PEOPLE: MAJOR CONTEMPORARY THEMES

CHAPTER 5

Leadership and Leader Development

WENJIN DAI AND ALEX TYMON

LEARNING OUTCOMES

After reading this chapter, you should be able to:

- explain the difference between the terms 'management', 'leader' and 'leadership'
- identify the significance of leaders and leadership in a variety of organisational contexts
- understand some traditional and emerging theoretical approaches to the study of leaders and leadership
- specify the importance and challenges of leader and leadership development
- critique approaches to leader and leadership development
- apply this knowledge to the work of the HR professional.

5.1 OVERVIEW

In Part 3 of this book, we focus on specific themes within the area of leading, managing and developing people. One might readily imagine that the concept of leadership will be pivotal in its own right and, furthermore, an important underpinning for subsequent topics; for example, the management of change covered in Chapter 6. The purpose of this chapter is to introduce the main theoretical approaches to the study of organisational leadership, and to provide an awareness of the strengths and shortcomings of these approaches. One such potential strength lies in the relevance of such approaches in a variety of work contexts, and we will stress that when we consider leadership, one size does not fit all. We also briefly outline current contributions to leadership understanding from academic research. Thinking on leadership moves apace and new contributions reflect the inherently dynamic nature of the topic area and also point to 'direction of travel' and, therefore, possible future developments.

The chapter begins with a discussion of the terms 'management' and 'leadership' as they impact on both the strategic purpose and direction of an organisation. We present several influential approaches to the study of leadership, identifying both traditional, and emerging, approaches. We will not only summarise the approaches but also discuss them with the aim of providing a critical awareness of their implications. Then we move to a discussion of the leadership development challenge, highlighting common issues, some of their potential causes and suggestions for improvement. Throughout the chapter links are made between organisational leadership in general, leadership development and the role of the HR professional in particular.

5.2 INTRODUCTION

This chapter focuses on leadership and leadership development in a business or organisation context, and their important roles in both devising and implementing organisational strategy. It considers how existing theories and frameworks help to address the questions of what is leadership, what could be identified as good or bad leadership, and how to improve the understandings of leadership development in a business or a working environment. As we noted in previous editions of this book, the notion of leadership has provided an enduring fascination; not only to academics such as psychologists and political or social scientists, but also to journalists, biographers, authors, dramatists and film-makers, for whom it provides a rich source of material both factual and fictional. We believe this still to be the case. Understanding leadership – the starting point of our chapter – can be legitimately regarded as one of the most important yet highly debated areas in organisation studies.

REFLECTIVE ACTIVITY 5.1

Before we delve into the academic literature on leadership, it may be helpful to review your own views on the topic through consideration of some prominent business leaders, for instance, Sarah Willingham (of TV's *Dragons' Den*), Larry Page (Google), Yun (Jack) Ma (Alibaba) and Martin Winterkorn (ex VW). Conduct brief research into your chosen leaders' business careers.

1   Can you identify common traits among these leaders? What style of leadership do you associate with these people?

2   Have they always been successful and brought positive influences?

5.3 UNDERSTANDING LEADERSHIP

Leadership is a word that people come across every day, yet many find it difficult to define; often it means different things to different people. For some, leadership is mostly about the 'leaders': the very few people who arguably have the most influence over others. Hence, studying leadership is focusing on that particular group of individuals – their personalities, traits, emotions, and more importantly, how to become one of them. However, some argue this perspective ignores the influence of followers who surround and support the leader, even come up with the ideas and follow them through thick and thin. In this perspective leadership is regarded as relationships between leaders and their equally important followers. Among the numerous definitions of leadership, most incorporate the idea that it involves achieving outcomes through the efforts of others (Yukl 2012). This stresses one of the simplest and most classic definitions that leadership is having followers, as leaders cannot be leaders without followers (Grint 2010).

Some criticise these traditional distinctions between leaders and followers and consider them as interchangeable roles rather than particular groups of people (Jackson and Parry 2011). Other current debates in the area include that leadership does not have to appear powerful or remain positive. The destructive and dark sides of leadership have realistic implications that many people experience every day. The blurring of the line between leadership and management in twenty-first century organisations is also topical. What practitioners and academics would agree upon is the contested and elusive nature of leadership. Nevertheless, these perspectives have made this subject open for continual and critical dialogues, and thus more appealing.

5.3.1 IS LEADERSHIP BETTER THAN MANAGEMENT?

Leadership has received a great deal of interest in recent decades, particularly when regarded as a distinctive aspect compared to management. In 1977, Abraham Zaleznik challenged the traditional view of management which focused on organisational structure and control. He argues that inspiration, vision and human passion are the essential leadership elements that drive great successes in organisations, but were omitted in the traditional view. Subsequently he claims there are fundamental differences between managers and leaders (see Table 5.1).

Table 5.1 The differences between managers and leaders

	Managers	**Leaders**
What they do?	Embrace process, seek stability and control, eager to resolve problems quickly	Tolerate chaos and lack of structure, want to understand issues more fully before resolution
Who are they?	Rational, persistent, tolerant problem-solvers	Creative thinkers, in common with artists and scientists
How they do it?	Take an impersonal, passive outlook. Negotiate and coerce, balance opposing views, design compromise, limit choices, avoid risk	Take a personal, active outlook. Shape ideas, alter expectations, set company direction, develop fresh approaches to problems, seek risk when opportunities appear promising
Why they do it?	To feel part of the organisation. Perpetuating and strengthening existing institutions	To feel apart from the organisation. Hope to profoundly alter human and economic relationships
Relation with others	Minimal emotional involvement. Subordinates perceive them as inscrutable, detached and manipulative.	Relate to others directly, intuitively, empathetically. Subordinates 'love' or 'hate' them. Relations appear intense, turbulent, disorganised and unanticipated

Source: Adapted from Zaleznik (1977, 1992)

These distinctions project negative and positive implications on to managers and leaders. Managers seem to be handling tasks and resolving problems in their boring mundane everyday life, whereas leaders are positioned to be a group of people arguably full of creativity and excitement which subordinates either 'love' or 'hate'. In John Kotter's article 'What leaders really do', he argued that 'leadership is different from management, but not for the reasons most people think. Leadership isn't mystical and mysterious ... Nor is leadership necessarily better than management or a replacement for it.' (1990, p103) Instead he argues leadership complements management: good management brings order and consistency while leadership is about coping with change and producing continuous change in our volatile world – so the real challenge in organisations is to balance strong leadership and good management (1990, 1999). Fundamentally the lines between leadership and management are increasingly blurred. Yet it seems nearly impossible to identify whether this is the manager's or the leader's job.

The tendency to describe managers and leaders as two types of people can be harmful sometimes, as it would be rather difficult to be a manager without coping with change, or a leader without bringing back order and consistency. As Gosling and Mintzberg (2003, p54) argue: 'the separation of management from leadership is dangerous. Just as management without leadership encourages an uninspired style, which deadens activities, leadership without management encourages a disconnected style, which promotes hubris.' Therefore it is important to understand the differences, also the underlying and inseparable connections between management and leadership.

5.4 LEADERSHIP AND MANAGING PEOPLE

There has been a revival of interest in the concept and application of leadership in recent years. Two decades ago, ambitious candidates for top-flight jobs in the world of business and public affairs might have enrolled on programmes to become Masters of Business Administration or to take diplomas in management studies. Today there is a burgeoning market in postgraduate degrees such as leadership studies, or business development and leadership. So an initial question to consider is why there is such renewed interest in the field of leadership, and how this could help us to understand modern organisations and organising processes. Perhaps part of the answer is to do with changing patterns of organisational life and similar changes in social expectations within the working environment.

Traditional organisations with strongly hierarchical structures are becoming rarer, and newer forms of both commercial and public sector organisations tend to be more flexible and task- or client-focused. What Handy (1976) described as 'matrix' organisations are generally considered to be more effective in a highly fluid commercial or operating environment; and the 'shamrock' style of organisation (Handy 1989) charts the move towards further operational flexibility. This type of organisational flexibility was also described by Atkinson (1984) in his model of the flexible firm, which disaggregates different organisational requirements and builds in a further form of organisational flexibility by outsourcing or subcontracting a number of its activities. This kind of articulated organisational structure works against the maintenance of strong hierarchies based around position (or legitimate) power (Mullins 2013), and often requires individual managers to exercise a different form of authority from that conferred simply by virtue of status or rank. Similarly, wider social attitudes towards authority have changed and, as in other walks of life, people generally expect to be consulted and involved in their work rather than simply instructed. In some circumstances these expectations are now supported by the law, for instance through the Information and Consultation of Employees (ICE) Regulations of 2005, which now apply to all businesses with more than 50 employees. Together, these trends may have renewed the interest in leadership as an important skill for those attempting to 'get things done through other people'. The importance of leadership is also reflected in the National Occupational Standards for Management and Leadership, which appear to show a transition between operational and/ or supervisory levels of management at levels 2 and 3, and a more strategic approach at levels 4 and 5 (Management Standards Centre). Thus, studying leadership and its development is important for HR practitioners.

For the purposes of this chapter, strategic leadership is taken to mean the activities involved in the initial creation of an overall business or organisational strategy, then directing and energising organisational resources towards the achievement of that strategy. Insofar as it then relies on others to carry out the strategy it may involve some management, but it is primarily about business vision and mission and engaging the energies of the workforce in pursuit of that vision. This means 'doing the right thing', creating the differentiators which, in people terms, involve becoming an employer of choice, an organisation which is able to encourage outstanding performance from its workforce and thus achieve superior results. On the other hand, managerial leadership is taken to mean activities surrounding the creation, maintenance and development of an appropriate infrastructure for business operations, including that which involves organising the work of other people. It means creating a working environment that can help a business or other organisation to achieve its objectives. In this sense management includes leadership to some degree: it is about 'doing things right'.

5.4.1 STRATEGY AND LEADERSHIP

As we saw in Chapter 2, the term 'strategy' is conceived as a means of identifying the ways in which an organisation seeks to pursue its purpose, or achieve its objectives. A prominent view of business strategy is 'resource-based', that is to say, mainly to do with identifying the key resources that give the organisation a distinctive capability and finding ways of applying those capabilities to parts of the market that offer the best prospects (Johnson et al 2011, Legge 2005, Boxall and Purcell 2011). Following from this, the key tasks in the strategic planning process could be said to be:

- analysing the organisation's environment and the changes that are expected over the plan period
- identifying and evaluating the organisation's key resources: those that are distinctive (by comparison to competitors) and those that are also important to delivering value to customers, taxpayers or client groups
- considering strategic options: ways of matching organisational resources to particular parts (segments) of the market, looking for the approach that is forecast to create maximum added value for shareholders, or to achieve the most effective use of public or donor money
- choosing the preferred strategic option
- re-aligning the organisation's resources (human and others) behind the chosen strategy: acquiring new resources, modifying existing resources and getting rid of those that cannot be economically reconfigured (which, of course, opens up questions about the ethical treatment of human resources)
- directing and energising those resources towards implementing the strategy
- responding to unexpected events during implementation.

Most of these activities are focused at the higher levels of a business or organisation, and are often the province of a single individual (for instance, in a small business or owner-managed enterprise) or a small group such as a company chief executive and board of directors. In the public sector, strategic management will be in the hands of those who exercise political power and the professional experts who advise them and find appropriate means of executing political decisions. They are activities which are primarily about making informed strategic choices, in other words responding to the question 'What is the right thing to do?' They are also about convincing and energising others to put their effort behind the chosen strategy, and in this sense involve many leadership skills. In terms of people management, this level of leadership is about defining approaches to ensure that appropriate talent is recruited and motivated to achieve superior results.

 REFLECTIVE ACTIVITY 5.2

List five personal qualities or attributes which you associate with successful leadership and place them in order of importance. Ask others (in your family, friendship group or class) to do the same, then compare the lists. How many attributes are common to all lists? Do you agree on the relative importance of these attributes? Do you think they are culturally specific, or relevant in all cultural contexts?

5.4.2 MANAGEMENT AND LEADERSHIP

Increasingly, leadership ability is defined as one of the attributes of the successful manager, along with the intellectual skills required for the assimilation of information, analysis and planning, technical and professional knowledge of the business area or sector, and a clear understanding of the specific organisation and its capacities.

The Management Charter Initiative (MCI), which developed as a result of the recommendations in the Handy and Constable and McCormick reports of the late 1980s, undertook a major analysis of the nature of management for the purposes of establishing a clear framework for managerial qualifications. Its work resulted in the adoption of a competency-based approach which quickly became highly influential in the field of management development in Britain (Frank 1991). The 1997 edition of the occupational standard was based around four major components: managing operations, managing finance, managing information and managing people, only the last of which could be clearly seen as requiring leadership skills. Ten years later, the MSC researched and developed a new set of standards, which also provide a functional map and set of units of competence which encompass the important knowledge and skill components of effective management. The significance of leadership is more clearly emphasised in the title of the new standards themselves: the National Occupational Standards for Management and Leadership. The six basic elements of the new standards, which can be viewed at the MSC website (www.management-standards.org), are:

- managing self and personal skills (depicted as a central aspect of the remaining five standards)
- providing direction
- facilitating change
- working with people
- using resources
- achieving results.

Leadership ability can be firmly associated with the second, third and fourth of these elements; and indeed the term 'working with people' has replaced 'managing people' in a way which might indicate the reducing of emphasis on formal control and the increased need for collaboration in present-day work environments noted above.

The CIPD Professional Standards recognise that soft skills are just as important as technical ones, and so these are better represented and thus reflect more fully aspects of leadership which are essential to good management practice. Nevertheless, these functions are qualitatively different from those required of strategic leadership which, as we have noted, appear at the higher levels of organisations. The majority of the Standards are much more concerned with 'doing things right' in the sense of providing an effective structure within which people can achieve high levels of performance for their organisation.

Now let us turn to some of the concepts and theories about leadership, and to identify how well they might support the development of the ability to work with people, either at a strategic or at a more operational level. The following theoretical discussions will be in two parts: firstly the traditional or established leadership theories will be described, then we will discuss some of the emerging leadership theories. The distinction between the established and the emerging is not definite, but please bear in mind some of the emergence theories are still being developed and some topics are under-researched (Dinh et al 2014).

5.5 LEADERSHIP: ESTABLISHED THEORETICAL FRAMEWORKS

It is useful at this point to remind ourselves of some of the key frameworks which have developed for the analysis and study of leadership. A summary of differing academic approaches to the subject is offered by several writers including Mullins (2013), Bloisi et al (2007), Hersey et al (2001), Huczynski and Buchanan (2013), Kreitner et al (2002) and Yukl (2012). Most offer a framework for leadership studies which identifies the following main schools of thought:

- the qualities or traits approach
- the leadership styles approach
- the situational approach and contingency models.

Taking each of these approaches in turn we can examine the general principles and models involved, and comment on their suitability in relation to either strategic leadership or managerial (operational) leadership.

5.5.1 QUALITIES OR TRAITS APPROACHES

This is essentially the 'great person' theory of leadership, and tries to identify the significant features of acknowledged leaders. Early approaches to the study of leadership (mostly undertaken before and shortly after the Second World War) dwelt on the personal qualities and characteristics of successful leaders in an attempt to isolate the 'magic ingredients'. They have not generally agreed on a common set of characteristics, although one or two, such as self-confidence and intelligence, did figure in a number of models (Kreitner et al 2002). However, we talk later about some emergent theories of leadership which indicate a resurgence of interest in traits as an approach to the study of leaders.

As a result, we might consider that trait theories offer few pointers which can help aspiring managers assess their potential other than by trying to decide if they possess the appropriate qualities, or can develop (or even simulate) them. Trait theories offer little help in terms of suggesting how managerial leaders can prepare and adapt themselves to the reality of work to be performed.

Adoption of the 'traits' approach also has implications for the role of people management in an organisation. If the development of successful organisational leaders is largely a matter of identifying those individuals who possess the desired characteristics and then offering the selected potential managers opportunities to develop and exercise these abilities, then the focus of people management will probably be on devising appropriate tests (such as psychometric or aptitude tests) which will help identify the 'right stuff', and devising systems of training and promotion which will support their development. More on leadership development will be explained later in this chapter.

5.5.2 THE LEADERSHIP STYLES APPROACH

Approaches to the study of leadership that analyse the differences between leadership styles are generally focused upon the leader's attitude towards people and the resulting behaviours which they exhibit in their day-to-day dealings with members of the team. This generates a range of possibilities, and the resulting classifications usually identify a range of styles, perhaps most succinctly described by Tannenbaum and Schmidt (1973).

They focused on the relative strength and power of leaders and followers (that is, subordinates) in terms of decision-making. At one end of the resulting continuum is 'boss-centred' (autocratic) decision-making where a leader largely decides what is to be done in a specific circumstance, and others accept and follow the decision. At the other end is joint (or democratic) decision-making, where a leader will define a problem or situation and then participate in the decision-making simply as a member of the team.

This model recognises the need for an understanding of the relationship between specific leaders and their teams from a basis of both leader and follower characteristics (such as personality, relevant knowledge, experience and a sense of security, etc) and permits the inclusion of circumstantial considerations (organisational and societal factors, etc) in the equation. In this respect it bears considerable similarity to the contingency models discussed in the next section. Insofar as it examines the skills and requirements for leading a team, the approach is not prescriptive, and is an appropriate tool for analysing and identifying the range of successful managerial leadership styles. It also offers some important messages about the importance of flexibility in terms of leadership style. These approaches have value but also shortcomings in terms of leadership development which are discussed later.

5.5.3 SITUATIONAL AND CONTINGENCY MODELS OF LEADERSHIP

Situational perspectives add another dimension on leadership studies: that of the circumstances, both organisational and environmental, in which the leadership activity occurs. This allows the development of what is generally termed the contingency approach to leadership; in other words an approach which might answer the question 'What type of leadership actions and behaviours are appropriate?', in other words 'It all depends on the circumstances'. Contingency approaches thus suggest a wide range of different but equally valid ways of leading and managing people. Some, such as Hersey and Blanchard's model of situational leadership (see Hersey et al 2001), focus on the appropriate leadership styles for groups or individual followers who are at different stages of readiness or maturity to achieve a task; 'readiness' being defined as a combination of both ability, willingness or confidence to carry out the task in question. As these vary over time, so the leader needs to choose and use the most appropriate style to fit the circumstances. The four styles suggested in the situational leadership model are summarised from Hersey et al (2001, pp182–87) as follows:

S1 – telling: this provides high amounts of guidance and direction but little supportive behaviour. This style is most appropriate for low follower readiness, including situations where followers are unable and/or unwilling. The leader structures the task and concentrates on step-by-step help and instruction.

S2 – selling: this requires high amounts of both directive (task) and relationship behaviours. This style is most appropriate for low to moderate follower readiness; particularly when followers are willing but still not fully capable of performing. The leader encourages more dialogue to achieve buy-in amongst the followers.

S3 – participating: this shows high levels of two-way communication and supportive (relationship) behaviour but low amounts of guidance (task behaviour). This style is most appropriate for moderate to high follower readiness: in other words situations where followers are competent but inexperienced, or competent but demotivated. The leader should focus on discussion, encouragement and facilitation rather than instruction.

S4 – delegating: this involves little direction or support; in other words, low levels of both task and relationship behaviours. This style is most appropriate for high follower readiness, in other words, situations where a leadership intervention is largely unnecessary (unless there are significant problems), and can focus on monitoring.

For instance, an HR assistant who is highly capable and confident about carrying out selection interviews would respond well to a delegating style of management in relation to this work. However, if they then find themselves in changed business circumstances and need to carry out redundancy interviews without having had much relevant experience, then a 'selling' style of managerial leadership might be more suitable, or possibly a 'telling' style if the individual was particularly resistant to carrying out the new task. There is also evidence that contingency approaches to leadership have particular relevance when considering inter-cultural situations. Kreitner, for instance, suggests that national culture is an important contingency and that cultural analyses such as those of Hofstede can be helpful in identifying appropriate styles for the needs of different cultural groups (Hofstede 1991, Kreitner 2001).

There seems, from Kreitner's research, to be some indication that the most widely applicable style is the participative one. It is well suited to many national cultures but particularly those such as that of the US and Sweden where there is limited 'natural' respect for hierarchy and seniority: what Hofstede would term a 'low power distance' culture. Nevertheless, it can be successful in a wider range of cultures than the directive style. The latter is more specifically suited to 'high power distance' cultures where status automatically commands respect (Kreitner suggests French and Indian cultures), and where subordinates will generally expect their leaders to have the answers by virtue of the expertise which has enabled them to achieve their status. The directive style translates poorly into 'low power distance' cultures or those where joint regulation or codetermination is the norm (for instance, the German one). He explains, however, that: 'Participative leadership is not necessarily the best style; it simply is culturally acceptable in many different countries . . . directive leadership turned out to be the least appropriate leadership style.' (Kreitner 2001, p613).

The contingency approach to leadership emphasises contextual factors as an important influence on leader success. Professor Joseph Nye, in a BBC interview ahead of the UK publication of his book *The Powers to Lead: Soft, Hard, and Smart* in May 2008, stressed the relationship between contextual knowledge and leadership power, explaining that contextual knowledge helps leaders to determine what balance they should strike between the use of what he terms 'hard' power (issuing commands) and 'soft' power (the ability to attract and retain followers). Contingency approaches remain highly relevant for the exercise of leadership in modern organisations however they are not easy to develop with limited time and experience.

A CRISIS OF LEADERSHIP AT THE BBC (PART ONE)

CASE STUDY 5.1

For 85 years the BBC has pursued its mission to 'inform, educate and entertain', not only in the UK but worldwide. It is funded by British licence feepayers through a sort of 'television tax' and is governed under Royal Charter by the BBC Trust. This arrangement makes it vulnerable on several fronts. Other commercial broadcasting and news media companies may consider that it has an unfair advantage in the market; it doesn't (indeed, is not permitted to) compete for advertising revenue in the UK. Licence feepayers may demand particularly high standards and responsiveness to a wide variety of diverse programming requirements; and its links with the government make it open to charges of political bias.

Leadership of this much loved, quintessentially British but sometimes reviled and criticised organisation is thus a difficult, but immensely important, job. In the words of veteran broadcaster David Dimbleby (2012), 'The Director General [DG] has to fight like a tiger to defend the BBC.'

In September 2012 George Entwistle took up the post after a competitive process managed by executive recruitment agency Egon Zehnder. He had been selected from a senior BBC role in July to succeed the outgoing DG Mark Thompson, but whilst both Thompson and Lord Patten (chairman of the BBC Trust) praised Entwistle as an outstanding and creative leader, some media commentators were surprised at his appointment. He was clearly an insider, having joined the BBC in 1989 as a trainee journalist, rising from reporting to editing news and factual broadcasts, including the flagship weekday *Newsnight* programme between 2001 and 2004.

But despite this long and successful service he was thought too 'quiet' for the role of BBC tiger – shy and uncomfortable in the public gaze, uncommunicative and an unimpressive public speaker (Brown 2012, Sabbagh 2012).

In October 2012, a storm of unprecedented ferocity hit the BBC squarely in Entwistle's area of expertise. Revelations on ITV about the late Jimmy Savile's sexual offences led to serious embarrassment for the corporation, which had withdrawn a *Newsnight* programme on that very subject as early as December 2011; to some, the BBC appeared to be attempting to cover up criminal behaviour which had taken place in its own backyard. Then, on 2 November, as further evidence of abusive behaviour came to light in the press, *Newsnight* broadcast what turned out to be an unfounded allegation of paedophilia against 'a very senior political figure' of the Thatcher era.

Whilst not naming the individual during the programme, the journalists concerned allowed a trail to appear on the Internet amid the following frenzy of speculation, prompting a public denial and legal action from the accused. The sole witness and accuser interviewed for the *Newsnight* report subsequently made a statement of apology, explaining that he had mistakenly identified his abuser from a photograph shown to him in the early 1990s.

The *Newsnight* team had failed spectacularly to follow the basic rules of journalism which are included in the BBC's own editorial guidelines. Checks had not been carried out by either the programme or station editors; nor had this controversial story been cleared by the DG. But the true test of Entwistle's leadership came during the aftermath.

After a week of turmoil, *Newsnight* finally had to broadcast a humiliating climbdown and Entwistle suspended all journalistic investigations by the programme team. He appeared complacent, claimed that the matter 'had not been brought to his attention' and seemingly adopted an overly bureaucratic and poorly informed, even uninterested, attitude to the management of the affair. This attitude was revealed during a radio interview on 10 November when his approach was publicly dismantled by interviewer John Humphrys, making his continued tenure as DG impossible. He resigned later that day.

Questions

1   Would you describe George Entwistle as a leader or a manager? Explain your reasons.

2   What might the situational leadership model have to tell us about the type of leadership required during organisational crises?

3   What benefits might an organisation gain from using external recruitment agencies to fill high-profile leadership roles such as this? What are the associated risks?

5.6 LEADERSHIP: SOME EMERGING PERSPECTIVES

In comparison to the leader-centric theoretical approaches as described above, there are many theoretical themes that consider leadership as relationships and processes which are classified as emergent approaches. Below we consider the most common:

- transformational leadership
- inspirational and authentic leadership
- servant leadership
- distributed leadership.

5.6.1 TRANSFORMATIONAL LEADERSHIP

Recent literature on leadership has noted the difference between transactional forms of leadership and transformational ones. This contrast relates back to ideas about the nature of leadership in a society which no longer accepts authority as the basis for command. If authority and 'position power' (French and Raven 1968) no longer works, what are the alternatives? One approach is to bargain: in other words to appeal to the self-interest of the followers. So-called transactional forms of leadership rely on the leader's capacity to negotiate appropriate follower behaviours based on legitimate rewards or punishments – although there is, of course, an inherent assumption that the leader has the appropriate authority to offer such rewards or administer punishments.

This is contrasted with transformational leadership, which is a process by which leaders create high levels of motivation and commitment by generating and communicating a clear vision and, often, appealing to higher ideals and values amongst followers. Rosener (1990, p120) defines it as motivating others by 'transforming their individual self-interest into the goals of the group' and by trying to make people feel part of the organisation.

Legge (2005) explains how this focus on a shared vision and personal commitment was, in the 1980s, part of a transformational leadership style which was characteristic of successful Japanese companies. It was reintegrated into American management culture (which was more focused on transactional leadership) via the work of the excellence gurus like Peters and Waterman, or Ouchi (1981). He charts the appeal of this style of leadership, and in particular its association with the American dream and thus some of the 'soft' HRM practices which facilitate the growth of an enterprise culture.

5.6.2 INSPIRATIONAL AND AUTHENTIC LEADERSHIP

It is impossible to discuss questions of leadership without considering the concept of inspirational leadership, which has regained some currency in recent years. In some ways this brings us back to concepts associated with trait theories, and in particular the characteristic usually described as charisma. Inspirational leadership, we are told by Adair (2003) and others, is about creating and communicating vision, having a passion and a dynamism that drives the leader and engages the enthusiasm and efforts of the led; even exhibiting unconventional behaviour and performing heroic deeds (Conger 1999). It includes the ability to take a long-term view, to inspire trust and confidence, which unlocks talent and enables the organisation to achieve exceptional performance. A recent trend in the world of management training and development that reflects this renewed attention to the highly personal nature of leadership, and in particular strategic leadership, is found in the growing interest in emotional intelligence as a relevant and learnable leadership skill.

Mullins (2013) and Legge (2005) both sound notes of caution in their consideration of inspirational leadership and draw attention to some of its drawbacks. Certainly it is difficult to see how charismatic leadership can be developed effectively. This is not to deny that many business founders have been charismatic and inspiring individuals, but their skills have often been better described as those of the champion which, as we have seen, relies on a wide range of business skills as well as the ability to protect and nurture a project. It is also less than wholly evident that inspirational leadership in itself results in significant benefits for organisational performance; in some cases it may be that the loss of the visionary results in the dissolution of the organisation. A specific attack on the cult of the inspirational leader was made by Beverly Alimo-Metcalfe at the HRD 2008 event, where she argued that organisations probably shouldn't choose leaders who are charismatic and inspirational because these qualities sometimes can be lethal. This view is supported by Evans (2008) who posits people at the top who are charismatic get there through the demise of others – they emasculate everybody else along the way. This kind of leadership can be toxic.

Adrian Furnham (2005) has also written about arrogance and egotistical leadership behaviour using the legend of Daedalus and Icarus. Inspirational leadership relies on a certain degree of emotional manipulation, and so its ethical status as a general management strategy might be open to challenge. It may also inspire less desirable characteristics in the followers, such as a high level of individual dependence on the approval and support of the leader; a fear of 'going against the grain' or groupthink; and a degree of enthusiasm for the vision which could encourage people to act in ways which stray beyond the boundaries of what might be considered ethical, or even legal (Conger 2002). Inspirational leaders can be bullies as well as visionaries; and the more powerfully they communicate their values, the less space there is for reasoned doubt or even opposition.

It is sometimes difficult to separate the concept of charismatic or egotistical leadership (with all its potential failings) from another idea which seems to have a more positive image – that of 'authentic' leadership. Authentic leadership is sometimes described as 'an expression of the leader's true self' – although of course the perception of authenticity might simply result from good acting (Ladkin and Taylor 2009). Techniques from the world of performance art are often discussed in this context; for instance, the Stanislavski method (ibid) and classically rooted concepts such as mastery and congruence (Ladkin 2008). All this might suggest that followers can never really know if the leader's display of their 'true self' is anything more than an illusion. However, illusions can be powerful things, and some researchers have noted that the outcomes of authentic leadership on followers' attitudes and behaviours can have significant predictive validity in terms of enhanced trust, job satisfaction and job performance (Walumbwa et al 2008).

5.6.3 SERVANT LEADERSHIP

Servant leadership as a term was initially used by Robert Greenleaf (1977) and has come to the forefront of research as the focus of leadership studies continues to move from the leader to the followers. The concept positions the leader as a steward rather than as a commander, and places him or her in a role which is defined by commitment to serve the organisation's needs rather than personal ambition; and to support the autonomy, growth and well-being of others. Key attributes therefore include humility, authenticity, empathy and a willingness to put the needs of others (the followers, the institution and society) above those of the self when providing direction. It also requires a recognition of the implications of organisational activity for the society (or, in an increasingly globalised world, the societies) affected by its operations. In this respect it has significance not only for the nature of the leader/follower relationship, but also for the ethical integrity of the organisation as a whole (Van Dierendonck 2010).

Whilst apparently somewhat idealistic, the notion of servant leadership is perhaps becoming attractive as an antidote to many of the widely reported failures of leadership, particularly in financial services organisations which, in 2007, sparked major disruption to the global economy, the repercussions of which are likely to last for a decade or more. Concern with the psychological flaws of chief executives has led to a line of research based on ideas of hubris, overconfidence and narcissism – the very opposite of servant leadership. This is well summarised by Bollaert and Petit (2010), whose exploration of the work seeks to move beyond an examination of this 'dark side' of executive psychology and appeals for a better understanding of (amongst other things) its causes:

> We believe that it is important to understand the contextual factors which may cause or aggravate hubristic tendencies, including the possible 'hubrisizing' effect of the executive function, as preventive measures could then be discussed in the context of corporate governance reform (Bollaert and Petit 2010, p373).

Negative or the dark side of leadership is now receiving increasing attention from researchers and practitioners, for a useful overview see Schyns and Hansbrough (2010).

5.6.4 DISTRIBUTED LEADERSHIP

As many have experienced in our lives, sometimes it seems rather impossible to identify one individual as the leader, as it could be shared among a group of people, or distributed across organisations. This approach is a shift from the traditional 'leader-centric' perspectives and many regard it as a potential solution to power abuse in organisations (Bolden 2011). As Bennett et al (2003, p3) argue:

> Distributed leadership is not something 'done' by an individual 'to' others, or a set of individual actions through which people contribute to a group or organization ... [it] is a group activity that works through and within relationships, rather than individual action.

Apart from shifting the focus in current leadership studies, distributed leadership also offers a new 'unit of analysis' that tends to see leadership from a holistic view rather than individual contributions (Bolden 2011, Gronn 2002). It was argued that leadership should be 'more appropriately understood as a fluid and emergent, rather than as a fixed, phenomenon' (Gronn 2000, p324). Similar to distributed leadership, other notions such as shared leadership, collective leadership, co-leadership are also looking at leadership as a social process that explores beyond individual agency.

Writing in the February 2008 issue of *Impact*, Linda Holbeche, the CIPD Director of Research and Policy, noted the evolving nature of management and leadership, and suggested that some important new themes are emerging from current research (2008b). Amongst these are the challenges created by the need to lead in situations of increasing complexity, ambiguity and uncertainty; the idea of building 'communities of leaders'; and the influence of leader values in shaping the behaviour of those around them. These ideas have clear implications for HR practitioners (HRPs), who are often charged with the responsibility for developing organisational leaders.

It is also evident that the question of leadership remains an important area for academic research. The growth of virtual organisations and teams has led to an interest in the practice of e-leadership, and this is likely to be of growing significance as technology offers more and better opportunities for work to be organised using geographically dispersed expertise (Avolio et al 2000). Ilze Zigurs has developed some ideas about the transfer of traditional team roles into a virtual environment, including that of leadership. If physical presence is an important means of signalling and reinforcing leadership in traditional teams, what happens when there is no such presence? The concept of 'telepresence' becomes relevant here; but as she explains: '... being telepresent is more than just keeping up a steady stream of email messages to team members. Leaders need to learn how to use the vividness and interactivity of media to make their presence felt in a positive way' (Zigurs 2003, p344).

HR professionals might be well placed to contribute to processes that attempt to identify the antecedents of hubristic behaviour and contribute to the necessary elements in corporate governance systems that would help to control their growth and impact. Whether we are concerned with traditional, virtual, inter-cultural, good or bad leadership, the academic field can offer the practitioner insights into useful approaches, as well as extending the range of knowledge and understanding about effective leadership in new contexts and situations.

 A CRISIS OF LEADERSHIP AT THE BBC (PART TWO)

CASE STUDY 5.2

Following the resignation of George Entwistle, the BBC appointed Tony Hall (Lord Hall of Birkenhead) as its new DG with a start date of April 2013 when the interim DG, Tim Davie, stood down.

Like Entwistle, Hall had joined the BBC as a news trainee in 1973 and worked there for 28 years before leaving to become chief executive of the Royal Opera House in 2001. This appointment was made without competition and as the result of a direct approach by the BBC Trust. One of his major challenges is to restore the confidence and morale of staff at the corporation, particularly those involved with news and current affairs programming.

5.7 DEVELOPMENT OF LEADERS AND LEADERSHIP

Many textbooks are devoted to the topic of leadership development (see for example: Gold et al 2010) and most management or organisational behaviour texts contain such chapters. The purpose of this section is not to replicate or produce a précis of these. Instead the aim is to simulate interest in further research and spotlight a few current debates on the topic of how leaders are trained and leadership is developed in organisations. These debates are important for HRPs, who may be held responsible and accountable for leadership development provision.

Leadership development is both a current and future concern, with over 50% of employers reporting that it is one of their top three priorities for the coming year (CIPD 2015g, Gurdjian et al 2014). Formal leader and leadership training programmes are used widely in an attempt to improve the way organisations are led with estimates of the annual spend on such interventions varying from $14bn in the USA to $50bn worldwide (Harrison and Auluck 2014, Raelin 2004, Yukl 2012). Often leadership development takes the lion's share of organisational training budgets and yet there is little evidence to demonstrate a return on this investment (CIPD 2014a, Yukl 2012). There is ongoing dissatisfaction with leaders and the state of leadership in most organisations, with less than 40% of organisations rating their leaders as excellent or very good (Boatman et al 2011).

Additionally, recent high-profile cases of poor leaders that have hit the media headlines suggest that things may be getting worse. The economic problems that started in 2008 increased the focus on leadership, but in many cases leaders were found wanting, with follower trust diminishing (CIPD 2013c, 2014a). At the very least there is more public debate and discontent with those seen as being irresponsible leaders. Cunningham (2010, p5) surmises: 'At the end of the first decade of the twenty-first century have we cracked the problem of leadership development? Not on the evidence so far.' He goes on to assert that organisations are no better led than 80 years ago.

So whilst there is a wealth of evidence that leaders and leadership are important to organisational success, and vast sums are invested in development, we are far from seeing better leaders in practice and we don't know why. Therefore this section of the chapter focuses on a selection of potential issues which could be contributing to this discontent and suggests ways these may be overcome.

The issues we have chosen to highlight are:

- The focus:
  - Who or what are we developing: leaders or leadership?
  - What is being learned: new paradigm or traditional theories on leaders and leadership?
  - What methods are being used: learning, training or development?

- The quality of learning needs analysis.
- The quality of learning evaluation.

5.8 THE FOCUS: LEADER OR LEADERSHIP?

The first issue we consider is linked to the leader or leadership debate (Day 2001). The term 'leader' refers to the individual, hence their learning increases human capital. 'Leadership' is far wider, recognising the importance of followers, and relating to the process or collective, with learning linked to social or even cultural capital (see Table 5.2 for more detail).

Increasing human capital of individual leaders can have an impact on the organisation, but this is likely to be limited in both scope and time. Scope is limited by the sphere of influence of leaders (how many employees they interact with and to what extent). Time is limited by a leader's tenure in the company (how long they remain in the organisation). With a focus on leaders, the organisation is reliant on select individuals acquiring desired knowledge, skills and attitudes and using transformed behaviours as a result; however, both of these assumptions should be challenged. As we discuss in Chapter 10, acquisition of new knowledge, skills and attitudes may not result in changed behaviour or transfer to the workplace, and even if it does, this behaviour may not be desired. Additionally, an over focus on the individual leader assumes one size fits all and ignores context; or that a successful leader in one situation will not necessarily be brilliant in another (Gurdjian et al 2014).

Table 5.2 Leader or leadership?

Comparison dimension	Leader	Leadership
Capital	Human	Social
Model	Individual Personal power Knowledge Trustworthiness	Relational Commitment Mutual respect Trust
Competence base/skills	Intrapersonal Self-awareness Self-regulation Self-motivation	Interpersonal Social awareness Social skills

Adapted from Day (2001, p584)

Conversely, increasing social capital through leadership development is more valuable to an organisation as the sphere of influence is far wider and longer lasting. New behaviours remain in the organisation and are adapted to meet changing circumstances, even if key individuals leave. Yet in most organisations the focus has traditionally been on individual leaders (Drath 2001), reinforcing a preoccupation with self-awareness and self-development at the expense of followers (Jackson and Parry 2008). Finite resources and the influence of power results in a focus on the top echelons of organisations, with an over-reliance on a limited talent pool or a few high-potential individuals with the importance of followers being ignored (CIPD 2013c, CIPD 2015g, Gold et al 2013). In the age of the protean career and increased mobility of employees this focus is unhelpful.

5.9 THE FOCUS: NEW PARADIGM OR TRADITIONAL THEORIES?

As discussed above, in recent decades theory has moved away from the idea that heroic leaders are the omnipotent force that single-handedly steer the organisation with a command and control or charismatic persona. Newer paradigm theories recognise that formal leaders are only able to effect change through others (Grint 2005). The theories of transformational (Burns 1978) and servant (Greenleaf 1977) leadership still focus on individual leaders, but put more emphasis on relationship-building and participatory approaches. This emphasises social awareness, using a collective empathy, service orientation and commitment to developing others with context, processes and systems aligned to maximise the effects of leaders' actions (Schyns et al 2011). Distributed or shared leadership (Gronn 2002) have also emerged as viable or even desirable alternatives to traditional bureaucracies, whereby employees without formal managerial responsibility are expected to lead from the front when appropriate (CIPD 2014a). These new paradigm theories change both the focus and content of leader and leadership development to empowering and enabling behaviours with an emphasis on collective ability and responsibility.

However, Implicit Leadership Theory (ILT) and the Romance of Leadership (RoL) indicate that although organisations may overtly state their preference for newer paradigm leadership approaches, in practice they may unconsciously be encouraging the opposite (Schyns et al 2013). ILT asserts that we all hold images in our minds of leaders' traits and behaviours; we then use these schema as a blueprint for assessing individuals to decide if we will grant them leadership (Eden and Leviathan 1975); and of course without followers there is no leadership. In contrast to expectations, ILTs have proven to be relatively consistent and, importantly, are dominated by traditional leadership traits from the 'great men' theories of a century ago (Schyns et al 2013). Traits such as charisma, vigour, self-confidence, strength, intelligence, tyranny, masculinity and attractiveness, as identified by Stogdill (1948), still prevail and are valued. Indeed, in some circumstances this value is magnified by RoL theory.

RoL theory asserts that we over-attribute success or failure of organisations or situations to individual leaders, ignoring other contextual factors such as the environment or followers (Schyns and Hansbrough 2012). Extreme examples are regularly seen in the sporting world, with, for example, football managers being sacked on the basis of a few lost matches, when realistically the players, the backroom staff and a host of other factors must have been influential on that outcome. Conversely, when things go well, they become the ultimate heroes (see, for example, the case of Jose Mourinho). Interestingly, in times of uncertainty RoL has been shown to increase (Bligh and Schyns 2007) as followers become more willing to abdicate responsibility and blame to those in formal leader positions. Therefore it is possible that the recent economic global crisis has caused resurgence in a desire for heroic leaders.

ROMANCE OF LEADERSHIP (RoL): JOSE MOURINHO

Jose Mourinho became a household name in the UK after joining Chelsea Football Club in 2004. On being appointed Mourinho said, 'I don't want to sound arrogant, but I think I am a special manager because I won the Champions league.' Following his appointment the club experienced significant success, which Mourinho was happy to take the credit for. This was, despite many other contributory factors, not least huge investments in new players and innovative support-staff changes. In 2007, Mourinho left the club after poor results at the start of the season, which he blamed on a lack of investment by the owner. But such is the nature of football that in 2013 he returned to Chelsea, much to the delight of fans, who were delighted to have the 'Special One' back at their club. In a *Daily Mail* headline in August 2012 it was reported that he felt this title was insufficient and should be changed to the 'Only One' because *he* had won so much. However, just seven months after Chelsea won the 2014/15 premiership title, the 'Special One' was sacked following a string of defeats.

These theories may mean that the content of leader and leadership learning is disconnected to organisational reality and practice. People may be learning about followership theories and practices, and organisations may proclaim this is what they seek, but in practice, traditional views of leaders abound and are embedded in recruitment, training and appraisal practices. If new paradigm behaviours are not recognised or rewarded, learning transfer is unlikely. This may provide one more reason for lack of satisfaction with outcomes of leader and leadership training and development.

5.10 THE FOCUS: TRAINING OR DEVELOPMENT?

Chapter 10 provides clarification of the terms 'training' and 'development', which are often used interchangeably. Table 5.3 sets out how they differ.

Table 5.3 The differences between training and development

Training	Development
Time-bound	More opaque, longer-term, nurturing perspective
Clear, relatively uniform, skills-based outcomes	Less prescribed and more flexible outcomes
Training objectives specified by the training provider	Personal learning aims specified by the learner

Leader training courses are very common, often provided as a series of off-job modules linked together into some sort of programme over a period of months, delivered by external specialist companies. Example modules include such topics as:

- coaching skills
- motivating for success
- communicating your vision.

Such off-job, formal training courses are easier for organisations to evaluate than on-job, in-company development interventions (McDowall and Saunders 2010), but we question their value in transforming the way organisations are led. Leader training has a focus on individuals' knowledge (knowing how) and skills (acting as a leader), but not enough on attitudes, emotions and values, which have proven to be important contributors in major organisational failures (Gurdjian et al 2014, Jackson and Parry 2008).

Leadership development, on the other hand, incorporates elements such as emotional intelligence, which has been shown to be important to effective leadership (Goleman 1995). Leadership development promotes a more holistic, multi-level, identity-based approach (Day and Harrison 2007). But this is messy: it has to be in-company, on-job and involve large numbers of employees. Leadership development lacks a clear beginning or end, with non-specific learning outcomes that change and adapt to organisational rhythms. This type of learning intervention is much harder to justify and evaluating success is notoriously difficult. But if messy leadership development is what is really needed, then investing in the easier option of leader training must result in dissatisfaction with the outcomes.

In reality, for meaningful organisational transformation to happen there is probably a need for a focus on both leader and leadership with both training and development interventions (McDowall and Saunders 2010). HR has a role to play in helping the organisation recognise what it is investing in and why, so that it can determine the return on this investment; in other words going back to basics with learning needs analysis and evaluation.

REFLECTIVE ACTIVITY 5.3

- What is the focus in your organisation? Leaders or leadership? Training or development?
- How helpful is this focus?
- How might you change the focus?
- How carefully is learning needs analysis or training needs analysis carried out for leader and leadership learning interventions?
- How well is leader and leadership learning evaluated in your organisation?

5.11 INSUFFICIENT NEEDS ANALYSIS

In Chapter 10 of this book we explore the lack of focus given to proper training or learning needs analysis (TNA, LNA). If the gap in knowledge, skills or attitudes is not known then there is a high risk that any training or development intervention will have limited value. At best, resources will be wasted, providing unnecessary inputs; at worst, learners are demotivated by irrelevant input and learning becomes devalued. When some organisations are devoting a large percentage of hard-squeezed budgets to leadership development then this has big implications. Lack of LNA or TNA may therefore account for some of the dissatisfaction with leader and leadership capability and effectiveness. Failure to identify needs upfront also affects the ability to evaluate investments in learning, training and development and it is well known that these tasks are poorly done in many organisations (CIPD 2015g, Roberts 2006).

CASE STUDY 5.3

TRAINING V DEVELOPMENT

Consider two typical examples of learning intervention.

A new employee is recruited as a forklift truck driver and he goes to an accredited external trainer to be trained in driving a forklift truck. Assessment at the end of the course is a series of practical tasks done to a pre-set standard and a test of important underpinning knowledge. Success in the assessment results in the award of a nationally recognised certificate of competence. He returns to work and carries out his job, with targets set for the quantity of items moved, within set timescales, and a clear requirement to do this safely as taught.

Simultaneously, the organisation starts a leadership development programme for all the middle managers in the company. This comprises a series of half-day off-job workshops, mentoring and on-job projects and assignments. Each manager has a personal development portfolio to record their learning goals and progress.

Source: Alex Tymon

Questions

1   What differences should there be in the LNA or TNA carried out for these two different interventions?

2   How easy is the evaluation of the forklift truck training?

3   What are the difficulties in evaluating the leadership development programme?

4   How would you carry out a return on investment or expectation calculation for both?

5.12 INSUFFICIENT EVALUATION

Only 7% of organisations in the UK complete a comprehensive evaluation of any of their training and development, 50% only do so at the most basic level of gauging reactions, and 50% do no evaluation at all (CIPD 2015g). Leader and leadership learning is the least likely of all to be evaluated (Gurdjian et al 2014, Jackson and Parry 2008). This is most likely due to the complexity and difficulties of evaluating such interventions, which begin to be highlighted in the Case Study 5.3. The forklift truck driver training is easily justified and evaluated, whereas the leadership development programme presents multiple challenges in this respect.

5.12.1 CHALLENGE 1: HOW TO MEASURE COSTS OF THE INTERVENTION?

In the forklift truck example, costs are fairly transparent: the direct costs of the training course; the time of the trainee; perhaps a small amount of on-job practice time; and increased supervision on immediate return to work whilst the new skills are honed. But for a leadership development programme costs are far from clear. For example, coaching is often cited as a valuable and effective method of developing leaders and leadership, yet how do we measure the costs? Is it just the direct costs of coaches' and leaders' time in formal sessions together? What about time spent by leaders on personal reflection? What about conversations with colleagues that might further enhance behaviour? And opportunity costs for leaders' time are much higher and more difficult to calculate than for other employees.

5.12.2 CHALLENGE 2: HOW TO MEASURE OUTCOMES?

In the forklift truck example, the outcomes are clear: safe movement of the required number of items, which are directly attributable to the training received and subsequent transfer of learning to the workplace (see Chapter 10 for more detail on learning transfer). But with leadership development outcomes are much harder to identify and thus quantify. Improved leadership should result in transforming the behaviour of followers, so it is their performance which needs to be measured. However, which followers doing what? There are many reasons why followers' behaviour could change, which may have nothing or everything to do with how they are led.

To overcome this challenge, many research studies and organisational evaluations use self or line manager reports to assess behaviour changes in leaders (Ely et al 2010), but how reliable and objective is this? And this still does not show measurable outcomes as a result of leadership development. If an organisation adopts the multi-level, identity-based approach to leadership development promoted by Day and Harrison (2007), we suggest that objective measurement of outcomes would be near impossible.

5.12.3 CHALLENGE 3: WHEN TO MEASURE OUTCOMES?

Our forklift truck training can be measured as soon as the driver returns to work. But leadership development is recognised as being 'slow burn'; with iterative, small lessons learned and then behaviour adjusted over time, it could be argued it never stops, so when is the outcome to be measured? And then there is linking inputs with outcome.

5.12.4 CHALLENGE 4: HOW TO PROVE CAUSE AND EFFECT?

An excuse given by many for poor evaluation of learning in general is the difficulty of linking outcomes back to training or development input, but in the leadership domain it is particularly acute. The long-term nature of leadership development and the once, twice or further removed behaviours of followers are hard to link, as many other factors could have affected outcomes.

An increasing number of recent studies have tried to truly evaluate leadership learning interventions using, for example, experimental methodologies or control groups (Santos et al 2015, Parry and Sinha 2005). However, these raise other questions such as the reality of experimental studies, generalisability of results and the ethics of excluding some individuals from learning interventions that might be valuable. But perhaps more importantly for HRD practitioners, these approaches are extremely complex and unlikely to be adopted by most organisations. Large companies with professional HRD teams may have the expertise and resources to carry out better quality evaluations and should be encouraged to do so, but the vast majority of UK businesses fall into the small and medium-sized category, and so evaluation is likely to remain a challenge. This suggests that a continuation of current practices is likely.

In the absence of systematic evaluation, decisions on what learning is provided by organisations reverts back to those who sign the cheques. Those individuals who attend expensive, high-profile, traditional off-job leader training tend to be top leaders, and therefore the decision-makers. These people are more positive towards these traditional methods than the organisations that sponsor them (CIPD 2013c). Hence there is a strong possibility that organisations will continue to use existing methods even if they are not satisfied with their outcomes (CIPD 2013c), unless of course a persuasive alternative is presented, and this is an opportunity for the HR function.

5.13 IMPROVING LEADERSHIP DEVELOPMENT: A ROLE FOR HR

The HR function has a chance to build its credibility by rising to the challenge of pushing for better quality leader and leadership learning. In short, the HR function can address some of the issues discussed thus far. Of course, this is much easier said than done, as this involves changing some very embedded attitudes and beliefs, exacerbated by the fact that these are held by the top people within organisations. But a real opportunity exists for those courageous enough and willing to model effective leadership behaviours and challenge the status quo.

5.14 CHANGING FOCUS: LEADER TO LEADERSHIP

The first step is to convince the organisation that leadership in its widest sense is the future. This will entail allaying fears, as those in formal leader positions will understandably be resistant to approaches that threaten their security. But promoting the view of Collinson (2006, p187), which 'views the identities of followers and leaders as inextricably linked, mutually reinforcing, and shifting within specific contexts' can start the process of acceptance. Reassuring formal leaders that their training will not necessarily be taken away, but instead enhanced, is essential. Individual leader development is a necessary foundation as better skilled formal leaders are able to use more sophisticated leadership, but there is also a need for developing collective leadership in teams and the broader organisation (Day and Harrison 2007). So the first role for HR is to help the organisation let go of the fixation on leader training and formal interventions that focus on only a small pool of top talent (CIPD 2013c) and look far wider. The paper by Dalakoura (2010, p436) provides a 'collective framework for leadership development' that could be valuable for HR practitioners attempting to start the process of widening views.

5.15 CHANGING PRACTICES: NEW PARADIGM THEORIES

HR also has a role to play in ensuring consistency in what is espoused as desirable in learning interventions and the reality of what is recognised and rewarded in organisation practice. ILT and RoL theory have the potential to undermine recruitment by allowing unconscious bias towards heroic or 'great men' traits to be sought at the expense of social awareness, collective empathy, service orientation and commitment to developing others.

HR can facilitate the design of processes and systems and provide training to overcome such biases. This should ensure that cloned recruitment does not occur and begin the process of changing the organisational culture to one that recognises and rewards collective leadership. This can then be reinforced by ensuring the content of learning interventions mirrors this message and develops the new paradigm skills required for all who need them. In short, many traditional methods of leader training used by organisations in the past need to be replaced by more effective methods aimed at leadership development. Quatro et al (2007, p439) caution: 'beware leadership development activities that may create narrowly focused leaders, asserting that a holistic approach is needed and go on to say that only the analytical facet of leadership can really benefit from off-job training approaches, the rest requires experiential development.'

5.16 CHANGING METHODS: EXPERIENTIAL AND INFORMAL LEARNING

An increasing weight of evidence suggests experience is key to effective leader and leadership development (Conger 2004, McCall 2010, Grint 2005, Raelin 2011, Yukl 2012) and concurs with much current HRD thinking in general such as the move towards more informal learning and the 70:20:10 approach (Jennings and Wargnier 2010), as discussed in Chapter 10. For leadership the experiential approach could be particularly appropriate because it recognises the importance of followers and a collective approach to development. As Grint (2005) suggests, there is huge potential for leaders to learn to lead from followers, in the way that parents learn to parent from their children. However, learning from experience is not automatic and on its own does not guarantee learning.

5.17 THE ROLE OF HR IN EXPERIENTIAL AND INFORMAL LEADERSHIP DEVELOPMENT

Experiential and informal learning needs conscious elements: a supportive organisation culture that develops individual interest and motivation to learn; management of experiences to maximise their learning potential; and the ability to reflect. HR has an important role to play in facilitating these elements, starting with the challenge of changing the learning culture of the organisation to one where experimentation and active informal learning become everyday activities.

Chapter 10 provides ideas on what is needed for a more self-directed learning culture to be brought about to increase individual motivation and interest in experiential leadership development. HR can further support this by facilitating the right type of experiences for effective learning. McCall (2010) stresses that, using experiential learning to develop leadership is more complex than it appears because certain experiences matter more than others. He cites the following as powerful because of the challenges they present:

- early work experiences
- short-term assignments and major experiences
- very good or very bad bosses
- hardships.

Hence, HR can really make a difference by ensuring an appropriate variety of tasks or assignments are available that present the right amount of challenge (Yukl 2012).

An additional role for HR is to facilitate the acquisition of reflective learning skills as this is critical for effective leadership development (Gurdjian et al 2014, McCall 2010, Sinclair 2007). Although not easy, reflective practice and critical reflection can be taught (Mackay and Tymon 2014). Alongside this, HR can argue for the time and space needed for experiential learning and put a focus on feedback to guide reflective learning from experience. Training people company-wide in the skills of giving and receiving feedback effectively could be a very worthwhile investment that should increase and enhance informal and active learning.

Ultimately, experiential leadership development is not a quick fix, but then things worth having seldom are. Formal training and off-job courses especially for the select few can be expensive, requiring external providers and off-job venues. Development approaches may not be cheaper but they are more effective at providing real organisational benefits. HR needs to take on a selling role and be open about the challenges, costs and benefits, but it can only do this if it has the facts and figures at its disposal. This entails thorough evaluation of learning, which begins with robust needs analysis.

5.18 IMPROVING NEEDS ANALYSIS AND EVALUATION

Changing the focus from leader to leadership means more people are involved in learning interventions, which presents challenges for resource-strapped organisations. One way to overcome this is to use more cost-effective methods, such as on-job, experiential and action learning approaches as already discussed. A second way to ensure effectiveness for a wider audience is to carry out better needs analysis and most training and HRD textbooks have useful chapters on how this can be achieved.

Robust needs analysis will identify:

- what leadership development is required
- for which individuals
- appropriate methods
- expected or desired outcomes.

Clarity on these points will help justify investment in training and development, both financial and in terms of time and space. The last point is critical, as this enables any intervention to be evaluated and the case for future investment in leadership development is much easier to make if past success can be demonstrated. Once desired outcomes are known then HR can tackle the challenge of seeking measurement of these. Due to the issues discussed earlier, this measurement and proving cause and effect will still prove challenging, but HR will have better metrics and thus more credibility in the eyes of the organisation.

5.19 IN SUMMARY

Leaders in twenty-first-century organisations have two competing challenges: getting things done to meet today's needs, whilst adapting what they do so that their business can thrive in the future (Heietz et al 2009). These are activities that require both personal ability and skills, but more importantly the support of others and committed followers, hence both leader training and leadership development. As Raelin asserts, 'The work-based learning process as a collective and reflective experience transforms leadership in kind toward a collaborative practice that can respond to contemporary demands' and ensure that everyone in the organisation can give all they have to offer (2011, p20). Organisations can increase the chances of success in leader and leadership development by defining what leadership means in their context and who is expected to lead with what skills and knowledge and in what way (CIPD 2013c). HR has a key role to play in this by embedding development in real work and measuring the impact (Gurdjian et al 2014) whilst ensuring the context and culture is conducive to learning (CIPD 2013c).

5.20 CONCLUSION

There is a global fixation with leaders and leadership. A search of the Amazon bookstore produces more than 5,000 non-fiction books with the word 'leadership' in the title. It is clear that there is a renewed sense of the importance of good leadership amongst those most concerned with setting standards for today's managers, be they in business, the public services, or elsewhere. This comes from economic, social and political changes, which have encouraged more aspiration towards leading others and one's self, and perhaps less obedience to traditional forms of authority.

It also stems from the need, as Handy predicted in 1989, for organisations to become more federal than monolithic, and for new styles of management and leadership to emerge to suit the changed environment, including the virtual one. It reflects a growing public interest in the standards of behaviour of those who run businesses and direct our lives through political decisions, and their competence to carry out the tasks entrusted to them. In this respect it links firmly with discussion about ethical standards and organisational practices considered elsewhere in this book.

HR professionals will be concerned to ensure good leadership in their organisations, to improve both the performance of the organisation itself and to enable it to attract and keep good staff. This means choosing appropriate frameworks for the selection of potential leaders, their initial training, managing the performance expected of them once in the job, appraising, developing and rewarding them, facilitating their careers and, sometimes, removing them. A coherent, fair and equitable approach to these tasks is thus essential.

KEY LEARNING POINTS

1 The relationship between leadership and management is a close one.

2 The way in which we analyse and understand leadership has important implications for personnel professionals, particularly with respect to the selection and training of organisational leaders.

3 An over-emphasis on charismatic leadership can result in undesirable organisational outcomes.

4 Understanding leadership is not just about a leader-centric approach; there are other leadership theories emerging which consider leadership from relational and process perspectives.

5 Leadership development takes the lion's share of most organisational training budgets, but with limited evidence of effectiveness.

6 Improving leader and leadership development requires better needs analysis, and clarity of what is being developed and for whom, alongside robust evaluation.

CASE STUDY 5.4

LEARNING TO LEAD IN SOUTHSHIRE SCHOOLS

Anil Gupta and Sandra Carter have recently been promoted to the headships of two primary schools in Southshire.

Leadership in modern schools is especially challenging as it requires high-level technical skills combined with well-developed relationship skills.

As part of the trend to free schools from local authority control and grant them

more autonomy, head teachers have had to learn a range of new technical skills including project management, HRM, financial and budgetary management, public relations skills and political sensitivity.

They need to be respected leaders of staff and pupils alike, and whilst they have scope to shape the strategic direction of their school, the increased autonomy has been accompanied by greater scrutiny and accountability.

Schools are a vital part of their local communities and their reputation among parents is a constant source of discussion and concern. Tricky issues abound: beyond a school's gates headteachers are expected to collaborate with other schools (some of which may be competitors for funding or pupils) and a host of agencies with responsibility for children's welfare.

Anil's background is in physics, and he has been teaching for 12 years, six of them in Southshire schools. He was made deputy head of the John Pounds Primary School (a city-centre school with a diverse ethnic mix, which takes approximately 350 8–11-year-olds) two years ago and has now been promoted to the headship of the school, which will become vacant at the end of the school year when the current head, Jim Graham, retires. Jim has been head for 17 years, and whilst well known and respected in the community, is somewhat traditional in his approach – a strong disciplinarian with considerable personal charisma. At the same time, Sandra (a modern linguist) is due to take up her first appointment as head of Teapot Row School on the outskirts of the city, which is of a similar size to John Pounds but with less of an ethnic mix. She has been promoted from a deputy headship of another school in rural Southshire. She has met the staff at Teapot Row, and whilst she finds them all to be friendly and devoted teachers, she thinks that the school has tended to rely on its reputation to attract pupils and may need to become more competitive and outward-looking in the future.

Schools in Southshire are able to draw on the resources of the Southshire Teaching and Leadership College (STLC). STLC offers a distinctive approach to leadership development: no two schools, or leaders, are alike and so STLC has adopted a highly personalised approach to leadership development. STLC has been asked to provide a suitable development programme for Anil and Sandra to facilitate their entry into their new leadership roles. Think about the design of such a programme, and consider the following questions.

Questions

1   How might leadership theories inform the content of the programme?

2   Which theories would you choose as the basis for this leadership development programme, and why? Are there any which you think are particularly unsuitable for the context?

3   How would you address the need to develop both the strategic leadership capability as well as the managerial leadership ability which Anil and Sandra are required to have as heads?

4   What possible learning and development techniques could be employed? Which would you consider most suitable?

5   How do you think the programme could be evaluated?

You may wish to refer to Chapter 10 to help with your answers.

REVIEW QUESTIONS

1   What do you see as significant differences between leadership and management? Must all good managers be good leaders? Do all business leaders have to be good managers?

2   How would you improve the development of leaders and leadership in your organisation? How might this be different to other organisations?

3   Think about someone you know who you would describe as a good leader, preferably in an organisational context. What makes them good in your view? Would the skills and attributes you identified earlier be suitable in all contexts?

4   Are you a member or leader of a virtual team? If so, try to analyse what sorts of leadership behaviour appear to be effective in this environment. If not, what challenges might exist for leaders of such teams, and how could an HR specialist help to identify them? You might like to consider if any lessons can be learned from the way in which virtual communities such as Facebook or Second Life operate.

EXPLORER FURTHER

Dinh, J.E., Lord, R.G., Gardner, W.L., Meuser, J.D., Liden, R.C. and Hu, J. (2014) Leadership theory and research in the new millennium: current theoretical trends and changing perspectives. *The Leadership Quarterly*. Vol 25, No 1. pp36–62. Offers a summary of recent directions in academic leadership research.

French, R. (2015) *Cross-Cultural Management in Work Organisations*. 3rd ed. London: CIPD. Includes a chapter on the implications of national culture for organisational leadership as well as some information about key authors on cultural differences, and the relevant findings of Project GLOBE.

Mullins, L. (2013) *Management and Organisational Behaviour*. 10th ed. Harlow: FT/Prentice Hall. This text offers comprehensive descriptions and discussion of all major conceptualisations of both management and leadership, including those relating to gender, as well as relevant case studies.

Nye, J. (2008) *The Powers to Lead*. Oxford: OUP. Harvard Professor of International Relations Joseph Nye considers leadership styles and skills, and also discusses the transferability of leadership between different arenas such as the military, politics and business.

Van Dierendonck, D. (2010) Servant leadership, a review and synthesis. *Journal of Management*. Vol 37, No 4. pp1228–1261. Provides an overview of the antecedents, behaviours, mediating processes and outcomes associated with the concept of servant leadership.

Yukl, G. (2012) *Leadership in Organisations*. 8th ed. Harlow: Pearson. Another comprehensive review of the nature of leadership in an organisational setting.

Information and press releases about the 2012 crisis at the BBC can be found on the BBC Trust's website at www.bbc.co.uk/bbctrust as well as those of most reputable newspapers.

International Leadership Association (www.ila-net.org) is a global network for leadership researchers and practitioners; it updates webinars and leadership related jobs regularly. It also offers some leadership resources and teaching activities to the public.

More case studies of leadership can be found on the CIPD website at cipd.co.uk/research/leadership.aspx

CHAPTER 6

Managing Change

GARY REES AND DAVID HALL

LEARNING OUTCOMES

After reading this chapter, you should be able to:

- explore the nature and types of change
- examine the context, process and content of change
- explore and examine change interventions
- examine change leadership and change capability
- examine the role of HR and change.

6.1 OVERVIEW

Change continues to take a front-of-stage role in both academic research and industrial practice. Whilst it is difficult to pinpoint a universally accepted definition of change, we are reminded that change management is not a distinct discipline with rigorous and defined boundaries, but more that the theory and practice of change management draws upon a number of social science disciplines and traditions (Burnes 2004). This chapter encapsulates the major theories in the field of change, adopting a strategic perspective, and considers how HR can impact upon change in organisations.

The appropriateness of change planning and intervention is dependent to some extent on how we fit theory into practice, and vice versa. Grint (1997, p1) sums up the argument particularly well:

- Theory is where you know everything and nothing works; Practice is where everything works,
- But nobody knows why;
- Here we combine theory and practice: Nothing works and nobody knows why.

Whilst it is unlikely that any one change model fits perfectly, there is scope to consider a more hybrid approach to change. There needs to be a move away from 'static' models of change, which stress the content and substance of change (Nelson 2003), to the dynamics of change, with the expectation that change occurs within a less certain environment, where flexibility is required to maintain or enable competitive advantage. These issues are explored throughout this chapter.

6.2 INTRODUCTION

6.2.1 DEFINING CHANGE AND CHANGE MANAGEMENT

Small-scale and relatively simple change, typically categorised as 'hard' problems, are usually managed within the day-to-day operational management activity. This type of change is not usually referred to as 'change' by managers, and the process of managing it is not described as 'managing change' or 'change management' within organisations.

Managers have to consider the many factors involved in a complex and dynamic situation before making decisions that implement actions that will influence the effectiveness, efficiency and ultimately the sustainability of their organisations.

Brech (1975, p19) defines management as:

A social process entailing responsibility for the effective and economic planning and regulation of the operations of an enterprise, in fulfilment of given purposes or tasks, such responsibility involving:

(a) Judgement and decision in determining plans and in using data to control performance and progress against plans;

(b) The guidance, integration, motivation and supervision of the personnel composing the enterprise and carrying out its operations.

Brech describes the four main elements of management as being planning, control, co-ordination and motivation. Fayol (1949) describes the function of management in similar terms, proposing five elements of management: planning, organising, commanding, co-ordinating and controlling.

Management can be described as, essentially, an intervention for controlling operational performance outcomes in line with an organisation's purpose and objectives.

In carrying out their responsibilities, managers deal with change on a day-to-day basis, which raises an interesting question: when does management become 'change management'? Is this purely an academic question (it will be for many managers), or is it helpful from a management and organisational perspective to understand what, if anything, differentiates the two?

Change may be defined simplistically as making things different, but needs to make explicit mention of actual and perceived change(s). Fincham and Rhodes (2005, p525) define change management as 'the leadership and direction of the process of organisational transformation – especially with regard to human aspects and overcoming resistance to change'.

The Society for Human Resource Management defines change management as: The systematic approach and application of knowledge, tools and resources to deal with change. Change management means defining and adopting corporate strategies, structures, procedures and technologies to deal with changes in external conditions and the business environment. (**www.shrm.org/templatestools/glossaries/hrterms/pages/c.aspx** [accessed 30 May 2013])

Therefore, managing change or 'change management' is a form of management control through the application of systematic management interventions that involve people to achieve a desired future state with defined performance outcomes in line with the organisational strategy.

From this definition, it is clear that there is a strong and inextricable link between organisational change, performance and strategy.

6.3 TYPES OF CHANGE

Dependent upon the perspective that has been adopted, a variety of models and concepts can be utilised in order to consider the types of organisational change. This chapter will consider the level of change, the size and scope of change, the nature of change and the momentum of change.

6.3.1 THE LEVEL OF ORGANISATIONAL CHANGE

Carnall (2003) suggests that there are three levels of strategic change. Firstly, organisation-specific changes, such as a new information system. Secondly, generic organisation-wide change programmes, such as business process engineering (BPR). Thirdly, generic multi-organisational change programmes, for example, mergers and acquisitions.

6.3.2 THE SIZE AND SCOPE OF CHANGE

Child (2005) provides a useful model on how to differentiate between the scope of change and type of change – see Figure 6.1.

Figure 6.1 Child's approaches to organisational change

Approaches to organisational change

	Planned	Emergent	
	BPR	Organic development (eg. start-up company)	Whole org.
Radical	Merger of departments	Changes to selection of new members made by teams	part org.
Incremental	Annual targeted improvements	Organisational learning	Whole org.
	Changes agreed in staff performance plans	Continuous improvement through project teams	part org.

It must be borne in mind that whilst radical and incremental change may be defined and measured, that often it is the perceived scale of change that may be more important than the 'actual' scale of change.

6.3.3 THE NATURE OF CHANGE – PLANNED OR UNPLANNED?

Whilst it may be assumed that all organisational change is both rational and planned, with control of nearly all processes and resources, there may be occasions when a less planned and logical method may be adopted. A parallel argument is one of adopting an organic approach to change (Burns and Stalker 1994) versus an expected mechanistic approach. If it is assumed that change can emerge, then one approach by management may be to throw a metaphorical hand grenade into the organisation, and then see what emerges.

For example, an organisation may deliberately set about rumour-mongering around restructuring and job cuts, then formally notify employees that all jobs have been red circled and that employees have to make applications for new posts. During this time, communication and consultation is deliberately kept to a minimum. Management then see what emerges after a period of time. A less contentious scenario could also be envisaged, where the management of an organisation simply let things run, without obvious intervention.

Change models tend to centre around planned change, which in itself will determine the various factors or characteristics that are then compared to, for example: strategic/

tactical and operational change; radical, transformational and incremental change; the rate of change (change momentum); and hard versus soft change.

However, complex large-scale change, usually driven by external factors and having a significant 'soft' change element, are planned and co-ordinated. The terms 'managing change' or 'change management' can be used to describe the application of systematic interventions to implement a planned change within organisations to achieve a desired future state. In the following section, several key change management models are considered.

The nature of change – hard and soft change

The 'hard' elements of change are the tasks within change management, which are defined and measured. 'Soft' factors, such as culture and motivation, may be more difficult to assess. Emphasis may be placed upon managing task factors at the expense of soft factors during change interventions; however, Sirkin et al (2005) argue that four hard factors correlate to the outcome of change interventions, namely: duration (length of time); integrity (reliance on managers); commitment (of all involved in change); and effort (within the opportunity of time allowed).

When characterising change, we have considered the speed and magnitude of change, and related this to the problem of complexity. The problems that change present to an organisation can be perceived by managers as 'difficulties', which are 'bounded' in that they can be well defined (specified) and can be dealt with without involving or impacting on the wider organisation.

Another category of problems are those which cannot be well defined and are 'unbounded' in the sense that the wider organisation is implicated and needs to be involved in dealing with these types of problems.

The nature of change – top-down versus bottom-up

Top-down change can stem from a managerial prerogative for maintaining control throughout the change. Change can be driven through by management, and resistance controlled and eliminated. Here change can become more of a political issue (Gioia and Thomas 1996). Lupton (1991) argues that a bottom-up approach has its benefits in that employees at all levels have skills and expertise that are often lost in change processes. A third option is a combination of top-down and bottom-up approaches.

Change momentum: magnitude and speed

The momentum of change, that is the combination of speed and magnitude of change, is a useful concept to analyse and characterise different types of change. As we have seen, change momentum is not always easy to predict, but if it can be anticipated (which is often the case) interventions to manage change may be considered from the options available. In other words, if managers are able to characterise the type of change an organisation will experience, this can be helpful in considering appropriate interventions to manage change in an effective way. We will consider change management interventions later, but let us return to characterising change. Figure 6.2 below represents a model of change momentum based on the two key variables of speed and magnitude.

'Smooth' and 'bumpy' change are both characterised by relatively small (and less complex) change, but differ in speed of implementation, with 'smooth' change happening over a longer period of time than the latter. Smooth change happens in small steps and is often described as being 'incremental', being barely noticeable in the day-to-day business of an organisation. Relatively minor changes to policies and procedures would be examples of this type of change. It is typically driven by internal factors.

'Bumpy' change is more noticeable, as the speed of change is fast and therefore requires a quicker response time by managers and employees in dealing with it. It is typically driven by external factors which require an organisation to move quickly to respond. Examples of this would include organisations responding to crisis, which require significant investment and/or changes in practice, for example, health, safety and the environment, regulatory reform or legal proceedings. Companies involved in fast-moving markets often have to manage this type of change as consumer opinion and tastes quickly change.

Figure 6.2 Model of change momentum

Magnitude of change

'Planned'	*'Big Bang'*
Large change	Large change
Slow change	Fast change
'Smooth'	*'Bumpy'*
Small change	Small change
Slow change	Fast change

Speed of change

Grundy (1993) describes three types of change related to speed of change. The first is 'smooth incremental change' as change that evolves slowly in a systematic and predictable way. He also describes 'bumpy incremental change' as periods of relative calm, that is, little or no change that is punctuated by accelerated change. The third type of change described by Grundy is 'discontinuous' change, which he defines as 'change which is marked by rapid shifts in strategy, structure or culture, or in all three' (Grundy 1993, p26). This equates closely to 'Big Bang' change in terms of change momentum.

Grundy's 'discontinuous change' and 'Big Bang' change describes many of the characteristics of what has become known as 'transformational' change – a type of change that involves the values, attitudes and behaviours of people that contribute towards shaping the culture of an organisation. This form of complex change focuses on the motivation and commitment of employees and their contribution towards performance outcomes. Leadership which emphasises these employee attributes in managing change is described as 'transformational leadership' (Bass 1985), to which we shall return later.

In conclusion, a range of differing variables have been used to examine the different types of change. However, there may be other more relevant comparators than the ones presented. It is necessary to examine the context of change as well in order to assess whether the most appropriate comparators have been used.

6.4 ANALYSING THE CHANGE CONTEXT

The question as to why organisations change is often determined by a combination of push and pull factors. Organisations sometimes have choices as to whether they want to change, or are sometimes forced to change, because of legal or other reasons. The importance of why organisations change is linked to the timing of change. Whilst there may be a range of comparators with which to analyse change dimensions, a potential metaphor is one which considers a combination of change interventions running concurrently – see Figure 6.3. The metaphor shows a range of change interventions, some of which start anew, some end, and all of which may impact upon each other.

Figure 6.3 Combination of concurrent change interventions

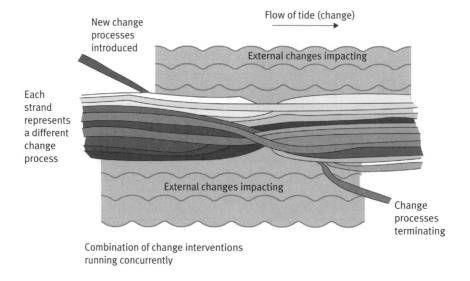

Whilst classic change models may posit a start, middle and end part of the change process, it is important to have to start at some point in terms of determining where the organisation is now and where it wants to arrive at in terms of change. Change models can either adopt a reactive approach ('this is why we need to change'), or adopt a proactive approach ('where do we want to get to as an organisation?'). Figure 6.4 demonstrates the iterative nature of change, and planning for change.

Figure 6.4 The iterative nature of change, and planning for change

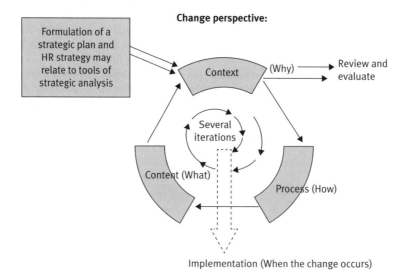

With strategic change, we may start with a strategic plan, or possibly a vision or mission statement, which leads to a strategic plan. When analysing why organisations change, there is often a trigger for change. The following factors are proposed here as triggers for change – see also CIPD (2009b):

- challenges of growth, especially global markets
- challenges of economic downturns and tougher trading conditions
- changes in strategy
- technological changes
- competitive pressures, including mergers and acquisitions
- customer pressure, particularly shifting markets
- pressures to learn new organisation behaviour and skills
- government legislation/initiatives.

When it comes to analysing the strategic context, a range of models can be utilised. Both the internal and external context need to be analysed.

Caldwell (2013) argues that change should be understood from a 'changing organisation' perspective, which places multiple, simultaneous adaptive demands upon individuals (employees) from many forces within the organisation, which in themselves may be planned or possibly unplanned.

6.4.1 EXTERNAL DRIVERS OF CHANGE

A useful tool to examine the external drivers of change involves the PESTLE taxonomy. The earliest known reference to a framework for describing the external business environment is by Aguilar (1967) who presents 'ETPS' as a mnemonic to represent the four sectors: Economic, Technical, Political and Social. Variations of this include 'PEST' and 'PESTLE', which adds the Legal and Environmental dimensions – see Table 6.1.

Table 6.1 PESTLE framework

Factor or driver	Typical considerations
Political	Taxation and other policies Current and future political support Funding, grants and initiatives Trade organisations Internal and international relationships
Economic	Economic situation Consumer spending Levels of government spending Interest rates, inflation and unemployment Exchange rates
Social	Demographics and social mobility Lifestyle patterns and changes People's attitudes and actions Media perception and influence Ethnic and religious differences
Technology	Research, technology and innovation funding Consumer behaviour and processes Intellectual property Global communication technological advances Social networks

Factor or driver	Typical considerations
Legal	Legislation in employment, competition and health and safety, etc Changes in legislation Trading policies Regulatory policies International protocols
Environmental	Clean technologies and processes Waste management and recycling Attitudes of government, media and consumers Environmental legislation Global warming and emission protocols

The PESTLE taxonomy provides a useful external environment scanning framework and a methodology for identifying and analysing factors that shape the external business environment. When combined with a SWOT (Strengths, Weaknesses, Opportunities and Threats) analysis, this evidence-based approach provides valuable information for strategic decision-making.

The external environmental factors identified from a PESTLE are typically considered as opportunities or threats in a SWOT analysis. Strengths and weaknesses are usually regarded as internal organisational factors which can be considered against the external opportunities and threats. This 'looking out' and 'looking in' approach provides a basis for internal–external organisation analysis and is an important part of the strategic management process, if carried out in a purposeful and rigorous manner.

6.4.2 INTERNAL DRIVERS OF CHANGE

Not all organisational change can be attributed to managers responding to a business environment comprising external factors. Internal drivers of change can also play a major role in initiating change and these include:

- new leadership
- new strategy
- new structures
- new business model
- organisation growth
- redesign of jobs
- redesign of business processes
- outsourcing
- change of location
- installation of new technology and systems
- changes to employees' terms and conditions
- being acquired or merged with another organisation
- redundancies.

These changes can be and often are influenced by external factors but they can also be triggered by decisions which are not made as a response to changes in the business environment.

Pettigrew and Whipp (1993) argue that environmental assessment is only one of five factors that determine the success of managing change. The other four factors are leading change, linking strategic and operational change, considering human resources as both assets and liabilities, and a central factor in all of this – coherence – pulling together the other four factors.

REFLECTIVE ACTIVITY 6.1

Duty of care

Change has been equated to bereavement (Marris 1986). Constant change may not allow employees time to grieve. It could be argued that organisations have a duty of care to ensure that the welfare of their employees is paramount and thereby limit constant and dramatic change. If an organisation does not constantly seek employee feedback and make an assessment through an organisational stress thermometer, then how will it know how much employees can take? Acas (2010) recommends that employees' emotions are taken into account when managing change, by including the following within every change process:

- create a vision
- lead (the change)
- consult (with employees)
- engage (employees)
- reflect upon the change process (including employees' views).

What are the implications for organisations when deciding upon the nature and type of change, and how change should take place?

It is important to differentiate between external and internal factors when considering change, with the key difference being that organisations and managers may have little, if any, control over the external factors. However, internal factors are typically management decisions which are designed to exert some form of control aimed at achieving certain performance outcomes.

Organisations lobby governments on many issues in an attempt to influence politicians' decisions and the outcomes that define the external factors which ultimately shape the business environment in which they operate. Climate change and the environment are examples of contemporary issues that continue to attract the lobbyists in the early part of this century.

Control is the primary motivation for doing this because if organisations can be a factor in shaping their business environment, this enables them to predict more accurately what this environment will look like. This, in turn, puts these organisations in a stronger position to be able to make informed strategic decisions to control their future direction and performance.

The UK Government's 'modernisation programme' of public services described in a 1999 White Paper set out a ten-year change programme aimed at delivering more responsive and high-quality public services which can be measured by better results. The NHS is probably the most widely publicised example of this modernisation agenda, having been subjected to a plethora of change initiatives and performance targets. A combination of external and internal factors typically drive this type of change in organisations.

6.4.3 CHOICE OF CHANGE INTERVENTION

After the context has been analysed, the choice of change intervention needs to be considered. Five different change management tools and techniques are discussed below in order to provide an understanding of how the organisation can manage change.

TROPICS test

The Open University (1985) describes two types of problems as 'difficulties' and 'messes'. Paton and McCalman (2000) use the terms 'hard' and 'soft' respectively to describe these same sets of problems, and devised the 'TROPICS' test as a guide to help determine the nature of change in terms of a continuum from hard to soft (see Table 6.2).

Table 6.2 The TROPICS test

Hard	Soft
Timescales clearly defined/short- to medium-term	Timescales ill-defined/medium- to long-term
Resources needed identified	Resources uncertain
Objectives specified and quantified	Objectives subjective and ambiguous
Perceptions of the problem shared by all	No consensus of problem
Interest in problem limited and defined	Interest in problem is widespread and ill-defined
Control within managing group	Control is shared with people outside of managing group
Source of the problem lies within organisation	Source of the problem is from outside the organisation

This test provides a useful reference framework to help characterise and understand the parameters involved when facing change. It is important to recognise that this is a continuum, and many change programmes will combine elements of hard and soft change.

When managers have knowledge and understanding of the issues involved in a change scenario, they are in a better position to be able to assess the situation and decide on an appropriate course of action to help control and manage the change process.

Lewin's three-phase change model

One of the earliest known models applied to managing change is a three-phase model by Kurt Lewin (1951) which focuses on the psychological aspects of behaviour modification:

1 *Unfreezing* – lowering resistance to change by recognising and accepting the need for change.

2 *Movement* – developing new attitudes to encourage behaviours necessary for change to occur.

3 *Refreezing* – stabilising, supporting and reinforcing the new change conditions.

This model presents a systematic approach to change management, describing a sequence of well-defined and interrelated processes. The premise for this model is that by identifying and understanding the key stages involved in the change process, the likelihood of effective change management is increased – by managers making better informed decisions about which interventions to use in managing change.

Lewin (1947) was also responsible for developing the Force-field analysis, a diagnostic technique which considered the forces or 'drivers' for and against change. At any time, there will be a number of forces in play that resist change and support the status quo, and forces that encourage change. These can be internal or external forces, or, as is usually the case, a combination of both.

When the sum of the forces 'for' and 'against' change are equal, they cancel each other out, resulting in equilibrium, that is, a steady state. However, when the forces driving change are greater than the forces of resistance (either by the driving forces increasing or the restraining forces decreasing) then change will occur, and the organisation will inevitably change and move to a new state, as shown in Figure 6.5.

Figure 6.5 Lewin's Force-field analysis

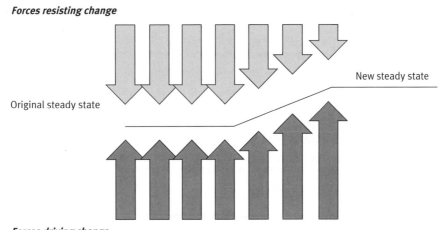

Although Lewin's model is criticised for over-simplifying change by describing a sequential linear process, its three stages of change are reflected in other more contemporary change-management models. French et al (1985) list eight components of a planned-change effort, which can be related to Lewin's model. The other main criticism of Lewin's model and other linear change models is that they describe the process of change transforming from an initial state to a final stage. Today, change is widely recognised as being a constant and continuing phenomena for all organisations, albeit at a faster rate for some compared to others.

6.4.4 RESISTANCE TO CHANGE

A multitude of factors could contribute to resistance to change. Prahalad, quoted in Allio (2008), cites three primary reasons for resistance to change in organisations. Firstly, the logic of management actions and behaviours is not always obvious. Secondly, if change occurs, the accumulated intellectual experience of the players becomes devalued and change is taken as a personal threat (so a safety net is needed). Thirdly, managers need to have their hand held while they are learning. Prahalad emphasises the need for managers to be constantly learning new skills.

French et al (2011) suggest that in order to minimise resistance in such cases, the change agent should make sure that the people affected by the change know specifically how it satisfies the following criteria:

- *Benefit*. The change should have a clear relative advantage for the individuals being asked to change; ie, it should be perceived as 'a better way'.
- *Compatibility*. The change should be as compatible as possible with the existing values and experiences of the people being asked to change.
- *Complexity*. The change should be no more complex than necessary. It must be as easy as possible to understand and use.
- *Triability*. The change should be something that people can try on a step-by-step basis and make adjustments throughout the process.

Frahm and Brown (2005) argue that one of the key aspects of creating strategic change is the receptivity of employees to organisational change. They argue that organisational communication can significantly help alleviate problems often associated with change fatigue and change resistance.

REFLECTIVE ACTIVITY 6.2

Your organisation (or an organisation of your choice) has decided to introduce job evaluation and performance management organisation wide. It is also operating a recruitment ban and pay freeze. As the HR business partner, use Lewin's model to identify some of the potential forces acting for and against this change initiative.

Kotter's eight-stage change model

John Kotter (1996) described an eight-stage change process for managing change in large organisations following his research into US organisations who had failed to manage change effectively:

1   Establish a sense of urgency – the need to change.

2   Create a guiding coalition – with authority and credibility.

3   Develop a vision and strategy – a clear aim and way forward.

4   Communicate the change vision – promote understanding and commitment.

5   Empower broad-based action – enable people to act and overcome barriers.

6   Generate short-term wins – to motivate and ensure further support.

7   Consolidate gains and produce more change – maintain change momentum.

8   Anchor new approaches in the culture – new values, attitudes and behaviours.

This model appears to be a linear and sequential set of processes, and has been criticised for these reasons. However, in the final two steps, Kotter attempts to address the problem of the 'refreezing' stage in Lewin's model by encouraging organisations and their employees to develop attitudes and values which help to promote the behaviours required to encourage and support further change. Developing an organisational culture that is proactive to change helps to create a feedback mechanism which transforms a linear change model into a continuous process.

Many change management programmes applied in organisations are based on systematic change management models comprising sequential processes similar to the examples outlined above. However, a common modification to these models in practice is to introduce an additional process at the end, which provides a feedback step from the final to the initiating stage. With this modification, these models describe a cyclical and continuous change management system.

A significant feature of Kotter's model is the role of leadership, particularly in developing and communicating the vision for change, which is critical to effective transformational leadership, and management of change in large-scale organisations (Bass 1985).

This type of approach to change tends to be effective for change that is predominantly 'hard' by nature, that is, as characterised in terms of the TROPICS test. Objectives, milestones and performance can be quantified and applied within the boundaries of a specific change programme, thereby offering a means to assess progress of the managed change programme.

Organisational development

There is another approach for intervening to improve organisational performance through managing change called organisational development (OD) that offers appropriate solutions to the 'softer' aspects of change. We must remember that hard and soft change is part of a continuum, and that the majority of change scenarios involve both aspects.

When managing change, organisations will apply a range of interventions often using both approaches described in this chapter. These different approaches are not mutually exclusive.

There are many definitions of OD, but the following definition is particularly useful in helping to develop understanding of the context, content and processes involved in OD as a change and organisational performance intervention.

French and Bell (1999, pp25–6) define OD as: a long-term effort, led and supported by top management to improve an organisation's visioning, empowerment, learning and problem-solving processes, through an ongoing, collaborative management of organisation culture – with a special emphasis on the culture of intact work-teams and other team configurations, using consultant–facilitator roles and the theory and technology of applied behavioural science, including action research.

CIPD (2009b) offers the following succinct definition of OD: 'planned and systematic approach to enabling sustained organisational performance through the involvement of its people'.

OD emphasises the management of culture and employee behaviour as the central interventions for sustaining organisational capability to deal with long-term change and improve performance. An examination of several definitions of OD reveals a number of common features which highlight the distinguishing characteristics of the OD approach to change:

- It has top management support and involvement – it is participative.
- It deals with change over the medium- to long-term – it is strategic.
- It applies to an entire organisation and its component parts – it is systematic within institutionalising change.
- It draws on the theory and practice of behavioural science – such as leadership, group dynamics and work design.
- It emphasises the transfer of knowledge and skills through training and developing people – using action-research and organisational learning methods.
- It is concerned with planned change but is adaptable to new situations – rather than prescribing a rigid process which must be followed.
- It is uses data to inform decision-making and progress – it is 'evidence-based'.
- It often makes use of change agents or OD practitioners to facilitate the OD process.
- It is aimed at facilitating planned change and improving organisational performance over the longer term.

The roots of OD can be found in the motivation theories of the 1940s and 1950s, which gave rise to the human relations school of management and organisation. It became popular towards the end of the last century as an alternative approach to the hard systems approach shaped by the models which flourished in the 1980s and 1990s. These models struggled to deal with the complexities and often unknown factors that were common components of the 'unbounded' soft and messy problems organisations faced as their environments rapidly changed.

OD focuses on managing organisational culture by promoting values and attitudes associated with personal and professional development, problem-solving, openness, engagement and commitment. The premise of this approach is that if an organisation's employees share such common values, this will manifest in desirable and normative behaviour at all levels: individual, team and organisation.

An example of where the application of the OD approach would be particularly relevant is in developing a 'high performance culture' within an organisation. By establishing a shared set of values which employees, particularly managers, agree to adhere to in the work environment, this provides a guide for what is regarded as acceptable employee behaviour, which, over a period of time, becomes regarded as normal behaviour by most employees.

The set of values would typically include values related to learning and improvement, working with others, being honest and respectful, etc, which ultimately influence individual and group behaviour to enable performance improvement. These values would typically be applied in performance management interventions, recruitment and selection, career development and progression, reward schemes and leadership development, to facilitate and embed an evasive organisational culture that encourages and supports high levels of commitment to performance.

This is a sophisticated and complex form of organisational control based on influencing normative behaviour which is acceptable to managers and employees. The principles of OD also facilitate management of the psychological contract, which is defined by Guest and Conway (2002) as 'the perceptions of the two parties, employee and employer, of what their mutual obligations are towards each other'.

Guest and Conway propose in their model of the psychological contract that the implicit nature of contract is moderated by the employees' and employer's sense of fairness and trust, and the belief that the employer will honour the unwritten arrangement between them. It is suggested that a healthy psychological contract will promote employee commitment and satisfaction and have a positive influence on performance.

How employees experience and perceive the workplace, and their relationship with managers and colleagues, will play a role in shaping their attitudes and consequent behaviour. OD, with its emphasis on values and attitudes as a means of managing culture and change, also presents an opportunity for employers and employees to develop positive psychological contracts to the benefit of both parties.

Although OD is an intervention for managing change and improving performance, because it focuses on the culture of an organisation influencing attitudes and values (and ultimately behaviour), it pervades all areas and activities of an organisation. With an emphasis on learning and improvement, at individual, group and organisational levels, through techniques such as action learning, it develops and sustains the performance capability of an organisation through its people asset (human capital) and prepares an organisation for dealing with continuous change, ie it develops a state of enduring readiness for change.

In doing this, OD shapes the culture of an organisation to encourage managers and employees not to resist change but to be accepting and even embrace change, and approach it in that way. In other words, OD influences the ethos of an organisation and its people in dealing with change. It is an approach which addresses the soft and often intangible aspects of managing change which, because of the complexity involved, the rationality-based linear change models do not adequately accommodate.

Organisations that take the OD approach towards managing change tend to rely less on specific and explicit change programmes, but approach change as a normal part of everyday business. In the UK, the NHS has attempted to take this approach, having undergone radical change since inception of the modernisation programme (see 6.4.2 'Internal drivers of change').

The OD approach implies that normal business is about change and that dealing with change is implicit in what organisations and their people do – it is 'business as usual'. This makes a lot of sense because if we accept that organisational change is a permanent phenomenon, employees will soon become exhausted and demotivated if they are presented with one change programme after another, and sometimes multiple change programmes at the same time.

That is not to say that organisations that adopt the OD approach cannot and do not roll out specific projects for introducing change. This would be a particularly appropriate approach for managing when hard changes are specific and contained, and lend themselves to being managed as a project with clearly defined and measurable objectives.

CASE STUDY 6.1

IMPRESS: MEETING COMPANY GOALS THROUGH STRATEGIC ACQUISITIONS

Impress is a privately owned worldwide manufacturer of metal food cans, operating in 21 countries, with 8,000 employees, and turnover of 1.6bn euros in 2006. Impress as a legal identity is based in the Netherlands, but has its head office in Paris, and operates primarily throughout Europe.

Its strategy is to be the best metal-can manufacturer as opposed to the most profitable or biggest, and places great emphasis upon values surrounding operational excellence. The corporate culture centres around trust, transparency and teamwork.

Impress adopts an acquisition strategy in order to meet company objectives, and not as a purpose in itself. After Impress has considered acquiring another organisation and has evaluated if there will be a resultant strategic advantage, questions around the target company's readiness to change are considered. All relevant parties are brought to the table, and HR, finance, legal, production, management and technical teams are consulted in an unaggressive and unobtrusive way.

Impress managers seek to understand the culture and management model of the organisation and its capacity for change, as well as explore the leadership of the change process. The reputation of the company in the local area is considered, employee behaviours and skills are analysed and consideration given to company values and how they are communicated throughout the company.

During the post-acquisition process, welcome meetings are arranged, existing signs and logos are replaced by the Impress brand, plans for integration of the two company structures set out, synergies and benchmarking sought, and restructuring plans made. Information is communicated as clearly and widely as possible in order to keep all relevant parties informed. Management changes are made as quickly as possible and a vision developed for the acquired company.

Impress use a 'learning by doing' framework for acquisitions, which facilitates the integration process and creates enough flexibility to allow processes and values to be influenced by the cultures of the company that it acquires and the countries in which it operates.

Source: Huws and O'Keefe (2008)

Questions

Consider the extent to which Impress adopts Kotter's approach when managing acquisitions and change.

Whilst the concept of a systems approach may on the face of it appear simplistic, systems models allow for a great deal of complexity and data to be analysed. Figure 6.6 demonstrates the key components of a process model of change.

A systems approach to change

Whilst there is a range of systems models available to the change agent, Mayon-White (1993) highlights the example of systems intervention strategy (SIS) as a useful tool for undertaking change. The diagnosis phase asks 'Where are we now?' (the description), then 'Where do we want to be?', which evolves the identification of objectives and constraints.

Figure 6.6 A systems approach to change

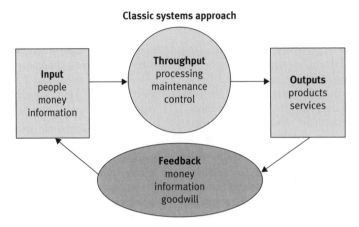

The question 'How will you know when you get there?' is addressed by the formulation of measures to achieve the objectives. In the design phase, we ask 'How can we get there?' in order to generate a range of options, then ask 'What will it be like?', where we can model options selectively. During the implementation phase, we consider whether we will like it, and then evaluate options against measures. Finally, we ask 'How can we carry it through?' then consider the design of implementation strategies and carry through the planned changes. Figure 6.7 demonstrates how the 'problem owners' fit within this model. Whilst McCalman and Paton (1992) argue that the problem owner may clearly define the nature of change, those affected by the change, the boundary and scope of the change and the relationships affected by the change, it could be contested that establishing who is affected by the change is not always apparent. 'Affected' could be considered in terms of job, role, task, function, etc, but may not account for emotional or cultural ties, etc.

Figure 6.7 Systems intervention strategy

Mayon-White (1993, p136) provides a chart showing the types of action and tools and techniques that are used in systems intervention strategy (see Table 6.3).

Table 6.3 The key features and methods of SIS

The three phases of the strategy	The steps of the strategy phases	What kinds of actions are appropriate to each step?	What tools and techniques are available to help?
Diagnosis	0. Entry	Start by recognising that change is a complex process.	Make use of the concepts of 'mess' and 'difficulty'.
	1. Description	Structure and understanding the change in systems terms. Get other points of view on the change problem or opportunity.	Use diagrams. Set up meetings (NGT, Delphi, etc). Create a model of things as they are.
	2. Identify objectives and constraints	Set up objectives for the systems that you are examining. Think of the objectives of the change itself.	Set up an 'objective tree'. Prioritise your objectives for change.
	3. Formulate measures for your objectives	Decide on ways of measuring if an objective is achieved.	Use '£s' or quantities where possible. Scaling or ranking methods elsewhere.
Design	4. Generate a range of options	Develop any ideas for change as full options. Look at a wide range of possibilities. Your objectives may suggest new options.	Brainstorming. Idea writing. Interviews and surveys. Comparisons with best practice in other organisations.
	5. Model options selectively	Describe the most promising options in some detail. Ask of each option: what is involved? Who is involved? How will it work?	Diagrams are simple models. Cost–benefit analysis. Cash flow models. Computer simulations.
Implementation	6. Evaluate options against measures	Test the performance of your options against an agreed set of criteria.	Set up a simple matrix to compare the performance of your options. Score each option against the metrics.

The three phases of the strategy	The steps of the strategy phases	What kinds of actions are appropriate to each step?	What tools and techniques are available to help?
	7. Design implementation strategies	Select your preferred options and plan a way of putting the changes into place.	Look for reliable options. Check back to 'problem owners'. Plan time and allocate tasks.
	8. Carry through the planned changes	Bring together people and resources. Manage the process. Monitor progress.	Sort out who is involved. Allocate responsibility. Review and modify plans if necessary (CPA, etc).

Source: Mabey and Mayon-White 1998

A range of models have been presented, some of which show signs of overlap; for example, systems intervention strategy includes Lewin's Force-field analysis. The choice of model(s) is up to the change agent and key stakeholders. It is possible to combine aspects of different models, for example, having a combination of OD and SIS, but caution needs to be expressed so that there is no confusion as to what the process actually involves.

 REFLECTIVE ACTIVITY 6.3

Many modern organisations operate within stringent financial controls and exercise both lean thinking and lean management principles. In simple terms, organisations need to do more with less. Classic work undertaken by Womack and Jones (1996) placed particular emphasis upon the needs of the customer, with five key lean principles:

- *Value* – specifying what creates value from the customer's perspective.
- *The value stream* – identifying all the steps along the process chain.
- *Flow* – making the value process flow.
- *Pull* – make only what is needed by the customer (short-term response to the customer's rate of demand).
- *Perfection* – strive for perfection by continually attempting to produce exactly what the customer wants.

Whilst these principles may be particularly suitable when applied to production processes, consider how this model could be applied to a charitable organisation or perhaps a small local authority organisation. In particular, consider who the 'customer' is and how the particular organisation (charity of authority) could change in order to meet the needs of the customer.

6.5 LEADING CHANGE

The choice of change agent is critical to the success of any change intervention. Whilst a universal definition of a change agent proves impossible to locate, characteristics, competences and skills can differentiate across change agents. In simple terms, Rosenfeld and Wilson (1999, p294) define change as 'the individuals or groups of individuals whose task it is to effect change'.

What does a change agent look like?

Whilst the determination of choice of change agent will be determined by a range of factors, Lessem (1989) provides a range of change agent characteristics:

- You are professional, with an in-depth knowledge and experience in a particular field, and often with greater loyalty to your profession than to your organisation.
- You learn from change, by observing, conceptualising, experimenting and validating. Also, by accommodating through flexible communications.
- You troubleshoot, rapidly identifying opportunities for change, and coming up with alternative courses of action to exploit them.
- You adapt to change, by mapping out the internal and external environment, and by creating systems and procedures for dealing with change.
- You experiment with change, by continually forming temporary project groupings and solving ongoing problems in interdisciplinary teams.
- You plan for change, by constructing long-term plans with contingencies built in, monitoring changes and adapting plans accordingly.
- You embody the spirit of change, and are respected as a free thinker. You also embody the organisation's cause.

 REFLECTIVE ACTIVITY 6.4

To what extent can the HR function adopt Lessem's seven characteristics and demonstrate these during a change process?

The historical nature of the role and significance of change agents has varied, from 'change masters' and 'transformational leadership experts' in the 1980s to 'catalysts of change' in the 1990s (Caldwell 2003). A useful model that progresses the definition and nature of change agents is provided by Caldwell (2003), who posits that a fourfold classification expands our understanding of change agency. His four descriptors are:

1 *Change leadership* – typically through identifying various traits and magical qualities associated with change leaders (akin to some leadership theories).

2 *Managers as change agents* – focusing on the role of managers (particularly middle management) in implementing change.

3 *Management consultants as change agents* – with particular emphasis on the role of project managers, often pitched at strategic co-ordination of complex and large-scale multiple change projects.

4 *(The emergence of) change teams* – facilitated by flatter structures and self-managed teams which combine knowledge and specialist expertise of internal and external consulting teams.

Whilst attempts to define what a change agent might look like appear plausible, the intentionality and integrity of this agent might determine their nature and subsequent actions and behaviour. Beckett (1999) highlights the notion that change agents seek to bring about change in order to enhance their own interests, and some of these actions could result in entrepreneurial activities and outcomes. Whilst no value judgement is made about undertaking entrepreneurial activities, the debate around change agents pushing boundaries beyond those expected of project managers could provide opportunity for further discussion and research.

REFLECTIVE ACTIVITY 6.5

As an HR professional, consider Caldwell's fourfold classification when applied to the process of recruiting and selecting a change agent for a complex change scenario. To what extent would this model help you to narrow down the type of change agent(s) required for the task?

Assuming that there is no singular and simple definition of a change agent, another approach to understanding what a change agent is and what they do may consider how change agents operate, and in particular, what tools they use when carrying out change.

Doz and Prahalad (1988) cite a range of tools that change agents can select from and use. Firstly, data management tools concern the manipulation of information, systems, resource allocation procedures, strategic planning and budgeting arrangements. These tools are used to guide decision-making. Secondly, management tools are a combination of hard and soft approaches. 'Hard' tools involve manipulation of key appointments, career planning and reward systems. 'Soft' tools include changes to management development and socialisation patterns. These tools dictate the rules of the game. Thirdly, conflict management tools involve relocation of decision responsibility, formation of business teams, task forces and co-ordination committees, the appointment of 'integrators', and establishment of procedures to resolve issues. These tools may be used more predominantly at different stages of a change intervention, where data management tools may prove most useful at the early stages of change, but conflict management tools may be used throughout some change interventions or perhaps during the 'movement' and 'refreezing' stages of a change process.

Buchanan and Boddy (1992) identified 15 competences that change agents adopt, clustered into five areas, namely: goals, roles, communication, negotiation and managing up. These competences sit within a framework which emphasises the political dimension.

The importance of both frontstage and backstage activity emphasises how the change agent has to manage their position continuously so as ensure their tenure and sustainability through the change intervention. Figure 6.8 displays the three critical agendas that may impact upon the determination of the change agent, where the content agenda relies upon technical competence (similar to Doz and Prahalad's data management tools), and the process agenda matches implementation skills, where communication, consultation, teambuilding, influencing and negotiation skills are key (similar to Doz and Pralahad's conflict management tools).

It could be argued that the more strategic the change, the more politically charged it will be and thereby draw upon more power bases. Balogun et al's research (2005) supports Hardy's argument (1994, 1996) that change agents address and engage the 'power of the system', mobilising existing power to negotiate power interdependencies to enrol staff to their cause. This parallels with Kotter's (1999) notion of forming powerful coalitions so as to effect a change agenda. Kotter argues that managers typically form powerful coalitions through network building and setting both business and personal agendas.

Figure 6.8 The expertise of the change agent

Source: Buchanan and Boddy (1992)

When making an assessment as to whether change agents could be recruited internally within an organisation, it might be useful to conduct an evaluation of whether there is a critical mass of the various skills within this context. If not, perhaps the necessary skills can be bought in.

The choice of who leads the change is a critical one, and should not rely purely on technical expertise. Endemic to this change process may be the setting of a vision or visioning statement by key player(s). If HR is to remove its reputation of being the bridesmaid, rather than the bride, then it needs to adopt strategic positioning, understand the business completely (business partnership), and adopt a leadership role (business leader).

CASE STUDY 6.2

HMRC

In an article from *The Times* (2010), Chris Mills argues that the radical change encountered by HMRC resulted in ineffective change management, attributed to the leadership rather than general competence.

Mills goes on to say that since the merger of the Inland Revenue and Customs and Excise since 2003, the organisation focused more upon tax-raising at strategic level, but lost the sense of purpose lower down. The lack of involvement of operational staff, where they drive the process quickly and effectively, was lacking. What is required includes strategic goals and a 'comprehensively thought-through model of the entire organisation, which encompasses vision, strategic performance measures, organisational structures, projects and business-as-usual activities, together with the right combination of skills, competencies and behaviours needed by all staff'.

Mills continues this line of argument by stating that the need to demonstrate clear alignment between all of these factors is crucial. The extent to which senior managers are more likely to be focused on building the profile of their own area (and themselves) may contaminate the effectiveness of the change process, despite having an overarching strategy and vision.

Another potential compounding factor is the Government's Efficiency Agenda, which attempts to maximise resources and ultimately save costs. Mills posits

that senior civil servants are often criticised for their apparent inability to translate good strategies into effective action, and sometime overuse consultants and other external staff in order to make things work, rather than providing the bursts of expertise for which they are better suited.

Source: Mills (2010)

Questions

Consider how the use of a change intervention, such as OD or systems intervention strategy, can assist in ensuring the strategic to operational alignment required to bring about effective change at HMRC.

6.6 HR VALUE ADDED AND CHANGE

Can HR establish and maintain a strategic-level involvement in organisations? The danger of pigeonholing functions is that some form of reductivism may result. If strategy was determined at a resource and capability level, then HR could perhaps fit more readily within strategic decision-making in organisations. However, Warren (2009) argues that OD needs to start with the business and HR's role is to facilitate it. HR and OD should be one and the same. It depends upon the level of importance that OD has within organisations as to whether OD impacts (and possibly guides) upon strategic planning.

For HR partners to take a leadership and proactive role, they will need to contribute towards key strategic decisions, and to do this, understanding of strategic change and change interventions is critical.

When bridging the strategic and tactical level, we can identify various ways in which HR professionals can endeavour to secure a successful role in the contribution made to change projects, namely:

- involvement at the initial stage in the project team
- advising project leaders in skills available within the organisation – identifying any skills gaps, training needs, new posts, new working practices, etc
- balancing out the narrow/short-term goals and broader strategic needs
- assessing the impact of change in one area/department/site on another part of the organisation
- being used to negotiating and engaging across various stakeholders
- understanding stakeholder concerns to anticipate problems
- understanding the appropriate medium of communication to reach various groups
- helping people cope with change, performance management and motivation.

There are perhaps many other areas where HR should impact upon change in organisations, such as learning from change, capturing appropriate knowledge and knowledge-sharing. Similarly, HR can facilitate teambuilding. Arrata et al (2007) argue that three critical elements are crucial to any change programme: thoughtful design; careful recruitment and development of personnel; and close integration between the change agent team and the organisational areas targeted for change. Successful communication underpins the effectiveness of the change team.

REFLECTIVE ACTIVITY 6.6

Concepts such as engagement and communication are vital within strategic and organisational change. It could be argued that HR has a central role in the day-to-day running of both of these concepts. In some cases, HR takes a leading role in implementing a range of change initiatives.

1   To what extent are there tensions for HR when managing change at both strategic and operational levels?

2   As a counter-argument, should line managers be largely responsible for engagement and communication within their respective divisions or departments?

CASE STUDY 6.3

MANAGING CHANGE THROUGH MARGINAL GAINS IN SPORT AND BUSINESS

A concept known as 'marginal gains' came to prominence during the London 2012 Olympics when the GB cycling team won a record eight gold medals. This outstanding performance followed similar success at the 2008 Beijing Olympics, and is attributed to the management approach adopted by Sir Dave Brailsford, the British Cycling Performance Director at the time of the 2008 and 2012 Olympic Games.

The concept of marginal gains can be neatly summarised in the following quote from Brailsford: 'Put simply... how small improvements in a number of different aspects of what we do can have a huge impact on the performance of the team' (Slater 2012). In other words, it is the aggregation of a number of small gains that result in a large gain in overall performance that can be significant in terms of outcomes and achievement. The application of marginal gains in sport is not confined to cycling and it has been adopted across many sports by individuals and teams. Well-known examples of sports that use marginal gains as an intervention to improve

performance include Formula 1 racing, rugby, athletics, swimming and golf.

Marginal gains is typically presented and discussed in terms of performance improvement, particularly when the context is competitive sport. However, the essence of marginal gains is change and the recognition of marginal gains as an intervention for managing change is often shadowed by the focus on performance and results. Many elements of marginal gains are key components of managing change, particularly in terms of continuous improvement and the application of metrics, such as statistical process control and quality management, are fundamental to the effective application of marginal gains. This case study highlights marginal gains as change intervention and discusses how this approach is applied in non-sport organisations with specific examples from a UK public sector organisation.

A strategy for change

To compare the use of marginal gains in sport with performance in business, it is helpful to consider the principles which underpinned the team's 2012 Olympic success. Sir Dave Brailsford provides insight into the systematic management approach applied at the GB cycling team: 'Firstly, you need a team with the skills and motivation to succeed. Secondly, you need to understand what you want to achieve. Thirdly, you need to understand where you are now. Then, you need to put a plan in place to see how you can get from where you are now to what you want to achieve' (BBC Breakfast, BBC1, 7 August 2012). This quotation captures the strategic and systematic management approach taken by Brailsford and his team. Understanding where the GB cycling team is now and planning future performance is based on the sophisticated application of metrics to track marginal performance gains. Marginal gains are sought from every aspect of the team's activities that contribute towards performance, including the technology that enables collection and analysis of real-time performance data. Performance improvement across such a range of areas demonstrates the holistic management approach taken by the team.

Theories in performance management and high-performance teams/organisations suggest that people need to be highly skilled and motivated to perform well (Katzenbach and Smith 2005). Brailsford states that the first requirement is a team with the skills and motivation to succeed. Elite sports teams are high-performance teams that are shaped by a high-performance organisational culture. The HRM literature describes the application of specific and integrated ('bundling') of high-performance work practices (HPWPs) in high-performance work organisations (HPWOs) to aggregate gains (Lawler 2005). Team GB cycling has successfully embedded continuous improvement practices in all aspects of its operation to realise aggregated marginal gains and, in doing so, is effectively managing change and performance.

Marginal gains at a UK Fire and Rescue organisation

To respond effectively to business challenges, major (destabilising) change may be required, but this type of change can be complemented by small evolutionary change ('incremental') that focuses on marginal gains. However, the goal of marginal gains may be obscured by the revolutionary strategic debate, rendering continuous change aimed at improvement through marginal gains passive rather than being driven by strategic intent. It is this context that sparked an interest in the concept of marginal gains at a UK Fire and Rescue organisation as an intervention opportunity to empower a more proactive approach towards organic change and improving organisational performance.

Specific examples of change and performance improvement at this organisation through a marginal gain approach include allowing on-call firefighters to text in their availability rather than having to visit the station, resulting in a significant increase in fire and rescue coverage across the area. Another example is the application of barcode readers to manage the organisation's assets, which has led to significantly improved legal compliance and management of over 30,000 traceable pieces of equipment. Changing station shift systems in tandem with increased managerial flexibility has led to a more productive working day. Less prescription over work routines has allowed adaptable and responsive services to be applied to changing community needs. All of these examples in isolation are small, incremental changes, but the accumulative effect through the aggregation of the marginal gains led to considerable improvements to community and firefighter safety.

Based on the success of marginal gains as a change and improvement intervention, this organisation has progressed to consider a more strategic management approach that identifies and connects marginal gains activities into larger programmes that are more strategically focused. Three key areas have been identified as a focus for discussion to take this forward:

- *Leadership gains*: small changes in overall strategic leadership and management that provokes new thinking in managers, and innovation within and between departments that improve efficiency, effectiveness and increased morale.
- *Technological gains*: introducing low-cost, undisruptive ICT or equipment changes that improve customer and service delivery experiences.
- *Process gains*: changing processes through lean thinking and application, along with the improved use of metrics to focus resources on the things that really make a difference and from which marginal gains can be determined.

To take a more strategic and proactive position on marginal gains, the organisation's management team believe that there are a number of common challenges to organisations. There may also be some that are more relevant to public sector organisations where the bottom line is more complex than profit, or in the case of sport, quickest time or points accumulated on the board.

Enabling organisation culture

One of the key challenges is to mindfully recognise margin gains within the overall strategic discussion and debate regarding continuous improvement. This must start with a discussion on the cultural norms that an organisation wishes to develop and promote. The focus needs to be on 'we're good, how do we get better?' and 'our people are good, how do we make them better?' Adopting this position sets a fundamentally different starting position from one that may often be focused on gaps and weaknesses. Although both approaches are focused on continuous improvement, the former is more likely to positively inspire, support higher levels of trust and allow empowerment to flourish. An example could be adoption of a strengths-based leadership approach to the development and management of our leaders that could produce the marginal improvements in personal performance and maximise talent.

Consider the intangibles

It is important that resources are fully accountable and used to their full potential: metrics are clearly important when indicating areas for marginal gains and measuring their success. However, whilst organisations can often sleepwalk into an approach whereby gains need to be fully justified and accounted for or, potentially, may be dismissed, introducing measurement frameworks and metrics may lead to innovation more focused on meeting targets (because individuals are held to account) than a more creative culture where managers are encouraged to innovate and to find marginal gains in all areas of their work.

This may be particularly relevant in the public sector where outcomes and outputs are sometimes less tangible and often intangible; it may need to be accepted that not everything can or needs to be measured. There is the danger that intended marginal gain may be quickly eroded by the bureaucracy needed to measure it. Sometimes it may take courage to allow the gain to be ill-defined; irrational, but emotionally valid. For instance, a feeling of self-efficacy in managers through greater empowerment is essential in creating improved performance but is extremely difficult to measure.

Conclusion

This case study proposes that a marginal gains approach to managing change offers a proactive and empowering approach to strategy for achieving continuous improvement. The incremental approach of marginal gains offers advantages for managing change, including encouraging and supporting employee involvement resulting in less resistance. This approach facilitates an organisational culture that supports high-performance behaviours in individuals and groups, which is essential to manage continuous improvement. Key to this approach is the recognition that many marginal gains can accumulate to deliver significantly greater terms of individual and group performance for an organisation.

Adapted from Hall et al (2012)

Questions

1   Can you identify where you could make marginal gains in the tasks you undertake (in work and out of work), and how would you prioritise these?

2   How would you monitor the gains you identified in question 1 to determine your improvement?

3   What would need to be in place to support you in taking a marginal gains approach to your individual work and the teams you are a member of?

6.7 CONCLUSION

Lloyd and Maguire (2002, p149) argue that, 'In future, the critical focus for sustainable organisational success will build on what the organisation knows about itself and its environment, and not on the transient structure and detailed processes. The successful organisations of the future will not be managing change but rather facilitating conversations for organisational learning and individual responsibility.' Hence the emphasis here is upon individual and team development, which sits comfortably within the scope and domain of HR.

'Change is ultimately about people – if they do not change, nothing significant happens' (Miller 2004, p10). Perhaps the argument for organisations having stronger and more sophisticated OD processes can never be understated. A positive employee attitude towards change is vital to a successful outcome. Tan and Tiong (2005) found that the highest correlated success factor was optimism, which they define as attitude towards change. HR, in partnership with line management, need to ensure that organisational change is planned, communicated and executed successfully on an ongoing basis in order to sustain business survival.

KEY LEARNING POINTS

1   There are numerous ways in which change can be analysed as far as the scope and nature of change is concerned.

2   HR professionals need to have an appreciation of the complex nature of several (sometimes contradictory) change interventions operating concurrently.

3   The context of change needs to be analysed in order to decide upon whether and which type of change intervention is needed or appropriate.

4   OD is a change intervention particularly suited to changing employees' values and organisational culture.

5   HR has a significant contribution to make to strategic change interventions, particularly when collating knowledge and learning emanating from change interventions, which can then be used on subsequent change interventions.

6   Change agents typically have to exhibit a range of skills and competences in order to demonstrate their credibility as a change agent, and simultaneously be aware of the political context within which they operate.

REVIEW QUESTIONS

1   Discuss the extent to which a vision and mission statement is important when an organisation is going through cultural changes.

2   Consider a change intervention with which you are familiar and consider what some of the barriers to change were, and where resistance to change was encountered. Try and classify these barriers and resistance factors into key categories.

3   What are some of the key skills that a change agent needs to exhibit? To what extent are these skills context-specific?

4   Think about how you could apply Lewin's change model to a change scenario of your choice. To what extent were there critical moments that defined the unfreezing, movement and refreezing?

EXPLORE FURTHER

Cameron, E. and Green, M. (2015) *Making Sense of Change Management: A complete guide to models, tools and techniques of organisational change*. 4th ed. London: Kogan Page.

Hayes, J. (2014) *The Theory and Practice of Change Management*. 4th ed. London: Palgrave Macmillan.

Hughes, M. (2010) *Change Management: A critical perspective*. 2nd ed. London: CIPD Publications. A sound textbook presenting a range of approaches to change.

Price, D. (ed) (2009) *The Principles and Practice of Change*. Basingstoke: Palgrave Macmillan. Provides a range of different perspectives on change by presenting some key articles and works on change.

CHAPTER 7

Flexibility and the Psychological Contract

RAY FRENCH

LEARNING OUTCOMES

After reading this chapter, you should be able to:

- define flexibility and understand the different meanings attached to this concept
- evaluate the importance of the psychological contract on employees' behaviour
- understand how flexibility and the psychological contract are interrelated; and
- explain how psychological contracts and flexibility can link with improved organisational performance.

7.1 OVERVIEW

In this chapter we examine several current concepts and issues which are central to good and effective management of people at work. An appreciation of the twin concepts of *flexibility* and the *psychological contract* help us in this regard in several important respects. It is, firstly, very important to understand current and emerging trends which affect the ways in which organisations operate. The notion of flexibility is certainly topical and frequently referred to, not only in business and management sources, but also more widely in mainstream news and specialist media.

To take just one example, the *People Management* online blog, in which practising HR professionals share views and experiences, provides a forum for divergent views on how flexible working plays out in reality. M'Pele (2015), in opening an online exchange on the topic, identifies the following potential benefits of flexible working, in particular the issue of remote work, where people are not based in a single workplace location:

- boost to productivity
- eliminates the necessity for absenteeism
- increases talent retention levels
- helps attract talent
- reduces costs.

However, contributors to this blog identify caveats; for example, noting that not all functions lend themselves to flexible working; M'Pele states that 'we're not yet ready to ditch the traditional office model once and for all'.

In this chapter we will therefore take a balanced overview as flexibility, while undoubtedly offering benefits for employers and employees, has also been associated with worsening work rewards and conditions. Once again, this debate was in full swing at the time of writing. Zero-hours contracts, in which people are paid for the work they do (and no more) and the actual time they take to carry out that work, are now widespread in the UK (see Arstein 2015 and Fleming 2015). There are significant advantages for workers in such arrangements. An Office for National Statistics (ONS) report in 2014 concluded that two-thirds of workers operating within such arrangements did not want to work more hours. Nonetheless, other commentators pointed to what they saw as the exploitative nature of such contracts, with the incoming UK Labour Party leader Jeremy Corbyn pledging to outlaw them during his 2015 leadership campaign, should the party win power at a subsequent general election.

Flexibility is not only important because it is topical. It also offers scope to allow people to work when they like (time) where they like (location) and enables workers to engage with work in different ways, for example as permanent employees, agency workers or self-employed homeworkers. It has the potential to revolutionise the working lives of many people worldwide. But it is definitely not a neutral term.

We will also explore the psychological contract concept – essentially an unwritten set of expectations of what an individual and organisation will give to and receive from each other in the course of their working relationship (Rousseau 1995, Tomprou et al 2015). While it can be viewed as a self-standing topic area, the notion of a psychological contract is linked to many others covered in this textbook, including flexibility. The level of commitment displayed by workers can be related to their psychological contract, and the state of that contract in turn influences workers' attitudes towards providing flexibility. There are important connections therefore between the two central topic areas in this chapter: flexibility and the psychological contract.

Just as flexibility is not a neutral term, so the psychological contract is also a value-laden term. At the simplest level, a psychological contract can be positive or negative. When expectations are not aligned a worker may seek to leave the organisation or reduce his or her input in some other way. In previous editions of this book we also unravelled potential in-built contradictions within this field. The desire for organisations to integrate HR policies with business objectives may, for example, sit uneasily with the move towards Atkinson's (1984) notion of the flexible firm, characterised by decentralised responsibilities and externalised workers. The client organisation in an outsourcing arrangement could find it difficult to manage, or even influence, the policies of a labour supplier. Gilmore (2013) records that flexible approaches to workforce deployment have often been coupled with an increase in part-time working, fixed-term contracts and outsourcing, making it potentially more difficult to secure organisational commitment. It has been noted that in much of the HR management literature, the typical focus had been on the remaining core activities and not on how non-core activities are provided (Marchington et al 2009).

The concepts discussed in this chapter are central to the core themes of the book, based around effective leadership and management of people. As such, material presented in this chapter is linked with themes and topics introduced elsewhere in the text. To take one example, the broad term 'flexibility' encompasses organisational and individual elements. In Chapter 8 we will see how people's experiences of work are affected by the organisational structure in which they operate, and of course, by the nature of work they do. In an important sense, therefore, organisational and job design lay out the context within which flexibility can be achieved. At the same time, the individual aspect of flexibility must be understood with reference to the subject of motivation, which we address in Chapter 12.

Meanwhile the promotion of all aspects of high-performance working, including flexibility, was addressed in Chapters 2 and 3. What can be said is that flexibility operates on both an organisational and individual level and that organisations and individuals (including managers and leaders) will have a keen interest in the topic.

We have, finally, an interesting issue regarding terminology and language throughout this chapter. How we choose to refer to the people – as employees, workers, or individuals – is context-bound, and arguably influences (or is influenced by) our thinking. Much of the current literature focuses on employees inside the organisation, yet as we will see, so-called networked organisations rely also upon people outside: for example freelancers, agency and outsourced workers. Even workers within the organisation can fall into the contingent category (that is, working without an ongoing contract). Examples here include temporary workers, seasonal staff and interns.

7.2 INTRODUCTION

Managing people in organisations has in recent years, according to many commentators, been carried out within a rapidly changing and turbulent environment; see for example CIPD (2012b) and Holbeche (2013). In many advanced economies there has been a move away from mass production of standardised products or even routine white-collar administrative work, with many such jobs moving to countries such as China and India. Concurrently, it has been suggested that people in organisations increasingly aspire to work more flexibly and wish to work in more autonomous and creative roles. A search for work–life balance by many employees results in a need for support from employing organisations in order to prevent burnout and maximise their work performance (French et al 2015).

Accelerating globalisation and technological advance has meant that the environment of organisations – both in the private and public sectors – has changed rapidly, resulting in a need for greater flexibility from organisations, their leaders and other workers (Thomas 2009, Thompson and McHugh 2009).

In this chapter we will examine a range of terms which have emerged as both diagnoses of current work practices and solutions to problems of managing people in the current competitive environment. Words and phrases such as 'flexibility', 'work–life balance' and 'work intensification' will be defined, analysed and their benefits and disadvantages highlighted. The debate on flexible responses to trends such as globalisation, technological advance and the 'marketisation' of public sector provision now has an established body of knowledge from Atkinson's (1984) notion of the flexible firm through to the CIPD report on 'smart and agile working' (CIPD 2014a). The area under consideration in this chapter continues to be academically relevant, topical and of personal interest to many of us.

 REFLECTIVE ACTIVITY 7.1

KPMG avoids redundancies through flexible working

Writer and researcher Charlotte Wolff notes how international professional services firm KPMG was particularly concerned to avoid employee redundancies following the economic downturn of 2008. David Conder, Head of People at KPMG, noted that: 'When we made redundancies alongside other, similar, firms in 2002/03, it constrained growth when the upturn came and it was also a very painful process for the organisation to go through.' KPMG's strategy now is to do the right thing for its clients, its people and the business. This means retaining talent, intellectual capital and the motivational level of its teams, thus ensuring continuity and top quality service.

KPMG's strategy now includes a 'flexible futures' programme using reduced hours and sabbaticals to manage the workforce flexibly during times when business is quiet.

Source: Wolff (2008)

7.3 FLEXIBILITY

Flexibility has been frequently identified as a key HR policy goal, along with strategic intention, quality and employee commitment, in order to ensure an adaptable organisation structure (Guest 2004). These HR goals are in turn held to generate 'a range of positive organisational outcomes, such as high job performance, high quality problem solving, successful change, lower turnover, absenteeism and grievance levels and high cost-effectiveness' (Iles et al 1996, p18).

On the one hand employers, encouraged by governments and non-governmental bodies, such as the International Monetary Fund and the World Bank, press the case for workforce flexibility in the hunt for efficiency, and on the other hand it is claimed that individual employees look for flexibility in working hours as they attempt to juggle the demands of home and work lives. It seems that the two agendas might meet in a unitary, though stressful, work–life balance (CIPD 2012d, Taylor 2002, Pollitt 2003) where employers' flexibility requirements can coincide well with the wants and needs of a great many employees. Truss et al (2006) found that workers who were on flexible contracts tended to be more emotionally engaged, more satisfied (with their work) and more likely to speak positively about their organisation. In addition, these workers were also less likely to quit.

When the concept of flexibility emerged, four main types of flexibility were identified (Blyton and Morris 1992):

1   Task or functional flexibility, where employees may be multiskilled.

2   Numerical flexibility, using different types of employment contracts and subcontracting, as in Atkinson's (1984) core-periphery concept.

3   Temporal flexibility, where the number and pattern of hours worked varies, for example zero hours, and annual hours.

4   Wage flexibility, where wages are individualised, and may be performance-related.

A notable early contribution to an understanding of contemporary attempts to change work and workers allocation was Atkinson's (1984) flexible firm model. This model posited committed core employees: highly regarded, well paid, with improved career prospects, and who offer in return functional flexibility, often through multiskilling. On the periphery are the distanced externals: the 'atypical', 'non-standard' or 'non-core' workers (described in negative terms) with low security to ease the organisation's needs for adjustments to market forces. There are important ethical undertones to such a distinction, with Clegg et al (2011) suggesting that the periphery itself comprised two sub-groups. These were firstly workers who were semi-skilled operating in the lower rungs of the supply chain and who could be easily dismissed and re-employed according to cost and demand fluctuations; and secondly an underclass working (possibly illegally) in poor conditions outside the formally recognised labour market. Such workers do not show up in official statistics or most research studies so remain outside the scope of most discussions of worker flexibility – but are real nonetheless. Later in the chapter we look again at the dark side of flexible working.

Current observations are that organisational forms are changing, with bureaucracies being dismantled and replaced by looser, networked organisational forms and processes, featuring partnerships and contracting out of activities. 'In the name of right-sizing, delayering and concentrating upon core competencies, the outsourcing of services continues to expand' (Marchington et al 2005b, p2) as organisations move from vertical towards horizontal integration. With this, come changes in the employment relationship. Marchington et al present an additional dimension to the understanding of employment flexibility, namely the extent to which the employment contract is under the influence of a single employing organisation or subject to control or influence by multiple employers, as might be the case with agency workers (see Figure 7.1). This axis is added to the previously accepted continuum depicting variations in the internalisation or standardisation of the employment contract (as in the core-periphery concept).

Figure 7.1 The twin dimensions of employment flexibility

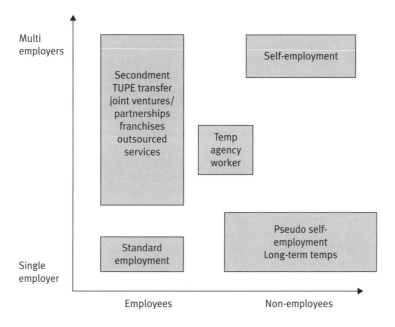

As the authors describe, the internalised, standard employment relationship is seen in the bottom left-hand corner. In the top right-hand corner is self-employment, 'where there is no contract of employment and where the self-employed individual sells his or her skills to a range of organisations and is, therefore, not dependent on a particular organisation for income' (ibid, p18).

The horizontal axis, from employees to non-employees, depicts the shift away from internalised full-time employees to a diversification of contracts including part-time, casual, temporary and self-employed workers. 'Part-time work might be considered to be close to the standard contract as there is nothing in principle stopping part-time work being organised on the same basis as internalised, full-time work with the same social rights and same regularity of employment' (ibid, p18). At the extreme of where the guarantees of employment and income are, at best, short term, are the so-called pseudo self-employed workers, who often work at a distance from the employer – such as homeworkers and freelancers – 'but who may be highly dependent upon one employer, even if there is no formal contractual guarantee of continuous employment or minimum income' (ibid, p19).

In the centre of the field we find temporary agency workers, in ambiguous circumstances: self-employed yet employed, where the agency is commonly regarded as the legal employer, even though it is the client who exercises control.

> The employing organisation, which acts as host to the temporary agency workers, directs their work activities side-by-side with those of direct employees on similar tasks ... This employment relationship ... [involves] both deviations from the status of direct employees, and control from more than one employing organisation (ibid, p19).

The top left-hand side 'covers an area where employment is internalised but where there is more than one employing organisation that can be considered party to the relationship'. Here 'there is a direct employment relationship but other employers – acting as agents or suppliers – may be involved in the employment experience, and even in controlling the employment relationship' (ibid, pp18–19).

7.3.1 WORK INTENSIFICATION AND WORK–LIFE BALANCE

Recent years have seen an increasing number of organisations in the UK offering a range of flexible working options to their employees. For many employers this has been a response to increasing interest in work–life balance, the need to be competitive in the labour market, and the introduction of legislation giving parents of young or disabled children and, more recently, carers, the right to request flexible working arrangements (Kelliher and Anderson 2010).

In a more critical vein, attention is drawn to other aspects of the work–life balance concept by Eikhof et al (2007) where 'beyond working time and the provision of flexible working practices to enable child care, there is little in the debate about the need to change work per se'. These authors also comment that the work–life debate 'narrowly perceives "life", equating it with women's care work, hence the emphasis again of family-friendly policies' (ibid, p326).

We can detect that flexibility, lying at the heart of the wage–work bargain, means different things to the different parties to the deal. Whilst conventional definitions are expressed from the point of view of the employer or organisation, descriptions of the consequences for the worker are required in the interests of balance.

It is possible to glimpse an unanticipated consequence of adopting flexible working practices – that of work intensification. Whilst reporting evidence that flexible workers record higher levels of job satisfaction and organisational commitment than their nonflexible counterparts, Kelliher and Anderson (2010) also report evidence of work intensification being experienced by both those who work reduced hours and those who work remotely. It is suggested that the apparent paradox of high job satisfaction and organisational commitment alongside work intensification can be explained by employees trading flexibility for effort. Employees respond to the ability to work flexibly by exerting additional effort, in order to return benefit to their employer.

Three means by which intensification may take place have been identified (ibid, p86). Increased effort may be imposed (as when workloads may increase following downsizing) or enabled (because flexible working patterns facilitate the exercise of increased effort), or it may be a reciprocal act on the part of employees in exchange for discretion over working arrangements.

Intriguingly, Kelliher and Anderson (2010, p99) suggest that in contemporary workplaces, with a 'prevailing rhetoric of greater personal autonomy', employees often see themselves as responsible for their own work intensification. To some extent the professional workers saw themselves as partly responsible and therefore did not voice opposition. However, other studies have also found that employees do not always respond negatively to intensification, especially where they believe they will gain some benefit as a consequence (ibid, p99).

REFLECTIVE ACTIVITY 7.2

Current research: experiences of intensification among Kelliher and Anderson's (2010) interviewees, from a number of UK private sector organisations, vividly illustrate the three means of intensification.

Imposed intensification

Workers describe why imposed flexible working on reduced-hours contracts has resulted in work intensification. Their workloads did not decrease in line with their hours when they moved to a reduced-hours contract and consequently they were doing something akin to a full-time job, but in fewer paid hours. This could result in both increased extensive and intensive effort.

One interviewee commented: 'There is enough workload to keep me busy for five days, but I only have three days to do it in, so I either work late, which I do sometimes, or I try and delegate some of it.'

Others described that they felt the need to be available at times when they were not scheduled to be working, but when the business was operating. This took the form of being prepared to take phone calls and checking emails at times when they were not working.

For example one interviewee reported: 'On a Monday, when I'm not at work, I'll typically put in 40 minutes to an hour just checking my emails to make sure that I'm on top of any issues that come up, or that came up over the weekend . . . so I check the email at least once if not twice during the Monday.'

The issue of email overload continues to be debated, with the noted psychologist Cary Cooper (2005) claiming that 'an inundation of often unnecessary emails, and the increasing ease and accessibility to work beyond the desk without any appropriate boundaries was damaging the UK's health. Cooper went on to claim that the nature of email communication (or how it had been adopted in many organisations) was that it demanded an immediate response leading to 'it managing us' rather than vice versa. Cooper (*ibid*) reported that something like a quarter of people are checking their emails on holiday and almost everybody is checking their emails home at night, long after they've 'left' work (Lewis 2015).

Enabled intensification

Although there is very clearly a problem for many workers in demarcating work and non-work time, others, typically remote workers, describe that working flexibly enabled them to work more intently, exercising both greater intensive and extensive effort. For example, one respondent noted that it was far easier to maintain energy levels and enthusiasm when working for three days or four days, as opposed to working for five days. The same person noted that, contrastingly, they were more likely to sustain efficiency over three or three and a half days, rather than five (Kelliher and Anderson 2010).

Intensification as reciprocation and exchange

Commitment levels of remote and reduced-hours workers are reportedly higher than those who did not work flexibly. The impact of commitment on effort is illustrated by a worker who reported greater extensive effort when she worked from home. This was due to that employee perceiving that she was valued as a human being, rather than seen as a nine-to-five machine by her employer. This led her in turn to exhibit a deep-seated loyalty and great levels of commitment (Kelliher and Anderson 2010).

Questions

1   As an HR manager, how would you respond to employees who have complained to you about their work intensification, and the impact that it was having upon their performance levels?

2   How might you devise a policy on email usage amongst employees, including ways of monitoring the policy's effectiveness?

7.3.2 THE BUSINESS BENEFITS OF FLEXIBLE WORKING

We commonly hear managerial descriptions, in unitary terms, of flexible working arrangements featuring options which allow employees to strike a work–life balance which fits with their needs, and yet gives the employer a say in the decision-making process (Wight 2007). Elsewhere we find descriptions of flexible working delivering improved business performance on service delivery and customer satisfaction, efficiency savings, and reduced recruitment and retention costs (Thomson 2008). Examples of this flexible working include part-time work, job-sharing, flexitime, working school hours, nine-day fortnights, mobile working and team rotas, which are claimed to give the employees choice in how, when and where they work (see Case Study 7.1).

CASE STUDY 7.1

BENDING THE RULES: SURREY COUNTY COUNCIL EMBRACES FLEXIBLE WORKING

As far back as 2007, Surrey County Council took steps to ensure that its workers could complete their daily tasks from spaces other than their desk at the office. Investments in technology allowed workers to log in at any PC or any telephone on a certain network, and all social workers were given a tablet PC to carry when out of the office. Anything the social worker recorded on the tablet was instantly added to a database back at the office and therefore became accessible to other staff. Staff were able to check their work emails from home, allowing the option of working from home, and also reducing their dependence on physical office space. Working from different offices or at home, working while travelling, and hot-desking in an office environment can all add flexibility to the working day.

The importance of giving the employees choice in how, when and where they work led to an improvement at Surrey

Council in terms of productivity, reduced sickness levels and financial gains. There was 4% reduction in staff turnover, and, it should be noted, 700 fewer full-time posts, leading to a decrease in staff costs. The council was able to rationalise its property portfolio and standardise IT systems. It has also seen an increase in morale amongst employees as they were given more freedom to choose their working hours, underpinned by trust that employees were able to self-manage a successful work–life balance.

Taking a broader view, the issue of flexible working has become an increasingly important topic as the Government re-evaluates the employment laws in the UK. All employees, regardless of circumstance, have a right to request a flexible working pattern from an employer. The employer has to weigh up the effect the application would have on the business as a whole. The employer has the right to reject an employee's flexible working request if it would be of detriment to the business.

Source: Wight (2007)

Questions

1 Give examples from your own experience of flexible working.

2 Were your feelings towards flexible working positive or negative – or a mix of the two – and why?

3 How can organisations balance greater employee freedom within flexible working with customer requirements?

7.3.3 FLEXIBLE WORKING AND PERFORMANCE

It is widely argued (see, for example, DTI 2005) that flexible working arrangements (FWAs) are good for business and the health and well-being of the working population. For decades researchers have attempted to assess the impact of FWAs on worker performance. A recent review of the literature on the link between FWAs and performance-related outcomes suggests that, taken together, the evidence fails to demonstrate a business case for the use of FWAs (de Menezes and Kelliher 2011). Whilst support for a link with performance has been most commonly found in relation to some aspects of performance such as absenteeism and job/work satisfaction, concerning other aspects of organisational performance (such as financial performance indicators, retention, individual productivity, organisational commitment, and health or well-being), the most common finding was no association. The authors conclude that, with the evidence to date, making causal inferences on this aspect of people management is problematic.

7.3.4 NEGATIVE ASPECTS OF FLEXIBILITY

We have already drawn attention to the dark side of flexible working and this was highlighted in the UK context by Toynbee (2008); see 'Appalling conditions' below. However, we follow this by conflicting evidence from 2015, indicating that impressions of what constitutes a 'dark side' is very much in the eye of the beholder.

Appalling conditions

Labour MPs representing the poorest parts of the country see how appalling conditions under bad employers can be. They see where agency workers are brought in to undercut existing wages – remember Gate Gourmet (the airline catering firm that was involved in a high-profile dispute with employees at London Heathrow airport in 2005)? Or where workers who want to be taken on permanently are fired and rehired to prevent them acquiring rights. They see outsourced NHS cleaners, and workers throughout the public sector being denied the chance they once had to work their way up. Agencies don't train people to fill higher-level jobs for which they are not contracted (Toynbee 2008).

CIPD research published in 2015 concluded that people working on zero-hours contracts (ZHCs) did not regard important aspects of their work in a negative light. Churchard (2015) summarised the findings, noting that ZHC workers expressed higher satisfaction scores on job satisfaction and work–life balance. They were less likely to feel under frequent excessive pressure at work than workers on permanent contracts (32% as against 41% respectively.) CIPD Chief Executive Peter Cheese commented that the report showed that type of contract was not the main factor driving satisfaction at work; this contrastingly linked more closely to how people are managed, the workload they are under and their relationship with their line manager.

Grey (2013) takes an interesting slant on flexible working, noting that it can be linked to organisational – or even professional – cultures. In this way, doctors, lawyers, academics, accountants (and HR managers?) will do whatever needs to be done to get the job done. By taking to heart 'a set of norms about values and behaviour, learned, certainly, through general education, but also through the organizational processes of their workplaces, professional associations and so on' Grey (2013, p77), such people may work intensively through non-work times including vacations to keep organisations going. Such workers are typically comparatively well-rewarded and may not think of themselves as exploited; rather as self-managed human beings. But in a sense one could say that they; in a paradoxical way, suffer from working conditions too.

An alternative to the conventional wisdom regarding the economic necessity of flexibility, at both global and individual levels, is provided by Giles et al (2010) in Case Study 7.2.

 THE FAILINGS OF FLEXIBILITY

CASE STUDY 7.2

For years, it has been the settled view in economics that, in most cases, flexible labour markets are best. More jobs might be lost in a downturn, but this cost is far outweighed by the benefits of flexible pay and the ease of reallocating jobs from dying industries to dynamic ones. Nobody was more closely aligned with such recommendations than the Organisation for Economic Co-operation and Development, the Paris-based group of developed nations. But now the OECD is modifying its view.

'We have been promoting flexibility, not for the sake of it, but for economic performance and for workers to get into new jobs,' says Stefano Scarpetta, the OECD's head of employment analysis. This motivation is allowing a change of view. 'Judging from the outcomes so far, short-time working schemes [such as in Germany, in which people work fewer hours while the government tops up their pay, although there are questions about whether this merely delays job losses] seem to have been rather successful in containing the job haemorrhage,' he says, adding that even his organisation is, 'a little bit more positive on public works programmes: we argue that as part of a labour market approach, they might be worthwhile.'

While this is not a wholesale repudiation of the OECD's former views, it reflects the fact that, according to the organisation's own analysis, the gains in employment flexibility of recent years have failed to protect employees from the economic crisis.

'There do not appear to be any clear grounds for concluding that workers, generally, are any better or worse prepared to weather a period of weak labour markets than was the case for the past several recessions,' the OECD concluded in its latest Employment Outlook.

Some top economists argue that the theory of superiority of flexible labour markets applies only at full employment. It will not work well when there has been a large shock to demand, output is well below potential and jobs are effectively rationed. In these circumstances, German-style institutions that cushion and spread the pain are probably superior.

Source: Giles et al (2010)

Questions

1   Identify the stated view taken on flexible labour markets by the main UK political parties in the lead-up to elections from 2016 to 2020. Can you identify significant differences between them?

2   To what extent do the political parties identify the stresses felt by self-managed professionals?

7.3.5 THE BENEFITS OF BEHAVIOURAL FLEXIBILITY

Most attention has been given to organisational and labour market flexibility rather than personal flexibility. For firms to be flexible they depend on the flexibility of the workforce: an orientation, attitude or style among employees, including team-oriented, lateral and autonomous perspectives (Iles et al 1996, p21). Anell and Wilson (2000, p168) suggest the following qualities might be required in employees: a desire to seek feedback on performance, a desire to improve, an ability to see multiple perspectives, a broad vision, an ability to visualise relationships, a readiness to accept responsibility for decisions, self-confidence, proactivity, a liking for change and a desire for co-operative independence.

Among senior managers, personal and strategic flexibility and internal characteristics such as problem-solving or creative thinking are desirable. These authors describe elements of 'behavioural flexibility' in managers in terms of the ability to manage complexity and uncertainty, adaptability, tolerance of ambiguity, openness, empathy, non-judgementalism, interest in others, and willingness to acquire new behaviours and attitudes. Sennett refers to 'a particular strength of character – that of someone who has the confidence to dwell in disorder . . . who flourishes in the midst of dislocation' (1998, p62).

In his book, *The Corrosion of Character* (1998), Richard Sennett examines the consequences for workers of the need for organisations to operate in highly competitive markets. He suggests that the flexibility they need to display, the willingness to accept change, and the loss of security that results, can have damaging effects on personal character.

Character, he argues, is an emotional experience that involves loyalty, mutual commitment and the pursuit of long-term goals. As society pursues immediate needs and businesses seek to respond to the consequent short-term goals, organisations find themselves regularly needing to restructure and redesign. In such a new economy he suggests that character traits are damaged with negative effects on workers' morale and motivation. People thus co-operate but without any underlying commitment: 'superficial co-operativeness'.

 CASE STUDY 7.3

PWC INCREASES EMPLOYEE FLEXIBILITY

Flexibility has taken hold as a concept in the twenty-first century and an early example was found in the case of professional-services firm PricewaterhouseCoopers (PWC). In 2001 PWC was described as a knowledge-driven organisation. PWC had concluded that when its employees left, the firm not only lost the training and knowledge they had built up, but also the client relationships they developed.

PWC therefore redefined its strategy based around choice for its employees, whose average age at that time was 27. Changes included a generous maternity and paternity leave scheme, childcare vouchers for returning mothers, and other benefits. Moreover, most employees were equipped to be able to work from home, and almost all of them chose to do this at least once a month.

The company also launched an in-house concierge service. Employees were offered a wide range of domestic services at discount price. These included activities such as waiting in for plumbers, builders and electricians. Take-up was greatest among company consultants, who often worked offsite for months.

PWC also introduced the notion of 'paid time off', rather than the more restrictive 'annual leave'. Employees could use their paid time off allocation for short-term illness, childcare and jury service, as well as holiday.

According to the author, the strategy initially appeared to be successful. Despite skill shortages in the consultancy sector, staff retention at PWC had improved by 4–5% over the previous year.

Source: Perry (2001)

Questions

1   What does this case show us about the benefits of flexibility to organisations and staff?

2   Is this type of flexibility restricted to the type of professional worker employed by PWC or could and should it have wider application?

The parties' responses to each other's requests for flexibility within the wage–work bargain, worker and 'employer', are likely to be inextricably interlinked. The concept of the psychological contract provides us with a suitable lens through which to view this aspect of leading and managing people.

7.4 THE PSYCHOLOGICAL CONTRACT

Although questions have been raised about its meaning and value (Guest 1998), the concept of the psychological contract has become a central theme of people management. Research continues to be conducted in the field (Tomprou et al 2015). In general terms, the concept characterises the employment relationship in terms of exchange – mutual expectations or obligations – in order to make sense of the range and degrees of commitment that flow in both directions. It is here that organisational policy and procedures mix with individual managerial and employee attitudes and behaviours, with complex outcomes.

There are two main definitions of the psychological contract (Marks 2001). The first is derived from the work of Argyris (1960) and Schein (1978) and refers to the perceptions of mutual obligations held by the two parties in the employment relationship, the organisation and the employee (or worker). The second definition, which is based on the work of Rousseau (1995, p9), asserts that the psychological contract is formulated only in the mind of the employee and is therefore about 'individual beliefs, shaped by the organisation, regarding terms of an exchange between individuals and their organisation'.

According to Rousseau (1995, p1) the ideal contract details expectations of both the employee and the employer, but these contracts are incomplete and so become 'self-organising'. A contractual continuum is commonly offered, from transactional (covering incentive pay and well-specified performance levels) to relational (including loyalty and concern for employee well-being). Transactional terms are exemplified by 'a fair day's work for a fair day's pay' and focus on short-term (and usually monetary) exchanges. The relational contract 'focuses on open-ended relationships involving considerable investments by both employees (company-specific skills, long-term development) and employers (extensive training)' (ibid, p91).

A useful typology is offered by Rousseau (see Figure 7.2), using the dimensions of timeframe and performance requirements, who says that four types of contract emerge 'with distinct behavioural implications for workers' (1995, p98):

- *transactional contracts* – of limited duration with well-specified performance terms
- *transitional or 'no-guarantees' contracts* – essentially a breakdown in contracts, reflecting the absence of commitments regarding future employment as well as little or no explicit performance demands or contingent incentives
- *relational contracts* – open-ended membership but with incomplete or ambiguous performance requirements attached to continued membership

- *balanced contracts* – open-ended and relationship-oriented employment with well-specified performance terms subject to change over time.

Figure 7.2 Types of psychological contract

| | Performance terms | |
	Specified	**Not Specified**
Duration Short term	Transactional (eg retail checkout operators employed during Christmas season) • Low ambiguity • Easy exit/high turnover • Low member commitment • Freedom to enter new contracts • Little learning • Weak integration/identification	Transitional (eg employee experiences during organisational retrenchment or following merger or acquisition) • Ambiguity/uncertainty • High turnover/termination • Instability
Long term	Balanced (eg high-involvement team) • High member commitment • High integration/identification • Ongoing development • Mutual support • Dynamic	Relational (eg family business members) • High member commitment • High affective commitment • High integration/identification • Stability

Source: Rousseau (1995)

In other words, the 'psychological contract' is a term for describing what is implicit in terms of reciprocity and exchange within the employment relationship.

It is suggested (CIPD 2012e) that employers have been encouraged to take the psychological contract seriously due to changes ranging from there being more employees on part-time and flexible work, to the survivors of downsizing having to do more, and 'human capital' becoming more critical to business performance.

7.5 IMPLICATIONS FOR THE MANAGEMENT OF PEOPLE

The CIPD (2012e) asserts that organisations have to 'get the most out of this resource (employees)' by knowing what employees expect from their work, by using the psychological contract as 'a framework for monitoring employee attitudes and priorities', and draws attention to the importance of the line manager role, in these terms: In order to display commitment employees have to feel that they are being treated with fairness and respect. Many organisations have concluded that they need to create a corporate personality or identity with a set of corporate values or a stated mission – an 'employee value proposition' or 'employer brand' – which employees will recognise and relate to. In practice, the employer brand can be seen as an attempt by the employer to define the psychological contract with employees so as to help in recruiting and retaining talent.

Recent work has emphasised the notion of engagement. This is defined by the CIPD (2012f) as 'employees internalising and emotionally connecting to the organisation's core purpose'. This CIPD survey emphasised the role of line managers in motivating via an engaging team-management style.

There is no doubt that increasing competition and changing expectations among employees have prompted a growing disillusionment with the traditional psychological contract based on lifetime employment and steady promotion from within. Consequently, companies must develop new ways to increase the loyalty and commitment of employees.

For instance, given the pressure to do things better, faster and cheaper, reward systems should recognise contribution rather than position or status. Reward strategies may also be used to rebuild commitment for survivors in downsizing organisations.

In addition, considering the shift towards decentralisation and empowerment, it is essential that individuals and groups are given more responsibility over salary decisions. Furthermore, rewards should be based on continuous performance and continuous improvement, rather than single events or past achievements.

7.5.1 CONTRACTS

Theories of the psychological contract have been built around full-time permanent employment and there is discussion about the extension of the concept to incorporate the experience of contingent workers. As Marchington et al (2005b, p78) point out: 'temporary agency workers attempt ... to satisfy their obligations simultaneously to two employers – the agency and the client'. This simultaneity raises questions about organisational commitment and loyalty.

'Forced' changes to contracts

Earlier in this chapter, we considered the 'imposed intensification' of work in relation to employees being subjected to reduced-hours contracts. Saunders and Thornhill (2006) explore the implications for employees' psychological contracts in conditions of a forced change from permanent to temporary employment status for some employees within an organisation. They suggest that permanent employees generally continue to exhibit relational forms of attachment to the organisation. These, 'the employees believe', are reciprocated by the organisation. Reactions from forced temporary workers are more varied. After a period of denial, some develop a more calculative approach to their interactions. Others maintain aspects of their previously developed relational attachments. Only some temporary workers appear to recognise that their future direction is no longer a concern of the organisation. Although only based upon one organisation, Saunders and Thornhill suggest that the process of psychological contract adjustment is likely to emerge through gradual reinterpretation, rather than through renegotiation.

Since commitment within the psychological contract is assumed to be based on volition, then a lack of volition, and conflicts of loyalty, will have an effect on psychological contracting among contingent workers. We might expect non-permanent staff to show a more transactional approach, and show less commitment, than permanent staff. Research evidence provides ambiguous results. In a call centre environment, Biggs and Swailes (2006) found that agency workers had a significantly lower level of organisational commitment compared with permanent workers. However, this is not necessarily the case according to MacDonald and Makin (2000, p89), who suggest 'the observance and commitment to the norms, symbols, and rituals of desirable groups is often higher among those just outside, but wishing to join, the group than it is among established members'. From the same authors we hear of higher levels of organisational commitment and job satisfaction among some temporary staff.

One possible explanation, it is suggested, may lie in the short tenure of non-permanent staff within the organisation.

Contract breach

To what extent can we come to understand the concept of the psychological contract through examining its being breached or violated? Coyle-Shapiro and Kessler (2000) describe a situation in which the majority of employees have experienced contract breach, in a large local authority directly responsible and accountable for a range of public services including education, environmental health and social care to the local population. This view was also supported by managers, as representatives of the employer, who further indicated that the organisation, given its external pressures, was not fulfilling its obligations to employees to the extent that it could. Overall, the results indicate that employees redress the balance in the relationship through reducing their commitment and their willingness to engage in organisational citizenship behaviour when they perceive their employer has not fulfilled its part in the exchange process.

Tomprou et al (2015) extend research on the psychological contract concept by exploring a model of 'post-violation'. The authors conclude that while many victims of violation remain with their employer, there are several possible responses to a perceived breach. These include reverting to the original contract pre-violation (the most positive outcome for the employer), formation of a more or less favourable new contract, or the collapse (dissolution) of the psychological contract.

Workplace transitions are thought to result in a fundamental shift in the employment relationship, and the impact of organisational change can be seen in terms of Rousseau's types of psychological contracts (PCs) (see Figure 7.2). Chaudhry et al (2011a) suggest that the ways in which employees make sense of organisational change influence whether employees revise their PCs. In their study, transactional and balanced PCs appear to be less affected by the contextual and cognitive factors related to the change, while changes occur in relational PCs.

A range of individual responses

There is a 'complexity of feelings' towards, and reactions resulting from, becoming a temporary worker, according to Saunders and Thornhill (2006, p452), where the attractions associated with obtaining greater freedom have also been associated with greater insecurity, potentially lower control over hours of work and working patterns, and a continuing to find new work. These ideas of preference for temporary work have been linked to workers' skill and knowledge levels to produce a typology of temporary contracts (Marler et al 2002 cited in Saunders and Thornhill 2006, p452):

- *boundaryless worker*: high preference for temporary work and a high skills/knowledge level
- *permanent temporary worker*: high preference for temporary work and a low skills/knowledge level
- *transitional worker*: low preference for temporary work and a high skills/knowledge level
- *traditional worker*: low preference for temporary work and a low skills/knowledge level.

This typology 'implies that personal preferences for temporary work are likely to influence feelings towards different types of psychological contracts. In particular, high preferences for temporary work would seem likely to accentuate positive feelings towards transactional-oriented psychological contracts, whereas low preferences for temporary work would accentuate negative feelings towards transactional-oriented psychological contracts' (ibid, p452).

There is interest in the state of the psychological contract during public sector restructuring and associated changes in employment relationships. Research (Wang et al 2010) into the effect of the 'transfer' process on employees' psychological contracts within the context of the move to a new employment relationship, as part of a public–private partnership, highlights that supervisors in particular have a strong influence on employees' attitudes and behaviour.

7.5.2 OLD AND NEW PSYCHOLOGICAL CONTRACTS

The terms of the new contract are still unclear, though the material so far in this chapter has provided us with insights; Maguire (2002) presents a number of distinctions between the old and new psychological contract, which are shown in Table 7.1.

Table 7.1 The distinction between 'old' and 'new' characteristics of psychological contracts

Old contract	New contract
Organisation is 'parent' to employee 'child'	Organisation and employee enter into 'adult' contracts focused on mutually beneficial work
Employees' identity and worth are defined by the organisation	Employees' identity and worth are defined by the employee
Those who stay are good and loyal; others are bad and disloyal	The regular flow of people in and out is healthy and should be celebrated
Employees who do what they are told will work until retirement	Long-term employment is unlikely; expect – and prepare for – multiple relationships
The primary route for growth is through promotion	The primary route for growth is a sense of personal accomplishment

As Maguire (2002, p168) puts it, the key differences between the 'traditional' and the 'new' psychological contract relate to the decreased expectation of paternalistic human resource practices, the replacement of the concept of organisational worth with 'self-worth', the substitution of personal accomplishment for promotion as the route to growth, and the decreased importance of tenure.

REFLECTIVE ACTIVITY 7.3

Thinking about the organisation you work for, or one with which you are familiar, to what extent is employment characterised by 'old' or 'new' contracts?

To what extent do you envisage your career developing with multiple employers? If you find this picture realistic, will your loyalty to any one employer be diminished?

The CIPD suggests (2012e) that in many ways the 'old' psychological contract is in fact still alive, and that employees still want security: interestingly, labour market data suggest that there has been little reduction in the length of time for which people stay in individual jobs. They are still prepared to offer loyalty, though they may feel less committed to the organisation as a whole than to their workgroup. In general they remain satisfied with their job.

It is commonly heard that the 'old' psychological contract, with its emphasis on employment security, has been held to have been violated because of extensive downsizing among white-collar employees from the late 1980s and early 1990s (Mumford 1995). This proposition has been examined by Beaumont and Harris (2002), using data from UK manufacturing industries for the years 1978–95. The authors call into question the view that historically high and sustained downsizing among white-collar employees was a leading cause.

Examining the psychological contract in terms of the parties' fulfilment of their obligations to each other highlights gaps in what employees expect and receive from their employer as well as what employees feel they owe the employers and actually give. This is again illustrated in Simon Caulkin's findings set out in 7.5.3 'Generational Differences: Baby Boomers and Millenials' below. Caulkin's work sheds a different light on the topic by opening up the possibility of demographic factors – in this case, age – having an effect on the nature of the psychological contract.

7.5.3 GENERATIONAL DIFFERENCES: BABY BOOMERS AND MILLENIALS

Loyalty of young workers: the new psychological contract? As far back as 2003, Caulkin reported on research by the Work Foundation on the motivation of the newest generation of workers, the 18- to 24-year-olds:

> Employers need to understand better how Generation Y, as the Work Foundation researchers term them, differs from previous cohorts of workers, and what that means for employment policies. For young workers, the new implicit contract of employability, rather than a job for life, is the only one they have known. And they have learned its lessons fast. Accordingly, they have developed a much more instrumental approach to employment than their predecessors. They have high expectations of careers development and gaining early responsibility and attach substantial importance to the employer's 'brand' – not just out of desire to work for a company that matches their own values, but also with an eye to improving their CV.

> The Work Foundation terms this 'gold-dusting': buffing their record to attract other employers. Loyalty to the organisation lasts only as long as they are achieving personal goals.

Huws (2013) suggests that in Western societies, an era of work beginning in 1945, when work was ideally viewed as involving 'some kind of meaningful activity under a permanent contract of work with benefits attached' had to a large extent ended. She goes on to express concern for current undergraduate students and graduates who were – or soon would be – working in an atomised labour market. Huws' conclusion echoes that of Caulkin ten years earlier; namely that a changing psychological contract was associated with the reality of the labour market and wider social trends endemic at any one time. One might reasonably be reminded of the phrase that every generation holds the key to its own world.

French et al (2015) suggest that Generations X (born after 1964), Y (born after 1978) and Millenials (Cogin 2012, Chaudhuri and Ghosh 2012), display a series of distinctive attitudes towards work. These included less loyalty to the employing organisation as a result of greater labour mobility. There is a clear link between this more instrumental attitude and the psychological contract concept outlined in this chapter. The predispositions of these three generational groups contrasted with the baby boomers (born between 1946 and 1955) and shadow boomers (born between 1956 and 1964). The boomers and shadow boomers are, despite the removal of compulsory retirement ages in many societies, in many cases about to leave the workforce, with a consequent loss of generational memory (Dencker et al 2008).

Papavasileiou and Lyons (2015) provide us with one further twist in the debate on the effect of demographics on work values, including organisational commitment and the fit between a person and his or her organisation, occupation and work environment. The authors conclude that millennial-aged Greeks exhibit 'some moderately unique work priorities, relative to their counterparts in other countries' (ibid, p2183), including a stress on intrinsic and social work values. Without going into detail on cross-cultural aspects of work values (see Broeways and Price (2011) and French et al (2015) for far greater detail and depth in this regard), one can conclude that culture is another potentially important influence on work values which underpin the psychological contract.

We can conclude that contextual factors, including cultural background and the geographical location of work, are key to understanding the psychological contract. If the employer is felt to have breached the contract, should we automatically assume that employee behaviour will necessarily be affected negatively? It seems that, in times of high job insecurity, employees may be less inclined to display negative behavioural outcomes due to the power disparity between the employer and employee, or to fear of redundancy, though attitudes towards the employer will be changed, if not translated into action.

CASE STUDY 7.4

THE PSYCHOLOGICAL CONTRACT AND RETENTION

Roger Eglin, writing in the *Sunday Times*, suggests that emotional ties – rather than just money – are vital in enticing good managers to stay with their employers.

A group of 476 Henley Business School alumni were questioned about their relationship with their employers. Of the replies, 11% were couched in what are described as transactional terms, while a compelling 52% came down in favour of a relationship contract. 'They want a more effective relationship with issues such as aspiration, equity and community remaining important . . . For those who have the talent and can make a choice this is what counts.'

With some jobs set to move to India, Barclays Bank has struck a deal with the Unite trade union to help those affected. But rather than losing people through redundancy, Barclays is offering them training and development opportunities to make them more 'marketable' within the bank.

Source: Eglin (2004)

Questions

Would you characterise your relationship with your current or previous employer as transactional, or is it based upon emotional ties?

7.5.4 FLEXIBILITY, PSYCHOLOGICAL CONTRACTS AND PERFORMANCE

The concepts of flexibility and the psychological contract are essentially transactional, involving reciprocal views concerning the quality of relationship between employee and organisation. It is now appropriate to revisit the links between people management and organisational performance.

Organisations seek to identify the link between people and performance (Purcell et al 2003), and the concept of high-performance working (HPW) (DTI 2005, CIPD 2014a) is characterised by references to flatter, non-hierarchical structures, moving away from reliance on management control, towards teamworking and autonomous working based on high levels of trust, communication and involvement. Whether the focus is on profit and shareholder value in the private sector, or on outputs and service levels in the public sector, performance is the topical currency.

Purcell et al's (2003) study on the impact of people management on organisational performance was intended to show the way in which HR practices – or what the CIPD terms 'people management', meaning all aspects of how people are managed – impact on performance. The study was conducted within a framework which claims that performance is a function of people's ability (knowledge and skills), their motivation, and the opportunity they are given to deploy their skills (referred to as 'AMO'). The authors concluded that a range of 11 HR policies and practices are required to turn this into action, and a model was devised, covering recruitment and selection, training and development, career opportunity, communications, involvement in decision-making, teamworking, appraisal, pay, job security, job challenge/job autonomy and work–life balance.

These performance-related HR policies encourage people to exercise a degree of choice on how and how well they do their job. In other words, they help induce discretionary behaviour which makes people work better and improve performance. This happens because the HR policies and practices develop positive employee attitudes or feelings of satisfaction, commitment and motivation (Purcell et al 2003, pix).

This material is taken from *Bringing Policies to Life: The vital role of front-line managers in people management* by Sue Hutchinson and John Purcell (2003), with the permission of the publisher, the Chartered Institute of Personnel and Development, London.

Figure 7.3 The people and performance model

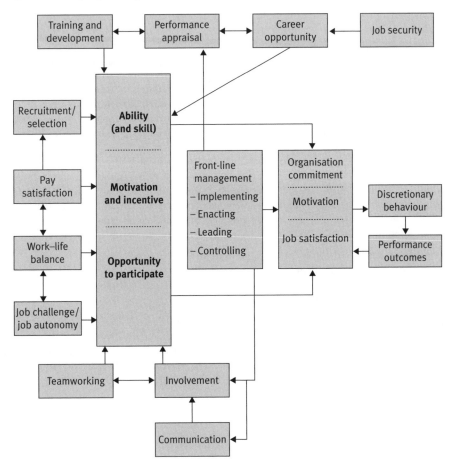

Some HR policies and practices were shown to be particularly important in terms of influencing employee outcomes like commitment, job satisfaction and motivation. These were those concerned with career opportunities, job influence, job challenge, training, performance appraisal, teamworking, involvement in decision-making, work–life balance, and having managers who are good at leadership and who show respect.

Among the implications for HR policy and practice is 'operational measurement' rather than 'remote' measures of profit: proving that HR contributes to performance is not a major issue, and measures which use profit or shareholder values are too remote from the practice of people management to be useful. What is important is operational measurement where a close link can be observed, and the regular collection of these measures covering people, operational, financial and customer areas is commonly done in the best firms (Purcell et al 2003, p72).

We can conclude that the responsibility for enacting the policies rests with front-line managers, since these are the people with whom workers theoretically interact. In Hutchinson and Purcell's (2003) framework, 'organisation process advantage'– the way these policies are implemented – is what makes a difference. Put another way: it's not what you do, it's the way that you do it.

7.5.5 FRONT-LINE MANAGERS AND THE HRM–PERFORMANCE CHAIN

A suggested causal chain linking policy inputs to performance outcomes (Purcell and Hutchinson 2007) draws attention to employee discretionary behaviour, sometimes referred to as organisational citizenship behaviour (OCB), being a consequence of HR practices and front-line manager (FLM) leadership behaviours: It is often observed that there is a gap between what is formally required in HR policy and what is actually delivered by FLMs. The way FLMs undertake their HR duties of selecting, appraising, developing, communicating, involving, etc, is inextricably linked to a wider set of what are increasingly called leadership behaviours, which aim to influence employee attitudes and behaviour and give direction. These two aspects of FLMs' roles can be brought together in the term 'people management' (ibid, p3).

Additionally, there is recognition that independent of FLM leadership behaviour, the HR practices as perceived by the employees will be related to organisational commitment and job experiences, and that the outcome effect on employee attitudes will be greater when both are positive. A possible people management-causal chain emerges, which seeks to clarify the distinction between policies, practices and employees' experiences of them. It is seen as follows (ibid):

- *intended practices* – designed by the organisation
- *actual practices* – and style of leadership behaviour
- *perception of practices* – in terms of satisfaction, fairness and legitimacy
- *employee attitudes* – in reaction
- *employee behaviour* – observable responses including OCB and attendance
- *unit-level outcomes* – organisational effectiveness and performance.

The authors conclude that the crucial link is between the employee experiences of people management, the formation or modification of attitudes towards the employing organisation and the job, and the inducement these provide to engage in certain types of discretionary behaviour (ibid, p16).

7.5.6 LEADERSHIP AND MANAGEMENT STANDARDS

The CIPD (2007a) Standards for Leadership and Management are placed in the language of performance infrastructure ('critical failure factors') and differentiators ('critical success factors'). The former describes what is needed to do things right (efficiency) and deliver acceptable levels of behaviour and legal compliance, although it is observed that mere adherence to process seldom generates high-performance outcomes. The latter describes what is needed to do the right things (effectiveness) and, the proponents claim, deliver 'genuine' people involvement, commitment, engagement and added-value contribution.

There are connotations of Herzberg's two-factor theory of motivation, which we discuss in Chapter 12, here: 'infrastructure' linking with hygiene factors and 'differentiators' involving motivators. The 11 policy areas (Purcell et al 2003) are seen as the performance infrastructure requirements, while the ways in which front-line managers deliver the policies – implementing, enacting, leading and controlling – are seen as the differentiators. It is claimed that these are 'directly related to the levels of commitment, motivation and satisfaction that employees report, and this, in turn, is linked to the vital area of discretionary behaviour' (Hutchinson and Purcell 2003, p3).

In 2010, the CIPD's report on sustainable organisational performance concluded that sustainable organisations would need to have a balanced short- and long-term focus and, crucially, agility to adapt to challenges and opportunities. It is clear that the notion of flexibility coupled with the need to ensure engagement via positive psychological contracts is crucial in this regard. The same report emphasised the need for leaders who regard employees as a core asset. We have seen that the management of flexible working should have at its centre a preoccupation with the people involved and should both be implemented and reviewed through consultation with those most closely involved.

There are very clear and important links between understanding the concepts, putting them into operation via effective management and subsequent organisational performance.

 CHILDCARE AND PARENTAL LEAVE

CASE STUDY 7.5

One million mothers would rather leave the workforce than stay in it, says Mintel, and only 20% return to work within a year of childbirth. Childcare costs, and the squeezed working and financial situation many parents report, all cause huge strain on the family dynamic, forcing men into a breadwinning role that society had been slowly easing them out of and, say the likes of Gillian Nissim (see below), putting parents at loggerheads. Most importantly, it is stifling diversity and, if it does force parents out of the workforce in significant numbers, has profound implications for the future health of the British workplace.

The effects are seen across both the much-discussed 'squeezed middle' of working professionals and in lower-paid positions where the economic benefits of work are lessening.

Gillian Nissim, founder, Working Mums

Your organisation started life in 2006. What's changed since?

A core of businesses have always seen the benefit of the family and flexible working, but the last few years have seen a rise in the rate of discrimination against

mothers. If workplaces were so brilliant, Working Mums wouldn't need to exist.

Do working women suffer more when they become parents?

Not always. But the real problem for working mothers is that they often don't go back to the same field, which means a lifelong loss of earnings. Many are working, at a loss, just to keep their toe in the door. Mothers should be able to get back to their careers.

We're seeing more men involved with parenting, but more could be working flexibly to alleviate pressure on mums. Government policy to extend paternity leave, and allow couples to divide their total leave, will put things on more of an equal footing, but men are not taking up their paternity entitlement.

Because childcare is still seen as a woman's role?

Maybe. I fear childcare is forcing family life to swing back to being female-led because of changes to child tax credits. We're hearing mothers really question their ability to continue working. It's got to the point where they're having to decide whether it's cheaper for them to stay at home. That will be bad news for families long term, as women will re-enter the workforce doing lower-skilled work.

Despite legislation, there won't be wholesale changes to family dynamics overnight. Families are at loggerheads.

In an ideal world it shouldn't be one person staying at home and the other not – it should be more of a conversation. Only when both parents have a choice will the work/family dilemma be solved.

What should employers be doing?

They must focus more on the benefits of a diverse workforce. More work is also needed around job design.

Mothers feel they have no way of resuming their roles after having a family. But women won't be able to work and have a family if there aren't more women in the pipeline.

Men need to demand more of a role in family life too, and there's nothing to be ashamed of for them in being a parent. HR shouldn't see flexibility as about gender – it's more about when and where all parents work.

Parental leave: What's next?

The changing legislative landscape explained

Since 2011:

A father can take up to 26 weeks' additional parental leave on top of his two weeks' ordinary leave, but it can only be taken 20 or more weeks after the child's birth and after the mother has gone back to work, and in a single block. He must have been on a continuous contract with his employer for at least 26 weeks by the end of the 15th week before the baby is due.

From 2015:

Employed mothers (who will still be eligible for 52 weeks' maternity leave) will be able to return to work after two weeks if they want to (four weeks for manual workers). Couples will then be able to share the remaining time between them by either taking it in turns to stay at home or by taking leave together (provided the total does not exceed 52 weeks). They will need to be 'open' with their employers and give 'proper notice' (expected to be eight weeks).

From 2018:

Ordinary paternity leave (two weeks) is scheduled to be reviewed.

Source: Crush (2013)

Questions

1 What impacts on employee attitudes and organisational performance might we see as a result of this dilemma?

2 How might the HR professional intervene in the interests of employee and organisation alike? How might the dilemma be resolved?

7.6 CONCLUSION

Organisations concentrate upon meeting the needs of their stakeholders: shareholders and customers in the private sector; government and service users – now increasingly 'consumerised' – in the public sector. Responsiveness to the 'whip' of the market, previously a private sector concern, is also now increasingly required in the public sector as it becomes 'marketised'. The organisation and its workers, internal or external, core or contingent, are required to focus on performing.

Agile response is the order of the day as timeframes are shortened, and so flexibility is sought, from collective and structural flexibility, to individual and behavioural. As organisations are re-engineered and downsized, and spans of control are increased, management attention is devoted to the increasingly autonomous worker, without losing control. To better understand the discretionary element of employment relationships, the psychological contract, and its management, has become a focus of attention.

It seems that the air is filled with managerial information and messages, suggesting what might or should be done. There are confident, sometimes strident, assertions and claims, based on research findings and examples of what appears to be best practice, and some of these might remind us of Pollert's (1991) 'desperate search for panaceas'.

Amongst this traffic it is possible to detect strengthening signals, describing increasing intensification of work and workers feeling pressurised. Where there is not a readily available pathway for workers to transmit signals of this sort, the alternative is to send messages through changed behaviour or attitudes. The reader, and the HR practitioner, then has the difficult task of listening and making sense of the sometimes conflicting information at his or her disposal.

KEY LEARNING POINTS

1 Developments in the global economy have resulted in a need for greater flexibility from organisations.

2 There are different types of flexibility including task, numerical, temporal and wage flexibility.

3 There are documented examples of unintended consequences of flexible working, and negative aspects of this notion more generally.

4 Managers can usefully be aware of the concept of the psychological contract, in order to enhance worker commitment and engagement.

5 A number of HR policies and practices, frequently carried out by line managers, influence worker commitment, loyalty and engagement.

REVIEW QUESTIONS

1 Critically assess the respective advantages and disadvantages to organisations and to employees of the different forms of workplace flexibility.

2 Identify and evaluate the specific actions that managers can take that will improve employees' psychological contracts with the organisation.

3 Evaluate the role of front-line managers in influencing the discretionary performance of individuals within the organisation.

4 How might the performance of outsourced workers be managed or controlled in order to sustain satisfactory outcomes for customers and service users in 'networked' private and public sector organisations?

EXPLORE FURTHER

Grey, C. (2013) Flexible employment contracts, the psychological contract and employee outcomes: an analysis and review of the evidence. *International Journal of Management Reviews.* Vols 5/6, No 1. pp1–19. This article provides a thorough review of evidence about the characteristics and consequences of flexible employment contracts and the role of the psychological contract.

Guest, D. (2004) *A Very Short, Fairly Interesting and Reasonably Cheap Book About Studying Organizations.* 3rd ed. London: Sage. This pocket-sized book, which the author suggests can be read on a longish train or plane journey, offers a critical take on much management literature and claims to say some things about organisations which seem to him to be true. Chapters 3 and 5 provide a wry commentary on the contexts underpinning flexibility and the psychological contract.

Tomprou, M., Rousseau, D.M. and Hansen, S.D. (2015) The psychological contracts of violation victims: a post-violation model. *Journal of Organizational Behavior.* Vol 36, No 1. pp561–581. This article is recommended as a piece of up-to-date research on the psychological contract which also contains a very extensive list of references detailing previous work in the field.

MANAGING PEOPLE: EFFECTIVE PRACTICE

Organisational and Job Design

RAY FRENCH

LEARNING OUTCOMES

After reading this chapter, you should be able to:

- assess the potential importance of organisational design and job design as part of the process of leading, managing and developing people
- understand models and research findings which aid effective practice in organisational and job design
- recognise the contribution both concepts can make to the development of flexible and committed employees
- point to emerging trends in organisational and job design; for example post-bureaucratic structures and 'enriched' jobs within the twenty-first-century global workforce.

8.1 OVERVIEW

In this chapter we examine organisational arrangements, in particular the ways in which organisations can be structured and jobs designed. These are important topics with significant relevance to leading, managing and developing people. In an important sense they form part of the backdrop of working life and set the context within which workers' contributions are framed. As we will see, organisations and jobs can be designed in very different ways and anyone involved in these activities can exercise a significant degree of choice. It is important therefore to understand contrasting models of structure and job design in order to make informed choices in these areas.

These topic areas contain insights derived from classical studies; some dating from early in the twentieth century. These remain influential and it is still important to consider them. However, thinking continues to evolve and there is a need to consider new and evolving thinking. In the area of job design, for example, a recent report on 'smart' or 'agile' working identified a new paradigm in some organisations, in which employees would be given ever greater flexibility in job design with decisions on job content placed in the hands of the job-holder (CIPD 2008a and 2014a). We deal with this topic in more detail later in the chapter.

It is also the case that topics covered in this chapter can have ethical implications with potential to become a matter of public concern. In 2015 the world football governing body FIFA was subject to allegations of corruption, with 14 current and former FIFA officials and associates indicted by the United States' FBI on charges described as involving 'rampant, systemic and deep-rooted corruption' (BBC 2015). This was followed by the arrest of seven current FIFA officials before their own conference in Zurich. While the allegations are under investigation at the time of writing and disputed, these events, and the more general suspicion surrounding the organisation, are highly damaging. Several commentators focused on FIFA's organisational structure as a source of its problems – over and above named individuals. Alvad and Bang (2015) claimed that reform of FIFA would need to go beyond a change of personnel, requiring fundamental change in the structure of the organisation. Pielke (2015) likened FIFA, in organisational terms, to a members' club, while noting that in scale FIFA was akin to a 'big business' or government organisation. The clear implication was that FIFA's organisational structure was no longer fit for purpose. It is important, both as practitioners and informed citizens, to keep abreast not just of new thinking, but also of current events, in order that our insights and recommendations are valid and up to date.

In practical terms there is evidence that structural arrangements and the design of jobs will have a strong influence on organisational performance. Mullins (2013) summarises the classical work of Drucker (1989), who argued that a poor structure would diminish an organisation's performance – even where one found good managers – and Child (2015), who also posits a link between the way an organisation is set up and strong economic performance. Child in fact goes further in concluding that the way organisations are structured also sends messages to the wider society about how people are and should be treated, so once again we see that there is an ethical component to the subject (see Chapter 4).

At the level of individual workers, much of the literature on job design also posits a link between the ways in which people's jobs are designed and their productivity. In this chapter we will see how people's attitudes and behaviour are shaped by their overall working context – including structure and job design. These attitudes and behaviour will have an impact on their motivation and engagement (see also Chapter 12) (CIPD 2012f).

From the perspective of leading, managing and developing people, organisational and job design are key concepts if people's experience of work can be shown to be strongly affected by the structure within which they operate and, of course, the nature of the work that they carry out. French et al (2015) locate this idea within their concept of a 'performance equation', which states that in order to perform well workers must firstly have the requisite attributes (skills and abilities). High performance is, secondly, conditional on people wanting to excel (levels of motivation). However, workers' performance is also affected by a third dimension, namely the organisational support provided for them. This last part of the equation deals with the backdrop to effective working. It encompasses the infrastructure of work, including the ways in which organisations are set up and jobs designed.

The topics examined in this chapter can appear abstract, maybe even 'dry', and less engaging than areas such as leadership and ethical considerations. However, organisational and job design are important concepts on several levels. If two friends, one working in a classical bureaucracy, the other in an 'adhocracy' (we will define these terms in more detail), compare their everyday experiences of work they will find that their working lives are indeed very different. As we will also see, organisation and job design are core principles underlying strategies of people management, so they are of interest to existing and future HR managers as well.

It is important to recognise that attempts to enhance performance through the application of design principles can founder through the law of unintended consequences. Linstead et al (2009) and Watson (2012), for example, both highlight what are termed 'dysfunctions' of bureaucracy. Bureaucratic structures are intended to foster efficient working through stability, predictability and fair treatment (both of employees and clients or customers). Bureaucracy is essentially conceived as a rational system of organisation.

The very features which are supposed to aid efficiency can result in reality in negative behaviour; for example defensive or even 'jobsworth' style behaviour among employees, resulting from over-adherence to rules, and moderate or 'get-by' performance as a consequence of slow and rigid promotion procedures. In this chapter we will advise against any assumption that implementing changes in organisation or job design will automatically result in positive outcomes. Notwithstanding this point, organisation and job design can be powerful tools for change.

We will, finally, show how recent work in organisation and job design has often sought to use these ideas to promote flexible working – an important theme within leading, managing and developing people in the twenty-first century. Gilmore (2013) notes that flexibility as a theme has come to permeate discussion about employment in general terms, and labour utilisation more specifically. The emerging concept of post-bureaucratic organisation is also underpinned by the idea of flexibility. The same author also notes that flexibility is associated with interesting tensions arising in the employment relationship. It is not a neutral or anodyne concept. Preece (2012) records that one reason for organisation redesign – in the form of post-bureaucratic structures – is to allow the job of managing human resources to focus on maximising benefits of working with a more flexible, temporary workforce. It is also very important to ensure that workers' knowledge and skills are deployed in ways that add value to the firm. The links between organisational design, job design and flexibility will be further drawn out in this chapter.

8.2 INTRODUCTION

We begin this section with a definition of some of the key terms which form the basis for an understanding of organisational arrangements.

8.2.1 ORGANISATIONAL DESIGN

Organisational design (OD) is defined as a planned activity in which designers, usually managers, maybe in conjunction with specialised consultants, attempt to adjust the formal shape of their organisation. There are many types of organisation and consequently many choices in organisational design. OD is defined by French et al (2015, p189) as 'the process of choosing and implementing a structural configuration for an organisation'. We see therefore that organisational design and structure are not synonymous but in a fundamental sense are linked concepts. OD creates organisational structure, defined as the intended pattern of tasks, responsibilities, lines of authority and networks of communication in an organisation.

It can be seen from this categorisation of structure that we are in essence dealing with formalised features of organisations. The classic way to depict an organisation's structure is via scrutiny of a chart or other diagram, in effect taking an impersonal view of what should happen in that organisation. The term 'informal organisation', contrastingly, denotes what actually happens in a workplace, which can deviate from what should occur within formal arrangements – for example, if people habitually ignore a bureaucratic rule or procedure.

'Organisation structure' as a term has several different sub-components within this overarching definition. These are set out below.

Formalisation

Formalisation refers to the extent to which an organisation stipulates the way work or particular roles comprising a job should be carried out. One guide to ascertain the degree of formalisation is the existence of procedural manuals or job descriptions pre-ordaining working styles and practices.

Specialisation

This aspect of structure refers both to the extent to which work roles involve a range of specialist activities and to the ways in which workers with similar or related roles and tasks are grouped together. Many organisations have historically operated in a highly specialised manner, typically by setting up discrete, functionally based departments.

Vertical differentiation

This sub-set of structure links to power and authority. An organisation could specify many levels within a hierarchy, each with distinct reporting responsibilities, or it might be designed as a relatively 'flat' organisation, with few hierarchical levels. The concept of span of control in which the ratio of workers reporting to managers is prescribed is also relevant here.

Centralisation

This deals with decision-making, in particular whether responsibility in this regard rests with senior managers, rather than it being cascaded throughout the organisation. Closely associated with this central idea is the degree to which tight control is exercised by a head office or whether, contrastingly, greater autonomy is granted to operating units or divisions.

Line and/or staff functions

In this element of structure there is a distinction between line functions, which are intimately connected with the primary purpose of the organisation, and contrasting (although complementary) staff functions, which supplement and further the aims of the organisation through the provision of ancillary services. In a large college, for example, the organisation's prime objective will be the education of students – so that lecturers form part of the line, while an HRM department may be categorised as a staff function.

We have looked at the implications of this distinction for HR in Chapter 2. The relationship between line and staff (and their relative importance) raises issues of horizontal (as opposed to vertical) co-ordination and control. Later in this chapter we will examine the ways in which organisational design – and hence structure – can be utilised in a positive way within the overall project of leading, managing and developing people.

 REFLECTIVE ACTIVITY 8.1

Look again at the elements of organisational structure listed above. How formal, centralised and vertically differentiated do you imagine the following types of organisation should be. Give reasons for your responses.

- the British Royal Navy
- an animal welfare charity
- a web-design and creative agency.

8.2.2 JOB DESIGN

Job design as defined by French et al (2015, p244) is 'the planning and specification of job tasks and the work setting designated for their accomplishment'. The authors elaborate on their definition by proposing that much contemporary writing on the subject views the objective of job design as facilitating meaningful, interesting and challenging jobs and that, within this perspective, a manager's responsibility is to design jobs that will motivate an individual employee. This finding underpins much academic research in this area, which often posits a link between aspects of jobs and employees' psychological well-being.

We will examine several examples of work within this tradition in this chapter. However, job design, as we will see, does not presuppose the design of enriched jobs – it can also lead to the splitting of tasks into routine, repetitive and unskilled work.

Watson (2006) draws a distinction between the terms 'job design' and 'work design'. He notes that 'job design' refers to task patterns that could occur in any part of a work organisation, while 'work design' is underpinned by more broadly defined principles which could reflect that organisation's culture and structure. This refining of terminology is useful in that it highlights the role of managerial choice in devising principles for organising work. Thus job design, and beyond this, work design, can form part of a more strategic approach to managing people. Watson makes the distinction in this context between direct and indirect control principles. In the former case, there is a stress on prescribed task procedures with only a minimal level of commitment required from employees. In contrast, indirect control principles emphasise far greater discretion for employees in the way they perform tasks; this is in turn dependent on their higher levels of commitment, leading to mutual trust between members of the organisation in question.

It would be true to say that for much of its history job design, and the broader concept of work design, has been associated with principles of direct control. In reading earlier work on this subject, one finds particular resonance of these ideas in the work of Frederick Taylor and his model of scientific management, often subsequently referred to as 'Taylorism'. As we will see, Taylor's work, together with principles associated with Henry Ford, contain assumptions that jobs can be designed on a rational basis in order to maximise workers' efforts with a view to quicken production, radically reduce costs and increase output to a very significant extent. It can be argued that mass production and consumption patterns have been predicated on these principles. At the turn of the millennium several commentators promoted the case for Ford as one of the key influential figures of the twentieth century, in part because of his impact on social trends due to the production of affordable cars, but also because many millions of people worked in jobs that bore the stamp of his (and Taylor's) vision. This tradition within job design has either minimised the issue of workers' motivation or put forward a model of needs at work which centre on maximising income, for example the concept of rational economic man.

Leach and Wall (2004) link different views of job design with specific epochs, making the distinction between traditional job design, which emphasises the design of jobs in order to minimise skill requirements and training times, with more contemporary job redesign, which, contrastingly, recommends increasing the number of tasks carried out by an individual worker such as through job rotation and 'enlarging' and/or 'enriching' individual jobs. However Huws (2013) claims that in Western societies the notion that work would involve some form of meaningful activity – prevalent since 1945 – had largely ended by the early twenty-first century (see also Chapter 7). Whichever analysis or combination of the two contrasting views are correct, it is clearly important to take a historical developmental perspective.

Organisational design and job design are, in summary, broad concepts and we go on to explore them in greater detail later in this chapter.

8.2.3 FLEXIBILITY

We have referred to this concept on several occasions already in this book and examine it in greater detail and depth in Chapter 7. This broad term refers to several discrete areas of business operations. It can be applied firstly to flexible forms of organisational structure –

implying a move away from a rigid bureaucratic form to one that can respond more speedily to demands emanating from its environment (Daft et al 2016). At the same time it refers to attempts to enrich workers' jobs through multiskilling, greater autonomy and responsibility with the general aim of fostering both better performance and greater commitment to the employing organisation. We will primarily examine the notion of flexibility with reference to these twin themes.

The term 'flexibility' is also, however, used in the area of employment itself, resulting in greater prevalence of such arrangements as part-time and fixed-term working, casual employment, outsourcing and teleworking. For some commentators, such as Bratton and Gold (2012), increasing flexibility of employment has led to heightened distinctions between a core and peripheral workforce.

A CIPD survey (2013b) included data on why employers chose to outsource parts of their employee resourcing activities, such as recruitment advertising and candidate sourcing and screening. Some of the more oft-cited reasons given for outsourcing included: increasing efficiency; reducing costs; freeing up HR managers to concentrate on more strategic activities; and increasing resourcing flexibility to meet peaks and troughs of demand.

One can see that there are powerful reasons for outsourcing work beyond individual organisations. However, some of the same reasons given for outsourcing, particularly increasing efficiency and reducing costs, were given as a justification for keeping activities in-house. There are no right answers and individual circumstances intervene; for example, a particular relationship with an external provider might make it advantageous to outsource.

8.3 MODELS OF STRUCTURE

Having defined the key terms used in this chapter, we now turn to look more closely at the topic of organisational structure, which is an essential component of organisational design. Bureaucracy has been a highly influential and long-lasting form of organisation structure: some writers see examples of it as far back as ancient Greek and Roman civilisations. In modern times, its key features were articulated by the sociologist Max Weber, who constructed an ideal type of bureaucracy, that is, what it would look like in an extreme or idealised form.

8.3.1 WEBER'S MODEL OF PURE BUREAUCRACY

- Tasks are allocated according to certified expertise, with resultant specialised (for example, departmental) structure.
- Jobs are defined through clear and often simplified routine tasks.
- Control is exercised through a hierarchical structure, typically with many layers denoting levels of authority.
- Rules and procedures are clearly set out in the form of written documentation.
- There are pre-set formal systems of communication via specified channels with hierarchical authority paramount.
- Employees are appointed and, where appropriate, promoted on the basis of clear criteria often relating to their qualifications.
- Managers are salaried officials and do not have a financial stake in the organisation.
- Rules are set and all decisions made rationally in an attempt to eliminate non-rational elements such as emotional involvement or personal preference.

In the late nineteenth century Weber claimed that organisations (in Europe) came to lay particular stress on rational decision-making. It was claimed that this distinguished them from the ways in which previous communities' workplaces operated more on the basis of traditional authority. Watson (2006, p38) states that, 'Out of this major cultural shift came bureaucracy. And bureaucracies are what modern organisations are.'

8.3.2 ALTERNATIVES TO BUREAUCRACY: ADAPTING TO 'CONTINGENCIES'

From the 1950s onwards, a wave of critical comment emerged centring on a perceived inability of bureaucratic structures to cope well in the face of changing circumstances. The underlying idea that organisation structures are influenced by 'external' factors, to which they must be adapted to ensure high performance, is commonly referred to as the contingency approach. Before examining the factors that have been identified as relevant situational events or contingencies, it is timely to look at some alternative structures which are either extensions of bureaucracy or radical alternatives.

Project team structures

Project teams are normally seen as temporary structures set up for a specific purpose where cross-functional expertise is required (see Needle 2015 for further detail). In some sectors – for example, consultancy – such structures could be seen as the norm, groups of employees from different functional areas routinely being assembled to provide an integrated service for a particular client. Another possible scenario in which such a structure would be relevant is where a project group comprising potential users of a new IT system, including representatives from different functional departments, work together to consider the implications of a new system for their own sub-unit. One advantage of such a structure is that it encourages workers to consider their contribution to organisational goals from a variety of perspectives and can therefore facilitate cross-fertilisation of ideas.

The matrix

Matrix structures are by no means recent phenomena, having been identified in significant numbers from the 1970s onwards. The key defining point of a matrix structure is multi-reporting, in that employees are required to consider at least two aspects of their job – typically their functional specialism and the products or services provided as part of their work. We have already referred to the distinction between line and staff functions, which is addressed directly in the matrix form, the notion of facing in different directions being reinforced in the structure of the organisation itself. Many students and academics reading this book will be familiar with the idea of the matrix since it is by no means uncommon in the higher-education sector (the author can identify examples from a number of different countries). A lecturer may form part of an academic department based on his or her academic subject area, but also have to report to senior managers whose remit could be courses (the product), or quality assurance, or international developments, or knowledge transfer. In such a case the individual lecturer could report to five separate managers.

The advantages of matrices are similar to those put forward for project teams in that they allow for easier collaborative working – and even synergy. On the other hand, the major criticism of matrix structures has centred on their potential for ambiguity and even outright confusion in reporting. The matrix idea could readily lend itself to transnational or global working, and this aspect is pursued more fully later in this chapter. The concept of a matrix is indeed similar to the ideal type of the 'global firm' based on divisional structure.

Divisional structure

The divisional form of structure, also known as the multifunctional model, was originally conceived as an alternative to the functional bureaucracy. In this form, entire divisions are set up to deal with all aspects of a product or service. It can be argued that the focus of such a structure is on outputs – that is, the end product – rather than on the inputs (all resources including human skills, knowledge and effort) needed to turn the end product into a tangible entity. General Motors (GM) for many years provided an example of this type of strategic approach to structure. GM's divisions were based on brand names and associated products. Individual divisions were largely self-contained and operated as profit centres. However, headquarters – sometimes known as 'the centre' – co-ordinated overall strategy and centralised other activities. The divisional nature of this multinational company became evident in 2009, when GM, following financial problems caused by global economic turbulence, sold off whole divisions of the company hosted outside the USA.

Organic structure and 'adhocracy'

The organic model was originally put forward, in a classical and still relevant research finding, by Burns and Stalker (1961) as a viable alternative to the classic bureaucratic structure in certain contexts. As we shall see in the following section examining the impact of contingent factors on organisational form, Burns and Stalker found that this type of structure, or rather its component features, would be effective when organisations operated in a turbulent environment of rapidly changing technology, fierce competition and uncertain customer demand. The main features of the organic model of structure were:

- network (as opposed to hierarchical) structures of control and communication
- knowledge spread throughout the organisation (rather than located at the top)
- employee commitment to their tasks (compared with loyalty to the organisation)
- knowledge, skills and experience applied to diverse tasks (compared with long-term specialisation)
- communication flowing up, down and across the organisation rather than being essentially top-down.

Burns and Stalker's organic structure is overall characterised by informality and flexibility. Originally applied to the fast-changing microelectronics sector of the 1960s, it has increasingly been advocated in other areas of the private and public sectors because their environments are perceived as more turbulent as a result of economic, political and technological change.

The adhocracy shares important features of the organic form. However, it may go further in that it can be defined as an organisational type that is not planned in the first instance, rather it develops spontaneously or in an *ad hoc* manner, hence the name (Clegg et al 2015).

Boundaryless organisations

We noted that the organic model identified by Burns and Stalker in 1961 represented a notable break from previous thinking in the area of organisational design both in terms of their stress on appropriate response to context and their advocacy of flexible structures. These insights continue to resonate at the time of writing. Bratton (2015) identifies four boundaries which organisations view as means of securing competitive advantage:

- vertical boundaries, which demarcate people in terms of seniority including through rank, status and title
- horizontal boundaries by which people are located by functional department or product group
- external boundaries separating the core organisation from its suppliers, customers and other communities

- geographical boundaries, including the preceding three boundaries but, in addition, applied across time, countries and cultures.

Bratton proposes that the boundaryless organisation model has accelerated in influence since the mid-1990s and is associated with the spread of a neo-liberal business model and, in particular, the phenomenon of globalisation. In this context, work organisations in many sectors need all four boundaries to be permeable, so that information can flow swiftly within and outside the organisation.

For our purposes, the boundaryless organisation model points to a less hierarchical structure, with a need to share information and learn from 'followers'. It also implies effective working is dependent on sharing of risk and cost, so promoting the idea of outsourcing.

Virtual network structure

In defining types of structure above, it became evident that organisations may not simply structure their operations so that they are bounded within a single entity. Rather, as we saw in the case of divisional structure, individuals might operate separately from headquarters in important respects. Virtual network structures take this principle further with organisations 'farming out' activities to other companies. They link to the concept of the boundaryless organisation considered in the preceding section.

As we saw when considering the boundaryless model, this phenomenon is often referred to as outsourcing. Whole areas of activity can be outsourced to another organisation, including accounting, marketing, design and, interestingly for our purposes, HRM. In some cases the organisation may not do what it is most famous for – Daft et al (2010) recorded that the fashion-wear company Nike produced very little or at times none of its own clothing.

Virtual network structures may involve the 'hub' organisation imposing its own patterns of structure on its partners or, contrastingly, might enable partner organisations to devise their own structure and indeed ways of designing workers' jobs.

Key relationships in the network structure are those running *across* organisations and managing such relationships effectively becomes paramount. Relationships can be contractual in nature, with deterrents put in place to avoid betrayal and other negative behaviour, or might be based on trust-based links, underpinned by knowledge of the partner organisation. In some cases the relationship can come to be based on goodwill and mutual obligation – akin to a successful personal relationship.

8.3.3 CONTINGENT FACTORS

There are many potentially distinctive forms of organisational structure: we have only outlined some general principles here. As suggested earlier, the essence of the contingency approach is that particular types of structure should be designed in the light of the contingent factors acting on the organisation in question. Although contingencies are by definition framed by unique circumstances, the overarching factors usually put forward are listed below.

Technology

The work of Joan Woodward, published in 1965 (but based on research carried out in the mid-1950s), identified a link between technology – here referring to production methods – and the ways in which the companies she studied were organised. Woodward's conclusion was that the production systems used by the companies she researched resulted in differences in those companies' structures. Woodward, in addition to demarcating forms of structure and linking them to technology, also, and very importantly, concluded that there was an optimal situation in which organisations that aligned their structures according to the technologies they used would be the most efficient. In other words, the structure would have to fit with this particular contingent factor.

Size of organisation

A research team from Aston University in England proposed that an organisation's size would be the most important determining factor in terms of its optimal structure (see Pugh and Hickson 1976, for an account of the research by members of the original group). The Aston researchers examined the extent of specialisation, the degree to which formal policies influenced work in reality, and standardisation in terms of procedures. The Aston academics then identified a number of points for comparison, all deriving from Weber's ideal type of bureaucracy, finally correlating these with statistical data from their own research sample. Their conclusion was that the independent variable which most strongly impacted on the dependent variable of organisational structure was size. The *post hoc* logic which purports to explain these findings was fundamentally that as organisations grow in size there is considerable pressure for them to become more bureaucratic – see also Chapter 3. Once again, the influence of a contingent factor pointed to an ideal structure depending on the nature of the specific organisation.

Organisational environments

As we have already noted, Burns and Stalker (1961) proposed their dichotomy of mechanistic and organic structures. The mechanistic category is very similar to Weber's model of bureaucracy, while the diametrically opposite organic form is flexible, is network-based and requires commitment – in addition to compliance and loyalty – from employees within this structure. The key contingent variable for Burns and Stalker was the particular environment facing the organisation. The more turbulent the environment, in terms of technological advance, competition and customer or client demand, the more organic the organisation should be, if it were to prosper and even survive in such a challenging milieu. Burns and Stalker identified organisations that had failed to adapt via changed structures, thus adding weight to their central proposition.

By 2015, there was a prevailing view that a very high proportion of organisations operated in turbulent environments with neo-liberal economic precepts and that the spread of globalisation created an environment in which there was 'a relentless accent upon change and post-bureaucracy'. Grey (2013, p105). This reinforced the conclusions of contingency theory, for example optimal structures depend upon the external context and also indicated a move towards post-bureaucracy in many, although not all, organisations.

In conclusion, organisational design offers a degree of choice to decision-makers who should consider the contingent factors faced by their organisations before deciding on structural arrangements. Nonetheless, such choices are themselves constrained as it has been shown that different structures tend to be more effective in particular circumstances, depending on factors such as size, technology and environment.

One should also be wary of assuming that organisations can only respond to contingent factors in a highly constrained way. There is a danger of interpreting the contingency model, which was conceived as a flexible idea, very much an antidote to the 'one best way' approaches of the 1950s, in an over-deterministic way. Child (1972) introduced the important idea of strategic choice, whereby managers or other senior figures within organisations made informed decisions about the conditions in which they chose to operate.

Child proposed that, in reality, large organisations could select and manipulate their environments. Daft et al (2010) use the example of the retailer Wal-Mart to illustrate this point, concluding that Wal-Mart had successfully lobbied the World Trade Organisation and UK and Chinese Governments for a reversal of policies on large store openings. This enabled them to maintain their global structure, whereas if they had simply adapted to their environment they might have merely complied with government diktat or conceivably not operated in those countries at all.

Child also proposed that structural responses to changes in technology could equally be viewed as the result of decisions on which tasks decision-makers wished to be involved in, while it was possible to break down large operating units into smaller sections, thereby making a positive choice on structure.

Notwithstanding the validity of Child's work, the contingency view of organisational design remains dominant in management thinking and it contains many valid insights.

 TAMING A LIFE-THREATENING ILLNESS

CASE STUDY 8.1

A few years ago a patient was admitted to a UK hospital for transplant surgery. The operation was deemed life-saving, so the oft-repeated cliché of work not being a matter of life and death did not apply. The ten-hour procedure was successful and the patient embarked on a lengthy recovery, which began with being confined to his hospital bed. As one can imagine, this rest period afforded an opportunity for deep reflection on a range of topics.

Our patient was a Professor of Sociology, and his reflections came to encompass both his professional training and his deeply personal concerns. So he began to ponder on how the human and social endeavour involved in saving his life had come to be. He could see: 'social acts of great learned skill and scientific knowledge, myriad social acts of humane and loving care, multiple social acts of practical activity – cleaning the floors, pushing trolleys with patients, providing food, keeping the plumbing going, welcoming the outpatients, organising beds, orchestrating a million little daily routines'.

In the course of its daily work, the hospital relied on so many roles: nurses, doctors, porters, ambulance drivers, social workers, phlebotomists, physiotherapists, transplant co-ordinators, administrators and ward managers. There are of course many more. Thousands of workers were organised through structure and job design in a massive division of labour in order to save people's lives.

Source: Plummer (2010, p5)

Questions

1   Hospitals are often categorised as bureaucratic organisations. What are the advantages of such a structure in a hospital setting?

2   Identify the contingent factors that impact on a hospital and show how they influence hospital structure. Could one ever envisage a non-bureaucratic hospital? Give reasons for your answer.

8.4 APPROACHES TO JOB DESIGN

Traditionally, job design principles have emphasised job simplification (Taylor 1911), interpreted critically by some writers as deskilling, while more recent contributions to the subject area have typically recommended expanding jobs in order both to increase employee job satisfaction, or at least to reduce boredom, and to engender greater flexibility in a workforce (Hackman and Oldham 1980). It is often proposed that such flexibility is desirable in view of changes in the wider business environment. In the UK context, Hutton (2004, p1) introduced this argument over ten years ago as follows:

'Britain's fundamental economic structures are changing; industries and services built around knowledge are growing, while those built around mass industrial production and raw muscle power are declining. Work is becoming more intelligent and an intelligent workforce is going to be one that wants to be intelligent about how it organises itself. The more autonomy and control it can have, the more content it will be.'

One should be wary of assuming that there is, or will shortly be, a proliferation of 'intelligent' work. On the contrary, the emergence of increasing numbers of workplaces such as fast-food outlets and call centres have mainly been associated with standardised repetitive 'Taylorist'-style jobs. Beyond such work with its associated routine tasks, one also finds what Clegg et al (2015) refer to as 'grunge jobs' comprising both work carried out in the lower reaches of the supply chain supporting global business, and that performed by an underclass of sometimes illegal workers operating in very poor conditions outside the formally recognised and regulated job market.

Nonetheless there is also evidence that increasingly many workers will be required to act as thinking performers and this segment of the workforce will form the main focus in this chapter. In such an environment it is posited that organisations seeking distinctive high performance should be involved in job design which contributes towards a positive psychological contract between employer and worker. This, it is suggested, can also aid and reinforce successful organisational performance. We have discussed both the issue of flexibility and the psychological contract in more detail in Chapter 7.

It is also necessary for all organisations to engage in job design as an 'infrastructure' task, to ensure that work is allocated into suitably sized role descriptions capable of being carried out effectively. At the same time, it is essential to ensure suitable demarcation of roles both vertically (in terms of skill, knowledge and hierarchical level) as well as horizontally (in functional terms). This aspect of basic job design is a prerequisite for minimal threshold standards of performance by organisations and is needed to avoid fundamental problems relating to the nature of work and roles.

 REFLECTIVE ACTIVITY 8.2

Read the statement below which appeared recently on a well-known supermarket's corporate website and answer the question which follows.

Making Our Company a Great Place to Work

We know that our people want four things from us:

- to be treated with respect
- a manager who helps me
- an interesting job
- an opportunity to get on.

This set of objectives is typical of those espoused by organisations in the retail sector (a major source of UK employment). They put forward a progressive vision of people management, incorporating recognition, support, opportunities for progression and also interesting work.

It might be thought, however, that the aim of securing interesting jobs in the supermarket context is the most challenging of the four aims set out above. In another section of the same website we hear from a customer assistant who says:

'... to be honest, I got a job [here] because I needed some money, but working here has been far more enjoyable and rewarding than I could ever have thought it could be.'

At the start of your study of this topic and without referring to material set out later in this chapter, suggest ways that supermarket managers could provide interesting jobs for store workers.

Answer from your knowledge of large supermarkets, as a shopper if you have no personal experience of store working.

It is possible to locate key developments in the approach to job design, although while these have been developed in particular epochs, each can still be applied to current work situations. It is now time to look at these approaches in more detail.

8.4.1 SCIENTIFIC MANAGEMENT

As indicated earlier, for its most famous proponent, Frederick Taylor, scientific management involved organising tasks into highly specialised jobs. Managers should take on responsibility for planning, co-ordinating and monitoring work, with the task worker restricted to the level of operative. Recruitment and training are simplified and workers are grouped together in large units such as factories or call centres, enabling a high volume of chiefly standardised goods or services. One example is the Fordist production line system, which, in addition to demarcating jobs, also controlled the speed of work. It is difficult to over-emphasise the significance of this model of job design. Henry Ford, in laying the conditions for mass production of cars, was able to reduce costs very substantially, which in turn led to greatly increased levels of car ownership in the USA.

This led to him being considered one of the pivotal figures of the twentieth century in the industrialised world.

Scientific management as a driver for job design has attracted much controversy and a good deal of criticism for the following reasons:

- it can lead to product inflexibility
- it has been criticised as dehumanising and for failing to recognise 'higher order' human needs such as self-actualisation
- it may foster compliance and an instrumental view of work as a means to an end, as opposed to engendering commitment and loyalty
- monotony and boredom can result in reduced performance outcomes.

REFLECTIVE ACTIVITY 8.3

Scientific management is perceived by some commentators as a particular direct form of control of work and workers by management. Braverman (1974) is prominent among writers who go on to assert that this concept of job design is fundamentally associated with an attempt to deskill workers. The notion of deskilling derives from the work of Marx – see McLellan (2000) in which owners and managers seek to maximise surplus value from workers, in essence exploiting them. Managers as a group are, in the nature of their role, concerned to control and regularise jobs and work. Nonetheless, not all jobs have been subject to this version of job and work design and the ability of particular groups of workers to retain or even enhance skill levels remains an important factor in job design.

1   How valid do you find the deskilling thesis, both as a theory and explanation of reality in work organisations?

Adler (1999) has put forward an interesting restatement of the impact of simplified 'Taylorist' jobs on employees' attitudes to their work situation. His research indicated that under conditions of scientific management, employees could still be motivated by a sense of a 'job well done'. For example, they were found to respond positively to managers encouraging them to compete with co-workers, both in terms of quality and output.

When they were respected and trusted by managers, the workers under study reciprocated with commitment and loyalty.

8.4.2 JOB REDESIGN

Job redesign emerged in part as a reaction to the perceived negative effects of scientific management. Its academic roots lie in the so-called 'human relations' school, which emphasised people's social needs which, it was claimed, could and should be met in the workplace. Herzberg's two-factor theory of motivation proposed that pure motivation derived from the content of work as opposed to hygiene factors such as pay, physical working conditions and quality of supervision. Hygiene factors, for Herzberg, were sources of dissatisfaction which could be lessened if, for example, pay was improved.

However, workers would only be truly motivated if their job or work met their needs for recognition, autonomy and achievement. Herzberg's view was that virtually all human beings would respond to work which was rich in motivating factors, if they had the ability to do the job and the opportunity to carry out meaningful work. We will, however, question this near-universal perspective later in this chapter.

In a highly significant contribution to this topic area, Hackman and Oldham (1980) proposed, on the basis of research, that five key characteristics could be used to identify the extent to which a job would, in reality, be motivating.

- skill variety – if different and diverse activities demanded the exercise of a range of skills and abilities
- task identity – the extent to which a job involves a whole and identifiable piece of work with a tangible end result
- task significance – the perceived value and effect of a job on other people
- autonomy – where a worker is free to schedule the pace of his or her work, have some choice in how the work is carried out and is relatively independent of supervision
- feedback – the degree to which a worker gets information about the effectiveness of their performance. This feedback could be gained through observation of their work outcomes.

It is argued that each key characteristic is linked to a positive psychological state which, in turn, leads to desirable work outcomes. For example, task significance could result in a feeling of satisfaction in the meaningfulness of work undertaken, with positive outcomes of work motivation and effectiveness following on from this psychological state. In summary, Hackman and Oldham stated that intrinsic motivation is dependent on individuals experiencing three critical psychological states: experienced meaningfulness (as noted above); experienced responsibility for work; and knowledge of the results of work activities.

Hackman and Oldham recognise that individuals can respond to the characteristics differently; they are after all a function of the individual's perception, so the motivating potential of a job may vary between people. Several factors will influence the manner in which any one individual will respond to changes in their job design:

- *Growth–need strength.* It is suggested that people vary in the extent to which they desire accomplishment and autonomy at work. People high in this category will therefore respond positively to enriched jobs; contrastingly, other workers might find newly enriched jobs a source of anxiety.
- *Knowledge and skill.* People who perceive they can perform adequately (known as a sense of self-efficacy) respond more positively to enriched jobs. This highlights the

importance of individuals' perceptions and also the development of knowledge and skills at work.

● *Context satisfaction*. Hackman and Oldham found that employees who were more satisfied with contextual factors such as pay and working conditions would be more likely to respond positively to job enrichment than fellow workers dissatisfied on these measures.

However, despite recognising potential differences in the ways particular workers might respond to job enrichment, in overall terms Hackman and Oldham's model sets out a clear agenda for managers and others to devise meaningful and varied jobs.

 REFLECTIVE ACTIVITY 8.4

How can Hackman and Oldham's model be applied to the following jobs?

● dentist
● railway ticket collector
● university lecturer
● tiler
● your current or previous job (assuming this is not one of the above).

The job redesign approach attempted to put forward a model which, through increasing the scope of jobs, could result both in greater efficiency and output (however defined) while also increasing the motivation of a workforce. Hackman and Oldham, while stressing the importance of 'moderating factors' which depress levels of motivation (for example lack of knowledge or skill), 'low growth need strength' and other negative factors in the work context, clearly advocate the design of jobs which can lead to psychological well-being among the people who perform them.

We have noted that Hackman and Oldham question whether, and to what extent, job-holders are likely to respond positively to jobs that are redesigned in this way. Their approach in addressing this issue is essentially a psychological one focusing on presumed needs and other psychological characteristics of human beings, which could vary. It may be, however, that individual workers can also choose work that, although comparatively meaningless, may offer the prospect of other desired rewards including pay, for wider reasons based on their calculation of costs and benefits. Support for this notion is provided by the work of Goldthorpe et al (1968), who identified a category of workers who took an instrumental attitude or orientation to work. Formed outside the workplace and influenced by, among others, family and peers, the instrumental orientation regards work as a means to an end, and workers within this category often make a conscious decision to enter psychologically unfulfilling but highly paid work. Thus many workers meet their higher-order needs off the job. With 168 hours in every week, work rarely consumes more than a third of this time for most people. There is ample opportunity for individuals with strong growth needs to find satisfaction beyond their place of work.

This is not to say that decision-makers should make no attempt to design satisfying work for job-holders; there may be considerable practical benefits in so doing. It is useful, however, to adopt a contingency perspective in this area; that is to understand that the nature of job design may depend on a variety of factors including the work itself and the chosen orientations to work as well as the psychological needs of the workforce.

It should finally be noted that enriched work with its hoped-for concomitant high commitment can itself be regarded as a form of subjugation due to the demands it imposes on employees working within its precepts. Grey (2013, p77) notes that: 'what now appears quite normal and natural is that managers will work long hours, do whatever needs to be done to get the job done and are motivated to do so by the intrinsic interest of their work, the payment they receive and, in general, a sense of responsibility and professionalism'. Grey goes on to paint a picture of managers stressed out by endless demands and locked into a particular set of corporate imperatives which, while in many respects preferable to that endured by workers in less enriched and self-managed jobs, themselves involve considerable sacrifices in many respects.

8.4.3 LESSONS FROM JAPAN

Any overview examining how job design has developed as a concept would not be complete without acknowledging the influence of ideas originating in, and imported from, Japan. The purpose here is not to provide an account of how Japanese techniques came to be commended to UK organisations from the 1980s onwards. Neither will we undertake a detailed analysis of what is a highly complex concept of management underpinned by deep assumptions within Japanese society. Rather, we will concentrate on how Japanese management principles have impacted on the specific area of job design, where it is claimed the following factors are particularly relevant:

- *Teamwork.* Japanese management techniques have often advocated the grouping of workers into teams, even in areas of work which would otherwise be organised on an individual basis. This concept can be extended to encompass task decision-making, for example, through quality circles.
- *Multiskilling.* The physical grouping of workers can also be extended to enable more similar job descriptions, that is setting a context of work in which employees are required to have generalised job skills. It follows that these jobs are minimally demarcated. We see here an early embodiment of the principle of flexibility.
- *Total Quality Management (TQM).* For our purposes the key element of TQM is the principle that quality control should be the concern of all workers and therefore form part of every employee's job role. This could be seen as one manifestation of job enlargement, building both additional duties and responsibilities into their jobs.

 REFLECTIVE ACTIVITY 8.5

TQM

Derived from Japanese management methods, and in contrast to other methods of monitoring the quality of a business's output, such as inspection and quality control, TQM is said to be a means of ensuring customer satisfaction through a process of continuous improvement of all work operations. Importantly for the study and leadership of people, to be successful its advocates point to the need for all employees to be involved in TQM. It requires creative thinking and the use of teamwork to solve problems and meet customers' needs. From this standpoint, competitive advantage and differentiation can be achieved through recognising the, often untapped, resource that organisations have in their workforces.

- To what extent could your own job – or one with which you are familiar – benefit from TQM applications? Give reasons for your conclusions.

Japanese work design principles have been incorporated within a wider philosophy including 'single status' employment conditions and lifetime, or at least long-term, tenure of employment. Some elements are not unique to the Japanese context, for example Swedish car-makers had also (quite independently) introduced small-group working into their production processes along with aspects of job enlargement. Nonetheless the Japanese system, as described, can be said to be a distinctive and coherent view on job design, the latter perhaps being seen as a differentiating factor. There have been well-publicised instances of Japanese practices being introduced to the UK, for example in the Nissan and Toyota car production facilities. Some of the principles outlined here have been widely adopted. While the economic difficulties experienced by Japan since the 1990s have cast some doubt on the extent to which they can be regarded as a panacea, many employers now assume that quality issues should be the concern of all workers and that this should be operationalised through job design.

One should take a realistic view of the extent of improvements emanating from such approaches to job design. These, it is claimed, centre on the twin benefits of greater productivity and more positive attitudes among job-holders. Important and commendable as they are, these benefits will not outweigh other factors affecting the organisation. One example is provided by figures indicating the comparatively strong productivity of Japanese-owned car plants in the UK. Rhys Murray-West (2002), in acknowledging their excellent productivity, noted nonetheless that measuring performance by productivity was 'using only a Soviet Union measure of performance. Productivity is a necessary condition of performance, but it is in no way sufficient to guarantee profitability. It hasn't stopped Nissan slipping into loss-making, which indicates the pressure they are under from the strength of sterling.' He also referred to the crucial importance of the desirability of the product itself!

8.4.4 BUSINESS PROCESS RE-ENGINEERING

Business process re-engineering (BPR), we will argue, should also be examined when considering approaches to, and influences on, job design. BPR emerged in the 1990s and is associated with Hammer and Champy (1993) and Davenport (1993). These writers advocate a radical approach to OD. In effect, they recommend ignoring past and current practice when considering how to both structure an organisation and design work. They place a strong emphasis on processes, and attention to these at the same hierarchical level.

Such chains of process are thus horizontal and often cross traditionally functional boundaries.

The focus on an absolute need to serve the customer can result in very dramatic changes to work processes and jobs. Buchanan and Wilson (1996) conducted a 'patient trail' in a British hospital. They found that a hospital patient might routinely have dealings with between 50 and 150 different members of the hospital's staff, becoming at different times the responsibility of most of the hospital's functional departments in the course of diagnosis, on-site treatment and aftercare (see also Case Study 8.1). Problems that arose from this complex process were attributed to hospital staff being quite naturally concerned primarily with what happens at their own stage of the patient's journey. Staff working within such a fragmented environment were not always aware either of what had gone on before or what would subsequently happen to the patient.

Examples such as that given above suggest that organisations should restructure away from vertical or functionally based departmental structures if there is to be a true focus on the customer (this ignoring the debate as to whether patients can be truly thought of as customers). But in addition to organisational restructuring, BPR also implies that jobs themselves should also be reorganised around principles of customer care and that employees should increasingly be empowered to make the decisions affecting a customer's relationship with the organisation.

8.4.5 GOAL-SETTING AND JOB DESIGN

Mullins (2013) notes that seemingly diverse methods of job design can in reality be interconnected with some extent of overlap between them. He also brings the concept of goal-setting into view as another approach to job design. This conclusion was also drawn by French et al (2015), who suggest that as goal-setting involves developing, negotiating and formalising employees' targets and objectives, it can readily be expanded to encompass goal-setting results in specific task goals. Locke's work on goal-setting suggested that specific and difficult goals supported by task feedback are more likely to lead to higher performance, although they should not be seen as too difficult or impossible and they would in any case only be effective if the worker had a feeling of self-efficacy.

8.5 SMART AND AGILE WORKING

At the start of this chapter we noted that the topic areas of organisational and job design continue to be debated, with new thinking and research findings put forward for our consideration on a regular basis. A CIPD report (2008a) summarises several recent trends in these areas under the heading of smart working.

Smart working is defined as 'an approach to organising work that aims to drive greater efficiency and effectiveness in achieving job outcomes through a combination of flexibility, autonomy and collaboration, while optimising tools and working environments for employees' (CIPD 2008a, p7). Smart working is, furthermore, identified as a new paradigm in which a critical mass of workers (in the developed world) experience increasing autonomy at work. The report goes on to identify a collaborative work experience in many organisations in which a customised work experience is developed for groups of workers informed by their individual needs and aspirations.

Agile working, as summarised in a 2014 CIPD report identifies a set of practices that enable the establishment of an optimal workforce. The notion of agile working reflects themes covered in this and previous chapters. Tools for agile working thus include an examination of work roles – with a recommendation to encourage multiskilling and job rotation. They also, and importantly, deal with *when* people work, *where* they work, for example in co-working or remote settings (see Chapter 7). The question of *who* is employed, for example permanent core or outsourced peripheral workers, was also very important. The CIPD report concluded that while agile practices were associated with quick and effective responses to change, only some organisations were planning to implement them, with a lack of flexibility and associated preoccupation with control prevalent in others, particularly in the UK public sector. The top barrier preventing moves towards agile working was operational pressure absorbing 'time necessary to develop and trial different ways of working' CIPD (2014a, p20).

The aforementioned report on agile working noted that one of the challenges with building agile workforces was the legacy of rigorous cost management. Many organisations were focused on cost reduction and becoming 'lean'; however, leaner workforces would not in themselves be smart or agile.

These recent contributions to the literature identify trends in the wider work environment which have helped promote new forms of working. These include the advent of homeworking, enabled by developments in technology and a sense that with less expectation of long-term employment with an individual employer, workers are more prepared to switch jobs if they feel that job design is neglected.

This is an optimistic note on which to end the main body of this chapter and it is hoped that the experience of organisations and jobs will become a happier one for more and more of us – not just a fortunate few. Nonetheless, the smart working report records that the job characteristics model – outlined earlier in this chapter – in which people are subordinate to a pre-existing job (which may be more or less autonomous and responsible) is still relevant. Moreover, it should be stressed that the reports did not deal with jobs and workplaces in the developing world where the picture can be a lot less rosy. In 2013, a lethal accident at a Bangladesh factory making clothing for several well-known UK fashion labels revealed jobs and management structures that were way below the standards aspired to in smart working or similar models (Nelson and Bergman 2013).

CASE STUDY 8.2

WORKING AT CAPGEMINI

Capgemini is a global leader in consulting, technology, outsourcing and local professional services. Headquartered in Paris, the organisation operates in more than 30 countries with 82,000 people across the globe.

Capgemini's consultants need to be able to work effectively from any location. Therefore all new recruits are provided with powerful lightweight laptops with wireless connectivity, mobile phones with email and Internet capability, easy access to teleconferencing facilities and the ability to access the intranet remotely.

Although consultants are often based on-site with clients and – as we have seen – frequently work remotely, there is office accommodation too. However, this is intentionally unusual, and the Soho office in London comprises 'hot desks' and collaborative work areas and flexible zones intended to foster 'accelerated decision-making and open and honest discussion'.

Capgemini provides people with a great deal of autonomy in their daily work. Consultants are often responsible for the planning and definition of projects in line with customer requirements and operate as self-managed individuals.

Consultants refer to mentors and 'reviewers' (a colleague who is a grade above) on development matters.

Leaders should be approachable, know their people on a personal level and Capgemini aim for a 'low politics environment'.

Capgemini's structure complements this context of work. The business operates a flat structure with six grades of consultants throughout the business. Performance is assessed against defined objectives and client expectations. Each grade has a set of behavioural competencies aligned with learning interventions, feedback and self-analysis tools.

The way in which jobs and structures are set out at Capgemini is underpinned by a distinctive organisational culture. Values of fun, modesty, solidarity, freedom, trust, boldness and honesty are celebrated and reinforced through recruitment, performance, recognition, learning and other processes and role-modelled by leaders.

Questions

1. Would Capgemini's structure and work arrangements be suitable in your own job (or in one you are familiar with)? Explain your answer.

2. Which element of Capgemini's strategy is more important – its structure or its culture? Why have you reached your conclusion?

8.6 CONCLUSION

The argument for linking principles of organisational design and job design to high performance and commitment workplaces can be summarised as follows:

- OD can achieve an organisational structure best suited to deal with that organisation's circumstances or contingent factors.
- A constantly changing and ever more competitive business environment means that work organisations in all sectors require multiskilled, proactive and customer-focused staff in order to be successful. These staff can be characterised as thinking performers – or possibly smart workers.
- An increasingly educated workforce, used to exercising discretion and choice in other areas of their lives will, in any case, demand jobs which are psychologically fulfilling.
- High-performance work organisations will therefore increasingly need to design, or enable their workers to design, jobs that provide variety, scope for initiative and autonomy and empower job-holders.

Noon and Blyton (2002) group these arguments under the heading of the 'upskilling thesis'. These writers go on, however, to question the extent to which this thesis is borne out in practice, proposing that there remain very wide differences both in terms of the range of tasks undertaken by workers and the degree of autonomy experienced across the labour market.

A contingency approach to the area, while recognising the value of 'humanising' jobs, would suggest that different models of job design are appropriate in different situations. For example, we should critically address the proposition that work has largely become more 'intelligent'. A large-scale research project carried out by Professor Peter Nolan into work patterns in the UK identified a more complex and subtle picture in the early years of the twenty-first century. Nolan (quoted in Wignall 2004) records that: 'we still have 10.5 million manual workers in this country. That's 40 per cent of the workforce. They're in warehouses, filling envelopes, filling shelves. Stacking shelves is something like the eighth quickest growing occupation ... people think we now have a service economy where everyone sits at a computer, and that's just not true. Jobs are being created by new technologies, but those jobs are the same kind of jobs that people were doing before.'

Nolan's conclusions were echoed in 2015 in a CIPD report on UK graduate employment. The report concluded that increasing numbers of graduates had significantly outstripped the creation of high-skilled jobs. This had resulted in graduates replacing non-graduates in 'less demanding jobs'. An increasingly well-qualified workforce would not, in itself, generate more high-skilled jobs. The mismatch of qualifications and skills had also led to one of the highest levels of self-reported over-qualification among graduates in Europe with several potentially negative consequences (CIPD 2015c).

It is not the intention here to dismiss the possibility that all jobs can be enriched or made more customer-focused; this is certainly true to an extent, and managers should develop ways in which this may be achieved. However, one should recognise the role of rhetoric – or even hyperbole – in some literature in this subject area, and the relatively unchanging nature of many people's work. Indeed, highly qualified employees are increasingly linked to less enriched work. Trends in job design are complex and non-linear.

One can also put forward a view that organisational effectiveness can be achieved through different models and indeed conceptions of organisational design. The fast-food sector provides a notable example of continuing simplification of tasks, albeit within a teamworking framework. Here, we have classical contingency principles operating – that is, the optimal structure of the organisation will all depend on the level of predictability required (both product and service), hierarchical relationships and the expectations of a workforce, many of whom in this case may have only short-term plans regarding their work and employment. In contrast, the nature of organisations and work in other sectors may lend itself far more easily to flat structures or even adhocracies, encouraging greater initiative and autonomy on the part of job-holders. Organisational design remains an important area; as Clegg et al (2011, p528) note: 'Organisation design matters just as much as any other kind of design . . . ugly organisation design produces bad managing.'

As we saw in Chapter 7 it has been argued that organisations should seek to implement and maintain functional flexibility, this concept encompassing job rotation, multiskilling and, where appropriate, teamworking as part of an overall strategy of flexibility or adaptability. Other aspects of flexibility included numerical flexibility, the precursor of many instances of downsizing, and financial flexibility, which, in an attempt to control salary costs, has seen numerous examples of subcontracting work, zero-hours contracts and even the wholesale movement of jobs to other parts of the world. However, even this seemingly inexorable logic may be contingent on particular circumstances. Clark (1993) suggests that there might be instances where workers' specialist knowledge is perceived as sufficiently important to justify retaining and bolstering it. The same author also notes that a worker's commitment to high-quality work can emanate from a feeling of ownership of that work or job. There is, in conclusion, a range of strategic choices available to organisational decision-makers when approaching the area of both organisational and job design.

KEY LEARNING POINTS

1   People's experience of work is affected by the organisational arrangements in which they operate and the nature of the work they do.

2   A variety of organisational structure models have been put forward in order to enhance performance.

3   Job redesign emphasises increasing the scope of jobs in order to increase efficiency and foster high levels of worker motivation.

4   Large numbers of people continue to work in jobs designed under principles of 'Taylorism' or scientific management.

5   A contingency approach to both organisational and job design, stressing the importance of recognising situational factors, is recommended.

1   List five advantages of the bureaucratic model of structure and five disadvantages. Do the advantages outweigh the disadvantages, or vice versa?

2   With reference to real-world examples, assess the usefulness of the contingency approach to organisational design.

3   Assess the importance of job design within the overall process of managing people. Give reasons for your answer.

4   How strong is the evidence that meaningful work will motivate a workforce?

EXPLORE FURTHER

Daft, R., Murphy, J. and Willmott, H. (2016) *Organization, Theory and Design*. 2nd ed. Andover: Cengage. The authors cover material dealt with in this book, so this is valuable as an alternative perspective on the two central topics. A range of case studies illustrate the concepts' inherently practical nature.

Grey, C. (2013) *A Very Short, Fairly Interesting and Reasonably Cheap Book About Studying Organizations*. 3rd ed. London: Sage. This book provides a thought-provoking and entertaining account of the development and application of many of the principles dealt with in this chapter.

Hackman, J.R. and Oldham, G.R. (1980) *Work Redesign*. New York: Adison-Wesley. Read this source text for an in-depth discussion of how job characteristics can affect workers' attitudes.

Recruitment and Selection

SALLY RUMBLES AND RAY FRENCH

LEARNING OUTCOMES

After reading this chapter, you should be able to:

- comprehend the potential importance of recruitment and selection in successful people management and leadership
- identify aspects of recruitment and selection which are needed to avoid critical failure factors
- understand the recruitment and selection policies and procedures which are said to be associated with high performance, commitment and successful organisational outcomes
- evaluate selection methods according to criteria of professionalism including reliability, validity and fairness
- appreciate the links between recruitment and selection and other activities which integrate workers within an organisation and ensure their longer-term successful working.

9.1 OVERVIEW

In this chapter we examine the important role of recruitment and selection within the process of leading, managing and developing people. Recruitment and selection is pivotal in this regard in certain important respects. At the most basic level our focus in this book is on people management within the employment relationship. Those charged with recruiting people to posts in work organisations take a crucial 'gatekeeper' role; only those people selected for employment can be led, managed and developed. So in the most fundamental sense the decision to employ (or not) underpins the whole area of managing people. Issues associated with exclusion from the workplace also highlight the need for professionalism, fairness and ethical behaviour on the part of those engaged in this activity.

Recruitment and selection also has an important role to play in ensuring worker perfomance and positive organisational outcomes. It is often claimed that selection of workers occurs not just to replace departing employees or add to a workforce, but rather aims to put in place workers who can perform at a high level and demonstrate commitment (Pilbeam and Corbridge 2010). We will elaborate on the sometimes complex linkages between recruitment and selction and performance later in this chapter.

Recruitment and selection is characterised, finally, by potential difficulties and it is necessary to keep abreast of developments in research in the field. Research from CIPD (2009a), for example, concluded that organisations should be increasingly inclusive in their employment offering as younger generations have grown up with the notion of flexible working, while older people have an interest in flexible working as an alternative to retirement. A CIPD *Labour Market Outlook* report in 2015 (CIPD 2015a), noted that following a 'long dark decade' the sun was finally shining for young jobseekers in the UK, with more employers turning to a wider range of younger recruits. However, the report alerted those involved in recruiting and selecting young workers to ensure the effective utilisation of their skills, as the UK had the second highest level of over-qualification in the OECD. This could result in productivity being undermined unless young people's skills were put to good use. These are just two examples of how an appreciation of current research can inform practice and also shows the critical importance of the social context in which recruitment and selection takes place.

9.2 INTRODUCTION

Recruitment and selection forms a core part of the central activites underlying human resource management; namely the aquisition, development and reward of workers. It frequently forms an important part of the work of human resource managers or designated specialists within work organisations. However, and importantly, recruitment and selection decisions are often for good reason taken by non-specialists such as line managers. There is therefore an important sense in which it is both the responsibility of all managers, and where human resource departments exist, it may be that HR managers play more of a supporting advisory role to those people who will supervise or in other ways work with the new employee. As Mullins (2013) notes, if the HRM function is to remain effective there must be consistently good levels of teamwork, plus ongoing co-operation and consultation between line managers and the HR manager. This is most definitely the case in recruitment and selection as specialist HR managers (or even external consultants) can be an important repository of up-to-date knowledge and skills, for example on the important legal dimensions of this area.

Recruitment and selection is often presented as a planned rational activity, comprising certain sequentially linked phases within a process of employee resourcing, which itself may be located within a wider HR management strategy.The two terms are commonly differentiated although there is a clear link between them.

Recruitment is commonly understood as a process by which a pool of capable people is generated, who then apply for employment in an organisation. Selection is the process by which managers and others identify and use valid instruments enabling them to choose potentially effective future employees from a pool of applicants. When selecting employees those reponsible will need to act in the light of given management goals within the organisation and and, of course, the legal requirements in place within a specific country and pan-national institutions, such as the European Union.

In setting out a similar distinction in which recruitment activities provide a pool of people eligible for selection, Foot and Hook (2011, p161) suggest that:

> although the two functions are closely connected, each requires a separate range of skills and expertise, and may in practice be fulfilled by different staff members. The recruitment activity, but not normally the selection decision, may be outsourced to an agency. It makes sense, therefore, to treat each activity separately.

Recruitment and selection as defined here, can play a pivotally important role in shaping an organisation's effectiveness and performance, if work organisations are able to acquire workers who already possess relevant knowledge, skills and aptitudes and can make an accurate prediction regarding their future abilities. If we accept this premise (which will be questioned to some extent in this chapter), then recruiting and selecting staff in an effective manner can both avoid undesirable costs – for example, those associated with high staff turnover, poor performance and dissatisfied customers – and engender a mutually beneficial employment relationship characterised, wherever possible, by high commitment on both sides.

Recruitment and selection is a topical area. While it has always had the capacity to form a key part of the process of managing and leading people as a routine part of organisational life, it is suggested here that recruitment and selection has become ever more important as organisations increasingly regard their workforce as a source of competitive advantage. Of course, not all employers engage with this proposition even at the rhetorical level. However, there is evidence of increased interest in the utilisation of employee selection methods which are valid, reliable and fair. For example, it has been noted that 'over several decades, work psychology has had a significant influence on the way people are recruited into jobs, through rigorous development and evaluation of personnel selection procedures' (Arnold et al 2010, p136). In this chapter we will examine several contemprary themes in recruitment and selection including the so-called competency approach and online recruitment.

Recruitment and selection does not operate in a vacuum, insulated from wider social trends, so it is very important to keep abreast of current research. The CIPD annual survey report *Resourcing and Talent Planning* (2015f) found that:

- UK employers are now operating in the most buoyant employment market experienced for some time. This is adding to the challenges that they face in recruiting and retaining talent. The majority of organisations report that the competition for talent has increased.
- Skills shortages are escalating and 78% of organisations reported having difficulties in filling vacancies. Senior management and technical staff vacancies were the most difficult to fill, but many respondents to the survey reported that they had experienced difficulties in recruiting all types of staff.
- There is an increased focus on retention of staff along with developing talent in-house.
- Half of organisations are recruiting from a much wider geography and an increasing proportion are actively trying to attract talent of all ages and backgrounds.
- Competition for well-qualified talent has increased according to 82% of respondents to the survey as organisations compete for key skills.
- These specific findings epitomise the very close link between recruitment and selection and the wider social and economic context.

This aspect of employee resourcing is characterised, however, by potential difficulties. Many widely used selection methods, for example interviewing, are generally perceived to be unreliable as a predictor of job-holders' performance in reality. Thus it is critically important to obtain a realistic evaluation of the process from all concerned, including both successful and unsuccessful candidates. There are ethical issues around selecting 'appropriate', and by implication rejecting 'inappropriate', candidates for employment. Many organisations seek to employ people who will fit in with their organisation's culture (French et al 2015); see also the IKEA case study below. Whilst this may be perfectly understandable, it carries important ethical overtones; for example, whether an employing organisation should be involved in shaping an individual's identity. We put forward the view in this chapter that, notwithstanding the moral issues and practical difficulties outlined here, recruitment and selection is one area where it is possible to distinguish policies and practices associated with critical success factors and performance differentiators which, in turn, impact on organisational effectiveness in significant ways.

WHY WORK AT IKEA? PART ONE

The following extracts are taken from the 'Working at the IKEA Group' section of the IKEA Group corporate website in 2015.

'COME AND BE YOURSELF WITH US'

'At IKEA we are looking for down-to-earth, straightforward people who have the desire to learn and grow personally and professionally right along with our business'.

'A positive team spirit'

'Working with us is like working with your friends. Our culture is based on the spirit of togetherness, enthusiasm and fun. And we're always looking for people who share our positive attitude and values.'

IKEA's website also stresses the importance of the company's inclusive, empathetic, open and honest culture, before going on to identify some specific IKEA values including:

- *Leadership by example*. Manangers act according to IKEA values, creating an atmosphere of well-being and expect the same from co-workers.
- *Togetherness and enthusiasm*. These values underpin the power to solve seemingly unsolvable problems which it is claimed they do 'all the time'.
- *Humbleness and* (*will power*). Humbleness is a precondition of respect; for each other, customers and suppliers.

- *Simplicity*. This involves taking an easy-going straightforward approach when solving problems, dealing with people or facing challenges.

It is clear that IKEA as an employer is strongly driven by values and will seek to recruit and select employees (co-workers) who identify with those values and are committed to making them work.

Questions

1 In what ways could an employer seek to assess qualities of empathy, humbleness, willpower and simplicity among candidates in the course of a recruitment and selection process? How accurate do you think judgements made along these measures are likely to be?

2 What selection methods could IKEA employ to assess whether potential workers can approach 'seemingly unsolvable' problems?

3 To what extent should an organisation like IKEA attempt to recruit and select workers who embody their organisational culture? Give reasons for your answer. Identify some possible negative outcomes of aligning selection with organisational culture.

9.3 EFFECTIVE RECRUITMENT AND SELECTION

We have already referred to the potential importance of recruitment and selection as an activity. Pilbeam and Corbridge (2010, p155) provide a useful overview of potential positive and negative aspects noting that, 'The recruitment and selection of employees is fundamental to the functioning of an organisation, and there are compelling reasons for getting it right. Inappropriate selection decisions reduce organisational effectiveness, invalidate reward and development strategies, are frequently unfair on the individual recruit and can be distressing for managers who have to deal with unsuitable employees.'

REFLECTIVE ACTIVITY 9.1

Getting it Wrong

In an attempt to check the robustness of security procedures at British airports, Anthony France, a reporter for the *Sun* newspaper, obtained a job as a baggage handler with a contractor subsequently named by the newspaper. In the course of his selection, France gave bogus references, and provided a fake home address and bank details. Throughout the selection process he lied about his past while details of his work as an undercover journalist were available on the Internet.

France then proceeded to take fake explosive material onto a holiday jet airliner at Birmingham International Airport.

This case provides a good, albeit extreme, example of the possible consequences of flawed selection procedures, or as happened here, when agreed practices, such as checking personal details, are not put into effect. Such consequences are potentially wide-ranging and encompass the trivial and comic to possibly tragic outcomes. One can certainly reasonably anticipate many of the negative outcomes listed below to follow when the predictions made about a candidate for employment fail to be borne out.

It is undoubtedly true that recruitment and selection strategies and practices have important consequences for all concerned, so what are the keys to maximising the chances of effective recruitment and selection? Some important factors are listed below.

9.3.1 RECOGNISING THE POWER OF PERCEPTION

Perception is defined as the process by which humans receive, organise and make sense of the information they receive from the outside world: Huczynski and Buchanan (2013), French et al (2015) and Mullins (2013). The quality or accuracy of our perceptions will have a major impact on our response to a situation. There is much data suggesting that when we perceive other people – particularly in an artifical and time-constrained situation like a job interview – we can make key mistakes, sometimes at a subliminal level. One key to enhancing effectiveness in recruitment and selection therefore lies in an appreciation of some core princples of interpersonal perception and, in particular, some common potential mistakes in this regard.

- *Selective perception.* Our brains cannot process all of the information which our senses pick up so we instead select particular objects – or aspects of people – for attention. We furthermore attribute positive or negative characteristics to the stimuli; known as the 'halo' and 'horns' effects respectively. For example, an interviewee who has a large coffee stain on their clothing, but is otherwise well-presented, may have difficulty creating an overall negative impression despite the fact that it might be that their desire for the new job that resulted in nervousness and clumsiness.
- *Self-centred bias.* A recruiter should avoid evaluating a candidate by reference to themselves as this may be irrelevant to the post in question and run the risks of a 'clone effect' in a changing business environment. The phrase 'I was like you 15 years ago' may be damaging in a number of respects and should not be the basis for employment in most situations.
- *Early information bias.* We often hear apocryphal stories of interview panels making very early decisions on a candidate's suitability and spending the remaining time confirming that decision. Mythical though some of these tales may be, there is a danger of over-prioritising early events: a candidate who trips over when entering an interview room may thus genuinely be putting themselves at a disadvantage.

- *Stereotyping.* This is a common short cut to understanding an individual's attributes, which is a difficult and time-consuming process. The logic of stereotyping attributes individuals' characteristics to those of a group to which they belong; for example, the view that because Italians are considered to be emotional, an individual Italian citizen will be too. Stereotypes might contain elements of truth, but may equally be entirely false since we are all unique. Stereotyping may well be irrelevant and, if acted on, also discriminatory.

It should be stressed that these, and other, perceptual errors are not inevitable and can be overcome. Many HR professionals study subjects like organisational behaviour as part of their career qualifications in which they are made aware of the dangers of inaccurate perception. Nonetheless, it remains the case that an understanding of this subject area is an important building block to effective recruitment and selection.

9.3.2 TAKING A STAGED APPROACH

Much prescriptive writing on recruitment and selection advocates viewing the process as sequential with distinct and interlinked stages. This model is referred to as the 'resourcing cycle'. The resourcing cycle begins with the identification of a vacancy and ends when the successful candidate is performing the job to an acceptable standard, that is, post-selection. It is a two-way process. Organisations are evaluating candidates for a vacancy, but candidates also scrutinise the organisation as a prospective employer. In recent years there has been an increasing focus on employer branding and image in attracting candidates. Organisations that gain a reputation for treating people well, offering stimulating and secure employment with the potential to progress stand a far greater chance of attracting, recruiting and retaining good people. Conducting the process in a professional and timely manner is necessary to ensure that not only is the best candidate attracted to apply and subsequently accept the post, but also that unsuccessful candidates can respect the decision made. If an unsuccessful applicant gains a favourable impression of the organisation, they may possibly apply for future vacancies.

The first step in the recruitment process is to decide that there is a vacancy to be filled. Increasingly, a more strategic and questioning approach may be taken. If, for example, the vacancy arises because an employee has left, managers may take the opportunity to review the work itself and consider whether it could be processed in an alternative way. For example, could the work be done on a part-time, job-share or flexitime basis? Alternatively, the job could be automated. The financial services sector in the UK provides one example of where technological developments have resulted in both significant job losses and changed patterns of work in recent decades.

On the assumption that a post does need to be filled, it will be necessary to devise specifications. Whether a competency-based approach (this concept will be defined later in the chapter) or the more traditional method of formal job descriptions and person specifications is chosen, a CIPD report (2007b) noted that specifications would need to reflect the duties and requirements of the job along with the skills, aptitudes, knowledge, experience, qualifications and personal qualities that are necessary to perform the job effectively. Consideration should also be given to how the recruiter intends to measure and elicit information regarding those skills. Are they essential to job performance or merely desirable and can they be objectively measured?

9.3.3 ATTRACTING CANDIDATES

The next stage in the recruitment cycle is the attraction of candidates as one important objective of a recruitment method is to realise an appropriate number of suitable candidates within reasonable cost constraints. Pilbeam and Corbridge (2010) note that there is no ideal number of applications and no intrinsic value in attracting a high volume of candidates, and neither is there a single best way to recruit applicants. The chosen recruitment medium needs to ensure that there are a sufficient number of suitably qualified candidates from which to make a selection without being overwhelmed with large numbers of unsuitable applications. Using a recruitment agency to find a small number of suitable candidates, particularly for senior or specialised posts, may prove a significantly more cost-effective and efficient method than a major web-based advertising campaign which generates a large response from unsuitable candidates. The choice of method will also be influenced by the availability of candidates; that is, is there likely to be a shortage or surplus of candidates? The upturn in the UK economy in 2014 had a significant impact on the availability of labour, with many organisations reporting a shortage of skilled labour and a lack of applicants for vacancies. This is in contrast to the tight UK labour market conditions experienced during the recession in the prior six years, where there were signficantly more applicants than vacancies. For example, in the highly competitive graduate recruitment market organisations will match the choice of methods to the nature of the vacancy, the university or course being targeted and the specific sector and other relevant factors. Small employers are more likely to carry out a targeted recruitment, while a large organisation (with a high-profile employer brand) will utilise a variety of methods to attract talent, in so doing accepting that they will receive a large volume of speculative applications (Suff 2012a).

 REFLECTIVE ACTIVITY 9.2

According to the CIPD (2015f), the most effective methods for attracting applications remain the company website and recruitment agencies. Sixty-five per cent of organisations have made improvements to their company website in order to attract candidates and there is an increasing use of new/media and technology. Organisations also report greater selectivity in their choice of recruitment partners in order to exploit limited budgets most effectively and attract the skills they need. The public and voluntary sectors are more likely to use traditional recruitment methods such as local newspapers for attracting candidates, whilst word of mouth and personal recommendations are seen as the most effective and most popular methods used by SMEs (Bergman 2012)

Look at the recruitment section of your local newspaper and a good-quality broadsheet. What sort of vacancies are typically advertised in each? Compare and contrast these with the types of vacancies advertised in online job boards or recruitment websites. What indicators are there in the wording of advertisements as to whether there is a surplus or shortage of candidates? What indications are there that online recruitment methods are replacing more traditional ways of attracting candidates?

Which method of recruitment should be adopted? There is no single best way, and a contingency approach involving an analysis of what might be effective in particular circumstances is advocated. In other words, 'it all depends'.

Human resources professionals should carefully consider and review which methods have been most effective in the past and which method(s) would be most appropriate for the current vacancy. They should also, critically, keep methods under review.

9.3.4 SELECTION

Selection is one of the last stages of the recruitment process and includes the choice of methods by which an employer will reduce a short-listed group following the recruitment stage, leading to an employment decision. For most people, this is the only visible stage of the resourcing cycle as their experience of it is likely to be as a subject or candidate rather than involvement in planning the entire process. While recruitment can be perceived as a positive activity generating an optimum number of jobseekers, selection is inherently negative in that it will probably involve rejection of applicants.

It would be prudent to argue that selection decisions should be based on a range of selection tools as some have poor predictive job ability. While it is almost inconceivable that employment would be offered or accepted without a face-to-face encounter, many organisations still rely almost exclusively on the outcome of interviews to make selection decisions.

To have any value, interviews should be conducted or supervised by trained individuals, be structured to follow a previously agreed set of questions mirroring the person specification or job profile, and allow candidates the opportunity to ask questions. The interview is more than a selection device. It is a mechanism that is capable of communicating information about the job and the organisation to the candidate, with the aim of giving a realistic job preview, providing information about the process, and thus can minimise the risk of job offers being rejected. Organisations seeking high performance in their selection processes should therefore give considerable attention to maximising the uses of the interview and, ideally, combine this method with other psychometric measures where appropriate.

9.4 VALIDITY OF SELECTION METHODS

It may appear self-evident that organisational decision-makers will wish to ensure that their recruitment (and in this case) selection methods are effective. We have already suggested, however, that making judgements on an individual's personal characteristics and suitability for future employment is inherently problematic and that many 'normal' selection methods contain significant flaws. There is also the question of what is meant by the terms 'reliability' and 'validity' when applied to recruitment and selection.

'Reliability' in the context of workforce selection can refer to the following issues:

- Temporal or 'retest' stability where the effectiveness of a selection tool is assessed by consistency of results obtained over time. An individual could, for example, complete a personality inventory or intelligence test at different times over a period of several years, although in the latter case it would be important to isolate the impact of repeated practice on results.
- Consistency, that is, can the test measure what it sets out to? Some elements of IQ tests have, for example, been criticised for emphasising a person's vocabulary, which might in turn be influenced by their education and general background rather than their innate intelligence.

Validity in this area is typically subdivided into the following aspects:

- Face validity has an emphasis on the acceptability of the selection measure, including to the candidate him/herself. For example, it is possible (although extremely unlikely) that there is a correlation between a person's hat size and their job competence. However, you would be reluctant to measure candidates' heads as part of their selection due to their probable scepticism at the use of this measure.
- Content validity refers to the nature of the measure and in particular its adequacy as a tool. For example, the UK driving test could be criticised for not assessing ability in either night driving or travelling on motorways.
- Predictive validity centres on linkages between results or scores on a selection measure and subsequent outcome – most commonly job performance at a future point. Here it is important to identify when the comparison will be made, for example, immediately in the case of a simple job requiring little training, or more commonly at an intermediate point, possibly after a suitable probationary period.

We argue here that validity, along with fairness, should be the overriding indicator of a selection method for high performance organisations and that it is important to obtain sophisticated data on validity in all its forms. Pilbeam and Corbridge (2010, p189) provide a summary of the predictive validity of selection methods based on the findings of various research studies:

1.0	Certain prediction
0.9	
0.8	
0.7	Assessment centres for development
0.6	Skilful and structured interviews
0.5	Work sampling
	Ability tests
0.4	Assessment centres for job performance
	Biodata
	Personality assessment
0.3	Unstructured interviews
0.2	
0.1	References
0.0	Graphology
	Astrology

However, they suggest that these validity measures should be treated with caution as they can be affected by the performance indicators used, and also the way the tools were applied. They indicate nonetheless both variability between measures and some overall degree of uncertainty when predicting future work performance during the selection process.

While it is recommended that validity should be the prime factor in choosing selection tools, it would be naive not to recognise that other factors such as cost and applicability may be relevant. How practical, therefore, is it to conduct any particular measure? As indicated earlier, an organisation aiming for high performance is recommended to adopt valid measures as opposed to merely practical or less costly ones. Again, one should recognise that recruitment and selection is contingent upon other factors such as the work itself. A 'high performance' organisation in the fast-food industry may legitimately decide not to adopt some relatively valid but expensive methods when selecting fast-food operatives. It should be noted that the oft-derided method of interviewing can in reality be a relatively valid method if conducted skilfully and structured.

9.4.1 RECRUITMENT AND SELECTION: ART OR SCIENCE?

Systematic models of recruitment and selection based on a resourcing cycle should not necessarily imply that this process is underpinned by scientific reasoning and method. As we have seen, Pilbeam and Corbridge note that even the most valid methods fall some way short of complete predictive validity. Thompson and McHugh (2009, p285) go further, taking a critical view on the general use and, in particular, the validity of employee selection methods. In commenting on the use of personality tests in selection, these authors state that 'in utilising tests employers are essentially clutching at straws and on this basis will probably use anything that will help them make some kind of systematic decision'. They identify now discredited selection methods, such as the use of polygraphs to detect lying and, other methods, such as astrology, which are deemed more appropriate in some cultures rather than others. It is indeed important to keep in mind that today's received wisdom in the area of recruitment and selection, just as in the management canon more generally, may be criticised and even widely rejected in the future.

The process of recruitment and selection continues nonetheless to be viewed as best carried out via sequential but linked stages of first gathering a pool of applicants, a screening-out process, followed by the positive step of actual selection. This apparently logical ordering of the activities is largely viewed as essential to achieve minimum thresholds of effectiveness.

9.4.2 INDUCTION AND TRANSITION

It is not always the case that selected employees are immediately capable of performing to the maximum level on their allotted job(s) and important stages in the resourcing cycle occur post-selection. When selecting, many organisations are making a longer-term prediction of a new employee's capability. This accounts for many organisations imposing a probationary period in which employees' performance and future potential can be assessed in the work setting. The resourcing cycle extends into this post-selection phase and the induction period and early phases of employment constitute a critically important part of both successful integration into the workplace culture and development as a fully functioning worker. The final stage of the resourcing cycle involves evaluation of the process and reflection on lessons learned from the process and their implications for the future.

9.4.3 RECRUITMENT COSTS

A concern with effectiveness in recruitment and selection becomes all the more important when one considers the costs getting things wrong. We begin with apparent costs which centre on the direct costs of recruitment procedures, but one might also consider the so-called opportunity costs of engaging in repeated recruitment and selection when workers leave an organisation. An excessive preoccupation with recruitment and selection will divert a manager from other activities he or she could usefully be engaged in. It is also useful to consider the 'investment', including training resources, lost to the employer when a worker leaves prematurely. According to the CIPD *Resourcing and Talent Planning* survey (2015f) the median recruitment cost of filling a vacancy is £7,250 for senior managers/directors, and £2,000 for other employees, although this rises to £10,000 and £3,000 respectively for vacancies in manufacturing and production. These costs are down on previous estimates and may reflect the more targeted use of recruitment agencies who typically charge between 20 and 30% of starting salary and the lack of real recruitment activity in the public sector where costs are considerably less.

Implicit costs are less quantifiable and include the following categories:

- poor performance
- reduced productivity
- low quality products or services
- dissatisfied customers or other stakeholders
- low employee morale.

The implicit costs mentioned here are, in themselves clearly undesirable outcomes in all organisations. In high-performing organisations 'average' or 'adequate' performance may also be insufficient and recruitment and selection may be deemed to have failed unless workers have become 'thinking performers'.

9.5 CONTEMPORARY THEMES IN RECRUITMENT AND SELECTION

9.5.1 THE COMPETENCY APPROACH

Typically, decisions on selecting a potential worker are made primarily with a view to taking on the most appropriate person to do a particular job in terms of their current or, more commonly, potential competencies. In recent years this concept has been extended to search for workers who are flexible and able to contribute to additional and/or changing job roles. This approach contrasts with a more traditional model which involves first compiling a wide-ranging job description for the post in question, followed by the use of a person specification, which in effect forms a checklist along which candidates can be evaluated on criteria such as knowledge, skills and personal qualities. This traditional approach involves, in essence, matching characteristics of an 'ideal' person to fill a defined job. There is a seductive logic in this apparently rational approach. However, there are in-built problems in its application if judgements of an individual's personality are inherently subjective and open to error and, furthermore, if these personal characteristics are suited to present rather than changing circumstances.

The competencies model, in contrast, seeks to identify abilities needed to perform a job well rather than focusing on personal characteristics such as politeness or assertiveness. The CIPD defines 'competency' as the behaviours that employees must have, or must acquire, to apply to a situation in order to achieve high levels of performance, while 'competence' relates to a system of minimum standards or is demonstrated by performance and outputs (CIPD 2012g). Torrington et al (2014) identify potentially important advantages of referring to competencies in this area noting that they can be used in an integrated way, so that following selection, competencies can be linked with employee development, performance management including appraisal and also reward activities. The key question to ask is what attributes are necessary to undertake roles, or what attributes are shared by the people who have already performed best in the role (Torrington et al 2014).

However, these authors go on to suggest that competency-based approaches can present a barrier to achieving an organisation's equality and diversity objectives. Where innovation and creativity are required, it may be better to recruit people with more diverse characteristics and an inflexible competencies-based approach may restrain this.

Competency-based models have, nonetheless, become increasingly popular in graduate recruitment where organisations in large part make decisions on future potential. Farnham and Stevens (2000) found that at that time managers in the public sector already increasingly viewed traditional job descriptions and person specifications as archaic, rigid and rarely an accurate reflection of the requirements of the job. There is increasing evidence that this popularity is more widespread. The CIPD *Resourcing and Talent Planning* surveys (2008–2015) demonstrate that next to interviews based on the contents of a CV/application form, competency-based interviews were the next most popular method for selecting applicants with nearly 80% of organisations now using competency-based interviews. The use of competencies for recruitment and development may also attract good candidates. PWC, for example, use their ten core competencies to 'sell' their organisation to prospective candidates on their corporate website by getting candidates to 'buy in' to their corporate philosophy. It is suggested that the competence-based model may be a more meaningful way of underpinning recruitment and selection in the current fast-moving world of work and can accordingly contribute more effectively to securing high performance.

9.5.2 FLEXIBILITY AND TEAMWORK

Many commentators refer to significant changes in the world of work and the implications these have for the recruitment and selection of a workforce. As far back as 2003, Searle (p276) noted that:

> Increasingly employees are working in self-organised teams in which it is difficult to determine the boundaries between different job holders' responsibilities. The team undertakes the task and members co-operate and work together to achieve it. Recruitment and selection practices focus on identifying a suitable person for the job, but... isolating a job's roles and responsibilities may be difficult to do in fast-changing and team-based situations.

There is here an implication both that teamworking skills could usefully be made part of employee selection and also that an individual's job specification should increasingly be designed and interpreted flexibly. It can plausibly be posited that we now inhabit a world of work in which unforeseen problems are thrown up routinely and on an ongoing basis and where is seldom time to respond to them in a measured fashion (Linstead et al 2009). In this type of business environment, decisions made can be 'rational' in terms of past practice and events but may in fact be revealed to be flawed or even obsolete when they are made in the new context.

If we accept this analysis of work in the twenty-first century, there is therefore an implication that organisations aiming for high performance may need to use selection methods which assess qualities of flexibility and creative thinking (irrespective of whether they are using a traditional or competency recruitment and selection model). Of course, many jobs may still require task-holders to work in a predictable and standardised way so one should exercise caution when examining this rhetoric. Interestingly, however, recruitment and selection practices should themselves be kept under constant review if we accept the reality of a business world characterised by discontinuous, rather than incremental, change. Organisations also need to ensure they do not infringe upon discrmination laws when trying to create the 'right' teams for their organisation.

 ABERCOMBIE & FITCH

CASE STUDY 9.2

How far should organisations go to attract the 'right' candidates?

Abercrombie & Fitch, the US-based clothing store, is known for its good-looking salesmen who often stroll with their tops off in or outside the shop. The clothing retailer has developed a highly successful market base by attracting (primarily) teenagers into their stores using sophisticated and targeted marketing. This involves the use of young, beautiful and predominantly white models and employees to attract younger customers. Mike Jeffries, head of the retailer, justified recruiting 'good-looking people' because they attracted 'other good-looking people': 'We want to market to cool, good-looking people. We

don't market to anyone other than that,' he said in an interview in 2006.

Over the past few years the company has been embroiled in various law suites across the world for alleged discriminatory recruitment practices based on looks. For example, in 2010 when Abercrombie & Fitch planned to open a store in Aberdeen, the company found itself at the centre of a discrimination row after posters were put up outside the store asking for 'cool and good looking people [to] come and represent our brands'. This came just months after the company was found guilty of harassment and unfair dismissal of Riam Dean, a disabled employee who was required to work in the store room only because of his disability. More recently, Michael Bustin, the pilot of the corporate jet, was fired for being 'untrendy and too old and the French rights watchdog investigated the company in France in 2013 for its recruitment policy in its flagship Champs Elysee store.'

It seems that Abercrombie & Fitch may have had enough of lawsuits as it announced in April 2015 major changes to its recruitment policies in its and its stablemate Hollister stores. The company will no longer be hiring store associates based on looks and body type, gone are the shirtless promotion activities and store staff will be called brand representatives and not models. A company spokesman commented that 'of course we will continue not to discriminate against any protected characteristic'.

Questions

1   Is there really anything wrong with targeting good-looking and cool prospective employees?

2   Would older workers genuinely want to work in an environment where the customers are predominantly teenagers?

9.5.3 RECRUITING IN THE VIRTUAL WORLD

The rise in the use of the Internet was probably the most significant development in the recruitment field in the early twenty-first century and its effects continue to grow apace. Whilst figures vary, recent surveys on recruitment practice (CIPD 2015f and Suff 2013a) continue to show that it is both the most popular and effective method for attracting applicants to organisations. There is mixed evidence that the Internet produces better-quality candidates, but it does deliver more of them, and employers increasingly report that online recruitment makes it easier to find the right candidate (Crail 2007, Suff 2013).

In November 2012 Facebook launched its jobs search app in the USA, which included around 1.7 million job listings. It was set up in conjunction with the US Department of Labor and three non-profit labour organisations as part of its social jobs partnership initiative. Facebook's entry into the 'jobs board' market is a reflection of the growing influence that these professional job sites are having on recruitment activities. In the UK, 80% of employers use job boards to help fill their vacancies; with Total Jobs, Reed and Monster being most popular with employers (Suff 2013b). Job boards, at around 30% usage, are seen as one of the most effective methods of recruitment (CIPD 2015f). The effectiveness and use of professional networking sites (such as LinkedIn) is increasing, with these now being surpassed by the recruitment agencies; wider social networking sites such as Facebook and Twitter are seen as being of limited effectiveness by employers (8%).

The benefits of online recruitment to employers include speed, reduced administrative burden and costs, and no geographical limits. Suff (2013a) also comments that applicants are more likely to know something about the organisation and its work if they use employers' websites. Employers value this aspect of online recruitment as it facilitates company branding. Indeed, developing a positive brand image is now seen as key to recruiting good-quality candidates, and the majority of organisations have made considerable improvements to their corporate websites in the last couple of years in order to improve their brand image (CIPD 2015f).

The benefits to applicants are that it is easier, faster and more convenient to post a CV or search a job site online than to read a selection of printed media (Whitford 2003). This is all very well if you have skills that are highly in demand, but if employers are tending to post vacancies on their own websites then candidates still have to trawl the web in order to find vacancies and even 'web savvy' applicants might be deterred by the perceived impersonal nature of online recruitment. There are, of course, still some people who are either not comfortable using the Internet or do not have ready access to a computer; thus there is still a role for conventional advertising (IDS 2006).

Whatever the pros and cons, online recruitment continues to expand and employers are now combining more traditional methods with online recruitment to attract suitable candidates. Other employers, such as Microsoft, are enhancing brand visibility and credibility by having a wider Internet recruitment presence. Microsoft uses its online tools to impact and influence its public image and reach a broader audience in order to help create a diverse workplace with varied skills and talents. One initiative is the introduction of corporate recruitment blogs. The idea is that potential job candidates may be attracted to the company through what they see on the blog and make contact through the specific blogger, who will initiate the recruitment process on behalf of the company (Hasson 2007).

The Internet is also being used more widely to attract applicants not only to organisations and their brand but also careers, as the following example from the Marriott Hotel Group demonstrates.

 REFLECTIVE ACTIVITY 9.3

My Marriott Hotel – a new way to attract applicants?

In June 2011 the first ever culinary social media game, My Marriott Hotel, was launched on Facebook to promote the Marriott International Inc. Developed in conjunction with Evviva Brands, a specialised brand consultancy, the game was designed as a tool for reaching employment candidates in countries such as China and India, where the service industry is growing, but hospitality is not a highly sought-after career. By managing a virtual hotel kitchen, players are given insights into the world of hotels and a culinary career at Marriott. Three weeks after the launch of the game, the Marriott jobs and careers page on Facebook had received over 10,000 'likes' and the game was being played in over 100 countries. Existing employees were also encouraged to share and promote the game within their own social networks.

The game was developed in response to feedback from surveys and focus groups that suggested that the company needed to enhance its online profile. Despite ranking in Fortuna's 'Best Place to Work', its brand recognition was low in many countries.

Would you be attracted to a career in hospitality management as a result of playing this game?

Adapted from Freer (2011)

9.6 FAIRNESS IN RECRUITMENT AND SELECTION

One factor shared by traditional and competence models of recruitment and selection is that both are framed by an imperative to take on the most appropriate person in terms of their contribution to organisational performance. This is, of course, unsurprising given the preoccupation of organisations in all sectors with meeting objectives and targets. However, when we consider what is meant by making appropriate selection decisions, other factors, including fairness, can also be seen to be important.

Decisions made in the course of a recruitment and selection process should be perceived as essentially fair and admissible to all parties, including people who have been rejected. There is evidence to support the view that applicants are concerned with both procedural justice, that is how far they felt that selection methods were related to a job, and the extent to which procedures were explained to them; and distributive justice where their concern shifts to how equitably they felt they were treated and whether the outcome of selection was perceived to be fair (see Gilliland 1993).

Fairness in this regard can be linked to the actual selection methods used. Anderson et al (2001) found that interviews, resumes and work samples were well-regarded methods, while handwriting tests (graphology) were held in low regard. Personality and ability tests received an 'intermediate' evaluation. This is linked to the concept of face validity: how plausible and valid does the method used appear to the candidate under scrutiny? It is reasonable to suggest that employers should take care in choosing selection methods in order to maintain credibility among applicants as well, of course, as assessing the predictive value of the methods.

Fairness in selection also extends to the area of discrimination and equal opportunities, as we saw in Chapter 4. In the UK, for example, current legislation is intended to make unlawful discrimination on the grounds of age, race, nationality or ethnic origin, religion or belief, disability, gender, marital status and sexual orientation. The law identifies both direct discrimination, where an individual is treated less favourably on the sole grounds of their membership of a group covered in the relevant legislation, and indirect discrimination, which occurs when a provision applied to both groups disproportionately affects one in reality. The Equality and Human Rights Commission highlights headhunting as one area in which indirect discrimination may occur. Headhunters may, in approaching individuals already in jobs, contravene this aspect of the law if existing jobs are dominated by one sex or ethnic group, for example. Compliance with equal opportunities legislation provides one example of performance infrastructure and would, it is surmised, reap business benefits, that is recruiting from the truly qualified labour pool and avoiding negative outcomes such as costly and reputation-damaging legal processes.

High-performance organisations may seek to go beyond the compliance approach and work towards a policy or even strategy of managing diversity (see also Chapter 11). As defined by CIPD (2006), a managing diversity approach:

> is about ensuring that all employees have an opportunity to maximise their potential and enhance their self-development and their contribution to the organisation. It recognises that people from different backgrounds can bring fresh ideas and perceptions, which can make the way work is done more efficient and make products and services better. Managing diversity successfully will help organisations to nurture creativity and innovation and thereby to tap hidden capacity for growth and improved competiveness.

It is thus important to ensure such a policy is operationalised in the field of recruitment and selection, as staff involved in this activity can be said to act as gatekeepers of an organisation.

CASE STUDY 9.3 · RECRUITMENT AT LV=

Liverpool Victoria Friendly Society was founded in Liverpool in 1843 by William Fenton, who started selling burial plans to the poor of the community to ease the burden of this expense for their families. The Society offered access to affordable financial products sold by agents who went door-to-door collecting premiums and building relationships with customers. For a long time Liverpool Victoria was known for its 'penny policies' and for providing savings products for people with limited financial means. Today LV= is still run as a mutual or friendly society, owned by its members rather than shareholders and for the benefit of its members and customers, and sells a range of insurance, investments and retirement products through its 17 offices situated throughout the UK. Great customer service is a fundamental part of the brand, which is focused on doing the right thing for their customers and members. LV= has expanded significantly since it began and now employs over 6,000 people, has 5.5 million customers and over one million members, and is the third largest provider of car insurance in the UK.

Recruiting the right people for this forward-thinking and dynamic business is fundamental to its continued success and to do this LV= has invested heavily in its brand image. In 2007 a major rebranding initiative changed not only the name of the company from Liverpool Victoria to LV=, but also created a strong brand image of the LV= tag line, LV= green heart, and the LV= green chair. Kevin Hough, Group Head of Resourcing at the company, believes that branding is an essential tool for attracting new employees in a highly competitive employment market as this allows prospective employees to get the look and feel of the organisation and engage with the company, its brand, its culture and its values. Kevin adds that branding helps reduce employee turnover because the employer–employee 'fit' is better.

There has also been a significant change in LV='s approach to recruitment. Back in 2008, 83% of hires came via recruitment agencies; this figure is now around 3% and agencies are typically only used for hard-to-fill and senior vacancies. Today LV= attracts most of its candidates through online methods such as the company website, with over 80% of attraction activities conducted this way. Indeed, LV='s careers webpages are not only colourful but give applicants a real insight into what it is like to work for LV=, including such things as employee and job profiles that bring the company to life for prospective applicants. The company also uses Instagram, Facebook, Twitter and LinkedIn as well as more traditional methods such as targeted advertisements in the press and professional publications, and monitors their success rates in order to better

focus its recruitment activities and budgets.

The application process is all online and this allows the company to respond to and process applications quickly. A large proportion of the vacancies are for customer service representatives who work in local offices answering customer telephone calls. Kevin Hough comments that he and his team continually assess the effectiveness of their recruitment activities in order to improve them. One example of this is that LV= has recently developed an online test that simulates a call-centre environment. This allows applicants to experience the work environment of the customer service representative and helps them decide if the job is right for them before they apply; according to Kevin Hough, this has increased the speed of recruitment and improved the quality of applicants to these positions. LV= recruitment methods are clearly working as over 94% of candidates offered jobs join the company.

Questions

1 In today's competitive recruitment market how important is it to use branding to attract good quality applicants? Why/why not?

2 Compare the careers and recruitment pages of LV= and other companies with which you are familiar. What does the information provided tell you about the organisations, their job roles and career prospects?

3 Consider whether you would apply to these companies based on the information provided on their website, why/why not?

4 Review the recruitment methods used by companies with which you are familiar, what evidence is there that recruitment is increasingly an online process?

9.7 THE EXTENT OF PROFESSIONAL PRACTICE

9.7.1 SMALL AND MEDIUM-SIZED ENTERPRISES

There is evidence to suggest that many human resources management (HRM) practices often prescribed in the academic literature are more common in some sectors of business than others and that the small and medium-sized enterprises (SME) group, in particular, are less likely to have in-house HR expertise and sophisticated systems in place (see Cully et al 1999). A study carried out by Cassell et al (2002) in SMEs in the north of England, focused on both the use and perceived value (by employers) of a range of HRM procedures. In the area of recruitment and selection, only 31% of firms in the sample used wide-ranging employee development and recruitment and selection procedures. Interestingly, 38% of the sample questioned said that they did not use recruitment and selection procedures at all. In the companies that did make use of them, 50% found that the procedures helped 'entirely' or 'a lot' in over half of the instances in which they are used. This is some way from the picture of widespread usage and the assumed universal benefits conveyed in some sources.

The reality of the context faced by managers of SMEs will frame their responses in an entirely understandable way, and prescriptive 'textbook-style' approaches may be viewed as inappropriate. It would, of course, be as damaging for SMEs as for any other organisation if a lack of high-quality practices in recruitment and selection were seen to inhibit performance and, indeed, SMEs have often been criticised for a lack of a proactive and integrated approach to managing people. However, any assumption that universally applicable approaches to recruitment and selection are needed may ignore the distinctive processes and practices faced by particular organisations.

 REFLECTIVE ACTIVITY 9.4

Lack of skills a major factor in UK recruitment and selection difficulties

A CIPD survey (2008b) reported that 86% of British organisations were having difficulty filling vacancies in spite of the financial and economic crisis which hit in that year. In part this was the result of a 'skills crunch', with 70% of the research sample citing a lack of necessary candidate skills as the main reason for recruitment dificulties. However, only half of the surveyed companies had a formal resourcing strategy to counter the skills-gap problem and struggled to recruit top talent. The situation has deteriorated further with employers reporting that skills shortages are escalating and in 2014 there was an increase in labour turnover reversing the steady decline observed in previous years (2015). This highlights the need to develop talent management strategies that incorporate not only recruitment but development and retention.

Deborah Fernon of CIPD also pointed to the importance of retention of talented workers noting that 'Organisations should have a look at their learning and development strategies which can help meet business demands in two ways. Firstly those employers who have development opportunities are more likely to stay, which reduces turnover. Secondly, a good learning and development culture will foster a strong employer brand, helping to attract key talent.'

This research highlights the importance of referring to contemporary evdence when analysing recruitment and selection in general terms and also points to the importance of the post-selection phase in retaining staff.

REFLECTIVE ACTIVITY 9.5

Employers are from Mars, Young People are from Venus

Stevens (2013) summarises a CIPD report (CIPD 2013e) highlighting a mismatch between the expectations of employers and young people in the recruitment process. This conflict of understanding hinders entry to the labour market for young jobseekers and contributes to high rates of youth unemployment, according to the report. The mismatch also fuels a 'ticking timebomb' of skills shortages for UK business, who might be unwittingly limiting their access to a diverse group of talent in the 16–24 age group.

Specific problems identifed by the report were:

- 'scattergun' applications from young people who had not researched the organisation and/or tailored their submissions
- a vicious cycle of employers asking for workplace experience in entry-level roles
- lengthy and untransparent recruitment and selection procedures meaning that young applicants were unaware of the stages involved
- poor careers advice and guidance in schools with resultant lack of awareness on how to improve chances of finding a job.

1   What steps can be taken to reduce the mismatch betwen employers and younger job applicants?

2   To what extent is it part of the role of HR managers to address a social problem such as the one identified in this report? Refer to both Chapters 4 and 9 of this book when devising your response.

9.8 RECRUITMENT AND SELECTION: A CONTINGENCY APPROACH

The underlying principle that organisational policies and practices need to be shaped within a particular context is often referred to as the 'contingency approach'. The argument put forward within this viewpoint is that successful policies and strategies are those which apply principles within the particular context faced by the unique organisation.

One example of a 'contingent factor' which can impact upon recruitment and selection is national culture. French (2015) draws attention to important cross-cultural differences in the area, for example, different cultures emphasise different attributes when approaching the recruitment and selection of employees. It is also the case that particular selection methods are used more or less frequently in different societies. For example, in individualistic cultures such as the USA and UK, there is a preoccupation with selection methods which emphasise individual differences. Many psychometric tests can indeed be seen to originate from the US. Furthermore, in a society which emphasises individual achievement as opposed to ascribed status (for example, through age or gender), one might expect a raft of legislation prohibiting discrimination against particular groups. Here the expectation is that selection should be on the basis of individual personal characteristics or qualifications. This may contrast with more collectivist societies, for example China, where personal connections may assume a more prominent role. Bjorkman and Yuan (1999) conducted one of several studies which reached this overall conclusion. It may also be true that selection methods are given varying degrees of face validity in different societies. A CIPD survey (2004b) on graphology discovered that, while relatively few companies in the UK used graphology as a trusted method of selecting employees, its adoption was far more widespread, common and therefore accepted in other countries, including France.

In summary, the contingency approach with the underlying message that managing people successfully depends on contextual factors – 'it all depends' – can readily be applied to the area of recruitment and selection. The increasingly large number of organisations operating across national boundaries; or who employ workers from different cultural backgrounds, can benefit from formulating policies within an awareness of cultural difference.

9.8.1 RECRUITMENT AND SELECTION AND ORGANISATIONAL CULTURE

It is unsurprising that the culture of a particular work organisation will influence selection decisions, with recruiters both consciously and unconsciously selecting those individuals who will 'best fit' that culture. In some organisations recruitment policy and practice is derived from their overall strategy which disseminates values into the recruitment and selection process. Mullins (2007) provided the example of Garden Festival Wales, an organisation created to run for a designated and short time period. This organisation's managers were particularly concerned to create a culture via recruitment of suitable employees.This is an interesting example as this organisation had no prior history and it indicates the power of recruitment and selection in inculcating particular cultural norms.

Other research has demonstrated that individuals as well as organisations seek this 'best fit', providing evidence that many individuals prefer to work in organisations that reflect their personal values. Judge and Cable (1997) and Backhaus (2003) found that jobseekers may actively seek a good 'person–organisation fit' when considering prospective employers. This, of course, provides further support for the processual two-way model of recruitment and selection. However, justifying selection decisions on the basis of cultural fit means that there are ethical issues to consider in terms of reasons for rejection: are organisations justified in determining who does and does not fit? It may be that practical concerns also emerge, for example in the danger of maintaining organisations in the image of current role models – which may be inappropriate in the future. Psychologists have also long recognised the threat posed by 'groupthink' where innovation is suppressed by a dominant group and a 'king's new clothes' syndrome develops, with individuals reluctant to voice objections to bad group decisions.

9.9 CONCLUSION

This chapter indicates the key importance of recruitment and selection in successful people management and leadership. An awareness of issues and concepts within this area are important tools for anyone involved with leading, managing and developing people, even if they are not human resource managers *per se*. A recognition of the importance of this aspect of people management is not new and success in this field has often been linked with the avoidance of critical failure factors including undesirable levels of staff turnover and claims of discrimination from unsuccessful job applicants.

It has been argued here that it is also possible to identify aspects of recruitment and selection which link with critical success factors in the twenty-first-century context, differentiating organisational performance and going some way to delivering employees who can act as 'thinking performers'. It is proposed, for example, that a competencies approach focusing on abilities needed to perform a job well may be preferable to the use of a more traditional matching of job and person specifications. In addition, many organisations may increasingly wish to identify qualities of flexibility and creative thinking among potential employees, although this may not always be the case; many contemporary jobs do not require such competencies on the part of job-holders. It is also the case that organisations should be preoccupied with the question of validity of selection methods, ideally combining methods which are strong on practicality and cost such as interviewing, with other measures which are more effective predictors of performance. It is proposed finally that a managing diversity approach, welcoming individual difference, may enhance organisational performance and create a climate in which thinking performers can emerge and flourish.

However, it is proposed that a contingency approach to recruitment and selection, recognising that organisational policies and practices are shaped by contextual factors, remains valid and that effectiveness in recruitment and selection may vary according to particular situational factors. In this regard it is noted that cultural differences could be an important factor in predicting the relative success of recruitment and selection measures.

 WHY WORK FOR IKEA? PART TWO

CASE STUDY 9.4

Return to the IKEA case study earlier in this chapter.

IKEA puts great stress upon recruiting employees who will complement its organisational culture.

1   What are the potential benefits of selecting a workforce in terms of an organisation's culture?

2   What are the philosophical and practical arguments against selection based on values and work culture?

KEY LEARNING POINTS

1   Managers involved in recruitment and selection of workers have a key gatekeeper role in giving or denying access to work.

2   Effective recruitment and selection is characterised by knowledge of social science topics such as perception.

3   A staged logical approach to recruitment and selection, seeing it as a process, is recommended.

4   We should examine the vaidity of different selection methods.

5   Fairness is a fundamentally important principle reflecting the ethically loaded nature of the activity.

1   Indicate with examples three ways in which recruitment and selection policies and practices can be used by an organisation aiming to develop staff as part of a talent management strategy.

2   Evaluate the evidence regarding the potential validity of biodata and personality assessment as tools for selecting employees.

3   What do you understand by the contingency approach to recruitment and selection? Provide two examples, from academic sources or your own experience, to illustrate this approach.

4   Evaluate the effectiveness of social media and online recruitment methods in comparision to more traditional methods. In what circumstances might more traditional methods be a more effective way of attracting applicants?

Arnold, J., Cooper, C.L. and Robertson, I.T. (2010) *Work Psychology: Understanding human behaviour in the workplace.* 5th ed. Harlow: FT Prentice Hall. Chapter 5 provides a clear and interesting discussion of different selection techniques and their validity.

CIPD (2015) *Resourcing and Talent Planning 2015.* Survey Report. London: CIPD.

Gilmore, S. and Williams, S. (2013) *Human Resource Management.* 2nd ed. Oxford: Oxford University Press. Chapter 5 takes a themed approach to the topic of employee selection.

Thompson, P. and McHugh, D. (2009) *Work Organisations: A critical approach.* 4th ed. Basingstoke: Palgrave Macmillan. In Chapter 19, 'Masks for Tasks', the authors take a critical perspective on the topics of how we assess others' attributes and how such perceptions are used in employee selection.

Developing Employees

ALEX TYMON AND MARGARET MACKAY

LEARNING OUTCOMES

After reading this chapter, you should be able to:

- explain the terms:
  - human resources development
  - learning, training and development
  - career management and career development
  - continuing professional development
- understand organisational and individual needs for training and development activities referring to contemporary debates and research
- identify where responsibility for training and development lies and why this is contested
- critique some of the more common training and development techniques
- explain the difference between career management and career development using three models
- identify the rationale for career development from an organisational and individual view
- evaluate the practice of continuing professional development.

10.1 OVERVIEW

The business case for investment in employee development is built on the need to sustain organisational performance in a dynamic environment. Global demand for a skilled and adaptable workforce of agile employees underpins the workplace as a critical learning environment. Proactive support for training and development can differentiate an organisation by leveraging superior employee performance and engagement and such outcomes can be viewed as an offensive strategy for sustainable success and industry leadership.

This chapter focuses on how individuals and teams can adapt through learning, and expand their skill capability to deliver innovative practices, products and customer commitment. We begin by defining key concepts, before highlighting the evolving emphasis on work-based, self-directed and informal learning – in contrast to more formal traditional training approaches and the impact this has on HRD practitioners. We also review perceptions of learning responsibility and talent development. In this regard we note a shift from corporate career management to individual career development. The chapter ends by considering the promotion of continuing professional development (CPD) as key to building flexibility and agility.

10.2 INTRODUCTION

10.2.1 CREATING THE FUTURE AND ADAPTING TO CHANGE

Top performing companies recognise that investment in employee learning can secure competitive advantage (Stewart and Cureton 2014) and as such dedicate a higher percentage of payrolls (as much as 5%) to training budgets than others (Cranet 2011, *Training Magazine* 2015). The CIPD (2015a) report considerable variation in learning and development budgets but the median figure is just £205 per employee, despite organisations expecting the HRD function to help them capitalise on the improved economic outlook since 2013 (The UK Learning Trends Index 2015). Spend on training does not necessarily equate to the quantity or quality of learning taking place, and it is recognised that increased use of informal learning may be both better and cheaper than traditional formal training. However, it is interesting that during the tough operating conditions following the 2008 global economic recession, many successful and well-known organisations bucked the trend and continued to maintain or even increase their learning, training and development budgets (Freifeld 2009).

The ways in which organisations develop their employees evolve in response to changes in the world of work, and this task is ever challenging as predicting the future is never easy. In the first decade of the twenty-first century there was an explosion in the number of jobs created in knowledge industries at the expense of many traditional roles (DCSF 2009a,b). We have some inkling of which jobs may disappear over the next decade for example: the Next Generation of Marcoms European report (2013) predicts that marketing agencies as we know them will cease to exist within the next ten years and by 2020 there will be five million fewer lower-skilled jobs in the UK than in 2010 (DCSF 2009a,b). Even traditional jobs that remain in name are changing in nature (see Case Study 10.2). But we do not know with certainty which new jobs will be around in 2025. The only certainty is that organisations and employees will need additional and perhaps radically different skills in the future, to meet the needs of 'agile, adaptable and ambidextrous organisations' (CIPD 2015c, p4). This means flexible and innovative approaches to learning and development will be required.

Other persistent themes are increased focus on individual responsibility for learning and a move towards just-in-time, experiential and informal development methods, with many organisations beginning to recognise the value of the 70:20:10 approach (Jennings and Wargnier 2010). In the era of the protean career, it will be increasingly rare for individuals to remain in the same occupation for their whole working life and certainly not in the same organisation. It is estimated that employees starting work in this decade will on average change jobs every two years (DCSF 2009a,b). Thus employment security and success of individuals will increasingly depend upon continuous lifelong learning and skills flexibility. Learning agility and taking responsibility for one's own development will be a necessity, with career management and continuing professional development growing in importance (Ashord and DeRue 2012, Day and Sin 2011, Povah and Sobczak 2010). It is therefore this overriding need to be adaptable and flexible in learning that we have chosen to focus upon in this chapter.

10.3 DEFINITIONS OF KEY TERMS

We begin by defining some key terms which underpin the area of employee training and development.

10.3.1 HUMAN RESOURCE DEVELOPMENT (HRD)

In simple terms, HRD can be viewed as developing the capabilities of people within an organisation in order to improve current and future efficiency, effectiveness and output.

There are many development methods, but the intended outcome is always learning and its application. It is therefore valuable to consider what is really meant by the term 'learning' and how it happens.

10.3.2 LEARNING

Definitions of learning suggest it comes about through the acquisition of new knowledge, skills and attitudes (KSA), through experience or practice and results in a relatively permanent change in behaviour (Stewart and Cureton 2014). A useful description of KSA can be found in Gold et al (2013, ch 5).

However, within this concept of learning there are caveats to consider because they make a difference for the HRD practitioner, three of which are:

Caveat 1: Behaviour change as a result of learning may be neither visible nor sustained.

Employees, via the process of learning, may have changed their capabilities and motivation, but what if the opportunity to use them is missing? Does a lack of visible behaviour change mean that learning has not occurred? For those involved in HRD, this issue of opportunity to use new learning, known as transfer, is a vital part of the process and as such is discussed more fully later in this chapter.

Caveat 2: The change in behaviour as a result of learning may not always be positive or desired.

All learning is not necessarily good for organisations. Employees learn short cuts and poor behaviour when they join an organisation just as quickly as desired behaviours, via informal learning. Formal or conscious learning takes place in the context of organised training or development activities and generates explicit knowledge and skills (overt or conscious knowledge and skills that are capable of being shared with a wider audience). Informal learning occurs through daily activities, leading to 'implicit' or 'tacit' knowledge or skills (those taken for granted or unconsciously held in the minds of employees). It is of course difficult to quantify but Burns (2008) reviewed numerous studies and surmised that the majority of workplace learning is in fact informal and the literature espouses the 70:20:10 model, where only 10% of learning comes from formal training interventions (Jennings and Wargnier 2010). The power of informal learning is an important consideration for those involved in HRD. From a positive perspective it presents opportunities to provide timely and cost-effective learning; from a negative perspective it has the power to undermine formal interventions.

Caveat 3: Not all adult learning requires the acquisition of new KSA.

Much adult learning only requires a slight adaptation or reinterpretation in existing knowledge or skills, but perhaps a more substantial change in attitude. This adaptation, reinterpretation or change is actually more difficult to achieve than providing new KSAs. For example, an update in technology will probably only require a small amount of new knowledge and it may actually require less skill than the old version. A clear example of this can be seen in the world's largest and most productive shipyard, Geoje in South Korea. Here robots now perform highly specialist skills, such as welding, with human employees relegated to lesser tasks. Accepting such deskilling is not always easy for employees and requires a major change of attitude. This is important for those involved in HRD as changing embedded knowledge, skills and attitudes can be difficult and more time-consuming than providing new ones, and may require different approaches. Reflective Activities 10.1 and 10.2 below provide examples of the challenges in getting existing staff to change behaviour compared to training new staff from scratch.

REFLECTIVE ACTIVITY 10.1

Who do you want to fly your plane?

An interesting research study by Hendrick (1983) compared the performance levels of both experienced and trainee pilots in a flight simulator. While both groups performed well when normal stick controls were in operation, the experienced pilots made significantly more errors when the stick controls were reversed. When increasing altitude, the experienced pilots made four times as many errors than the trainee pilots. This study concluded that experience in a task resembled a 'double-edged sword', with lengthy experience resulting in embedded habits. Hendrick concluded that experienced pilots were more vulnerable to error when flying a new type of plane, due to these embedded, and difficult to change, habits. So who would you prefer to fly your plane, and why? The answer may point to complexities and contradictions in the area of learning theory and its practical application.

REFLECTIVE ACTIVITY 10.2

Teaching the teachers?

There is a wealth of research identifying challenges with the implementation and adoption of new technologies; ironically, much of this is situated in the context of education. Moerschell (2009) identifies a number of reasons for resistance to new technologies in academia, most notably the lack of learning motivation shown by established staff. Cohen et al (2005) describe 'old-timers' who employ delay tactics to avoid learning about new technologies, much to the chagrin of newer staff. In reality these educators should be more open to learning than most and responsive to taking on new knowledge and skills, yet in reality it appears changing their attitudes is the stumbling block. However, this phenomenon is not restricted to academia: IT training consultants often report that training new recruits is far easier and quicker than existing staff.

10.3.3 TRAINING, EDUCATION AND DEVELOPMENT

Training, education and development are distinct techniques (McDowall and Saunders 2010) at the disposal of the HRD professional and individual to enable learning. The definitions of these terms can be explained using an analogy:

Schools in the UK are required to provide sex and relationships education to children, and whether or not we approve, most of us have a view of what it involves – in essence the passing on of information, but in a very general way. Most definitions of occupational education concur that it is focused on inputs and therefore has non-specific outcomes. It involves a planned process of providing access to concepts, ideas and knowledge.

However, what if your child was to come home saying, 'We had sex training at school today'? What images could flash through your mind? Such images may be disquieting, because training is very different from occupational education. It is still a formal process, but it is focused on outputs not inputs, such as the output of skill development. To quote Holst (2009, p332), 'training is the mastery of action (practice)... it is about building skills, understanding and confidence of people'.

Consider too your reaction if your child said, 'We had sex development at school today'. What images might be created now? Again, they could well be alarming ones. Development is also focused on outputs and implies getting better at something or becoming more advanced. It is the process of growing an individual and preparing them or equipping them for different, better or bigger things.

The interrelationships between these terms are important. Training has clear outcomes and adopts a shorter-term perspective compared to development, which may also have desired outcomes, but these are likely to be less specific and could adopt a longer-term, nurturing perspective development (McDowall and Saunders 2010). But this argument could depend upon the organisational context. If a medical consultant takes 13 years to qualify, would this be considered to be training or development, or possibly both? What is probably most important is that training, education and development are all considered tools to be used within HRD in order to facilitate learning, and which one to use will depend on the learning need identified.

10.3.4 LEARNING THEORIES OF VALUE TO THE HRD PROFESSIONAL

Many theories are of value when deciding the best methods of facilitating learning, from the early behaviourist theories of the 1920s through to more recent theories of cognitive, social and experiential learning. Most HRD and organisational behaviour textbooks contain accessible chapters on these topics. Illustrative of valuable theories to HRD practitioners facilitating employer-provided training are the following three:

1   Hierarchy of learning/cognitive levels (Bloom 1956, Entwistle 2001), which explain that the deeper the level of learning needed the more time, effort and investment in training is required.

2   Unconscious incompetence to unconscious competence (Howell 1982) informs us that to ensure new skills become second nature to employees, sufficient reinforcement is needed, which necessitates investment in time and resources for practice and feedback. If an organisation is not able or willing to provide the necessary level of investment, then the original need for the training should be questioned.

3   Learning styles theories including cognitive style, learning preferences and learning approaches; referring to the ways people approach tasks, process information and adopt different learning strategies (Wilkinson et al 2014).

Although richly criticised, these may be relevant to both learners and trainers, as they encourage consideration of different learning and training methods. A special edition of the journal of *Education and Training* (2006) Vol 48 No 23, provides several articles that explore the uses and importantly criticisms of learning styles.

REFLECTIVE ACTIVITY 10.3

- Provide three examples of things you have learnt in the last year.
- What opportunities have you had to use this new learning?
- How did this learning occur: was it formal or informal?
- Did the learning involve training, development or education?
- To what extent did you need completely new knowledge, skills or attitudes?
- How easy is it to adapt or change existing attitudes?

10.3.5 IDENTIFYING LEARNING NEEDS

The MAGIC Model (Figure 10.1) is a tool which can be used to identify when it might be necessary for an employee to undergo a learning experience, and therefore it might be prudent to consider carrying out a Training Needs Analysis (TNA) or Learning Needs Analysis (LNA). TNA and LNA is the process of identifying a gap in KSA that can and should be filled by a training, education or development intervention. Techniques for doing so are extensively covered in most training and development textbooks.

Figure 10.1 Times when consideration should be given to LNA

Mandatory skills and knowledge are those required by all new employees and include induction/ orientation, basic job learning to reach competent employee status and legislation-driven learning such as in health and safety_ So whenever a new employee comes on board, thought should be given to learning needs analysis.

Adapting to changes in processes, materials, equipment, demand levels, etc could all lead to a need for new or amended KSA. So whenever any organisational changes are planned, learning needs analysis should be considered.

Growing into a new role or developing for future career moves will inevitably demand changes and development of KSA. So learning needs analysis should be part and parcel of any career planning activities, either company or individually driven.

Improvements to current work practices and activities may require new or amended KSA. So both day-to-day performance management and the formal review process should include learning needs analysis as standard.

Corrective coaching for shortfalls in performance may require an intervention to increase or refocus KSA. So any poor performance or conduct issues may flag up the need for learning needs analysis.

10.3.6 WHO IS RESPONSIBLE FOR PROVIDING LEARNING, TRAINING AND DEVELOPMENT?

Until very recently, it was assumed that employers were totally responsible for employee training and development, and indeed many organisations took this responsibility seriously, providing comprehensive interventions. Training was something that was 'done to employees' because it was good for the organisation, and traditionally employees expected their employers to provide it as part of the psychological contract (see Chapter 7). Many organisations still subscribe to this view, seeing the main role of learning, training and development to 'provide the knowledge, skills and behaviours required for sustainable success' (CIPD 2015a, p7).

But the changing world of work discussed above is changing the extent to which employers invest in or support development of skills that appear to benefit the employee in the main, as they might be wary of making their staff highly attractive to other employers. This means it is increasingly difficult to be clear where responsibility for training and development sits. One way to clarify this might be to try and establish who benefits most from the training and development and then assign responsibility accordingly.

Knowing who benefits from learning may also dictate the best methods to use. Clearly, if the organisation is the main beneficiary, it will be responsible for the training or learning provision which is likely to be more formal and structured. This ensures the organisation can guarantee that those employees who need the learning get it and that records can be kept. On the other hand, if the employee is the main beneficiary, they must take some responsibility for its provision themselves, and because the learning will be more individual in nature, the development techniques may be less structured and formal.

SAP TRAINING

The training consultancy Development by Design has been involved in implementation of SAP in over a dozen organisations in the last decade, by managing and/or delivering training to end users. SAP, the all-encompassing computer management system, has the potential to affect the jobs of virtually all employees in an organisation if their job involves the use of technology, but in different ways dependent on the specifics of their role.

Development by Design has seen very different approaches taken to SAP training design and delivery by organisations. Some adopt a 'sheep dip' approach and provide a standardised programme to all employees regardless of job role, so that most staff receive some training that is not wholly relevant to them. Other organisations make hard decisions about who receives what training, restricting this to 'must have' needs only with no time or resources for 'added value or nice to have' content (Kearns 2005). This results in different training provision by category of employee; for example, finance staff being trained on the SAP finance package, procurement staff receive the supply chain package, HR staff the HR package, etc, with a few staff getting no training at all. A few organisations take a hybrid approach, providing compulsory training for all employees in specific jobs but tailored to their roles and then optional additional generic training for any staff who request it. The two latter approaches, with training targeted at specific job roles, might appear to be more tailored, but there is little evidence of any truly individualised training as all staff in a given category receive the same programme regardless of their past experience or skills.

Interestingly, all organisations have opted for a trainer delivered solution for their SAP implementation, despite the fact that computer skills ought to be a prime candidate for an e-learning solution.

Source: Frances Nichols, Development by Design

Questions

1. What are the potential advantages of the 'sheep dip' approach to training?

2. What are the potential disadvantages?

3. How would you categorise SAP training using the MAGIC model (see Figure 10.1)?

10.3.7 WHO BENEFITS FROM LEARNING?

Few would argue that basic job training for new employees and corrective coaching for employees who are underperforming are anything other than a business necessity. Therefore referring to the MAGIC model (Figure 10.1), mandatory KSA and corrective coaching are very clearly in the interests of the organisation if it wants optimal performance from its employees.

Learning for growth, on the other hand, could be viewed as much more in the interests of the employee, because it will lead to enhanced employment prospects, which could be outside the organisation, even if the organisation will also benefit through more robust succession planning.

Adapting to change, however, could be viewed as in the interests of both organisation and employee, dependent upon the specifics of their job role. In Case Study 10.1, providing tailored training packages relevant to different job roles of employees is seen as essential to both organisation and employees because this is an inherent part of their day-to-day job. However, some organisations chose to provide optional SAP training to all employees. In these cases the training is viewed more as in the interests of the employee.

Similarly, training for improvement (doing tasks above and beyond those expected) could benefit both employee and organisation. For example: enabling a call-centre operative to coach newer colleagues could improve operational performance whilst at the same time affording greater job satisfaction for the employee, and is hence a shared benefit. But getting the same operative to shorten call durations would be of prime benefit to the organisation because this would increase productivity by enabling the operatives to take more calls. Yet for the same reason it could be viewed as of no benefit or even a negative for the operatives themselves, if the only reward for efficiency was more calls.

10.3.8 A PARTNERSHIP APPROACH

These examples begin to demonstrate that deciding who benefits from learning is not as straightforward as at first it may seem. As demonstrated in Figure 10.2, mandatory training and corrective coaching are overtly in the interests of the organisation, but they are also covertly in the interests of the employee, as without them their employment is vulnerable. Growth may overtly be in the interests of the employee, but covertly it also benefits the organisation by providing better skilled and potentially more motivated employees.

Figure 10.2 MAGIC Model: overt benefit or covert benefit

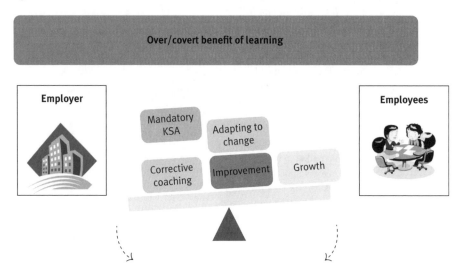

What is becoming increasingly clear is that in the twenty-first century it is unrealistic to expect employers to be totally responsible for HRD activities. It also appears that skills development is much more effective and successful if it is viewed as a partnership approach between the organisation and the learner; this is highlighted by the literature on the move from training to learning.

10.4 FROM TRAINING TO LEARNING

The historical view of training as an activity that is 'done to' an employee is making way for more contemporary approaches which emphasise learning as initiated and driven by individuals. To appreciate this change it is useful to explore the predominant discourse before: systematic training approaches.

10.4.1 THE SYSTEMATIC TRAINING CYCLE

As a result of the Industrial Training Act 1964, a tool heavily promoted in UK organisations was the four-stage Systematic Training Cycle (STC). This promotes systematic use of TNA, design, delivery and evaluation to ensure that training provision is both effective and efficient (the right things are trained in the most appropriate way). Numerous authors provide detailed descriptions of the four stages (Buckley and Caple 2009, Harrison 2009, Reid et al 2007) and the STC is by no means the only systematic model in existence: Cowell et al (2006) provide an overview of seven alternative systematic training models.

Stringent criticisms of the cycle include the fundamental charges that it is unresponsive to change, slow and costly in terms of resources, and more generally, cold and clinical with a basis in scientific management (Rayner and Adam-Smith 2009). Yet despite criticism there are many examples of organisations that continue to use the principles of the STC achieving some excellent results. The annual learning awards use the STC as a foundation of their judging criteria and provide numerous examples of exceptional organisational training and learning interventions (**www.learningandperformanceinstitute.com/events-2/learning-awards/**).

These positive examples could imply that it is not the STC model that is faulty but the way in which it is used, or rather, misused. Design and delivery are the active and visible activities often enjoyed by trainers and recent interest in neuroscience (CIPD 2014b) has increased excitement in these two phases. The less 'sexy' TNA and evaluation are often the poor relations. As Roberts (2006, p489) reports, 'although the [HRD] profession espouses the "bookend" phases of analysis and evaluation, these two phases are the ones that consistently get short changed', yet they are arguably the most important. For example, Iqbal and Khan (2011) present a useful conceptual model of TNA highlighting the value for a whole range of HR activities, including cost savings. Most HRD textbooks explain in detail the importance of proper evaluation of training (see, for example, Gold et al 2013 and Stewart and Cureton 2014) and yet 50% of organisations admit a superficial approach at best with just 7% completing a comprehensive evaluation including return on investment and expectation (CIPD 2015a).

10.4.2 ALTERNATIVES TO SYSTEMATIC TRAINING

It is likely that most organisations would prefer not to provide training: it is not a core activity and requires investment of scarce resources. There are also alternatives; McClernon (2006) lists the following examples:

- recruit people who already have the required KSA
- align compensation and reward more closely with performance to improve motivation
- improve communications and performance management to ensure effort is appropriately focused
- redesign work methods, increase technology or outsource, to reduce or remove the internal need for KSA
- improve work climate to increase engagement and commitment.

Or, as Sutherland (2009) suggests, make better use of the skills that their employees already have.

Supporters of the STC might claim that these activities are not really alternatives but could in fact be outputs of a thorough TNA or LNA, yet again suggesting misuse of the approach rather than the philosophy itself. McGuire and Gubbins (2010) argue that formal learning, such as that supplied by effective use of the STC, is still important in modern organisations. However, even if organisations use the STC effectively, some less formal employee development and learning is still likely to be needed and evidence suggests such approaches are being used more frequently (CIPD 2015a).

REFLECTIVE ACTIVITY 10.4

- How is TNA or LNA carried out in your organisation?
- To what extent does LNA or TNA identify alternatives to learning or training interventions?
- Are there examples when a more thorough LNA or TNA might have prevented the provision of costly training?
- How well is training evaluated in your organisation?

10.4.3 AWAY FROM SYSTEMATIC TRAINING

In recent years interest has moved away from formal training and the 'jug and mug' metaphor (McGuire and Gubbins 2010), in which knowledge and skills, from the overflowing jug of the trainer, is poured into the empty vessel or mug, which is the learner. More attractive to some is the learner-centred approach, or the 'sower and seed' metaphor (McGuire and Gubbins 2010), with learning seen as facilitated growth. Beard and Wilson (2006, p4) propose a model called the 'learning combination lock'. This model highlights the complexity of learning for individuals and the multitude of factors which can affect its success, demonstrating how the 'one size fits all' or 'sheep dip' approach of traditional training cannot hope to meet the needs of individual learners. The suggestion therefore is to move from formal, instructor-led content-based interventions to self-directed, work-based, informal process (CIPD 2015b). This supports the idea of andragogy by Knowles (1990), who speculated that adult learners such as employees within organisations need much more involvement in the learning process for it to be effective. And research shows that competitive advantage can be gained when individuals are co-producers of their learning (Drucker 2005, Sloman 2007).

10.4.4 TOWARDS SELF-DIRECTED LEARNING

Research into self-directed learning attempts to quantify the steps needed to encourage this approach. Of interest to HRD professionals may be the paper by Ellinger (2004) which discusses the implications for integrating self-directed learning into HRD practices. One particularly important aspect is a supportive environment and organisation and culture which facilitate the following:

- tolerance for errors and experimentation, using everyday work as an opportunity to learn
- participative leadership, delegation and open communication
- individual motivation and commitment to learning
- a fit with business goals
- systems that encourage teamworking.

(Confessore and Kops 1998, CIPD 2005a, Harrison 2009)

REFLECTIVE ACTIVITY 10.5

- How does your organisation measure up against these requirements for a self-directed learning culture?
- What do you see as the downsides to self-directed learning?
- How motivated and committed are you to self-directed learning?

10.4.5 THE POWER OF SOCIAL AND GROUP LEARNING

Increased interest in self-directed approaches and just-in-time learning as opposed to traditional training has placed renewed focus on social learning theory and practice (CIPD 2015c). This theory argues that new behaviours are learnt through and with others (Bandura 1977). Social learning is particularly powerful in connection with group and team-based learning, which are concisely reviewed by Stewart and Cureton (2014). These methods enable organisations to leverage both the explicit and tacit knowledge and skills of their employees. This can be very powerful for organisations needing to be fast and flexible in anticipating and adapting to change (CIPD 2015c), as well as motivational for employees who consistently report their skills are under-utilised (Sutherland 2009). Although social learning can and does happen successfully informally, successful organisations are more likely to facilitate this through developing the learning agility of their employees and other interventions such as promoting action learning (Revans 1982).

 JOHN LEWIS PARTNERSHIP (JLP)

CASE STUDY 10.2

JLP has 93,000 employees, known as partners, generally accepted as being some of the best in the retail sector. With excellent product knowledge and exemplary customer service skills, partners made a visit to a John Lewis store a pleasure. But, the retail sector has seen a revolution, driven by development of online trading so that even for JLP, web orders now make up one-third of sales. Five years ago the focus for JLP staff training was product knowledge, but now technology means staff can acquire this very easily. For example, partners are given tablets on the shop floor so they can brush up on knowledge in less busy periods. JLP is also a big advocate of the 70:20:10 principle, believing active, informal, social and on-job learning can bring benefits for all. This just-in-time approach means training is always up to date and partners engage in learning that is relevant to them and the business.

The role of the JLP learning and development team has also been revolutionised, with its focus now being on learning agility. Because of the fast pace of change in the sector, they believe teaching partners to learn will help both them and the business in the future and they measure their success on how quickly partners can acquire new skills.

They take a 'lifelong' approach to learning and feel responsible for the continuation of partners' employment by making sure they are equipped with the right skills and capabilities.

To develop the right learning culture the learning and development team has provided a self-service system, allowing partners to access training on demand. They do not start with the top talent and work down; any partner can use JLP's mentoring database and online courses from Ashridge Business School.

Source: *People Management* (June 2015).

Questions

1   What impact might the changes in learning and development culture and practices at JLP have on learning transfer?

2   How might your organisation learn from the JLP approach?

3   What are the potential disadvantages of the JLP approach?

4   What are the potential challenges with relying on technology for learning solutions?

10.4.6 DEVELOPING LEARNING AGILITY

Case Study 10.2 provides a practical example of how JLP has moved from training to learning approach. It emphasises how this involves helping individuals 'learn how to learn', and the concept of ownership for personal development – a recurring theme of this chapter. An analogy for this type of sustainable development could be:

> Give a man a fish and you feed him for a day. Teach a man how to fish and you feed him for life (attributed to Lao Tzu the founder of Taoism).

If learners can develop learning agility, not only will organisations find it easier to train and develop them, but the individuals themselves will find it easier to embark on the journey of lifelong learning. The twin themes of contribution to organisational effectiveness, and personal development, have made lifelong learning a topical concept and a theme which is continued later in this chapter. The focus on moving from training to learning leads one to consider the methods of development which might enable this to happen.

10.5 CHOICE OF LEARNING AND DEVELOPMENT TECHNIQUES

Choosing development techniques – and the choice is vast – will be influenced by a number of factors such as the extent and type of learning need, organisational culture, resources available and learner-related factors including learning theories and models, discussed earlier in the chapter.

Peter Honey (1998) describes over 100 different techniques in his *Manager's Guide to Work-based Learning* text. Cheetham and Chivers (2001) list almost as many in their paper 'How professionals learn'. Both are useful sources of ideas for those planning development activities. In addition, many textbooks have useful chapters for those wishing to design and deliver learning interventions (see, for example, Stewart and Cureton 2014). But evidence shows that some techniques are more widely used than others and some are regarded as being more effective than others. On-job training is still the most commonly used intervention (48%) closely followed by in-house development programmes (46%) and coaching by line managers or peers (CIPD 2015a) and effectiveness ratings of these are high. Formal off-job training interventions are still widely used in many organisations with 27% citing them as their most common method (CIPD 2015a) but effectiveness ratings are lower.

The popularity and effectiveness of on-job and in-house methods is almost certainly due to the in-built ability to practice and gain feedback in real time. This links into learning theory (Howell 1982), which shows that practice and feedback are essential for new skills to become unconsciously embedded. But the situation is more complex. E-learning has long been heralded as the ultimate individualised, learner-centred technique with inbuilt practice and immediate feedback. Many years of CIPD surveys have reported that organisations intended to increase the use of such technologies. Yet in 2015 only 12% of respondents regarded it as an effective learning method (CIPD 2015a) with managers reporting that 'it was not a substitute for face to face or classroom learning' (McNair 2012, p10).

10.5.1 IS TECHNOLOGY THE FUTURE?

Technology certainly has a role to play in increasing effectiveness of learning. It has the potential to reach employees in the 24/7 global world we live in and for the increasing number of jobs that are technology-based, it is an obvious solution, or is it? Think back to our definition of learning above: yes, technology can provide access to huge amounts of current information or knowledge, but are new skills or attitudes developed? And does this result in a relatively permanent change in behaviour? Not necessarily. In the Case Study 10.2, technology has been embraced at JLP, with partners able to update their knowledge at any time. But the culture change in the organisation, a focus on developing learning agility and a learning and development team who are confident and capable with technology has accompanied this and is probably the reason for success. There is certainly some evidence to suggest that not all organisations are likely to see such value from technology-based solutions. Case Study 10.1 is an interesting example, where it would be assumed that an e-learning solution would be used, but in reality organisations and employees want a traditional trainer-led approach. The CIPD (2015a) reports that although 75% of organisations believe technology-based solutions could be helpful, only 24% of learning and development professionals feel confident with them. If organisations are going to reap the huge potential benefits of future generations of mobile technologies, then these professionals need to build their own competence and confidence first to be both able to use the technology, but more importantly recognise the support needed to make sure real learning and its transfer occurs.

10.5.2 IMPORTANCE OF THE TRANSFER OF LEARNING

Whatever development technique is selected, one essential factor for effectiveness is the transfer of learning. Indeed, most of us could cite examples of training interventions that have been enjoyed, the participants having changed their KSA, but which led to no marked change in performance when back at work. Consider the manager who returns from a two-day management skills workshop brimming with enthusiasm to use new project management techniques or to start coaching and mentoring their team, but within days the enthusiasm is gone and the new techniques put on the back-burner. This could be due to lack of transfer, which Yorks et al (1999, p56) tell us 'has long been the Achilles' heel of HRD'. There are multiple reasons for this lack of transfer: time pressures, resource shortages and culture mismatch being just a few. One prime reason is how much the newly trained employee is encouraged to use his or her new knowledge or skill, a real issue with off-job formal training. Transfer is far more difficult to achieve, with such traditional training, where trainees undergo a 'one size fits all' intervention, not tailored to them and lacking the realism of their everyday work experience. This could be key to why on-job, self-directed, social and team learning are thought more effective, because they address this issue: learning is just-in-time, completely tailored with in-built practice and feedback.

 REFLECTIVE ACTIVITY 10.6

Think about training programmes you have attended. How was learning transfer facilitated?

From your experience of work-based development and training, what methods are employed to assist in translating experiential and other learning into relevant workplace activity?

10.6 CAREER AND PROFESSIONAL DEVELOPMENT

The debate about responsibility for learning leads on to a discussion about investment in career and professional development. This is the focus of the rest of this chapter.

10.6.1 WHAT IS A CAREER?

The term 'career', in its most general sense, is interpreted as upward progression through a series of job roles with increasing levels of responsibility or managerial control. In essence, a career is a structured sequence of work experiences that promote employee development and advance organisational capability.

10.6.2 WHAT DOES A CAREER LOOK LIKE?

The concept of a career provides a useful focus for employment and future goals that drive a sense of purpose. There is no doubt that a perspective on career significance is uniquely personal and for some people of resounding meaning: 'careers are what we judge our lives by' (Inkson and Arthur 2001, p48).

By contrast, some individuals see employment as a connection of different work projects, locations and even job roles in increasingly competitive global labour markets. For example, research by the Resolution Foundation tracks the rise of self-employment with individuals 'forced to go it alone' (D'Arcy and Gardiner 2014, p3). Which view do you take?

REFLECTIVE ACTIVITY 10.7

1 How does a career differ from a job?

2 What are the distinctive features of a career?

3 What does a career mean to you?

Individuals often make sense of their employment history through a retrospective construction of career decisions. These career stories may grant coherence to a serendipitous employment experience of different roles or sectors. Media coverage of overnight career success often belies the years spent toiling for recognition. Even Harrison Ford, known for his remarkable good fortune in transitioning from carpenter to leading actor after a chance encounter with the film producer George Lucas, had previously spent 15 years as a cabinet-maker trying to start an acting career.

The rise in different employment contractual relationships, as highlighted in the introduction, through increasing part-time working, outsourcing and the use of flexible working arrangements, has altered assumptions about careers (Greller 2006, Harrison 2009). Hall (2004) declared the career in terminal decline, yet there is limited evidence of the widespread abandonment of career structures in organisational practice (Sullivan and Baruch 2009, Baruch 2004, 2006). The relevance of career models is shifting in a global economy where diverse career patterns often transcend occupational and national boundaries. The internationalisation of labour markets places more demands on the HR function to operate strategically within these business trends. It also offers significant opportunities for HR specialists to advance the professionalisation of the HR field and respond to the organisational challenges of talent management and development (Farndale et al 2010b, Mackay 2015b).

10.7 CONTEMPORARY CAREER MODELS

Three prominent career concepts follow: the traditional career, the boundaryless career and the self-managed career. These academic constructs provide a useful framework to explore current debates around career development.

10.7.1 TRADITIONAL CAREER

The image of a traditional career is of a pattern of jobs within a single organisation that follow a linear and predetermined path. This is often depicted as a hierarchical ladder that an employee climbs acquiring greater levels of expertise and managerial accountability (see Figure 10.3). In this model the employer assumes a paternalistic role and employees' self-worth is defined by the organisation (Tams and Arthur 2010, Sullivan and Baruch 2009).

Figure 10.3 Traditional career ladder

Key characteristics of a traditional career structure are specific entry criteria linked to education and qualification attainment, a planned and co-ordinated structure of job experience, and a coherent reward strategy. Reward is provided through the extrinsic acceleration of pay, increased benefits and role seniority. Additionally, intrinsic rewards flow from public recognition of an individual's promotion and achievement.

10.7.2 TRADITIONAL CAREER LADDER

Employee success is measured in progressive movement up the career structure that mutually satisfies organisational objectives and individual career growth. Examples of careerists flourishing within a single organisation are firstly Lord Browne, who began work with the oil giant BP as a graduate trainee and rose through the organisation hierarchy to become CEO, and secondly Sir Terry Leahy, who joined Tesco as a management trainee and similarly worked his way up to CEO within the supermarket chain. Such examples indicate the value of company-specific knowledge to career progression, and are a potent indicator of individual worth to the business.

This traditional model is equally valid within the public sector (Baruch 2004a). The employer provides relative security of employment and career advancement in exchange for superior performance and firm allegiance to the organisation. However, the removal of many mid-level positions has affected the available rungs in the career ladder.

10.7.3 BOUNDARYLESS CAREER

The unpredictability of lifetime employment has affected expectations of a stable career pattern. The concept of career-growth without limits of a single company is labelled boundaryless (Tams and Arthur 2010). The boundaryless career crosses multiple companies, sectors and locations which differs from a traditional career path; for example, a steady path of development in the Royal Navy from junior rating to senior commander of a ship. The boundaryless career is multidirectional shaped by opportunity. An individual creates a career in various organisations through a process of development along a path of experience (Sullivan and Baruch 2009). An individual example is Adam Crozier, who in public interviews has joked that his career path might suggest someone who doesn't quite know what he wants to do. Crozier began employment as a graduate trainee at Mars Pedigree Petfood, and has moved across diverse organisations from the *Daily Telegraph* to Saatchi & Saatchi, to the Football Association, to Royal Mail and to chief executive at ITV. Crozier's industry-switching is connected by the transfer of integrated business and change management skills.

10.7.4 SELF-MANAGED CAREER

The self-managed career emphasises the individual as master of his or her own destiny rather than the organisation. Hall (2004) developed the concept of a protean career, so-called as Proteus, the Greek god of the sea, changed form to match the environment. Following the analogy, as the business environment evolves and requirements change, individuals must similarly adapt by renewing their skills and updating their knowledge. Success is gauged by the individual's vision and values as the career contract is with oneself; an alignment of personal aspirations and work (Hall 2004). A Protean career is characterised by continuous learning. Sir Richard Branson, founder of the Virgin Group, is arguably Britain's best-known example of such adaptation. Branson has directed Virgin's evolution from music to airlines, shops, telecoms, drinks and even bridalwear.

Similarly, a portfolio career is where an individual makes a deliberate choice of personal independence, working on a variety of contracts with clients and organisations. The freelancer identifies with clients, groups or collaborators, and this working identity forms a career (Ibarra 2004). Individual investment in project activities, learning development and the perceived value of employees' knowledge competence is termed 'career capital' (Maurer and Chapman 2013, Mackay 2015a). Review the online report, 'Career Capital', by Accenture (2014), available at **www.accenture.com/IWD2014**

In a dynamic business environment an economic view of development makes use of a set of competencies to shape and influence effective career management (Seibert et al 2001). These are framed as open career questions.

- Know why – values, attitudes, internal needs, identity and lifestyle
- Know how – career competencies: skills, expertise, capabilities, tacit and explicit knowledge
- Know whom – networking, relationships, how to find the right people
- Know what – opportunities, threats and requirements
- Know where – entering, training and advancing
- Know when – timing of choices and activities.

Another perspective on career is one that sees learning as a collection of knowledge gained from work experiences over time that enables people to adapt their behaviour and career strategy (Tams and Arthur 2010, Sullivan and Baruch 2009). This collected learning constitutes a career rather than the biographical succession of work experiences. Sir Alan Sugar, the successful entrepreneur, when asked for his personal career advice emphasised that experience accumulated is what matters. From this perspective every worker has a career built through successive jobs of his or her working life. Yet there is tension in such a view, because it implies that all individuals are equally capable of deriving skill enrichment from accumulated experience. Individual entrepreneurs such as the easyJet founder, Sir Stelios Haji-Ioannou, demonstrate that some are more skilled than others in making use of their experience.

10.7.5 WHAT IS THE BUSINESS RATIONALE FOR CAREER MANAGEMENT?

The rationale for career management is the effective nurturing of talent, specific company knowledge and the successive deployment of workforce capabilities to best serve the business. Companies such as Waitrose, the John Lewis Partnership, Caterpillar and the Hilton Group spend considerable time, money and effort turning fresh recruits into loyal company men and women who will internalise and promote organisational values. Although 'career management' and 'development' are often used interchangeably, they are differentiated by career ownership and direction.

Organisations rely on talent development and nurturing this human capital of individual employee development can add value to the company's ability to compete in global markets. Thunnissen et al (2013, p1757) argue that: 'Talents are a long-term corporate asset and should be treated like one'. This pinpoints the business rationale for career management as harnessing employee skills and knowledge capability boosts organisational productivity and success. Features of systematic career management include succession planning, formal mentoring arrangements and secondments. Effective career coaching embedded in the performance review process links an individual's development planning to the organisational charting of future resource allocation. Review the CIPD research insight *Managing careers for organisational capability* (2011) for further examples of career management.

Organisations invest in employees' education providing work experiences that expand competences and target development through in-house training and corporate universities. Return on this career investment is assessed against expected career trajectories. For example, in a global bank executive officers' career progress was measured against a predicted speed of reaching branch manager position within a number of years. If this position had not been reached, early severance was encouraged. This demonstrates the organisation's risk management of a career to assess whether an individual remains an evolving asset.

Many organisations need to build expertise through successive job experience and exposure to distinct environments. For example, the medical and legal profession demand intensive training and applied practice to achieve operational competence. Organisational investment in developing pilot skills may be questioned, as technological advances and auto-piloting have decreased individual skill reliance. However, the emergency US Airways jet landing on the New York Hudson River in 2009 dramatically demonstrates the value of an individual pilot's seasoned expertise. The pilot Sullenberger, a captain of 29 years' airline experience, saved the lives of all 150 passengers and crew members. By contrast, when the cruise liner Costa Concordia struck rocks in 2012 the evacuation training and leadership capability of the captain Francesco Schettino was severely criticised and charged with a range of offences including manslaughter and abandoning ship.

Although the concept of career management is straightforward, the execution may be more complex. Career oversight is often shared by different business units, managers and mentors and the locus of control for career management may vary in practice. Consider this employee's view of a career structure: 'The career management is really about who knows who at the moment. There's no real formal structure to the career management' (CIPD 2010c).

- What are the career interventions in your organisation?
- Who develops the career path?
- What navigates you through the organisational maze?
- What are the challenges of developing career paths in distinct operating areas?

There is an apparent tension between organisations' promotional use of career opportunity to attract new recruits and the reality of what a promised career delivers. An employment climate affected by recession has further obscured career structures through recruitment and promotion freezes. Read the following example (CIPD 2010c) and consider the implications for an individual employee:

> The career path that we are describing for the future is more come to us, learn some things, gain some skills, go somewhere else, move on and maybe rejoin us later in your career as a senior leading scientist.

This is an opaque route and places the map firmly in the hands of the individual protagonist to chart his or her course. In addition, mergers and acquisitions can affect a maturing career plan that runs counter to the changed requirements of the business. Pressing business demands may include sourcing external expertise to find the right skill sets. If employers are ceding control of career management, then increasingly individuals are encouraged to be proactive in their own career development. The career literature emphasises individual agency in career planning and self-directed learning which assumes the individual will continue to develop their core competencies and update their skills. One example that synthesises the literature perspective of self-directed learning is a career management skills framework; see Hirschi 'The career resources model' (2012, p376).

Career development marks a shift from directing to enabling development that increases or sustains employees' current productivity. Career development is a critical lever in attracting, engaging and retaining talent. As noted earlier, economic fluctuations demand career resilience (Sullivan and Baruch 2009). Resilience is acquired by a constant updating of skills that enables employees to anticipate change and remain competitive (Mackay 2015a). This assures an individual's employability within the company and outside (Ghoshal et al 1999). Positive career development resonates with the need for continual learning, as highlighted in protean and self-managed careers, and summarised in the CIPD model shown as Figure 10.4.

Figure 10.4 Rationale for career development

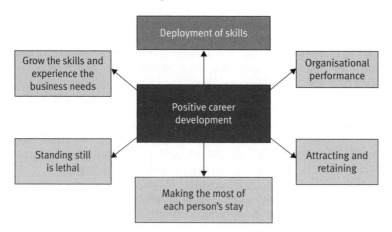

Source: CIPD (2005a)

Career development is portrayed as symbiotic, offering the potential for both individual career advancement and the enhancement of organisational capability. The CIPD depicts this as positive career development.

The extent of the employer's responsibility in providing career development tools, opportunities and funding is debatable. Although it is assumed that HR practitioners will provide career support, this may vary in practice. 'HR departments are, of course, heavily involved in giving career advice and information to individuals, and assessing and advising on their development needs' (CIPD 2009a). Moreover, financial results or conflicting business priorities may overtake development needs. Similarly, line managers differ widely in their competence level as career coaches, and in their enthusiasm for acting as organisational guides. Factors critical for employee career development support and success are summarised below:

- managerial support
- mentoring guidance
- peer and organisational network support
- organisational investment
- opportunity for extending skills
- inclusive access to development experience
- diversity of staff profile in expected career progress
- harmony of business needs and individual aspirations.

Alternatively, an individual not finding opportunities or support may encounter barriers that limit career growth. Line managers may inhibit career movement, as the employee seeking guidance may become a rival for promotion. Research by the Work Foundation (2010) indicates that access to development and training opportunities is skewed, with managers and professionals five times more likely to receive work-based training than people with no qualification or in an unskilled job. Few employers regard investment in training and employee development as similar to long-term physical assets, although in a knowledge economy the potential gain in organisational currency is significant.

10.8 CAREER DEVELOPMENT STRUCTURES

Career success is in the eye of the beholder with progression implicit in the psychological contract. Boxall and Purcell (2011) argue that the construct of a deal is in the mind and subjective interpretation of individual employees and therefore cannot be viewed as contractual. Career success is complex because career aims change over time. Employee ambitions change with age, family life and employment circumstances (Maurer and Chapman 2013). Success may be measured in progress consistent with personal aspirations, the achievement of professional excellence or preference for meaningful work (Sullivan and Baruch 2009).

For some it is the extrinsic reward of power and remuneration, for others reward through internal feelings of worthiness and achievement (Baruch 2006). Line managers and HR practitioners need to provide clear plans for career progression so that employees are aware of what is required to gain career advancement.

Employee expectations may be satisfied through the trade-off of long journeying hours for the future assurance of career uplift – for example, to achieve partnership status in accountancy firms. Yet the 'big four' accounting firms, Deloitte Touche Tohmatsu, Ernst & Young, KPMG and PricewaterhouseCoopers, all have predominantly male senior partner staffs. Professional women spend more time working flexibly, and have less linear career paths. Moreover, although the organisation wants to nurture talent and fast-track potential leaders, it may also need to balance this growth with the intake of fresh blood. For example, the fashion house Givenchy broke from reliance on in-house expertise by hiring the young designer Alexander McQueen to reinvigorate the company's style.

As discussed earlier, the ability of HR professionals to expand their expertise drives business expectations and key areas for specialist knowledge are identified as: data analytics; recruitment and resourcing; organisation design; and reward; see *Personnel Today* (2014) 'Four areas to grow your HR career in 2014'. In short, what matters for career growth is that HR professionals broaden their business knowledge and acumen across the organisation.

Nonetheless, career promotion may be a simple case of managerial expediency in response to operational or political pressures rather than reward for effective on the job performance.

Thus three pertinent questions emerge about career development structures:

- Is there a match between the organisation's needs and the individual's aspirations?

- Is the career framework transparent to all?
- Can the career offer remain valid and affordable for the business?

10.9 THE OWNERSHIP OF CAREER DEVELOPMENT

Career ownership revolves around control and direction; and perceptions of career-orientation and control may stem more from individual mindset than external environment (Briscoe and Hall 2006). Yet there is potential ambiguity and competing expectations in the purpose of career development for the organisation and for the individual; can personal growth and development readily transfer to corporate advantage?

International career development may call for distinct approaches in managing across borders. Expatriation is managed according to the organisational strategy for particular expertise – for example, international career structures at the oil company Shell, the Foreign and Commonwealth Office, and Nestle. Research in international careers has found that the primary motives for going to work abroad are personal interest, a search for new experiences and an interest in the external environment (Suutari and Brewster 2000). Consequently, there may be a mismatch between individual values and organisational pressure that provoke a career crisis. For example, a BBC journalist may refuse a political assignment in Israel when the individual's interests are focused on social development in Brazil. These individual career aspirations can change with family circumstances, educational requirements, health, financial commitments and personal interests. Moreover, for businesses in recession an increased pressure on developmental budgets may restrict investment in career development to employees identified as talent; and members of a talent pool. For example, BT has a workforce Talent Deal which sets out the expectations of contributions from talent pool members in return for the support they receive in career planning.

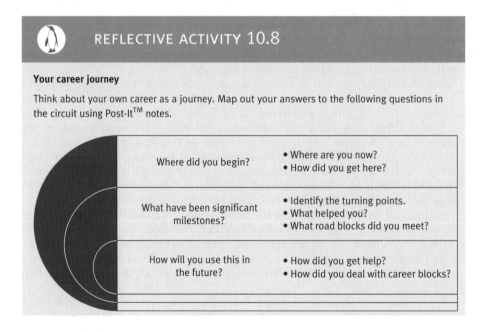

REFLECTIVE ACTIVITY 10.8

Your career journey

Think about your own career as a journey. Map out your answers to the following questions in the circuit using Post-It™ notes.

Where did you begin?	• Where are you now? • How did you get here?
What have been significant milestones?	• Identify the turning points. • What helped you? • What road blocks did you meet?
How will you use this in the future?	• How did you get help? • How did you deal with career blocks?

A self-managed career demands high levels of self-awareness and personal responsibility (Hall 2004). It also makes significant demands on an individual's ability to adapt in terms of performance and learning, as evidenced in this statement:

Our graduate scheme will give you everything you need to build the kind of career you want. But it's up to you how it goes. You'll be the one in charge, putting forward your ideas, taking on responsibilities and making choices about how you get the job done (IBM Graduate Scheme 2013).

Certain individuals have a greater tolerance for ambiguity that suits an entrepreneurial approach to career invention. For others, self-directed career management is a burden resulting in mounting stress levels (Cooper 2005). This reveals why many employees wish to keep the traditional psychological contract for the job security that it offers (McDonald et al 2005). Workers at Cadbury's chocolate factory in Bourneville may have believed their specific company knowledge and experience would secure future employment until Kraft's takeover undermined such prospects.

Nonetheless, there is debate as to how much individual development and learning can be effectively harnessed by the organisation, and managed as an organisational resource (Thunnissen et al 2013). The unpredictability of organisational career paths shifts the emphasis to individuals' personal investment through continuing professional development.

10.10 THE CONCEPT OF CONTINUING PROFESSIONAL DEVELOPMENT

Continuing professional development (CPD) has been defined as a constant updating of professional knowledge throughout one's working life by means of systematic, ongoing, self-directed learning (CIPD 2012e). This professional enrichment is depicted in Figure 10.5.

Figure 10.5 Professional expansion

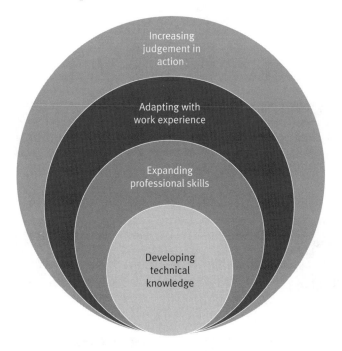

10.10.1 UNDERSTANDING CPD

CPD promotes the ongoing attainment of effective job performance through targeting current and emerging development needs. There are diverse definitions of CPD which often overlap with 'principles of lifelong learning, professional education, personal development, career advancement and workplace learning' (Mackay 2015b, p2). In short, CPD represents good practice and represents a professional value for HR practitioners. It can be argued that the product of CPD is essentially 'personal property'. Inkson and Arthur (2001) support the validity of self-interested professional development in what they termed career capitalism, that is, the return on investment in a career. The understanding is that by recognising and taking advantage of development opportunities this will lead to career success (Tams and Arthur 2010, Briscoe and Hall 2006). As a result an individual who understands the marketplace, and can adapt to what is in demand, can increase the yield on personal capital.

Continuing professional development can therefore be seen as a virtuous circle of improvement (see Figure 10.6). We can assume that development momentum is generated by individual and economic self-interest to improve professional capability and performance (Megginson and Whitaker 2007).

However, development improvements may be difficult to evidence in soft skills, such as influencing skills, and increased agility in mediating people management issues of conflict. This may be one explanation as to why many performance reviews annually record the same developmental needs. How can the virtuous circle of continuous development focus on the required specific competencies that will matter in the future? For example, semi-skilled manufacturing workers who need to acquire advanced digital skills that are in demand. Increasingly HR professionals are expected to meet the international challenges of sourcing, managing and retaining talent in globally competitive markets (Farndale et al 2010b). Consequently for HR specialists this pivotal role in talent management within the organisation underlines the individual need to sustain organisational trust and collective credibility through ongoing professional development.

Figure 10.6 Virtuous circle of improvement

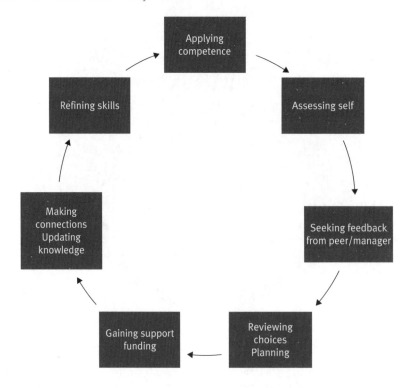

As noted earlier, the Leitch Report (2006) recognised the importance of skills for productivity, and noted that gaps in learning and skills were a collective reason for organisations' failure to compete in global markets. Furthermore, the Department of Innovation, Universities and Skills identified skills and learning gaps as the primary cause for individual lack of participation in economic activity (Gold et al 2010). This corroborates continuing professional development as an organisational defensive strategy against the prospect of sector decline or industry changes. In addition, CPD offers the protection of employability for the individual.

REFLECTIVE ACTIVITY 10.9

1   Provide examples of CPD from your own experience.

2   What has this learning enabled you to do differently?

3   Who, in your opinion, is the prime beneficiary of this development?

10.10.2 EVALUATING CPD

Given organisational investment in training and education, the business wants to harness professional learning to affect improved performance. As discussed above, evaluating development of learning and soft skills is a complex challenge. Nonetheless, as CPD evolves there is greater recognition of the importance of professional development to support longer working lives and sustain employability. The CBI's Education and Skills Survey (2015, p10) reports: 'most jobs created in the decade to 2022 will be high-skilled ones – filling these and improving the UK's productivity track record will mean many people already at work will need to add to their skills'. This emphasis on continuous development for skills currency is central to enhanced capability in adapting to fast-changing business environments. CPD practice underpins the expansion of skills, knowledge and competence to ensure talent growth in a global context. For as the CBI (2015, p11) point out: 'across the world current and emerging competitor nations are looking to grow talent through their education and training systems and strengthen the skills that contribute to competitiveness, innovation and growth'.

10.10.3 CPD AND PROFESSIONAL BODIES

The revised CIPD Code of Professional Conduct (July 2012c) states the expectation of 'a firm commitment to continuous professional development'. The professional body highlights the critical role of CPD in ensuring human resource specialists strengthen their professional agility through continuous learning. Many professional bodies enforce the practice of CPD as a condition of active membership, and to ensure consumer protection. Professional status is accredited, and assures the public of their role as a legitimised expert. In certain cases CPD is a legal requirement and represents individual professional liability: for example, the Association of Chartered Certified Accountants (ACCA).

Review the following example of CPD from the Royal College of Veterinary Surgeons (source: **www.rcvs.org.uk**):

The RCVS Guide to Professional Conduct makes it very clear that veterinary surgeons have a responsibility to ensure that they maintain and continue to develop their professional knowledge and skills. CPD is therefore the personal obligation of all responsible veterinary surgeons and should be seen as the continuous progression of capability and competence.

The recommended minimum CPD is 105 hours over three years with an average of 35 hours per year. It is appreciated that most veterinary surgeons will do considerably more than this.

By contrast, the Chartered Management Institute declares a broad approach to CPD (**www.managers.org.uk**): 'The Institute is not prescriptive as to the content, approach or effort an individual member puts into their development but offers advice and practical support.'

REFLECTIVE ACTIVITY 10.10

Review a range of professional bodies for examples of CPD practice. You might want to look at the Royal Institute of British Architects (RIBA), the Institute of Fisheries Management (IFM) or the Chartered Institute of Environmental Health (CIEH).

Then, in a study group, answer the questions below; compare your findings on CPD requirements and methods of recording evidence.

1   What are the advantages of identifying specific CPD categories?

2   Discuss the possible limitations of these approaches.

Table 10.1 gives an example from the Chartered Institute of Plumbing and Heating Engineering (CIPHE) of the requirement for a plumbing engineer to log 30 hours of CPD annually (**www.ciphe.org.uk**).

Table 10.1 Sample CPD hourly log

CPD category	Maximum hours for CPD claim
Training courses and workshops	30 hours
Conferences and seminars/lectures	14 hours
Attending exhibitions	8 hours
Technical writing	15 hours or 30 for books
Mentoring	20 hours
Private study	8 hours
Qualification studies	30 hours

10.10.4 CPD PRACTICE: STICK OR CARROT?

Two models of continuing professional development are evident in professional bodies: the compulsory approach or the voluntary. Whereas voluntary practice appeals to members' enlightened self-interest, obligatory practice allows for the audit of CPD records. A survey conducted in 2008 found that 50% of professional bodies made CPD mandatory (*Personnel Today* 2008). CPD was measured by task hours or study units completed, and sanctions included suspension. But 25% of survey responses stated that they did not measure CPD practice. The resistance to compulsory CPD can denote the balance of professional power – for example, in the medical field (Megginson and Whitaker 2007). By contrast, the 2014 XpertHR Survey of HR roles and responsibilities shows respondents being proactive in CPD and focusing on improving the HR function (2014b). For example, 73% agree that CIPD qualifications are vital for advancement in the

HR profession. As one recommends: 'No matter how proficient and experienced you are in HR, the more awareness and understanding of the business you have, the more credible – and therefore successful – you will be' (**www.xperthr.co.uk/survey-analysis/hr-roles-and-responsibilities-2014-xperthr-survey/152858**).

10.10.5 CONSTRAINTS OF CPD

Even if CPD practice and recording is systematic, the outcome and application of such development remains subjective. An inspection framework attempts to judge professional development through quantitative measures. Clocking learning hours and course attendance is easy to verify. Yet exposure to specialist knowledge through conferences may be insufficient for professional advancement in context. Improvement through CPD participation is difficult to evaluate without an assessment of learning.

This highlights an inherent conflict between the demonstration of competence levels and the ongoing need for further development. It is in the interest of the professional body to promote its members' competence, and generate demand for management learning in its role as a provider of professional courses, or as a learning academy (Cervero 2001). There may be little inclination to publicise members' skill gaps or atrophying knowledge. The risk is of CPD deteriorating into a form-filling exercise dominated by process. CPD must be a meaningful account of learning development and skill acquisition beyond a record of attendance at training events. How can continuous professional development become a portfolio of value and not just an overlooked record?

10.10.6 BENEFITS OF CPD

The main benefits of CPD for the individual are updating, increasing competence and enhancing mobility (Sadler-Smith et al 2000). Professional development contributes to greater self-confidence and competence in a job position and CPD serves as an auditable record within organisations of development activity. The potential rewards of CPD must be apparent to both the individual and employers in supporting learning development. For an individual, ongoing development can provide intrinsic motivation, elevated status as well as broader options through transferable skills (Mackay 2015b, Woodall and Gourlay 2004). The individual incentives for CPD are shown in the thought bubbles of Figure 10.7.

Figure 10.7 Subjective reward of CPD

Maurer and Chapman's longitudinal research (2013, p463) indicates that 'employees who participate in development activities over time may experience more promotions'. From an organisational perspective of knowledge resources, CPD can cultivate in-house talent and capitalise on exponential learning. Is there then evidence of a convergence of interest for employers and employees in the widespread adoption of CPD?

For practitioners CPD knits together educational learning and work practice (Mackay 2015b). Having current skills and knowledge enriches the possibilities of a self-managed career. However, the individual imperative to update skills and acquire qualifications is often a response to job demands that will ensure contract renewal. Despite the heralded benefits of professional development as self-empowering, individuals may be entirely instrumental in learning as they seek to demonstrate career relevance. CPD is increasingly seen as an investment for employment continuity (Rothwell 2005). An individual between jobs needs to acquire marketable experience that will differentiate them from other job candidates, such as herding elephants in Kenya. The individual works on CPD as a personal investment in learning from experience; illustrating learning agility and self-reliance through a colourful CPD portfolio.

The CIPD (2012l) points to continuing professional development as 'an essential part of professional life, not as an optional extra'. Individuals who choose to embrace continuous development discover an invigorating process of learning throughout life. Because CPD represents such an integral feature of contemporary working life, it can be illustrated (Figure 10.8) as interconnecting gears within the organisation.

Figure 10.8 The dynamics of learning and development

 REFLECTIVE ACTIVITY 10.11

How can an organisation maintain the smooth interplay of the three cogs (learning, earning and growing) in this model?

Review the mini case study examples of Davenport et al (2010) (available online at **https://hbr. org/2010/10/competing-on-talent-analytics**). How is investment in employee development tracked? What is the impact of learning on job performance? What are the challenges of these approaches in diverse sectors or international contexts?

As is evident from this reflective activity, mutual commitment is required to meet the demands of a dynamic economic environment and adapt to constant movement. Learning can increase capability for potential earning. Earning sustains business competitiveness and continuous growing. Growing can expand learning and be life-enhancing.

CASE STUDY 10.3

CAREER DEVELOPMENT IN PRACTICE: A ROADMAP FROM WASHINGTON, DC

The US government agency, Enduring Defense, based in Washington, DC, recognised employee retention was an issue. The agency employed over 3,000 staff combining civilians, military personnel and contractor employees. Attracting talented scientists and bright engineers was not a problem, but holding on to them was challenging. Many specialised staff were frustrated by a slow climb up the agency career pyramid. Some felt that if they couldn't move up, they would move out. As a result they took their cutting-edge technical knowledge and unique skills out of the door.

In the past the agency always agreed to fund staff requests for training and development. Some conferences in Hawaii or Australia appeared to be remote from their departmental job focus. Staff looked at this funding as a networking opportunity for future external consultancy work. Expenditure control and development consistently anchored to mission objectives was a problem.

To address these issues, the agency set up a new corporate university as an umbrella for professional development specifically linked to mission goals. External consultants designed and implemented an organisation-wide competency framework. A set of career guides was rolled out for each function defining job broadbanding and relevant resources for individual development.

Stan Allport worked in the facilities function in charge of logistics. He had attended the career guides roadshow, and was optimistic about his career track. Stan had worked for the US Air Force before joining the agency, and after two tours in Afghanistan felt entitled to protected employment in a steady job.

But when Stan looked through his career guide he didn't find what he wanted.

The guide featured employees' self-improvement through mentoring and on-the-job projects. There were suggestions for skill updating, continuous learning and knowledge acquisition. Skill proficiency assessments were designed for the line manager and employee to agree on a personal development plan. Stan was disappointed by a lack of specific job vacancies. The guide emphasised employees' development aligned to the mission, not the plan for his career. Rumour was spreading that the severe restrictions on defence spending meant relocation of the agency to Huntsville, Alabama. This was not in Stan's vision of the future. He knew that his wife Kelly, a doctor at the children's hospital, and twin daughters would never leave the vibrant capital city for a sleepy southern state.

Stan emailed his line manager for an urgent meeting. He wanted to underline to her that the agency had promised him a career when he signed up. This self-improvement was a fuzzy concept; it was too uncertain. Where was the career map? He didn't really want to work on special assignments or extra projects. Stan had done his years of hard graft. It was payback time. Stan really wanted to know when he'd get his next promotion, and how his career mapped out until retirement.

Source: Margaret Mackay

Questions

1   What are the benefits of this development approach from an agency perspective?

2   What are some of the tensions of individual career development in practice?

3   If you were Stan's line manager, how would you explain the career guidance?

10.11 CONCLUSION

Learning and effective employee development can maximise opportunities for business survival and success. Managing talent and harvesting dedicated organisational knowledge can be vital. Yet such development activities are often challenged by a dynamic environment.

In a context of worldwide challenges for effective corporate HR (Farndale et al 2010a), continuing professional development is critical in advancing respect for the professionalism of the HR field. The HR function has a central role in fostering appreciation of the value of learning and enhancing workforce skills. As organisational guardians of CPD, HR also needs to nurture informal knowledge development and company-specific skills.

To be effective, HR's management of talent and ongoing development ranges from traditional training provision to harnessing informal learning for both employee career development and organisational advantage. A renewed interest in sustainable career management and innovative support for professional development can retain talent and foster engagement. Workplace learning offers mutual benefits for both the organisation and the individual; it increases organisational capability whilst enhancing individual employability. A starting point for agile HR practitioners is to embrace the concept of lifelong learning, to ensure their own skill sets are current and relevant, thus providing a role model within their organisation. In doing so, HR professionals are able to effectively manage the challenges of diverse staffing needs, global mobility and competitive talent management.

KEY LEARNING POINTS

1 There is a robust business case for investment in employee development to increase competence and ensure organisational competitiveness.

2 The impact of the knowledge economy demands continuous learning and skill currency.

3 Successful employee and talent development demands a shared approach.

4 The emphasis for employee development has shifted from formal training to broader concepts of learning, and values the impact of informal learning.

5 Organisations need to proactively support career development to increase motivation and retain talent.

6 The individual is increasingly responsible for career-orientation and direction.

7 Continuing professional development is integral to individual learning.

REVIEW QUESTIONS

1. How can informal learning be managed in order to capitalise on talent development?

2. How can the HR function address the demands of business leaders who only value formal training?

3. How can HR promote sustained professional development?

4. What is the business rationale for career management?

5. How can line managers address the tension between individual development and organisational needs?

6. How can HR practitioners encourage talent development that embraces a diversity of education, experiential learning and development?

EXPLORE FURTHER

Gold, J., Holden, R., Iles, P., Stewart, J. and Beardwell, J. (2013) *Human Resource Development: Theory and Practice*. 3rd ed. London: CIPD. Explore learning theories and how these impact on training, development and CPD.

Megginson, D. and Whitaker, V. (2007) *Continuing Professional Development*. 2nd ed. London: CIPD. Extend strategies for continuous professional development.

Pedler, M., Burgoyne, J. and Boydell, T. (2007) *A Manager's Guide to Self Development*. 5th ed. Maidenhead: McGraw-Hill.

Explore self-development activities to support individual career planning and development:

- Listen to this podcast: BBC Radio 4 *The New Workplace* (August 2015). Five episodes discuss contemporary changes in the workplace and impact for employers and employees. Select episode 4 'The New Workplace, The New Employee', online at: **www.bbc.co.uk/programmes/b066fqcw**
- Listen to this podcast. CIPD Podcast 101 *CPD for HR* (5 May 2015). Listen to a conversation on how 'the world of continuing professional development is changing... and how smart organisations are turning what can be a pointless box-ticking exercise into a golden recruitment and retention opportunity'. Online at: **cipd.co.uk/hr-resources/podcasts/101-CPD-HR.aspx**
- Think about the following statement from the CBI/Pearson 2015 Education and Skills survey:
- 'In today's world, education has become a continuous, lifelong process through which skills are regularly upgraded to adapt to fast-changing environments.' (CBI 2015, p11)
  - To what extent do you agree with this view?
  - In what way does your experience support or differ from this viewpoint?
  - What is the role of HR in responding to the skills challenge for talent attraction, development and retention?
- Review Chapter 1 'The education and skills landscape 2015' and Chapter 3 'Skills are an increasingly urgent priority' online at **news.cbi.org.uk/reports/education-and-skills-survey-2015/education-and-skills-survey-2015**

CHAPTER 11

Managing the Employment Relationship

SALLY RUMBLES AND PETER SCOTT

LEARNING OUTCOMES

After reading this chapter, you should be able to:

- specify the importance of the contract of employment and its limitations for the management of employees
- explain differences in how conflict at work is viewed and some of the implications for managerial action
- assess the key implications for managers of recognising trade unions as representatives of employees
- understand the importance of management style and management practice to the effective management of employees
- understand the difference between equal opportunities and diversity
- Appreciate the complexity of managing a diverse workforce.

11.1 OVERVIEW

The objectives of organisations may be expressed in different ways. In the private sector these typically relate to profitability or market share, while in the public sector account must be taken of budgetary constraints imposed by politicians. Voluntary bodies may express their objectives in terms of service delivery to vulnerable groups in society. All organisations, however, employ people to achieve their objectives irrespective of how they are expressed. Employees also have needs that they want to be met in their work, and expectations about how they will be treated. In this chapter we explore some key features that shape the employment relationship between employers and employees. Some of these elements are determined by employment law which places constraints on management action. However, there still remains considerable choice in the way that employees may be managed, and this choice is influenced by managers' beliefs and their attitudes towards their staff. One key decision that must be made is whether employees are to be treated in the same way as other organisational resources, or are viewed as a special kind of resource that can provide a competitive advantage. Much contemporary HRM literature is based upon the latter view, and we identify three current themes that are consistent with this perspective: partnership, employee engagement and diversity management. We begin with an overview of the employment relationship and the nature of the contract of employment between the employer and employee.

11.2 INTRODUCTION

11.2.1 THE NATURE OF THE EMPLOYMENT RELATIONSHIP

The employment relationship is concerned with the features of the relationship between employer and employee, and the ways in which it can be managed. Thus an understanding of employment relations is important for those who are responsible for the effective management of people at work.

In essence, employment relations is concerned with the 'wage–work bargain'; that is, what work an employee will do in return for the wages paid by the employer. The term 'wages' refers not just to the pay received, but also to other terms of employment such as holiday entitlement and sick pay. It may also refer to other rewards that the employer may provide, such as subsidised private health insurance and free childcare places. Similarly, 'work' has a wider meaning than the employee's job. Employers have expectations about both the quantity and quality of the work. Some explicitly define specific behavioural characteristics of tasks, particularly in what are called 'customer-facing' jobs. A well-known example can be found in the passenger airline industry, where many airlines compete on standards of customer service. This is reflected not only in their marketing policies, but also in the criteria they use to recruit, select, train and manage front-line staff. The expectations involved in the exercise of this type of work has been referred to as 'emotional labour' (Hochschild 2012).

11.3 THE CONTRACT OF EMPLOYMENT

A useful starting point for our understanding of the terms of the wage–work bargain is through the concept, or idea, of the contract of employment. Each individual has a contract of employment with his or her employer, and the contract specifies the terms and conditions under which the employee works. However, the nature of the contract of employment is often misunderstood. Very few employees in the UK have a written contract which contains all their terms and conditions of employment in one document: most of us have a contract whose terms can be found in a number of sources. Figure 11.1 depicts some of the main sources of the contract of employment.

When employees refer to their 'written contract of employment', what they often mean is a formal written statement of the main terms of employment. This document is not the contract, as shown in the *System Floors v Daniel* case, heard by the Employment Appeal Tribunal (EAT). In its judgement, the EAT concluded that 'this statement did not constitute a written contract between the parties. It was merely a document that stated the employer's views of the terms' (Sargeant and Lewis 2014, p52).

The written statement is important, nonetheless, since the Employment Relations Act 1996 requires it to specify the most important terms of employment, including pay, hours of work, holidays and sick pay.

The Act also allows employers to refer employees to other documents that contain these terms, or which provide more details. Thus, the other possible sources shown in Figure 11.1 may need to be examined if we are to have a clearer picture of the terms of the contract.

REFLECTIVE ACTIVITY 11.1

Sources of the contract of employment

Obtain copies of as many of the documents shown in Figure 11.1 as you can, but especially offer letters, written statements and employee handbooks.

Read through these, and try to identify examples of statements that refer to employees' duties or responsibilities – that is, what is expected of the employee. Also, identify examples of the pay and other benefits that an employee will be entitled to under the contract of employment.

It is common, especially in larger organisations, for the HR department to produce an employee or staff handbook. This often contains details of employees' rights and duties. For example, it might explain what an employee is to do if they are unable to work through illness and what pay they will receive while sick. Similarly, employees who have a work roster may find that their actual times of work are provided by a notice.

Figure 11.1 Some possible sources of the contract of employment

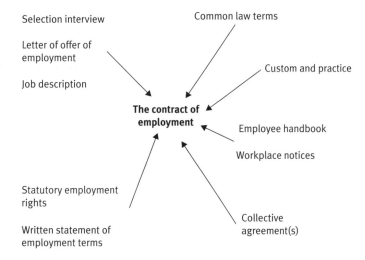

Where an organisation uses job descriptions, these include the main duties and responsibilities of an employee: thus they seek to clarify the 'work' element of the wage–work bargain. At the selection interview, there may be discussion about the terms of employment. These may cover both the work expected of an employee and the pay they will receive. For example, a candidate might ask about opportunities for overtime work and be told by the line manager how that is arranged. Although such 'spoken promises' can become terms of the contract, the problem is that it may not be easy to be sure what was said. The avoidance of such problems was one of the reasons why legislation requires employers to provide the written statement so that there is less doubt over the terms of the contract. Similarly, the need to formalise what is agreed with an employee accounts for HR departments providing letters of employment offers and specifying details in employee handbooks.

However, some terms may still not be written down. Custom and practice refers to possible employment terms that arise because they have operated for some while. For example, an office may have a custom that all workers finish at lunchtime on Christmas Eve, but this has never been written down in any formal documentation. Suppose, then, a manager tells her staff that they will need to work till 17.30, their normal finishing time. Is this lawful? If an employee challenges this decision in a court, it may be decided that the custom is part of the terms of employment.

REFLECTIVE ACTIVITY 11.2

Custom and practice

In the example of custom and practice given in the text about finishing work early on Christmas Eve, what factors do you think the courts might take into account to decide if it was reasonable for the employees to finish at lunchtime?

Other terms may be implied by judges to exist in a contract of employment. These are sometimes referred to as the 'common law terms' (Collins et al 2012, pp96–98). For example, all employees have a duty to use reasonable skill and care in their work. It will be for the courts to decide what is reasonable, but, as we have seen above, job descriptions might be used to specify the standard of work expected of an employee. Another duty of employees is to give faithful and honest service and not commit misconduct. Many organisations will produce a list of disciplinary rules which seek to clarify what this common-law term means for employees in reality, and these are often included in the employee handbook. The need to set standards of expected behaviour is both good practice and, as we see below, important in unfair dismissal claims. The important point to note, however, is that even if these are not specified in any document, the duties still exist as part of the employee's contract of employment.

Statutory employment rights refer to those that are provided through legislation, emanating from both national and supra-national levels; for example, the European Union (EU). Their purpose is to provide a minimum 'floor of rights' for all employees, and employers cannot offer terms that are worse than those provided by legislation. Some of these relate to specific parts of the wage–work bargain; for example, the UK national minimum wage and the EU Working Time Directive, which was implemented in the UK through the Working Time Regulations. The latter specifies maximum hours of work. Other statutory employment rights are concerned with the way in which employees are managed. These include maternity rights, the right not to be unfairly dismissed (see below), and thus how disciplinary action should implemented by a manager, and legislation that seeks to prohibit unlawful discrimination on certain grounds; for example, race, sex, religion and belief. We explore discrimination in more detail later in the chapter, and also deal with the issue in Chapters 4 and 9.

REFLECTIVE ACTIVITY 11.3

Employment rights

For many managers the growth of employment rights has become an accepted part of organisational life. However, there are critics who believe employment regulation is having a damaging impact on UK business's competitive position. This view has become an increasing theme in some government initiatives and policies since 2010. The unofficial Beecroft (2011) report, undertaken for the Department of Business, Innovation and Skills (BIS), suggested various ways to make it easier to dismiss employees and proposed exemptions from some employment laws for small businesses. The Growth and Infrastructure Act 2013 introduced a new employment status of employee-shareholders, who would gain shares in a company in return for relinquishing some of their employment rights. The 2010–15 Coalition Government ran a Red Tape Challenge, which invited interested parties to nominate regulations that constituted a 'burden on business' and should be repealed. This eventually turned its attention to the area of employment law. The current Conservative Government, which includes deregulation as one of its priorities, has continued the spirit of this initiative in BIS's new Cutting Red Tape programme. On the other hand, some government initiatives point in the opposite direction. For example, the Conservatives' July 2015 budget increased direct government intervention in the area of minimum wage-setting, introducing what is effectively a new national minimum wage rate for employees aged 25 and over, and proposed increases in this rate over the course of the 2015–2020 government.

The final source of employment terms, shown in Figure 11.2 below, is collective agreements. These can be found in organisations that recognise a trade union or unions, and where terms of employment such as pay and holidays are negotiated between the union and the employer. The outcomes of the negotiations are called collective agreements since they cover the collective group of workers represented by the trade union. A collective agreement normally covers all the employees in a particular occupation or grade, whether or not they are union members. Where unions are recognised, the employer has a relationship with both individual employees and the trade union.

Figure 11.2 The relationship between the contract of employment and collective agreements

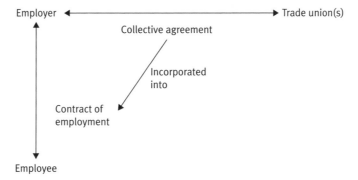

Collective agreements are not normally legally enforceable between the employer and trade union. However, the substantive terms of these agreements – for example, pay and hours – are incorporated into individual contracts of employment. Where an employer has collective agreements with a trade union these agreements can be an important source of an employee's contractual terms.

11.3.1 THE WAGE–WORK BARGAIN REVISITED

The effective management of the employment relationship requires managers to understand the nature of the contract of employment. In particular, it is important to recognise that the terms of the contract may be found in a number of different sources. However, Williams (2014) points out that there are two major problems with viewing the employment relationship simply as a contractual one. First, a contract implies that the two parties come together in a free and equal way. However, those seeking work are clearly in a weaker position than the employer, who has the freedom to offer the job to a number of applicants (see also Chapter 9). Furthermore, once an employee has taken a job, he or she is then required to obey the employer's commands or orders. The second problem with a simple contractual view of the relationship is that it is not possible to specify, at the outset of the relationship, all the obligations of the parties. The contract is thus open-ended, and the relative power of the parties will be important in deciding how the relationship is shaped. Thus, it is also important to recognise that the employment relationship has a power dimension, and that there is potential for differences, or conflict, to emerge in the relationship. Of course, the relationship is also characterised by co-operation between the employer and employees. The latter have an interest in the success of their employer which will help secure their jobs.

11.3.2 TERMINATION OF THE CONTRACT OF EMPLOYMENT

If an employer terminates the contract of employment, employment legislation allows the employee to claim at an employment tribunal that the dismissal was unfair. Tribunals decide whether the dismissal was 'fair and reasonable in the circumstances'. If the tribunal determines that the dismissal was unfair it can require the employer to reinstate or re-engage the employee, or make an award of financial compensation. In most cases employees will need two years' continuous service before they can make a claim.

The Employment Relations Act 1996 specifies five fair reasons for dismissal:

- misconduct, for example, where an employee breaks company disciplinary rules
- lack of capability, which is concerned with the employee's work performance and is explored in detail in Chapter 12
- redundancy
- statutory bar to employment, for example, where a company driver is disqualified from driving
- some other substantial reason which might include an employee's refusal to accept changes to their contractual terms in times of business difficulty.

The first two reasons are those that are most closely concerned with managing and leading people.

The employer must show that, in addition to having a fair reason, the dismissal was handled reasonably. This can be achieved by demonstrating that the dismissal followed the principles of natural justice. In employment this means:

- the employee was made aware of the standards of behaviour expected, hence the need to explain these at the start of employment
- the employee was informed of the allegation or complaint
- an investigation was undertaken to establish the facts of the case
- the employee was given an opportunity to explain their view of the case
- the employee was offered the opportunity to be accompanied by a fellow employee or trade union representative
- the penalty was proportionate to the offence
- the employee had the right of appeal to a more senior manager.

In order to effectively manage problems with employee behaviour and demonstrate that they have incorporated the principles of natural justice into their employment practice organisations draft disciplinary rules and procedures, often including these in employee handbooks.

11.3.3 THE ROLE OF PROCEDURES

The purpose of employment procedures is to create a 'problem-solving pathway'. They allow managers to consider an employee complaint, or, in the case of disciplinary action, provide managers with the opportunity to change or correct an employee's behaviour. Formal procedures allow appropriate action to be taken to solve a problem, rather than employees feeling they must express their disagreement with management through other means; for example, by being absent from work or performing below their capability. Procedures seek to ensure that managers deal with employment issues in a fair and consistent way, and are one of the ways in which managers seek to control or contain conflict in the employment relationship. Grievance and disciplinary procedures are the two most common ones found in organisations. However, there may be separate procedures covering specific employment matters: capability, to distinguish these issues from those related to conduct; harassment and bullying; equal opportunities; pay grading if a job evaluation scheme is used; and appeals against performance appraisal ratings, especially if this is linked to pay.

The unfair dismissal provisions of employment law have emphasised the importance of formalising disciplinary rules and procedures. The Advisory, Conciliation and Arbitration Service (Acas) has produced a Code of Practice (Acas 2015a) which is taken into account by tribunals hearing unfair dismissal claims. If the tribunal decides that the provisions of the Code have not been followed by either the employee or employer they can adjust any financial awards by up to 25%. Although not having the same status as the Code, Acas has also published a guide to handling grievances and disciplinary matters (Acas 2015b). Both publications provide valuable advice to HR managers

11.3.4 TRADE UNIONS AND COLLECTIVE BARGAINING

The narrow re-election of a Conservative government in 2015, committed to policies of labour market deregulation and further restricting the power of trade unions, suggests that trade unions and employment relations are likely to become more prominent public policy issues than they have been for some years. Government policies, together with broader economic and social changes, have had a significant impact on trade unions. To take one example, it is interesting to look at union membership figures which have declined significantly in the UK since the peak of some 13 million in 1980. At that time over half of all employees were members of a trade union, and collective agreements set the terms and conditions of about three-quarters of the UK workforce. In 2014 some six and a half million workers were union members, which accounted for 25% of the workforce. These figures represent a significant change. Union membership remained stronger in the public sector, however, where about 54% of employees were members. In the private sector membership was under 15% in 2014 and mainly confined to larger employers (Department of Business, Innovation and Skills 2015, p5).

As we saw above, collective agreements arrived at through negotiation between trade unions and employers can be a major source of an employee's contractual terms. Collective bargaining refers to the process where employers and unions jointly agree the terms and conditions of employees. For the employer, collective bargaining can be an efficient means of determining contractual terms since it does not require negotiation with each individual employee, and can assist in containing the conflict that may arise over employment terms. In addition, since the union has made the agreement, it has an interest in ensuring its members (the employees of the organisation) accept the terms that are agreed. Collective bargaining, then, is a key function of trade unions, and is a process that can provide greater equality of power in the employment relationship.

Collective bargaining is concerned with both parts of the wage–work bargain. It determines important parts of the wage the employee receives. As well as pay, hours and holidays it may cover matters such as overtime and shift premiums, sick pay, redundancy payments, pensions and health and safety (van Wanrooy et al 2013, pp80–82). These terms are the *economic* aspects of the contract, or 'wages'. However, collective bargaining can also determine *work* issues. For example, as well as redundancy pay, a collective agreement may specify how staff would be selected for redundancy, should that situation arise. In addition, it is not uncommon for there to be collective agreements covering staffing plans, equal opportunities and performance appraisal schemes. Thus, collective bargaining has a managerial aspect which means that these matters are determined by joint agreement, not by managers alone. This provides an example of how gaps in the open-ended contract may be filled.

As well as collectively bargaining with employers on behalf of employees, trade unions have other functions. They may provide specific services to their members as individuals. These may include legal and financial advice for both work and personal matters. Trade unions in the UK seek to represent their members outside the workplace in wider social matters. This might include lobbying for improved social policies to help eliminate child poverty, for example, and campaigning to improve the employment conditions of migrant workers. One further role of trade unions, important to those managing employment relations, is that following the principles of natural justice noted above, trade union officials typically represent their members in formal grievance, disciplinary and similar matters.

 REFLECTIVE ACTIVITY 11.4

Find out more details of the role of trade unions. The easiest way to do this is to go to the unions' websites. If your employer recognises a union or unions, this would be a good starting point. If not, perhaps visit the webpages of two or three unions you have recently heard about in the news. Most can be found simply by typing their name into a search engine or visiting the Trades Union Congress website, which lists many unions (**www.tuc.org.uk/britains-unions**). For each union, identify how it describes its role and seeks to achieve its objectives, the types of workers it recruits and how many members it has. From your research, consider what are the main similarities and differences between how the unions you have looked at see their roles, priorities and objectives, and what the reasons might be for any differences.

11.4 CONFLICT AND THE EMPLOYMENT RELATIONSHIP

We have noted the potential for conflict to arise in the employment relationship, so how do managers view the reasons for its existence? Before exploring the answer to this question, undertake the following Reflective Activity.

 REFLECTIVE ACTIVITY 11.5

Conflict at work

For this activity, you are asked to reflect on the following four statements on conflict between employers and employees. For each, identify the values or beliefs of those people who hold this view. Which of these views most closely reflects your own view? Why?

Conflict between an employer and employee is:

- a dysfunctional factor in an otherwise healthy organisation
- largely preventable, provided organisations take a proactive approach to developing policies and practices which take account of employees' needs and expectations from work
- an inherent feature of organisational life, but one that can be largely institutionalised and managed through recognising that differences of interests exist between the two parties
- a reflection of the fundamental divisions and inequalities in the wider society.

Each of the four views reflects different explanations of the causes of conflict between employers and employees and how they are to be managed. These views are based on 'frames of reference': a term first attributed to Fox (1966, 1974) to distinguish between the beliefs held by managers that influence their approach to the management of employees.

Those that believe that conflict is dysfunctional are characterised as holding a 'unitary' view. Often using the team or family analogy, those with unitary perspective expect co-operation from their staff since the goals of the organisation and employees are the same: employees must understand and accept their role, and also accept that the leaders of the organisation are best-placed to make the important decisions. With its emphasis on co-operation, the unitary view would see conflict as a result of poor communications, or, significantly, as the result of trouble-makers, like trade union activists, who generate conflict in an otherwise harmonious organisation.

As human resource management theory and practice has developed, some authors have adopted the term 'neo-unitary' to capture the beliefs that underpin this approach to managing the employment relationship (Farnham and Pimlott 1995). This perspective has much in common with the traditional unitary view in that co-operation and harmony between employers and employees is believed to be the normal state of affairs. However, as the statement in the activity suggests, conflict can be prevented, but only if managers are proactive in developing policies and practices that take account of the needs and expectations of employees. Managers will thus need to utilise the knowledge provided by the Human Relations school of thinking to engender employees' commitment to their work and the organisation's objectives (Edwards 2003).

Those who believe that conflict in the employment relationship is inevitable are said to hold a 'pluralist' perspective. While not disputing that there is scope for co-operation between managers and employees, pluralists point to the differences in interests between employers and employees. For example, employers will naturally wish to minimise wage costs while employees will, equally naturally, wish to maximise their pay. The key concern of pluralists in the employment relationship is to find ways to manage the conflict so that disruption – for example, in the form of strikes – is limited. For those with a pluralist perspective, trade unions are not the cause of conflict. Rather, they have a legitimate role in representing one interest group, employees, in the relationship. The task for managers is to build a relationship with trade unions, and develop procedures so that disputes and differences can be resolved through the process of negotiation.

Those holding a Marxist view of conflict see this as the result of workers being exploited in the employment relationship. The development of procedures with trade unions to prevent and resolve expressions of conflict is, at best, only a temporary solution. Conflict, it is argued, will be eliminated only when the distinction between the owners of capital and workers is removed.

11.4.1 MANAGEMENT STYLE AND EMPLOYMENT RELATIONS

The distinction between unitary and pluralist perspectives provides a basis for understanding different management styles. According to Purcell and Ahlstrand (1994, p177) '[management] style implies the existence of a distinctive set of guiding principles, written or otherwise, which set parameters to and signposts for management action regarding the way employees are to be treated....' 'Style', then, describes the choice that is made as to how the employment relationship is to be managed. These authors identify two dimensions of management style: individualism and collectivism.

Individualism

Two broad extremes of individualism can be identified, based on the extent to which managers view employees as individuals with needs and aspirations. Those that are described as having 'high individualism' or an 'investment orientation' towards staff would typically emphasise the following policies and practices:

- employees seen as an important resource
- a focus on internal labour markets
- employee development, appraisal and individual systems of reward
- empowerment.

This management style is based on a neo-unitary view where conflict and differences can be prevented, and, as we will see later, is aimed at generating employee engagement.

In contrast, managers who have a low concern with individual employees, a traditional unitary view, would adopt a 'cost minimisation' approach with the following characteristics:

- labour as a commodity to be bought from, and returned to, the external labour market as economic activity dictates
- an emphasis on numerical flexibility
- limited, if any, training
- tight control over pay.

Collectivism

Purcell and Ahlstrand (1994) also draw a similar distinction on the collective dimension of management style which seeks to capture the extent to which managers accept that employees have a right to act collectively – for example, by joining a trade union – and are willing to negotiate and consult with employee representatives. At one extreme, typical of the traditional unitary approach, there would be resistance and hostility towards trade unions. At the other end of the spectrum the relationship sought by management is highly co-operative with the union, and would include: regular consultation with union representatives on strategic plans; extensive information exchange; and the use of joint working parties to manage employment matters. The contemporary term for this approach is 'partnership', and we examine this below. Between these extremes lies what Purcell and Ahlstrand (1994) refer to as 'adversarial relations'.

Adversarial relationships may exist in organisations where unions have been recognised by the employer for many years, but where managers would prefer not to have to negotiate with them. The primary concern of managers in these firms will be to protect their right to make decisions without the involvement of unions, sometimes called the 'managerial prerogative' (Storey 1983). Control and stability of the employment relationship, through formally agreed procedures, are important characteristics in such businesses, and the issues on which unions can negotiate are usually carefully and tightly drawn.

11.4.2 PARTNERSHIP AGREEMENTS

We have already noted the importance of collective agreements as a source of employment terms, and that these can be arrived at through either adversarial or co-operative relationships between the employer and trade unions. In recent years there have been some examples of so-called 'partnership agreements' between employers and unions that appear to be the result of a more co-operative approach between the two parties. As Williams (2014, p194) notes, the main idea underlying partnership working is that it promotes 'co-operative relations between managers and unions, to the supposed benefit of all parties, including the employer, the recognised union, and the workforce'. In practice, however, such agreements are often somewhat vague and aspirational, and more concerned with mechanisms of enabling employees to have a say and other such 'process' issues, rather than giving guarantees about employment security or similar substantive matters (Williams 2014, p195).

REFLECTIVE ACTIVITY 11.6

Partnership agreements

List what you believe to be the benefits of partnership agreements to: the employer, the trade union, and the employees of the organisation.

Each of the elements of partnership agreements justifies a little more explanation. The first can be little more than empty rhetoric. However, if it genuinely reflects a greater level of trust between the parties, it may lead to improved employment relations. The development of communication and consultation processes can take different forms. Such processes may, for example, provide for trade unions to be more closely involved in the decision-making processes of the organisations, at least to the extent that union representatives are consulted on those matters that may have an impact on employees. Also, they may provide for representatives of all employees, not just those that are union members, to be informed and involved in business decisions.

The final two elements seek to meet the key needs of the employer and employees. Employees may be reluctant to be more flexible in their working arrangements if they believe that this could put jobs at risk. Thus flexibility comes if the employer is willing to agree to some level of employment security. Not, perhaps, a commitment that employees will keep those specific jobs as a result of organisational change, but that alternative jobs will be available – hence 'employment security'. These two components, then, combine to establish a degree of mutuality in the partnership agreement since each meets the respective key need of the employer and the employee.

As businesses struggle in the difficult economic climate, we have a good opportunity to see how well partnership agreements work in practice. Do they allow the business to survive when faced with poor trading conditions, and provide employees with higher levels of job security than would have been the case without it? Alternatively, are the espoused benefits of partnership working only enjoyed when economic conditions are favourable for organisations? This suggests that the central plank of partnership is the trust needed between the parties in the employment relationship. Without this, partnership is unlikely to succeed.

THE IMPLICATIONS OF PUBLIC SECTOR PAY RESTRAINT

CASE STUDY 11.1

An important part of recent governments' drive to reduce public spending has been various moves to control the wage bill in the public sector. They have, for example, reduced staff numbers, made changes to pension entitlements, introduced public sector pay freezes for the 2011–12 and 2012–13 pay round, and has since sought to limit the annual increase in the pay bill to an average of 1%. The pay limits have also been applied to those public servants, such as teachers and most NHS staff, whose pay and conditions are supposed to be determined by recommendations to government from independent review bodies. The July 2015 budget extended this 1% average annual limit effectively for the duration of the current Parliament to 2020. One proposed way of keeping within this overall average is to end the practice of annual incremental pay progression, based on length of service and to relate pay progression within pay grades much more closely to individual performance. Such changes have occurred for local authority-controlled school teachers within England and Wales from 2014. A government attempt in the same year to limit a 1% pay increase only to National Health Service (NHS) staff already at the top of their pay scale triggered an industrial dispute; because health is a function devolved to the four nations of the UK. Confusingly, the different settlements of this dispute in the various nations that make up the UK has now resulted in three sets of pay rates for the same NHS grades between the four nations: one set applying to England and Northern Ireland, and more generous settlements for Wales and Scotland respectively (Sharp 2015).

The various initiatives raise a number of issues for the recruitment, retention and motivation of staff in the public sector that are relevant to the subject matter of this text. These include whether it is either possible or desirable for government to try to exercise such tight central control over public sector pay over such a long period of time, particularly when similar controls are not in place for the private sector. What, if any, incentives can be offered to attract staff if skill shortages in key areas start to emerge? Should pay be more closely related to performance, and how can one reliably define and measure what is meant by performance in the public sector anyway? Is annual incremental pay progression really just a second, 'hidden' pay rise, or is it an important way to retain the accumulated skill and expertise over time of staff?

Questions

1   How realistic do you think it is for government to try to limit centrally the amount of pay increases in the public sector over a period of several years? What are the main objections that could be raised to this and what do you think could be the main unintended consequences of such a policy?

2   List the various arguments in favour of a) retaining annual progression pay increments, and b) making pay rises within grades more conditional on staff performance. Which case do you think is more convincing, and why? Draft out a case you could make in favour of your preferred alternative to try to convince someone who supported the opposite alternative?

3   As an HR manager, you have been asked to prepare a report that suggests ways of retaining and motivating hard to recruit staff in an era of low overall pay increases. What would be the main strategies and policies you would put in such a report?

11.5 EMPLOYEE ENGAGEMENT

As we pointed out at the start of this chapter, the management of employment relations implicitly includes three current themes. We have referred to the first of these, namely partnership, in the preceding sections. We go on to look at the third of these – diversity management – in greater detail later in this chapter. We now turn to our second theme of employee engagement.

The management of the employment relationship characterised by an 'investment orientation' towards employees is designed to elicit their commitment to the organisation. Where managers are able to achieve an engaged workforce it is claimed that this can lead to both organisational success and employee well-being (MacLeod and Clark 2009). Indeed, there is now a substantial body of literature that supports this view, with practitioners and academics agreeing that the consequences of employee engagement are positive; however, there is little agreement on a definition. A CIPD-commissioned research report (Alfes et al 2010, p5) identified engagement as having three dimensions:

- intellectual engagement – thinking about the job and how it might be done better
- affective engagement – positive feelings about doing a job well
- social engagement – actively seeking opportunities to discuss work-related issues.

Where organisations are able to effectively engage their employees on these dimensions, the authors claim that three important outcomes can be identified which can assist organisations in the achievement of their objectives. Firstly, engaged employees are likely to perform better than those who are not. Respondents in the survey claimed to have good levels of job and social skills, were willing to take on extra work and tended to have high ratings in their performance appraisal. Secondly, engaged employees are more likely to be innovative at work. This might include searching out new methods of working, generating enthusiasm for innovative ideas and transforming such ideas into meaningful applications. Thirdly, engaged employees are more likely to want to stay with their employer.

How then can organisations generate employee engagement? Holbeche and Matthews (2012) suggest four 'drivers' of engagement:

- *Connection.* Employees need a sense of identification with, and pride in working for, the employing organisation; there has to be a common purpose and shared values.
- *Voice.* Managers need to keep employees informed of the organisation's progress and of organisational change, and listen to employees' views so that they feel involved in the business.
- *Support.* Employees need to be treated as individuals and enabled to do their job; they should feel they are valued and receive a fair deal from their employer, and believe their employer is concerned with their well-being.
- *Scope.* Work should be purposeful and provide employees with the opportunity for growth and accomplishment; it should allow for autonomy and be underpinned by mutual trust.

Alfes et al (2010) came to similar conclusions and highlighted the importance of meaningful work and employee voice to creating an engaged workforce (see also Chapters 8 and 12). Employee voice is the foundation of sustainable business performance increasing engagement which enables effective decision-making and drives innovation. To do this organisations need to create a climate of trust in engagement that fosters opportunities for both collective and individual voice to be heard, or more simply put, talking and listening to their employees (Rees et al 2013). Management style is instrumental in fostering employee engagement and employee voice. Through communication, managers can help employees place their own work in the context of the organisation's objectives. Similarly, establishing and maintaining effective communication and consultation channels can both reinforce employees' view of the value of their work and enhance social engagement. It is perhaps no surprise then that they emphasise the importance of line management style in creating employee engagement. Line managers, it is suggested, are the crucial link between the employer and employees, and their behaviour is central to levels of engagement. Their key tasks in this respect are selecting the correct people for the job, regular communication with their staff, relevant training and development, and ensuring reciprocity of effort and reward.

REFLECTIVE ACTIVITY 11.7

Employee engagement – how engaged are you?

Access one of the many free employee engagement surveys available online (for example the Gallup Q12) and review the results to see if you are engaged at work. What factors does the survey measure and how do these in your opinion contribute to employee engagement? If you were tasked with improving employee engagement in your organisation what would you do? If your organisation undertakes staff or engagement surveys you could also look at the results of these surveys to help you answer this question.

11.6 DIVERSITY AT WORK

11.6.1 INDIVIDUAL DIFFERENCES AND MANAGEMENT STYLES

Management style also affects the way in which managers handle the individual characteristics of employees. We would expect those who have an 'investment orientation' towards employees to take account of individual differences to the benefit of the organisation. Such an approach is analogous with the management of diversity. Before examining the meaning of diversity we briefly consider the legal provisions on discrimination.

We noted earlier that statutory employment rights are an important source of an employee's terms, and that specific legislation makes for unfair discrimination if it is based on the grounds of sex, race, age, religion and belief, sexual orientation or disability. As we have seen in Chapters 4 and 9, managers regularly discriminate between employees; for example, in choosing between job applicants. The legislation prohibits discrimination which has no connection with the work to be done (in legal terms, which is not a 'genuine occupational requirement'), and distinguishes between direct and indirect discrimination. An example of direct discrimination would be a job advertisement that states that only women can apply for the post. Indirect discrimination arises when a requirement or condition that cannot be justified is applied to a situation where members of one or more of the protected groups cannot comply. An example of this was the previous requirement for applicants to the UK police force to be a minimum height; male recruits had to be 1.78m and female recruits 1.63m. These requirements were gradually phased out during the 1990s because being tall isn't a necessary requirement for the job and the policy was found to be discriminatory and unlawful to both individuals from certain ethnic groups who were less capable of meeting the minimum height requirement, as well as to men. At the time of writing, the shortest police officer in the UK is 1.52m tall (*Express & Echo* 2014).

11.6.2 EQUAL OPPORTUNITIES

The concept of equal opportunities underpins many organisational approaches to equality in the UK, which have been developed in response to the legislation introduced by successive UK governments since the mid-1970s to address unfair discrimination in the pursuit, obtaining and retaining of employment, as well as other workplace practices. The result is a legal framework developed around a definition of inequality that draws heavily on the idea of indirect discrimination: 'discriminating against people on grounds that are irrelevant to the jobs they doing or for which they are applying' (Chryssides and Kaler 1996, p89). To reduce the disparate treatment by managers, the HR profession has focused on establishing specific procedures to ensure legal compliance and demonstrate equal treatment (Harris 2005). Thus the 'neutral treatment' principle of much anti-discrimination legislation has become the cornerstone of organisational policies and procedures which are designed to achieve sameness of treatment in resourcing decisions (Foster and Harris 2005, p6).

An equal opportunities approach is seen as one of 'compliance' with the law. It typically focuses attention on groups that may be unlawfully discriminated against, and features such initiatives as target-setting, positive action and redressing past discrimination. Its attraction for line managers is that it offers a certain simplicity and ease of application by reducing the scope for exercising discretion and providing the essential means of defending their decisions against claims of less favourable treatment (Wilson and Iles 1999). Its limitation is that it has led HR specialists and operational managers alike to focus on consistency of process or procedural justice, even though consistency is a relative principle, whose pursuit alone will not act as a catalyst for progressive employment practice (Foster and Harris 2005). Relying on a principle of consistency is problematic as it does not require individuals to be treated well, only alike, and allows for situations where all employees are treated equally, but equally badly (Fredman 2001).

In order to meet its EU membership requirements, equality legislation in the UK has expanded to take account of a growing number of specific groups in the workforce (Foster and Williams 2011). The EU continues to be highly influential in this respect since managing diversity is a key component of the 2009 Lisbon Treaty. In the UK we now have the Equality Act 2010, aimed at safeguarding the rights of groups who share so-called 'protected characteristics'. Other legislation, such as the Children and Families Act 2014, introduces rights that relate to personal circumstances rather than to protected characteristics: for example, parental leave rights. The resultant increased legal complexity has meant that managers need to be aware not only of individual rights, but – as we saw with an investment orientation to employees – a concern with individual needs at work. In other words, a managing diversity approach. Managing diversity in this context is framed as a strategic response arising from demographic change, and is differentiated from equal opportunities on the basis that organisations should focus on the individual rather than the potentially disadvantaged group to which the employee belongs. Thus diversity encompasses a whole range of differences beyond those associated with disadvantage or covered by anti-discrimination legislation (Tomlinson and Schwabenland 2010).

 REFLECTIVE ACTIVITY 11.8

Equality and diversity in practice (1)

Go online and research the equality and diversity statements on the websites of the TUC (**www.tuc.org.uk**) and one or two of the largest trade unions, such as Unite (**www.unitetheunion.org**) or Unison (**www.unison.org.uk**). What evidence can you find about their view on equal opportunities? Read the next section on the nature of diversity and research the websites to see if there is any indication of a diversity focus; consider what role trade unions play in fostering equality and diversity in the modern workplace.

11.6.3 THE NATURE OF DIVERSITY

Equal opportunities (EO) initiatives in the UK are aimed at developing a level playing field for disadvantaged groups, but it is claimed that they have failed to achieve the goal of greater organisational inclusion of minorities for two reasons. First, they do not cover adequately all disadvantaged groups, and those that they do (such as women and non-white employees) are treated as homogeneous, often stereotyped, groups. Second, EO fails to generate the involvement and commitment of managers who perceive it simply as a compliance issue (Ahmed 2007). Managing diversity is claimed to overcome these limitations, and to provide a powerful set of arguments with which to mobilise management interest in the needs of members of minority groups (Kandola and Fullerton 1998). At the same time, writers such as Belbin (1991) found that culturally diverse teams were more effective than homogeneous ones, thus providing the basis of a business case for diversity. French (2015) summarises research showing that the performance of multicultural groups at work was typically either much better than that of monocultural groups, or significantly worse, highlighting the importance of careful management of such groups, if they are to be effective.

Unlike EO initiatives, a diversity approach recognises that everyone is different even though some may share certain characteristics such as ethnic origin, gender, etc. Diversity therefore consists of visible factors – for example, race and age – but also non-visible personal characteristics including background, culture, personality and preferred work style. The diversity argument is founded on the premise that 'harnessing these differences will create a productive environment in which everybody feels valued, where their talents are being fully utilised and in which organisational goals are met' (Kandola and Fullerton 1998, p40). The CIPD defines diversity as 'valuing everyone as an individual – valuing people as employees, customers and clients' (CIPD 2010b, p2). In principle, diversity management encourages the development of more innovative HR policies and practices, which offer greater reciprocity in the employment relationship by addressing individual needs. This HR approach appears more relevant to the flexible behaviour required of employees in the less predictable work roles that are a feature of contemporary working life (Foster and Harris 2005). The problem for today's managers then is that there is no single best way of treating employees, because each one will have their own personal needs, values and beliefs.

11.6.4 ORGANISATIONAL BENEFITS OF DIVERSITY

Three main reasons are typically used to justify an organisational approach for making equality and diversity an important management issue:

- the business case
- the impact of the demographic time bomb
- the social justice argument.

The business case for diversity

According to the CIPD (2010b), there are three business reasons for organisations exceeding legal requirements on discrimination: people issues, market competitiveness and corporate reputation.

1   *People issues* – creating an open and inclusive workplace culture in which everyone feels valued helps to recruit and retain good people. People aspire to work for employers with good employment practices and to feel valued at work. To be competitive, organisations need to derive the best contributions from everyone. Skills shortages and difficulties in filling vacancies are forcing organisations to recruit from more diverse pools and to offer different working arrangements in the 'war for talent'. Managing diversity creates a recruitment pool that improves the chances of getting the right person for the right job. Diversity also creates engaged employees working in a climate of productivity and commitment, with low turnover and sickness absence rates. In turn, creativity and innovation are increased.

2   *Product market competitiveness* – a diverse workforce can help to inform the development of new or enhanced products or services, open up new market opportunities, improve market share and broaden an organisation's customer base.

3   *Corporate reputation* – healthy businesses flourish in healthy societies and the needs of people, communities and businesses are interrelated. Social exclusion and low economic activity rates limit business markets and their growth. Thus businesses need to consider corporate social responsibility (CSR) in the context of diversity. The

overall image of an organisation can be important in attracting and retaining both customers and employees.

Arguably, the business and social justice cases for diversity are complementary, because unless people are treated fairly at work they will feel less committed and may underperform. Despite many criticisms of the business case, researchers claim that it and social justice arguments can co-exist to produce a case for diversity that is capable of achieving greater social equality. In some organisations – for example, in the voluntary sector – the business case and social justice is largely the same thing (Tomlinson and Schwabenland 2010).

Studies have found that not all HR diversity practices are associated with increased workforce diversity and that attitudes to diversity in large corporations have been, at best, mixed. For example, managers in some organisations have tended to see its value in recruitment and selection, but have not applied it to other working practices. There is also a wide recognition of the supposed value of workforce diversity, but mixed evidence on its impact on business performance. A report for the Department of Business, Innovation and Skills (2013) found that firms have reaped business benefits from equality and diversity practices including improved financial performance, but not all firms in all context at all times. However, others argue that there is limited empirical data to prove an association between the outcome of HR diversity practices and improved organisational performance (Shen et al 2009). Despite the apparent attractiveness of the business case it appears that organisations still see legislation as the main driver for making changes in practice, and view diversity management as a cost rather than a driver of organisational success. If that is the case, it suggests that arguments for the business case need to be communicated more effectively and its profile raised as a strategic business lever (CIPD 2007b).

 REFLECTIVE ACTIVITY 11.9

Equality and diversity in practice (2)

Go online and research the equality and diversity statements of your employer and one or two other employers. What indication do they give as to whether their approach is more equal-opportunities- or diversity-focused? Identify some examples of the business case for diversity for your chosen organisations. With the improved economic outlook what might be the drivers for taking a managing diversity approach?

Demographic changes

The UK workforce is ageing; the proportion of the working population aged between 50 and 64 is at its highest level since the 1970s. This trend is continuing, with predictions that by 2033, 23% of the population will be aged 65 and over with only 16% aged 16 or younger. In addition, there is a sharp tapering of people in the workforce between 30 and 40 years old due to low birth rates in the 1970s, and there are fewer white able-bodied men under 45 years of age With the expansion of the EU there has at the same time been an increase in the number and mix of ethnic groups within the UK, particularly from Eastern Europe (ONS 2014). Put simply, changing demographics mean that if there are fewer white males available for employment, employers need to consider broadening their search for employees. The latest CIPD *Resourcing and Talent Planning* survey (2015f) confirms that organisations are experiencing skills shortages at an ever increasing rate and the 'war on talent' is a key priority for many chief executives. Twenty-first-century organisations require a flexible, highly skilled workforce, adaptable to change and able to compete in the global marketplace. Consequently, employers need to be fishing in the widest possible talent pool to ensure they have access to the breadth and depth of skills available, which meet their business needs. The demographic time bomb created by falling birth rates and longer lifespans means that fewer younger people will be employed to provide the taxes to support an ageing population. Even though changes in retirement ages may enable people to have the right to work longer, the statistics predict that proportionately fewer people will be in paid employment.

11.7 MANAGING DIVERSITY – HOW TO MOVE EQUALITY FORWARD

One of the main criticisms of managing diversity is that it requires significant resources with no guarantee of success. There is no instant formula for its achievement because it is a complex task and every organisation will approach it differently. The CIPD (2005b, 2007b and 2012h) suggests that, in common with other strategies for employee engagement, it needs to be led from the top of the organisation. Further, it requires systematic management action that moves from minimal legal compliance to a focus on the development of an open workplace culture in which everyone feels valued and can add value. The key is to make managing diversity a mainstream issue, owned by everyone so that it influences all employment policies, practices and drivers.

The CIPD suggests the following tips for implementing a successful managing diversity strategy:

- ensure that initiatives and policies have the support of senior management
- remember managing diversity is a continuous process, not a one-off initiative
- develop a diversity strategy to support the achievement of business goals which addresses the diverse needs of customers
- focus on fairness and inclusion, ensuring that merit, competence and potential are the basis for people decisions
- review policies and update with changes in law.

REFLECTIVE ACTIVITY 11.10

How diverse is the workforce?

Diversity: the state of play:

There are 10.3m people aged over 65 in the UK today – this will rise to 12.5m by 2020. In the past ten years, the employment rate of the over-50s has risen by almost 25%.

- Just under half (48%) of UK employees are women compared to two-fifths in the 1970s.
- The gap between full- and part-time men's and women's hourly rates of pay is 22%.
- One in eight UK employees has a disability. People with a disability or long-term illness are over twice as likely to face bullying or harassment in the workplace as non-disabled people.
- In 2011, one in five people (20%) identified with an ethnic group other than white British, compared with 13% in 2001. Asian and black and minority ethnic (BME) staff are more likely to recommend their employer as a good place to work than white staff, but are still under-represented at senior management levels.
- Unemployment is twice as high among people from ethnic minorities, and there are proportionately more unemployed Chinese, Indian and black African graduates than white graduates. Interestingly, however, only 12% of white men are in professional occupations, as opposed to 21% of Chinese and Indian men.

- White men have the lowest rate of participation in full-time education between the ages of 16 and 24 (37%) followed by white women (40%).
- Forty-one per cent of white women in employment work part-time, but only 7% of white men do so, as opposed to 38% of Bangladeshi men.
- One-third of the UK workforce now work flexible hours and part-time workers now constitute 31.9% of the UK workforce.

(Sources: Office for National Statistics, CIPD, UKCAE)

Consider the above statistics and compare them with those in the organisation for which you work. How diverse is your organisation in comparison to these statistics? What initiatives are taken by your employer to encourage diversity; for example, part-time working, flexible hours, etc? What initiatives could your employer consider in future to encourage a more diverse workforce? For example:

- address work–life balance needs to the benefit of the organisation and the employee by offering suitable choices and options
- encourage ownership, creating a culture of empowerment so that decisions are not passed up without good reason
- develop guidelines for managers to help them respond flexibly and appropriately to diversity needs
- link diversity management to other initiatives such as Investors in People and quality management
- be aware of the international context and the influence of national cultures on work.

The social justice argument is examined in more detail in Chapter 4. It is essentially an ethically driven approach incorporating CSR. It is often associated with compliance measures directed at disadvantaged groups, target-setting and positive action (Gilmore and Williams 2013). As such, the social justice argument has frequently been linked with equal opportunities measures targeting groups rather than the individually focused orientation of diversity management.

LOOKISM – HOW FAR SHOULD EQUALITY GO?

CASE STUDY 11.2

We judge people on their appearance at work every day, and the online dating community **www.beautifulpeople.com**, which specifically targets 'good-looking' people, has now capitalised on this by launching an employment agency linked to its online dating agency. Greg Hodge, its managing director, argues that there are business benefits to employing attractive staff including winning more business and increased revenue generation. The employment agency, launched in 2013, allows companies who count appearance as a key factor in selection of staff the opportunity to target its 750,000 members. Employers are able to advertise their vacancies through the website to members and the assumption is that the result for the

employer will be 'good-looking' applicants

Stories like this prompt the debate as to whether lookism should somehow be brought within the anti-discrimination legislation. Legislating for 'personal appearance', however, would be problematic. In the fashion retail sector, for example, businesses such as Abercrombie & Fitch often want to create a particular 'face' for their brand. To what extent should that be permitted, providing it doesn't breach existing equality legislation? Many would argue that lookism is the new racism and there is far too much scope for lawful bias against unattractive employees and job applicants where their looks are frankly irrelevant to the job.

Questions

1   List the advantages and disadvantages to extending the current equality legislation to include personal characteristics.

2   Compare your view with that of a colleague or others in a small group and debate your main differences in your views. Then,

working together, consider how you would:

● legislate against lookism
● incorporate opposition to lookism into HR policies and practices
● in both cases, what do you think would be the main likely unintended consequences, and how could you overcome them?

11.8 CONCLUSION

The management of the employment relationship is a complex task. Managers have considerable choice in the way in which they structure the relationship, including the extent to which they view employees as a resource, and whether to deal with trade unions as representatives of employees. One key factor that may influence that choice is the market within which the business operates. Employers with tight product or service margins may decide that the costs of investing in employees cannot be afforded. Similarly, they may decide that trade unions will limit flexibility and add to labour costs. It is also important to note that although an investment orientation that includes recognition of individual differences is claimed to improve business performance, there is mixed evidence about the extent of this success.

KEY LEARNING POINTS

1   Beliefs shape management style and influence whether employees are seen as a resource or a factor of production, and whether trade unions are perceived to be legitimate representatives or a source of conflict.

2   To build a workforce that is trusting of management and committed to the success of the organisation requires managerial initiatives to develop an appropriate culture, supported by relevant policies and practices.

3   Three contemporary developments which reflect strategies to achieve the commitment of employees are partnership agreements with trade unions, employee engagement and diversity management.

4   Discriminatory decisions taken at work need to be made on factors relevant to the work itself and not on personal characteristics such as age, sex, race, etc.

5   An equal opportunities approach can be portrayed as one that seeks compliance with legislation, and typically focuses on identifying the groups who are more susceptible to unfair discrimination. It utilises procedures that are designed to meet legal requirements on equal treatment.

6   The managing diversity approach focuses on the individual with the aim of creating a work environment where everyone feels valued, where their talents are fully utilised and where organisational goals are met.

REVIEW QUESTIONS

1   With regard to the following scenarios, identify what you consider to be typical features present in respect of the management of the employment relationship:

● where employees are seen as a resource that can provide competitive advantage
● where trade unions are recognised for collective bargaining
● where employees are viewed as a 'factor of production'
● If possible, you should draw on your own work experience.

2   What action can an HR manager take to prevent conflict arising within an organisation? If it does arise, what options exist for its resolution?

3   A line manager has asked you to help her understand the importance of the contract of employment, and how far she can rely upon it to ensure she gets the best out of her staff. How would you reply?

4   Evaluate the evidence that managing diversity is good for business using examples from academic sources or from your experience. If you were an HR professional, what arguments could you make to your employer in support of the business case?

5   How might trade unions and other employee representative groups reconcile the needs of their collective body (equal treatment for all) with the needs of individuals (valuing individual needs)?

EXPLORE FURTHER

CIPD (2015) *Resourcing and Talent Planning Survey Report*. London: CIPD.

French, R. (2015) *Cross Cultural Management in Work Organisations*. London: CIPD.

Gennard, J. and Judge, G. (2010) *Managing Employment Relations*. 5th ed. London: CIPD. This is the CIPD text on the subject.

Gilmore, S. and Williams, S. (eds) (2012) *Human Resource Management*. 2nd ed. Oxford: Oxford University Press. Chapters 10 and 11.

Kirton, G. and Greene, A. (2015) *The Dynamics of Managing Diversity: A critical approach*. 4th ed. Abingdon: Routledge.

Konrad, A., Prasad, P. and Pringle, J. (eds) (2006) *A Handbook of Workplace Diversity*. London: Sage.

Williams, S. (2014) *Employment Relations: A critical introduction*. 3rd ed. Oxford: Oxford University Press. Takes a thematic approach to the subject area.

Websites

● Department for Business, Innovation & Skills (BIS): **www.gov.uk/government/organisations/department-for-business-innovation-skills**. This is the government department responsible for employment policy.
● Trades Union Congress: **www.tuc.org.uk**. The TUC is the umbrella organisation for most of the trade unions in the UK.
● Confederation of British Industries: **www.cbi.org.uk**. The CBI is the national representative body for UK employers.

- Advisory, Conciliation and Arbitration Service: **www.acas.org.uk**. Acas provides a range of impartial advice and publications on employment relations. Their website includes both the Code of Practice and Guide on discipline and grievances.
- CIPD: **cipd.co.uk**. Contains research and other documents on employment relations and managing diversity.
- Equality and Human Rights Commission: **www.equalityhumanrights.com**. The Commission has responsibility for monitoring the effect of equality legislation.

CHAPTER 12

Performance Management, Motivation and Reward

GARY REES AND ALEX TYMON

LEARNING OUTCOMES

After reading this chapter, you should be able to:

- identify the different ways that performance management (PM) can be defined and interpreted by organisations
- understand the assumptions which underpin the application of PM
- recognise the contribution of organisational theory, industrial engineering and behavioural science systems to the development of PM
- understand the relationship between performance, motivation and reward
- evaluate the extent to which PM can assist in improving organisational effectiveness and efficiency
- consider the contribution that HR can make to PM.

12.1 OVERVIEW

Organisational effectiveness and efficiency is rarely, if ever, off the management agenda in work organisations, and assumes an even higher priority during times of economic austerity. PM is one process that can enable organisations to produce greater quality of product or service. It is a potentially pivotal topic within the broader managing people area.

However, PM must not be regarded as the universal panacea for improving organisational effectiveness. This chapter places PM in context, and weighs up the pros and cons of adopting PM as a means to improve productivity or service by motivating employees to perform better and, at the same time, considers the arguments for the use of reward as a motivator.

Contemporary issues such as employee engagement and commitment are discussed as part of a focus on motivation theories and approaches, while we keep in view the underlying question of how HR can make a difference in adding value through PM.

12.2. INTRODUCTION

There is little doubt that most organisations in the twenty-first century share some common objectives in order to ensure their survival, so that by producing a consistent product and/or service – which raises more in revenue than it costs to provide – they will attract and retain customers and encourage them to keep spending. Not-for-profit organisations share some of these aims, such as the need for consistency and the requirement to minimise costs for the provision of their product or service. What is also beyond doubt is the role of people in helping to meet these objectives. PM is all about managing employees effectively and there is a wealth of research which demonstrates that well-managed employees increase revenues and decrease costs (see, for example, Coombs et al (2006) and Subramony (2009), two meta-analytic studies). A very persuasive example from the not-for-profit sector is also provided by West et al (2002), who demonstrate the link between PM and patient mortality in hospitals.

The ongoing economic turmoil post-2007 has further increased the spotlight on PM, with questions posed as to the robustness of PM in the light of the 'reward for failure' practices that accompanied the collapse of the banking industry. Wain (2009, p17) cites the CIPD's research, which demonstrated that 92% of its survey thought that closer scrutiny of poor performance accounted for the rising interest in PM.

In this chapter we consider the concept of PM and the theories of motivation that underpin it, along with its implications for managing and leading employees.

12.2.1 WHAT IS PERFORMANCE MANAGEMENT?

There are myriad definitions of PM, but one of the best known is that of Armstrong and Baron (2005), which has been adopted by the CIPD (2012i, p1):

> A process which contributes to the effective management of individuals and teams in order to achieve high levels of organisational performance. As such, it establishes shared understanding about what is to be achieved and an approach to leading and developing people which will ensure that it is achieved.

This definition informs us of two important factors: firstly, the all-encompassing nature of PM – it has been suggested that all activities within a business should be contributing towards better performance and that managing the performance of employees is 'running the business' (Mohrman and Mohrman 1995); and secondly, the implication that PM can be viewed as a 'continuous process' (Biron et al 2011, p1295), involving identifying, measuring and developing employees in line with organisation strategy.

The extent to which PM impacts upon performance is contingent upon the context and the interconnectedness and interlocking of various supporting mechanisms. The ultimate aim is to maximise organisational effectiveness, especially within the ever-changing context of the modern organisation (Budworth and Mann 2011).

The all-encompassing nature of PM can be seen by examining the people–performance link. A classic approach is demonstrated by the Boxall and Purcell (2008) AMO model (see Figure 7.3), in which performance is a function of ability, motivation and opportunity. Therefore, the role of the employer, their agent, or the manager has to be to maximise these three elements in order to enhance performance. However, it could be argued that the terminologies adopted by Boxall and Purcell (2011) need to be brought into line with current HR thinking and practice. Incorporating the elements of employee engagement (see Chapter 11) alongside employee commitment and job satisfaction allows us to expand the AMO model and recognise the increased complexity of high performance (see Figure 12.1). The nature of motivation will be discussed in more detail later in this chapter.

Figure 12.1 Some of the activities which could maximise ability, motivation, opportunity, satisfaction, commitment and engagement (AMOSCE)

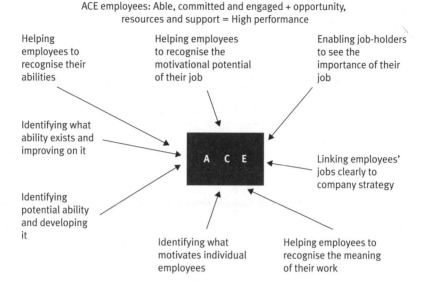

In the context of high-performance work organisations (HPWOs), research indicates that the activities presented in Figure 12.1 are representative of those demonstrated by top performing businesses. For example, Jamrog et al (2008) found that in a survey of 1,369 organisations, HPWOs have well-established values that are typically well understood by most employees and are key drivers of employee behaviour. They also report that HPWOs are clear about what behaviours employees need to exhibit in order to execute organisational and departmental strategies, and identified that managers need to:

• set clear goals
• understand employees' abilities
• guide and coach employees.

Although the relationship between these management activities and organisational performance is complex, and there are different levels of outcomes dependent on business sector and type of employee, there is evidence to show that PM is interpreted as an investment in staff, which leads to discretionary effort (McClean and Collins 2011).

The PM process includes the alignment of objectives and performance through measurement, assessment and monitoring. Where there is a gap between objectives and performance, appropriate HR supporting mechanisms are required (Figure 12.2).

It could therefore be argued that HR as a function can add value through the range of supporting mechanisms that it can provide.

Another method of considering the strategic nature of PM is through the 'balanced scorecard', which attempts to link employee rewards to performance in the areas of finance, customers, internal business processes and innovation, learning and growth.

According to Chavan (2009, p396), 'In some instances, companies see the non-financial measures as of such importance that a threshold level of performance is set for each of the non-financials. Only if an individual exceeds these threshold levels can they qualify for performance-related rewards linked to financial performance results.' The importance of organisational culture and vision also has a part to play in how the organisation considers and addresses performance.

Figure 12.2 HR supporting mechanisms

12.3 PERSPECTIVES ON PERFORMANCE MANAGEMENT

From a managerialist perspective, where the manager has to ensure the most effective and efficient use of resources (including people) in achieving business objectives, PM can be seen as a tool to control and manipulate; very much a top-down process. The assumption underlying this perspective of PM is that the organisation, in the form of a controlling manager, can make a positive impact upon an individual's work performance. Within this assumption, managers are expected to demonstrate both general management skills as well as skills directly related to the PM process. The latter could include task skills such as objective-setting, understanding technical aspects of the job.

12.4 MONITORING PROGRESS AND MEASURING RESULTS

General management skills, in contrast, could include leadership, mentoring, coaching (see Chapter 10) and interpersonal relationships. Managers may demonstrate strong task skills, but are often lacking confidence in the softer interpersonal and social skills (Bowles and Coates 1993).

The managerialist perspective also assumes a hierarchy of control, with a direct relationship between manager and subordinate. This is more difficult to achieve in complex organisational structures, such as multidimensional matrix structures. For example, a subordinate may report to several different line managers, who are all based in different locations. The control aspect of PM is legitimised through the perceived objectivity of the process. This objectivity then becomes the driving force for achieving performance outputs (Levinson 1970, 1976).

12.4.1 THE ETERNAL TRIANGLE

Herzberg (1968) presents the eternal triangle perspective, in which there are three general philosophies of personnel (or HR) management: organisational theory; industrial engineering; and behavioural science.

The organisational theorist Weber (1947) believed that human needs are either so irrational or so varied and adjustable that personnel management has to be as pragmatic as the occasion demands. Herzberg cites the example of job design, where, if jobs are organised in a proper manner, the result will be the most efficient job structure, and the most favourable attitudes will follow. Alternatively, within the eternal triangle theory, the industrial engineers (Taylor 1911) believe that humankind is mechanistically orientated and economically motivated, and therefore we need to attune the individual to the most efficient working process. Here we need to design the most appropriate incentive system and design the most appropriate working system for the human machine. Behavioural scientists (eg Schein 1984) focus on group sentiments, the attitudes of individual employees and the organisation's social and psychological climate, with the emphasis on instilling healthy employee attitudes and an appropriate organisational climate. This model illustrates a useful analogy for the use and possible misuse of PM as means to improve performance in organisations.

12.5 PERFORMANCE MANAGEMENT AS A PROCESS

PM can also be viewed as a process by looking at the employee lifecycle and the management activities which could contribute to improved performance at each stage. The advantage of this approach is that it can provide guidance to organisations on which activities to introduce and when.

Before recruitment and during the selection process, some of these activities are understood and are embedded in many organisations, others less so. For example, how any organisations provide sufficient information to enable prospective employees to 'self-select' themselves out of the recruitment process thereby potentially saving costs and effort of managing employees who cannot or will not be successful? How many organisations are explicit in looking for employees whose values are aligned to that of the business and are therefore more likely to be committed? How many organisations make the conscious effort to test for potential at the recruitment stage?

During formal induction, when organisations run induction or orientation schemes, to what extent is the robustness of these schemes measured and subsequent action taken? Is there recognition that this is the stage at which employees learn both the formal and informal rules of behaviour and the difference between the overt or stated expectations of the organisation, and the reality of what will be tolerated in practice? A robust induction process can be invaluable in making performance standards and expectations explicit.

Research around the 'induction crisis' identifies problems which may manifest themselves in both the short term and long term. For example, the Reed Consulting Survey (2004) demonstrated that 4% of new starters walk out of the job because of poor or non-existent induction programmes, and 93% of the 5,700 respondents in their survey believed that a poor induction had a continuing adverse effect on their productivity at work.

During the period, to what extent do line managers appreciate the true value of the probationary period? All too often, it consists of a form-filling exercise initiated by the HR department. The manager signs to say that the new employee should have their position confirmed but without having any idea of how they are actually performing.

Then a few months later the manager is complaining that the employee is underperforming, or worse still, is asking HR how they can remove them. During formal reviews and appraisals, how many managers recognise the value of constant feedback, both positive and developmental? Behaviourist learning theory (Skinner 1953, cited in

French et al 2011) demonstrates the power of positively reinforcing desired behaviours: employees are much more likely to repeat actions that gain them positive recognition. Positive reinforcement has also been shown to increase employees' 'self-efficacy beliefs', which in turn, increases performance (Bandura 1993).

However, there appears to be a blockage against recognising when an employee has performed to standard, a belief that employees should exceed before they receive recognition. A typical comment on supervisor training courses is: 'Why should I recognise an employee who has just reached the standard? That is their job.' But if we employ someone and ask them to reach a certain standard and they do, then this should be recognised and the danger of not doing so is that performance and standards will slide.

The power of positive feedback is the theory supporting appreciative inquiry (see below), but many managers appear to spend their time and effort looking for and acting on the 5% of jobs that people do badly, whilst ignoring the 95% that they do effectively.

An excuse sometimes cited for lack of feedback is the idea that people learn from mistakes, and it is certainly true that allowing people to fail can be useful in some circumstances. Control theory (Carver et al 2000) indicates that failure can even motivate more than success. Learning organisation theory (Ellinger 2004) suggests that freedom to fail is an important factor to enable an organisation to grow. But there is a lot of difference between giving employees space to experiment accompanied by constructive feedback and abdication management. According to Geal and Johnson (2002, p26):

> What do people learn from mistakes? What not to do, so they need to try something else. But, what else? A manager able and willing to give developmental feedback so they can improve is both necessary and motivating when handled well.

So using the excuse of allowing people to learn from mistakes could be viewed as lazy at best, and at worst could be incredibly costly for the organisation. In summary, the balance between allowing experimentation and providing appropriate feedback needs constant review.

At any time in the employee lifecycle, there may be the need to manage poor performance or conduct. This raises the question of how many managers are able and willing to manage poor performance or conduct in a positive way before it becomes a major issue. An organisation may well have a 'capability and conduct' procedure, which will undoubtedly espouse the wisdom of dealing with performance and conduct issues informally and early. But how many organisations train and support their managers to run these informal 'improving poor performance/poor conduct' discussions?

Table 12.1 Performance management as a process

Employee activity	Timeline and action	Manager/employer activity
Gains knowledge of expectations and culture Self-selects in or out	Before recruitments: Job descriptions, person specifications, adverts, company information	Gives signals of expectations on job performance standards, conduct standards and culture
Demonstrates ability and motivation Conscious or subconscious alignment with values Self-selects in or out	During selection process: Interviews/assessments, etc	Tests ability and motivation Checks values alignment Seeks potential

Employee activity	Timeline and action		Manager/employer activity
Learns conduct expectations Adapts to the culture	During formal induction/ orientation	At any time: Possible poor performance or poor conduct intervention	Formalises conduct expectations, terms and conditions/ handbook, etc
Learns performance standards Develops knowledge and skills	During mandatory training		Provides standards of job performance Provides knowledge and skills Provides feedback
Becomes a productive employee Adapts to the culture	During probation period		Team briefing and communication Reinforces performance and conduct standards Provides feedback One-to-one reviews Provides ongoing training and coaching
Reviews performance Agrees objectives Identifies learning needs Considers aspirations Possibly gains reward	During formal reviews and/ or appraisals: Annual or more regularly		Reviews performance Sets objectives Agrees learning needs Identifies potential and aspirations Possible link to reward
Continuous improvement Develops self-feedback mechanisms Achieves potential	Ongoing: Business as usual		Team briefing and communication Reinforces performance and conduct standards Provides feedback One-to-one reviews Ongoing training and coaching

12.5.1 APPRECIATIVE INQUIRY

Drawn from research into positive psychology (Seligman 1998), appreciative inquiry suggests that when employees are encouraged to focus on their strengths, then they are more likely to succeed and enjoy greater job satisfaction (Bryce 2007). For a practical example, see Arkin (2005b).

CASE STUDY 12.1

PERFORMANCE APPRAISAL AT SODASTREAM

Operating in over 30 countries, SodaStream is the world's largest manufacturer, distributor and marketer of home water-carbonation systems. A change in HR personnel led to a project aimed at designing a new appraisal process. Focus groups were carried out to understand issues with the existing scheme and to answer a key question: What are the conditions that can make our performance evaluation process a success? The majority of employees described the existing system as an unpleasant and unhelpful experience; however, they also believed that it was crucial to have a performance appraisal process that was able to: positively energise employees; include follow-up; raise employee motivation; and be short and simple. As a result of this feedback, the HR team at SodaStream commissioned a new process building on the concepts behind appreciative inquiry and positive psychology, which was piloted with 64 employees and 26 managers.

Strength-based performance appraisal (SBPA) – the principles

The goals of the new system were: to improve organisational performance and business results; focus on employees' strengths but without neglecting problems; reflect the double meaning of appreciation, that is, valuing good performance and increasing value; and support knowledge management within the organisation.

To this end, seven principles were adopted: feed forward; reflected best self-feedback; happiness research; developing strengths; the 3:1 positive to negative emotion principle; a win–win philosophy; positive organisational core; and collective efficacy.

The SodaStream performance appraisal

The SBPA system at SodaStream contains six steps:

- supervisor–employee meeting including success stories told by the subordinate and enthusiasm stories told by the supervisor
- a joint questionnaire and preparation of reports
- a second supervisor–employee meeting involving a strength-based evaluation discussion looking for new ways to use strengths and agree goals to achieve win–win outcomes
- creation of an organisational strengths map
- a celebration party to recognise strengths
- a follow-up process.

An initial evaluation

Benefits of the new system as reported by subordinates included: increased quality time with managers; a positive experience of performance evaluation; a focus on strengths; goal-setting; increased learning; and better matching of competencies to tasks.

For the organisation, reported benefits included: increased levels of motivation and performance; better goal-setting; improved organisational culture; increased collaboration; and improved manager–employee relationships.

Source: Bouskila-Yam and Kluger (2011)

Questions

1   How does the SodaStream performance appraisal process differ from ones you are familiar with?

2   What would need to be in place in an organisation in order to adopt this type of process?

REFLECTIVE ACTIVITY 12.1

Think about an organisation with which you are familiar. Using Table 12.1 as a guide, consider the evidence for a clear PM process being in place. What evidence exists that it has been implemented in an effective manner?

However, there is more to PM than just the actions involved. Effective PM is not only dependent upon *what* is done, but also upon *how* it is done. Purcell et al (2003) provide research evidence to support the proposition that no one particular HR practice is critical to organisational success, but rather that good management by line managers, applying various approaches effectively and appropriately according to the context, is the key factor. Committed and capable line managers are, therefore, essential to successful PM (Hutchinson and Purcell 2003). These managers need to know the 'how' of PM as much as the 'what'; that is, the answers to questions such as:

- How can we define performance?
- Who should define performance?
- How can we measure performance?
- What is the link between motivation and performance?

12.5.2 DEFINING PERFORMANCE

For performance to be managed it has to be defined and measured. This demonstrates that what the organisation measures is indicative of what the organisation values (Johnson et al 2011).

There is no single, universal definition of performance; it depends very much on the particular perspective adopted. For example, some definitions relate to the organisation and various expectations in terms of outputs: Performance should be defined as the outcomes of work because they provide the strongest linkage to the strategic goals of the organisation, customer satisfaction, and economic contributions (Bernadin et al 1995).

Other definitions emphasise behavioural aspects, in addition to outputs or results: Performance means both behaviours and results. Behaviours emanate from the performer and transform performance from abstraction to action. Not just the instruments for results, behaviours are also outcomes in their own right – the product of mental and physical effort applied to tasks – and can be judged apart from results (Brumbach 1988, p389).

12.5.3 WHO DEFINES PERFORMANCE?

It is not only a question of *how* performance is defined, but also *who* within the organisation is, or are, responsible for defining performance standards. Often, it is the organisation itself that determines performance and how it will be measured. Performance requirements are often part of a strategic planning process, cascading top-down through the organisation from senior management (Humble 1972). However, this does not have to be the case. Semler (1993) describes a bottom-up approach, where employees at Semco were allowed to set their own performance targets and define appropriate rewards. There is also the possibility of a combined top-down and bottom-up approach, with mutual adjustment of goals and objectives (Nonaka and Takeuchi 1995).

Other stakeholders, such as shareholders, and customers, will have their own views on performance standards or achievements and their views may be contradictory. The parties involved have different perspectives, expectations and experience of performance. For example, shareholders are interested in long-term value of stocks and assets. Middle management may have an interest in protecting and advancing their own position, power and rewards. Customers are increasingly demanding high-quality, customised products and services. In addition, all of these stakeholders may adopt different roles at different times or have multiple, simultaneous roles. Therefore, the agreement of what constitutes effective performance may be difficult to reach.

A more integrated approach may help to overcome some of the problems inherent in defining performance and performance standards. It is generally accepted that involving employees in the setting of objectives and targets is more likely to gain commitment to their achievement. Fundamentally, though, for the organisation to succeed, someone, somewhere needs to combine the targets to ensure that the organisational objectives are indeed being met. This is a line management responsibility, but HR might need to empower and ensure that the process is taking place.

12.5.4 WHAT ASPECTS OF PERFORMANCE CAN BE MEASURED?

What an organisation chooses to measure, and when, depends on the PM framework adopted within the organisational context and on what the organisation values in its employees; for example, to what extent is learning valued as part of the PM process? But a robust PM process typically relies on the setting of definable and measurable goals and targets, which raises challenges as it is impossible to measure all aspects of an employee's performance. For example, how does an organisation measure knowledge-creation, creativity and innovation? PM too often assumes explicit performance measures and cannot always incorporate tacit inputs, throughputs and outputs at individual, group and organisational levels.

Similarly, there are temporal barriers. Performance targets are typically set in time and the timescale might in itself affect accurate measurement. How does one allow for long-term performance improvements and outcomes within an annual appraisal cycle, for example? The critical issue then becomes when we measure and record performance.

In addition there is the challenge of the traditional PM emphasis on the individual, whereas the increasingly interdependent nature of work, and the consequent emphasis on team and groups, makes measurement more challenging. It is not just individual performance that is important, but also the contribution that the individual makes towards group effort, and the combined output of the group as a whole. So team targets are an area that needs to be explored.

An example of these complexities can be seen in a study by Rosen et al (2011), who explore the challenges of managing and measuring adaptive performance in teams. This is potentially a very important aspect in the modern business environment; however, it can be difficult to measure behavioural dimensions over time, across groups of employees – as opposed to individuals.

12.5.5 PITFALLS OF DEFINING PERFORMANCE TARGETS

There are many pitfalls with objectives and targets. Reeves (2008) used the term 'targetology' to describe the fixation of the then British Government and many organisations with targets. He agrees that targets can be helpful, citing the reduction in hospital waiting times as an example, but he questions the number of targets which are used:

> One or two clear targets can be powerful. A hundred targets is a recipe for confusion, stress and disaster. . . Just because targets are good, it does not mean that more targets are better.

Hall (2009, p10) argues that 'Focusing organisation and individual activity on what really matters, through the use of targets linked to strategic aims, can be a powerful management "tool" but careful consideration needs to be given to what is targeted, how targets are applied and who targets are applied to.'

Research by Professor Yves Emery (2008) identifies some common issues with both defining targets and attaining them: policy deployment, quality versus quantity targets, goal displacement, individualisation effect, goal override and limited influence. An example of each is provided in Table 12.2.

 REFLECTIVE ACTIVITY 12.2

Analyse the targets or objectives that you have been set during a PM process. To what extent do the pitfalls listed in Table 12.2 apply to these? How could your targets be improved upon?

12.5.6 MEASURING PERFORMANCE

The PM process (Table 12.1) shows that measurement or performance review and feedback should be an ongoing activity, so that positive reinforcement or corrective action can be supplied as soon as it is justified. Normal management activities such as walking the floor and one-to-one reviews can enable this measurement to happen and ensure that one of the 'golden rules' of appraisals is followed: 'No surprises', that is, anything discussed in a period review or appraisal concerning performance should be expected by both parties.

This is important as 'surprised employees become angry employees, and angry employees sue' (Segal 2010, p76).

Table 12.2 Pitfalls of target definition

	Example
Policy deployment The difficulties of translating strategic goals into meaningful bottom line targets. Not all objectives are easily split and can become meaningless if broken down too much	A common strategic goal, such as 'increase market share', which may well translate into specific objectives for senior managers, but is almost impossible to be a meaningful objective for a back office employee such as a payroll data entry clerk
Quality versus quantity targets With quantity targets being easier to set and therefore being used in place of quality targets which may be more beneficial	An HR officer may be set a target to ensure 95% of employees who leave the organisation complete an exit interview: a very SMART target. But actually what is really wanted is quality of data from exiting employees about why they are leaving, so that meaningful decisions can be made
Goal displacement Where the measures become seen as the goal	In a call centre the goal may be to improve customer service and one measure of this is to answer calls more quickly. It is easy for employees to 'lose calls' – that is, drop them as soon as they are answered – in order to improve the call-answering statistics, which actually results in even worse customer service

	Example
Individualisation effect Where competing goals set up unintended competition between staff, especially competition for scarce resources	A cable TV sales team may be measured on the number of customers they sign up, and to ensure quality of sales the customers have to stay for a minimum time period of six months. However, the technicians who install the product in the customer's home are measured on speed of install and the quicker the install, the more likely there will be a problem, which in turn leads to customers disconnecting
Goal override Where employees only focus on goal achievement and neglect other important responsibilities. It may become necessary to have a relatively complex measurement system in order to ensure that the 'day job' carries equal weight	A hotel maintenance team may be targeted on the completion of reported repairs and may go flat out to achieve these targets. As a result they may neglect the preventative maintenance jobs, which are a part of their job description, because they are not overtly measured
Limited influence Where employees have very little control over the targets set, or at least perceive this to be the case	In a retail environment where product range, price and advertising are all centrally controlled a shop assistant may easily perceive that they really have very little control over the actual sales that they make and this perception may actually be real. It has also been argued that employees are just the delivery system and that 90% of the impact of their endeavours comes from the system!

Another measurement technique, which is often overlooked, is self-measurement. Although different theorists may argue why, they do mostly conclude that participation in goal-setting can lead to improved performance. The research that supports the idea of autonomy and participation in goal-setting is also well known and includes the work of Herzberg (1968), Hackman and Oldham (1980) and Locke and Latham (1990), to name but a few. For example, Locke (1968) in Hollyforde and Whiddett (2002) identified the value of goals as a motivator and performance enhancer suggesting that specific rather than general goals and participation in goal-setting are important in improving performance. Locke also identifies self-regulation or self-measurement and management as being powerful enablers, an idea supported by Bandura (1993, p128), who states that:

> Most human motivation is cognitively generated. People motivate themselves and guide their actions anticipatorily by the exercise of forethought... Forethought is translated into incentives and appropriate action through self-regulatory mechanisms. This suggests that self-measurement is an everyday activity.

Latham (2007) provides a useful summary of some of the research around this area, but the message appears to be that although the effects are mediated and moderated by other factors, such as personality, involving employees in goal-setting and facilitating self-feedback can and does result in higher performance. This perhaps provides an argument for the use of more self-appraisal and for developing ways in which employees can access their own feedback on performance.

12.5.7 APPRAISAL AS A PERFORMANCE MANAGEMENT TOOL

The more recent literature (for example, Aguinis 2009), calls for a wide view of PM, including performance planning, assessment and review, identifying that it is more than simply appraisal. But some form of performance appraisal is nearly always incorporated with the aim of improving performance, motivating employees and/or allocating rewards.

An honest and accurate assessment of current performance can be a strong driver for further learning, development and performance improvement. As discussed earlier, feedback and the setting of improvement targets can itself be a strong motivator (Locke and Latham 1990), and for there to be equitable distribution of rewards some fair method of comparing contributions between individuals is required. The potential impact of fairness is highlighted by Adams' equity theory – see 12.6.1 'Motivation Theories' below.

The whole PM system should therefore ensure that employees perceive equity of treatment and fairness, none more so than in the appraisal process and distribution of rewards. This supports the argument that PM and reward policies need to be transparent. The role of perception means that extra attention must be paid to how the process is communicated so as to ensure that the message is clear and universally understood.

However, there is a wealth of evidence that points to negative aspects of performance appraisal and at least three recent books that have called for an end to them (Bouskila-Yam and Kluger 2011). Very careful consideration is therefore needed when choosing a performance appraisal process and planning its implementation.

12.5.8 TYPES OF APPRAISAL

Different types of appraisal include: top-down, self-appraisal, peer appraisal, bottom-up and multi-rater, such as 360-degree and 720-degree feedback. The most common is a top-down approach with the inclusion of self-appraisal, usually as a preparatory activity for the employee. There are many benefits of a multi-rater approach, which in theory will produce a more rounded outcome, but the time and expense involved often rules this out as an option.

Appraisal methods can be divided into two main approaches: those oriented towards results (outputs); and those oriented towards competencies (inputs). Results-oriented appraisal is based on the setting of quantifiable, achievable and time-bounded objectives, most often agreed between manager and subordinate, and geared towards achieving organisational objectives. Competency-oriented appraisal is based on the demonstration of certain key skills and behaviours thought to be associated with high performance. These skills and behaviours, agreed by manager and employee, may also include the use of multi-rater instruments. The trend in recent years is towards combining both results and competency-based approaches in an attempt to deliver the dual benefits of achieving immediate performance targets and supporting longer-term development of key skills and capabilities.

Appraisals and the link to development and reward

PM systems differ in the emphasis they give to rewards or development. The trend is for increasing emphasis on development rather than reward, and de-emphasising the link between PM and pay (Armstrong and Baron 2005). PM and development are overlapping and interdependent processes. Performance reviews, whether they are periodic appraisals or continuous day-to-day interactions between managers and employees, provide encouragement for learning and development. Development may take the form of informal training, self-managed learning by the individual employee, coaching by the manager, or more structured training and development interventions. Whatever the form, development is intended to have a direct impact on performance capabilities and can also have a powerful motivational effect (CIPD 2012i).

However, multiple perspectives on appraisals lead to conflicts. Reconciling PM as a developmental process and as a pay decision-making process is not straightforward. Linking performance appraisal to pay reduces the focus on development (Kessler and Purcell 1992). An employee is less likely to highlight a development need if it might be seen as a weakness and therefore detrimentally affect their pay award.

12.5.9 POTENTIAL PITFALLS WHEN EVALUATING EMPLOYEES

Appraisals ask for evaluations to be made, and accordingly there are potential pitfalls, some of which are highlighted below.

Rating scale issues

In appraisal systems where a rating scale is used, there are constant issues with people being unhappy with the 'average' rating. Standard distribution dictates that not everyone will be at the top, some people will be at the bottom and most people will be in the middle. But being rated as 'competent', 'satisfactory', 'C' or '3/5' is unsatisfactory for people who can see 'exceptional', 'A' or '5/5' on the scale.

The Swiss Federal Administration trialled a new system with the following grades:

A++	Far beyond expectations
A+	Beyond expectations
A	Objectives fully reached
B	Objectives partially reached
C	Objectives missed

Although people psychologically still want to be A++, most employees will be rated as an A, which is psychologically better than a C (Emery 2008). However, despite all the research into improving rating scales, there is little evidence that one is better than another, and recent focus has moved onto trying to minimise rater bias (Budworth and Mann 2011).

Appraiser bias

Appraisers all have their own biases. Some have tendencies to rate everyone kindly or everyone harshly, which can raise issues, especially when rewards are linked and comparisons are made with other teams, whose managers have rated differently. In addition, there are those who struggle to differentiate between any employees, wanting something for everyone, known as the 'watering can effect'. Furnham (1997) identified 13 different 'perception errors', which he said could negatively influence an appraisal system.

These pitfalls can severely affect an employee's sense of equity and cause dissatisfaction with the system, which in turn is likely to diminish performance. Furnham's 13 systematic perception errors are:

1 First impressions – rather than how the appraisee has performed.

2 Halo effect – only focusing on one favourable behaviour or quality.

3 Horns effect – contrary to halo effect; a negative rating.

4 Contrast error – comparison with selected employees, often star performers.

5 Same as me – rating appraises highly due to sharing common attributes with appraiser.

6 Different from me – contrary to same as me.

7 Recency effect – judging only recent behaviour, then generalising.

8 Central tendency – rating everyone in the middle of the scale.

9 Leniency in rating – generous to everyone to avoid conflict.

10 Strict rating – consistently strict in appraising performance.

11 Performance dimension error – where two aspects of the appraisal follow, score two distinct qualities the same.

12 Spillover effect – based on previous appraisal.

13 Status effect – giving better ratings to higher-level employees.

Much of the training provided to appraisers attempts to reduce and minimise the impact of these types of rater bias.

 REFLECTIVE ACTIVITY 12.3

Peter Cheese, CEO of the CIPD, argued in a blog article entitled 'Putting the human into HR' (2015) that managers who see established companies such as Accenture and Deloitte scrapping enshrined practices, like the annual performance review and performance rankings, would consider following suit. Cheese questions the validity and usefulness of long-established practices like PM, where there is now a need to remove the emphasis from control to enablement, which sounds plausible, but may not be so easy to bring about in practice.

1 During the 1980s, the concept of 'empowerment' was prevalent in some quarters and may have seemed to some managers to be the way forward. To what extent is Cheese's assertion of enablement simply a repetition of the notion of empowerment?

2 Consider the implications for management and leadership if we were to reduce or possibly abolish management tools, like the performance management system.

12.5.10 REWARD PITFALLS

Whilst not all formal appraisal systems are overtly linked to rewards, there are many potential issues with appraisal systems being linked to rewards. Fixed quota systems, where evaluation is based on the amount of reward available and not on actual levels of performance, can lead to meaningless appraisals for employees, especially if the total amount of money available is limited. Evidence suggests that less than 10% of annual salary has a very limited effect on motivating people to higher performance (Emery 2008). In the current economic climate, the question has to be asked as to how many organisations can make budgetary arrangements for this amount of money. If a smaller 'pot' is to be distributed in such a way as to offer more than 10% to some employees, are managers willing or able to differentiate enough between their employees?

Dependent upon organisational structure and context, the practice of team reward may inhibit or adversely affect individual motivation (for further reading, see the CIPD website).

Do employees who are less confident and think they cannot achieve the standards to attain a bonus actually work less hard, so in effect the reward becomes a demotivator? Which leads to a fundamental question: do rewards such as pay and other recognition schemes actually motivate employees at all?

12.6 MOTIVATED TO PERFORM?

It must be remembered that PM is, in itself, simply a process. Human beings don't always follow rules and do exactly what they are told. In order to maximise performance by employees themselves, we need to understand the human psyche by considering key aspects such as motivation, commitment and engagement.

12.6.1 MOTIVATION THEORIES

Content and process approaches

Content theories focus on what (outcome or reward) motivates people. Common examples of content theories include: existence-relatedness-growth (ERG) theory (Alderfer), achievement theory (McClelland), two-factor theory (Herzberg), and hierarchy of needs theory (Maslow). In contrast, process theories concentrate on how people are motivated, or the cognitive process used to connect effort with outcomes or reward. Goal-setting theory (Locke 1968) is an example of a process theory, as are equity theory (Adams) and expectancy theory (Vroom), which are both discussed below. For an in-depth treatment of content and process motivation theories, see Mullins (2013). Effective management interventions combine both content and process motivation theories as they are complementary not opposites (Hollyforde and Whiddett 2002).

Equity theory

Adams' (1965) equity theory contends that employees consider the inputs, for example, abilities and effort they bring to work, in relation to the outputs (perceived rewards they gain as a result), and then go on to compare the ratio of these two factors with referent others, through the use of the distributive justice concept (see Chapter 4).

A perceived injustice motivates the individual to take action – they can increase or decrease their inputs, or seek to increase or decrease the inputs of others. Alternatively, they can seek to change the outputs for either themselves or others. In extreme circumstances they may choose to leave the organisation. Leaving the organisation may also include psychological withdrawal, for example, turning up for work but spending all day on Facebook. It is important to note the critical part that perception plays in equity theory, so the injustice may not be perceived by others (Mullins 2013).

All through the twentieth century, theorists argued about the capacity of money to motivate employees towards greater performance (Latham 2007). Money, or what it can supply (money can be a status symbol or a sign of recognition), appears in all of the 'content' theories of motivation and therefore it is implied that money is a motivator (see 'Reflection theory' below). Barber and Bretz (2000) suggest that money is among the most important factors for people when deciding on a job.

REFLECTIVE ACTIVITY 12.4

Think about yourself and talk to others you know. What was it that made you and they think about looking for a new job?

This activity may give some insight into the complexity of the question as to whether money is a motivator. One only has to consider the 70,000 'games-makers' who volunteered to work during the Olympics and Paralympics of 2012 to recognise that money is not always the single motivator. These people were driven by other factors, and whilst without doubt some were driven by extrinsic drivers such as social or status needs, for many, the motivation would have been intrinsic, such as a sense of achievement or development and growth.

Expectancy theory

A process theory of motivation seeks to explain the cognitive process of how an individual is motivated to increase performance. A common example by Vroom (1964) is explained through the formula:

F = E I V

F is the force of motivation, ie how much effort will be applied ('how hard I am willing to work'). E is expectancy, ie the belief that extra effort will result in better performance ('if I work harder, my output will increase').

I is instrumentality, ie the belief that better performance will lead to a reward ('if my output increases, I will get a reward').

V is valence, the perceived value of the reward ('how much I want the reward'). Valence links back to content theories of motivation, which tell us that individuals are motivated by a multitude of factors (needs and wants), including money, but also security, affiliation, power, achievement, status, growth and more.

Source: Buchanan and Huczynski (2010)

Contemporary views of motivation

Motivation theories never die, but some of them certainly age. Despite the ongoing criticism of Maslow's theory of the hierarchy of needs, many organisations still adopt this framework to unpick and understand human motivation. If we ignore the need to satisfy each level, starting with basic hygiene factors, then elements of esteem needs and self-actualisation may be associated with newer concepts, like 'employee engagement'. The 1990s saw the emergence of three psychological conditions (Kahn 1990), which impacted upon engagement (and disengagement): psychological meaningfulness, psychological safety and psychological availability. These three terms can be interpreted as: firstly, feelings of worthwhileness, being valued and useful to the organisation. Safety relates to carrying out work without losing face, and maintaining dignity and respect within working relationships. Psychological availability includes the sense of emotional, physical and psychological resources to engage at a given time.

Nohria et al (2008) argue that people are driven by four basic emotional needs or drives, which underpin everything that we do:

1   *The drive to acquire* – mainly physical goods, like money, which enhances our social status and then allows us to compare ourselves to others.

2   *The drive to bond* – people need to have a positive emotional bond to their organisation and people within it too.

3   *The drive to comprehend* – seeking meaning and contribution, seeking challenges and the scope to learn and grow.

4   *The drive to defend* – by promoting justice and feelings of security, as well as the need to maintain the status quo. Nohria's drives are not hierarchical in nature, but are relevant upon key 'levers' of motivation, namely: culture, job design, the reward system and performance management processes.

REFLECTIVE ACTIVITY 12.5

Review Maslow's (1943) Hierarchy of Needs model. Compare and contrast this with Nohria's Four Basic Drives of motivation model. What are the key differences, and do these reflect changes within a more contemporary society?

The importance of intrinsic motivation

The resurgence of interest in intrinsic factors such as meaning, purpose, spirituality and commitment and, more recently, engagement, has emphasised the importance of work as a motivator in the organisation (Fox 1994, Lockwood 2007, Meyer and Herscovitch 2001). Intrinsic motivation is the spontaneous satisfaction individuals derive from the activity itself. Extrinsic motivation, in contrast, requires tangible or verbal rewards (Ankil and Palliam 2012). Intrinsic motivation can lead to more engaged and committed employees and the four most critical intrinsic rewards are: a sense of meaning and purpose; a sense of choice; a sense of competence; and a sense of progress (Chalofsky and Krishna 2009). In terms of meaningfulness, people with the highest levels of productivity and fulfilment view themselves as inseparable from their work, intrinsically motivated by the work itself and professionally committed to and engaged with the organisation (Chalofsky and Krishna 2009).

So, there is evidence to suggest money can reduce the effectiveness of intrinsic motivation and there are circumstances when it appears not to. The deciding factor, as is so often the case, is not what is done, but how it is done. Even if money is a motivational factor, it is commonly linked to equity theory (as discussed earlier in this chapter), ie employees compare their rewards with colleagues and if they perceive unfair treatment, they are motivated to act. Transparency in how rewards such as pay are implemented is therefore very important. In addition, expectancy theories of motivation (see below) also provide potential guidelines on implementation of reward policies and practice.

Commitment and job satisfaction

Defined by Koster (2011, p2838) as: 'the decision to participate', organisational commitment can be seen as the psychological bond between an individual and an organisation. Meyer and Herscovitch (2001) concluded that employees can be committed to different targets, including their occupation, team or manager in addition to or in place of their organisation. The positive benefits of increased employee commitment are well documented and include: increased performance outcomes; enhanced organisational citizenship behaviours; and reduced labour turnover (see, for example, Meyer Herscovitch 2002).

Meyer and Allen (1991) expanded the concept of commitment to explain why it leads to positive outcomes, outlining three components: affective commitment – emotional attachment to the target; normative commitment – moral obligation to the target; and continuance commitment – a perceived lack of choice on whether to leave the organisation. Mayfield and Mayfield (2012) argue that affective commitment is the most powerful of the three components.

Job satisfaction, a more established concept, deals with how a person feels about their job or work experience (Locke 1976). High levels of job satisfaction are not thought to increase performance directly; however, job satisfaction has been shown to increase commitment, reduce grievances, lower labour turnover and contribute to engagement.

Hackman and Oldham's (1980) job characteristics model in French et al (2011) links five job characteristics – skill variety, task identity, task significance, autonomy and feedback – with positive psychological states (see also Chapter 8). This model provides a platform for linking meaningful jobs with higher levels of job satisfaction.

12.7 THE LINKS BETWEEN REWARD AND PERFORMANCE

The topic of reward is in itself a significant area for research and debate. For further in-depth discussions, see Perkins and White (2011).

12.7.1 PAY AND INTRINSIC MOTIVATION

According to Kuvaas (2006), the link between pay and performance is mediated and moderated by employees' personal levels of intrinsic motivation. It is suggested that money, an extrinsic motivator, may actually decrease long-term intrinsic motivation and so have a detrimental effect on performance.

Two conflicting meta-analyses were published in 2001, both trying to establish the link between extrinsic rewards and intrinsic motivation, and the results are mixed. According to Deci et al (2001), the use of rewards as a motivational strategy is a risky proposition, as this disengages interest and self-regulation. Cameron et al (2001) counteracted this by stating that rewards are not harmful to motivation to perform a task (see Latham (2007) for a summary of the debate). Interestingly, recent evidence from a multiple employer study showed that performance-related pay (PRP) was positively related to intrinsic motivation, which can shape the workforce. Employees for whom PRP is a motivator will self-select to work in organisations which offer this benefit (Fang and Gerhart 2012).

12.7.2 PERFORMANCE-RELATED REWARD – EXPECTANCY THEORY IN ACTION

A classic use of expectancy theory is to define and execute a performance-related reward scheme, in order to improve short-term performance. An example could be an attempt to increase sales of sports shoes in a sports shop in the lead up to Christmas: the employer wants to increase the amount of effort (force) that employees will put in. For this to work employees need the following:

- A belief that putting in extra effort, talking to customers, learning about stock, etc will result in making extra sales. So they need training, goal-setting and feedback to this effect (expectancy).
- A belief that the extra sales they make will be recognised by their manager and result in a reward. This could be extra pay, prizes, recognition, promotion, a permanent contract, time off, more interesting work, etc. There needs to be a system for individuals to record their sales that actually result in the promised reward being given (instrumentality).
- A belief that the reward is worth having to them. This is a good reason to offer a choice of rewards if possible (valence).

 REFLECTIVE ACTIVITY 12.6

Why is pay important to an individual member?

Does pay provide the mirror by which an employee reflects images of power, status, value and succession? The meaning that pay holds is largely deduced from employees' personal characteristics (values), pay level (relative to others) and the level of familiarity the person experiences with the pay system (pay system knowledge). These meanings are expected to influence employee outcomes such as satisfaction, motivation and performance (Thiery 2001, in Salimaki et al 2009).

This view is supported by anecdotal evidence of practitioners pointing to exit interview data and proclaiming that lack of money is the reason for demotivated people leaving an organisation. However, more detailed analysis may produce a different picture. People who have decided to leave an organisation may well quote the 'bigger and better' pay packet as the reason for joining a new organisation, but if a different exit interview question is asked – 'What made you start looking for another job to start with?'– then other factors begin to emerge. People become dissatisfied and demotivated with jobs due to poor management, lack of opportunities and boredom. Therefore HR responding to management requests to match pay offers from competitors in order to retain employees seldom works, especially in the longer term.

Is performance-related pay right for your organisation?

As both performance and motivation are affected by many factors, PRP (or any other intervention) cannot be linked in a causal manner. Williams (1998, p173) argues that managers' and employees' views need to be considered in order to analyse the effect of PRP on motivation and performance. Whilst the debate around PRP continues, it is worth considering some of the operational difficulties that have been associated with reward practice.

The following set of questions has been raised by Williams (1998, p176) and adapted to fit the categories provided.

With regard to organisational culture, teams and individual attitudes to PRP:

- Is PRP appropriate to all organisations?
- Is there a climate of trust (particularly in line manager–subordinate relations)?
- What effect does PRP have on team and co-operative building?
- Does a focus on individual performance lead employees to place self-interest ahead of those of the organisation generally?
- Does PRP create divisiveness?
- Does PRP encourage short-termism?

He similarly raises questions about the PM process itself:

- What criteria should be used for measuring performance? Outputs? Inputs? Both?
- Can individual performance be measured objectively and fairly?
- Can performance be defined comprehensively?
- Do line managers have the willingness and ability required to operate PRP?
- How much of performance is within the individual's control?
- How should average performers be treated?

Questions related to the value of rewards also need to be addressed:

- What amount of pay constitutes a significant increase in the eyes of employees?
- Will PRP diminish the value of intrinsic rewards?

It may be relatively simple to provide an answer to each of these individual questions. However, when considered together, the complexity of linking PRP to performance becomes much more evident. Thus simple, prescriptive solutions cannot be found.

So the question of whether money is a motivator that can lead to improved performance is a very complex one and the answer is by no means clear (Latham 2007). At best, it can be said that there is a connection between money and satisfaction, which may under certain circumstances increase commitment and perhaps performance. More important is the fact that all employees will be motivated by different factors, as highlighted by the 'content theories'. The effective manager will recognise this and work towards helping employees gain maximum motivation at work, using the principles of expectancy theories and equity theory to make this happen.

TOTAL REWARD AT ARUP

CASE STUDY 12.2

Arup is a global design and engineering consultancy. The company employs around 10,500 people in 37 countries, around half of whom are based in the UK. At Arup, which is employee-owned, the reward package includes a global profit-sharing scheme as well as a range of other benefits.

Although the organisation did not formally publish a total reward policy until 2007, Arup has been practising a total reward strategy for much longer, and offers online total reward statements to its employees around the world. Tony Hatton-Gore, director, group remuneration and benefits, joined Arup in 2001. At that time, there was an awareness of total reward within the organisation and, soon afterwards, Arup decided to adopt this approach.

There were three key reasons behind the decision to introduce total reward statements:

- total reward statements were seen as an effective way to ensure staff understood the make-up and the value of their employment package
- in line with its values of honest and fair dealings with staff, and in the interests of transparency, Arup wanted people to understand what was available within the organisation as an employee-owned firm
- as an engineering and design consultancy, the organisation wanted to take a holistic 'total design' approach to reward.

Total reward statements

Hatton-Gore explains that although there are some elements of the benefits package – such as the global profit-share scheme and global retirement policy – that are determined centrally, the benefits vary by country, and are based on the company values in combination

with what Arup needs to compete in the local labour markets.

The total reward statements are tailored for each individual employee. They include details of salary, profit-share payments and in some cases more than 20 items to which the employee is entitled. The items included are mainly those on which a value can be placed, and these are totalled to give a monetary value for the overall employment package.

Other benefits, such as holiday allowance or the availability of flu vaccinations, are included on the statement but not given a cash value.

Hatton-Gore notes that some of the benefits listed on the statement are included because the organisation wants to make sure that employees are aware of what is available: for example, the employee assistance programme.

He says: 'We have not attempted to put a monetary value on these things.'

However, while training and development opportunities are viewed as part of the employment package, these are not included on the total reward statement. Hatton-Gore explains that reward in a monetary sense is just one part of what working for the organisation is about; the career and personal development opportunities, and the chance to work on interesting projects, are part of the overall experience rather than another element in the reward list.

Arup's formal total reward policy combines both the monetary and the non-monetary benefits of working for the organisation. The policy was published in a company magazine when it was formally launched in 2007, and is also available to employees via the intranet.

Hatton-Gore says if somebody finds a way to put a value on some of the other, less tangible, elements of the employment package – such as career opportunities – this would be a 'very interesting idea', but says it is a challenge that has not yet been cracked.

Source: Sharp (2009)

www.XpertHR.co.uk

Questions

1   To what extent can Arup's total reward strategy be truly transparent?

2   How will this reward approach be received across all 37 countries? What happens after PM?

If a standard formal appraisal interview occurs with the appraisee, a range of actions or options is available to superiors and subordinates alike. As we have suggested already, there may be a portfolio of approaches that interact within the PM process, such as 360-degree feedback, self-appraisal, upward appraisal, coaching and mentoring interventions.

Companies may operate a system of forced ranking, or forced distribution, whereby groups of employees are compared against each other and ranked from best to worst, instead of being judged against independent performance standards. Although this approach is more common with appraising managers, it can be applied to any area of work. Employees who are placed in the lowest category (for example, the lowest 5%) may be dismissed from the organisation or given a fixed time to improve their current performance to the expected organisational standards. Conversely, the top-performing employees may be provided with significant learning opportunities, career growth and perhaps significant financial and personal rewards (Boyle 2001).

12.7.3 HOW CAN PERFORMANCE BE IMPROVED?

Dependent upon the source(s) of the performance problem, the organisation needs to decide on the type and scope of problem intervention. There may need to be consideration of the macro-level issues affecting the broader organisational context, or attention given to micro-level, individual issues.

Some of the techniques available include:

- learning
- development
- training
- coaching and mentoring
- teambuilding
- culture change programmes
- reward schemes
- structure, process, systems, job redesign, etc
- management approach.

12.8 ARGUMENTS AGAINST THE USE OF PERFORMANCE MANAGEMENT

There is increasing evidence that PM can have a positive impact on organisational performance (Armstrong 2000, Molleman and Timmerman 2003). However, evidence is not universally positive (Furnham 2004, Hazard 2004, Morgan 2006). Some studies suggest performance appraisal and pay to be the least effective HR policies, as perceived by the employees (Hutchinson and Purcell 2003). Pulakos (2009) reports that more than two-thirds of employees are dissatisfied with their PM system and believe it has no impact on improving their performance. This mixed picture may exist for multiple reasons: the spectrum of different PM approaches adopted across organisations; the issues of implementation, that is, the *what* may be right, but the *how* is neglected; and the difficulties of proving cause and effect between the use of high-performance working practices (HPWPs) and improved organisational performance (see, for example, Guest 1997, Koster 2011). So PM should not be regarded as a simple 'best practice' solution. Rather than adopting mechanistic, off-the-shelf approaches or processes, organisations need to ensure their PM approach and processes are implemented in a way that suits their context, giving due consideration to organisational culture (Haines and St-Onge 2012).

12.8.1 MEASUREMENT AT WHAT COST?

PM is not without potentially significant costs in terms of staff time and administration. Not only are implementation costs to be considered, but also the long-term maintenance costs of any PM system once established. To what extent do organisations consider the total costs of the PM system versus the impacts, both positive and negative, on performance outcomes? An example would be the internal focus of systems within the automotive manufacturing industry, where the needs of customers were ignored to the long-term harm of the organisation. Organisations may assume that a PM system will have a positive impact, but any improvement needs to be offset against the often substantial costs of running the system itself.

12.9 THE ROLE OF HR AND BEST PRACTICE WITHIN PM

Research suggests that world-leading companies adopt a more strategic approach to PM as opposed to a tactical one, and this linking of daily operations to strategy translates into increased employee commitment, engagement and performance (Biron et al 2011). Therefore, although HR should support line managers in the implementation of PM processes, success is dependent on full involvement of senior managers within the organisation, requiring them to 'walk the talk', so that employees receive clear signals that this is important. Without this, PM can easily become a painful and negative form-filling exercise, with HR bullying and nagging line managers to complete what they see as a timewasting process. Therefore perhaps the most important role for HR in PM is working with senior management to facilitate commitment so that they can model the required behaviours.

HR also has a key role in designing, communicating and training the PM process and there are interesting ideas emerging about how to improve this: for example, aligning the process to employment engagement strategies (see Gruman and Saks 2011). In this way, HR managers can demonstrate the 'thinking performer' skills expected of the HR business partner. Another interesting stream of research looks at PM from the employee perspective (see, for example, Buchner 2007), a valuable route for the increasing number of less hierarchical organisations employing knowledge workers.

Other important contributions that HR can make include: facilitating communication and training for both appraisers and appraisees, as this enables a more inclusive and positive process; communication of company strategy, which will lead to individual objectives; and helping employees see how their own values align with those of the organisation in order to build commitment and engagement.

CRITICAL REFLECTION 12.1

Global competition places greater pressure on the cost of employment (by driving costs down), with arguably employees expected to work harder and be more productive (output driven). Underlying this is the expectation that employees work longer hours, beyond their stated contracts of employment. Assuming that PM lies primarily within the remit of line managers, how can the HR function work with line managers to ensure that employees are not overworked, to the point that employee burnout may emerge within departments or divisions?

12.10 CONCLUSION

The employment relationship continues to change in differing organisational contexts and climates. Performance remains at the centre of organisational strategies and plans, but what is expected of employees in terms of outputs has perhaps heightened. Talent management and developing future leaders remain key issues for organisations and these are undoubtedly (if not sometimes, subtly) linked to PM.

From an HRM and HRD perspective, the emphasis should be on developing people rather than on the job itself. However, the challenge for employers may be in retaining employees for the duration of their most productive work (while they add value) and no longer. The choice of a global talent pool remains attractive for some organisations, but the reality for most organisations remains the need to drive down (not simply control) the cost of employment, with many public services in the UK enduring a pay freeze over the last few years, manufacturing companies competing on cost with the rest of the world.

The HR (and HRD) strategy has to encompass all aspects affecting performance, at contextual, organisational, team and individual level. To do this, it has to be part of the main business strategy, closely aligned to organisational culture and supported by appropriate mechanisms – such as organisational structure, HR policies and procedures – and be strongly aligned to the HRD strategy.

More flexible and fluid arrangements will be necessary, within which there is a greater appreciation of the subjective, tacit, multi-stakeholder aspects of performance. From a more strategic perspective, the resource-based view of HR (Boxall 1996, Boxall and Purcell 2003) suggests ways in which organisations can build upon unique clusters or 'bundles' of human and technical resources in order to improve levels of performance and thereby achieve competitive advantage in the marketplace. The agility highlighted by Dyer and Shafer (1999) and adapted by Boxall and Purcell (2003) may provide an insight as to how organisations can use PM within a bundle of HR activities.

The HRD strategy could also be enhanced to incorporate ways in which HRD and HRD professionals can assist in motivating employees (Buchner 2007), and move away from what is 'being done' to employees and move towards how the employees can grow in their capabilities, skills and competences.

PM may contribute to the success of the firm, but the vital issue is how the talents of employees can be retained, developed and utilised so as to add value to the organisation. Whilst we may concentrate on the output measurement from PM and deal with its consequences, the question to be answered is 'How do we increase performance?' The answer may take us back to developing and nurturing the organisation's greatest asset – employees: a theme we developed in Chapter 10.

KEY LEARNING POINTS

1   PM is only a process. The perspective that senior management adopts will impact significantly on how the process is implemented and the consequences of the process followed through.

2   Emphasis needs to be placed upon the employees' expectations throughout the whole PM and appraisal process. These expectations may link to the psychological contract and organisational culture influences.

3   When it comes to setting performance targets, there is a strong requirement to readjust to contextual changes and maintain a realistic perspective, or the targets themselves may negatively impact upon performance.

4   The question of who defines performance is a critical part of the PM process. The relationship between the appraiser and appraisee needs to be clearly defined and professionally maintained.

5   There needs to be a sensitive and pragmatic balance of PM, motivation and reward systems to affect appropriate performance outcomes.

6   Managers (including HR professionals) need to understand not just what motivates employees, but why they are motivated.

REVIEW QUESTIONS

1   Critically assess the role and contribution that HR makes to the PM process.

2   What motivates you at work, and how would you classify these motivators in terms of content and process theories?

3   To what extent is 360-degree feedback a fad that is unsustainable as a true and workable practice (in relation to manager–employee interactions)?

4   Do you believe that everything surrounding and including PM places too much emphasis upon the individual, at the expense of teams, divisions, organisational cultures, etc?

CASE STUDY 12.3

JOHN LEWIS PARTNERSHIP

Highly praised and much loved, the John Lewis Partnership (JLP) has more than 80,000 partners in the best-known and arguably most successful example of employee ownership in the UK.

The partners (all permanent employees) co-own 276 Waitrose supermarkets and 36 John Lewis stores, an online and catalogue business, a production unit and even a farm. The workforce is retail-dominated, but also comprises distribution workers, head office staff and specialist buying, IT and finance functions. The workforce is stable, with lower turnover than its competitors and longer service. People who join JLP tend to go on to build careers through the organisation.

Andrew Clark, head of reward, is in no doubt that JLP's success is down to its partners and the competitive advantage they bring. They are, he says, 'what differentiates us from other organisations'. One of Clark's key priorities, however, is to further unlock the competitive advantage of partners to ensure JLP retains its successful position and, although this is an HR issue generally, he is certain that reward has a central role to play.

A key part of the reward strategy is pay and benefits positioning and Clark, along with the partnership council, has thought very carefully about where JLP positions itself in the market and how it rewards good performance through its PRP approach rather than reward basic levels of performance. JLP now pays above national minimum wage across the country regardless of local conditions that may allow them to pay minimum rates. And while there is, says Clark, pressure to be market-leading on recruitment rates, this is not the approach JLP has decided to take.

While some competitors may pay slightly higher starting rates, there is often very minimal pay progression beyond that point, whereas at JLP, through individual performance-driven progression, partners can, over time, achieve earning rates substantially ahead of their starting pay. So for Clark it is about being competitive on base pay, market-leading on benefits, but being really distinctive on overall earning potential. By way of illustration, he says: 'What we want is to be distinctive on rewarding excellent performers and to allow earning potential without having to be promoted. So if we've got an excellent furniture saleswoman who is of real value to the business, why shouldn't we be paying her a really great rate? Why should she need to go and be a section manager somewhere else, when actually her skills

are best suited to her job and she can really drive her own earning potential?'

Getting these 'nuts and bolts' of pay right, says Clark, is the 'rock of solidity' underpinning the whole employee value proposition. In his view, if partners are paid right, they understand it, and if they think their pay is fair, consistent and equitable, this allows the organisation and partners to move on to discuss other things – from developing the benefits proposition to engagement and high performance.

As well as getting base pay positioned right and pay progression driving individual performance, JLP's total reward package is pretty exceptional.

Although it was lower in 2011, the universal partnership bonus was still 14% of salary (the equivalent of more than seven weeks' pay). There is a vast array of benefits on offer, from store discounts, subsidised holidays and leisure activities to life assurance and a final-salary pension scheme.

Innovative ways of presenting total reward statements – using QR codes so partners can access them via their smartphones, for example – are reaching those partners who may not engage with benefits through traditional media. Ultimately, though, Clark is unequivocal about the bigger picture: 'Customers keep coming back to us because of our partners. That is the key focus for the business, for HR and for reward.'

What JLP is executing in its reward strategy is all about putting the partners at the centre of this hugely successful business.

Source: CIPD (2012j)

Questions

1 How does the concept of a 'partner' possibly change the employment relationship and attitude towards rewards?

EXPLORE FURTHER

Armstrong, M. and Baron, A. (2005) *Managing Performance: Performance management in action*. London: CIPD. Remains the frontrunner of PM texts. Particularly useful on the 'how to' approaches.

Buytendijk, F. (2008) *Performance Leadership: The next practices to motivate your people, align stakeholders, and lead your industry*. New York: McGraw-Hill Professional. This text provides a broader perspective on PM and is strong on highlighting its pitfalls.

Cokins, G. (2004) *Performance Management: Finding the missing pieces (to close the intelligence gap)*. New York: Wiley and SAS Business Series. This text provides a pragmatic approach to PM and introduces a range of techniques and approaches that HR professionals should find both interesting and useful.

Hutchinson, S. (2013) *Performance Management: Theory and practice*. London: CIPD.

Perkins, S.J. and White, G. (2011) *Reward Management: Alternatives, consequences and context*. London: CIPD. Read the latest edition of the CIPD Annual Reward Survey for insights as to what is changing and what is remaining the same in relation to benefits and reward available and adopted.

White, G. (2014) Reward Strategy and Managing Performance. In: Rees, G. and Smith, P.E. (2014) *Strategic Human Resource Management: An international perspective*. London: Sage.

PART FIVE

CONCLUSION

Summary Themes and Future Trends

RAY FRENCH AND GARY REES

LEARNING OUTCOMES

After reading this chapter, you should be able to:

- identify some of the key challenges and themes impacting on HR
- indicate some possible future HR developments
- highlight key research findings that impact upon HR (this learning outcome is embedded throughout the chapter).

13.1 OVERVIEW

Material contained throughout this book aims to strengthen readers' understanding of people management by reviewing major research findings and theories and linking these to effective practices and positive outcomes. In this final chapter, we will revisit and highlight recurrent themes from earlier sections of the book, in order to identify the key challenges facing those who lead, manage and develop people in the contemporary workplace. As we have seen, responsibility in this area may fall to a designated HR function. In some cases, though – for example, in many smaller organisations – line managers take the leading role in managing workers. An alternative model is to outsource this activity to specialist providers. We noted at several points throughout the book that this outsourcing model has become increasingly prevalent. In reality, a combination of line and HR expertise is required in many situations in order to effectively manage people at work, and so in Chapter 2 we examined the possible *shape* of HR activity – who actually carries out the work? – in greater detail.

In conclusion, though, whoever undertakes the people management role will be required to operate in a pressured situation. Based on consistent trends, identifiable since 2000, they will almost certainly be faced with competing demands to secure high worker performance leading to perceived added value, while at the same time securing employee engagement. As we noted at the very start of the book, managing people within such a demanding context is no easy task. As a result we look again at key external developments facing HR in this final chapter, together with suggestions for effective people management in a very challenging era.

We strongly counsel readers to keep a very sharp lookout for emerging issues affecting HR management as we operate in an inherently topical field where events move apace. To take just one example, at the time of writing in late 2015, there was considerable focus on 'name-blind' worker selection. Crush (2015) summarised progress in this area, where several major organisations, including HSBC and KPMG, had pledged to recruit on a name-blind basis. Such a practice would involve removing 'signposts' to a job applicant's identity beyond their skills, experience and qualifications. UK Prime Minister David Cameron, in a speech to the 2015 Conservative Party conference, highlighted bias where 'white-sounding' applicants were twice as likely to receive a call back from recruiters compared to those with 'ethnic-sounding' names. The Prime Minister in his speech noted the unacceptability of such findings, giving the example of 'one black girl [who] had to change her name to Elizabeth before she got any calls to interviews', which he said, 'in 21st-century Britain is disgraceful'. This is just one example of emerging trends and issues at the heart of managing people. Please continue to look out for similar issues, trends and events long after you have finished reading this book.

How can we most effectively lead, manage and develop people? While we counsel against regarding the latest fad (whatever that may be) as a panacea, there is a need to evaluate major contemporary research in HRM and HRD as well as valid theories and models in areas such as motivation and how people learn. Sometimes these models highlight central findings which have remained valid over many decades, while in other cases recent research points to new and developing insights. The challenge for students, and of course managers, is to appreciate what is changing and what is enduring in this subject area. In this chapter we highlight findings and theories which can help aspiring and existing managers.

The chapter concludes with a look at the possible future of HR with reference to recent research such as the CIPD (2015d) *Landing Transformational Change* report. As the core book for CIPD's Leading, Managing and Developing People module, we trust that this chapter will serve as a useful revision tool for both students and tutors.

Please also refer to **cipd.co.uk** for additional resources.

13.2 INTRODUCTION

In this book we have examined a very wide range of topics. The breadth of coverage reflects the all-encompassing nature of leading, managing and developing people. When examining the management of employees we have considered the nature of the employment relationship (Chapter 11), recruitment and selection (Chapter 9), training and development (Chapter 10) and performance management and reward (Chapter 12).

There are, in short, many different and varied aspects to employing workers – although in Chapters 2 and 3 we saw how such disparate threads might be subsumed within a strategic focus or 'bundles' of connected policies.

Beyond the specific subdivisions of HR work listed above, we have also stressed the broader importance and role of leadership as an activity (Chapter 5). Linked with leadership is the need to think and act professionally and ethically when leading and managing people (Chapter 4).

We have also argued that the ways in which people are managed are influenced in a most profound way by wider economic, political and social developments – see our quote from David Cameron above. The drive for flexibility (Chapters 7 and 8), emanating from work organisations – and externally from national governments and supra-national bodies – has been particularly influential in this regard. Increasingly, flexibility becomes part of the mindset of employees too and we have shown how the desire for, or even expectation of, flexible working can impact on workers' psychological contracts. Managing flexible work arrangements sensitively and efficiently brings a new focus to HR.

It is also necessary to consider the role and place of HR within organisations as all the topical knowledge and cutting-edge skills possessed by managers would be ineffective if HR does not have a defined role and status within a workplace. Only if this role and status exists can those who manage people have a positive influence on organisations' people management strategies, policies and practices. In 2015 the report *Landing Transformational Change* once again highlighted a need for HR involvement concluding that: 'senior HR managers were critical in directing the change but not leading it {rather} acting as expert facilitators' (CIPD 2015d, p28). The role of HR in change processes was likened in this report to stage directors, 'critically appreciated by all involved in putting on a production of change but not front of stage'. At any rate this recent report once again shows that HR has to be 'close to the action' in order to have impact.

We have seen how HR can be both a specialist and 'line' role and how it has developed from a support administrative function focused on compliance to, in many cases, a fully integrated business partner role. That role continues to be developed and redefined and once again we see a 'moving picture' with new research data emerging.

In view of the broad topic coverage of this book, implicit in the subject area we will, at this point, select particular areas for further scrutiny in our concluding chapter.

Although key external factors facing HR are numerous and ever-changing we have, in a number of places, highlighted the concept of globalisation and its potentially wide impact on employment, both in terms of creating clusters of key knowledge workers but also the continued presence of more routine work and standardised workers. We also focus on the role of macro-economic factors; for example the widespread pressure to 'do more with less' when managing people in both private and public sectors, drawing on material presented in Chapter 3.

We also return to look at particular themes which are threaded through the book. It is increasingly a routine part of HR managers' life to work with a diverse workforce and we summarise issues surrounding diversity raised in previous sections, particularly Chapters 4 and 11. The theme of conflict is also revisited, because although types of conflict may ebb and flow with time, some degree of conflict is inevitable within workplaces. Conflict is by no means a negative phenomenon and can be managed to drive up organisational performance. We deal also with the phenomenon of outsourcing and the sensitive areas this flags up for HR.

One overriding important theme is change. In Chapter 6 we concluded that it is vital to plan, communicate and execute change successfully if a business was to survive. Organisations may wish to change or, alternatively, are compelled to, due to altered legal obligations or some other changing external driver. As change is ultimately about people, HR in partnership with line managers has a key role in change management. In this chapter we identify some important changing trends as they affect people management. However, what is more important than identifying specific examples of change is the recognition that HR managers need to have a positive attitude or mindset towards change, given the inherently changing nature of leading, managing and developing people.

13.3 HR CONTEMPORARY CHALLENGES

13.3.1 GLOBALISATION AND TALENT CLUSTERS

All organisations need to confront the key issues emanating from the external environment. In the early twenty-first century one key environmental factor is globalisation, powered by the strategic aim of companies to seek out new market opportunities, while attempting to use changes in the environment to their advantage.

Such an evolutionary trend reflects better communication and accessibility provided by the Internet, development of sophisticated and standardised software (so-called 'microsoftisation'), improvements in infrastructure, and decades of tough competition necessitating cost-cutting in all sectors. As these trends evolve, all organisations become challenged to achieve sustainability in their marketplaces.

In essence, globalisation is underpinned by profoundly important economic, sociocultural, technological and political factors. It is a deep-rooted phenomenon which has impacted on business in different but always important ways and is predicted to evolve – paradoxically in unpredictable ways – in future.

Linstead et al (2009) characterise globalisation as an increased blurring of boundaries of all sorts including those between nation states, economies, industries and work organisations. A sense of greater interconnectedness between different parts of the world has implications for all aspects of business. For our purposes, though, we can identify two: first, the pressure to drive down employment costs in the face of significant overseas competition; and second, freer movement of workers across the globe resulting in a more diverse workforce.

Profound consequences for HR can follow. For example, some private sector organisations in Western economies have recognised the lower cost-base of other economies such as India and responded by relocating particular business operations there.

This is by no means a one-way process. Bawden (2009) notes how companies including BT, Powergen, Santander and Orange repatriated call centre jobs back to the UK from India in effect reversing a trend which might have appeared inevitable. However, there has been a clear trend since the mid-1990s to relocate white-collar jobs from the UK to emerging and developing economies.

At the same time, much routine manufacturing work has similarly been outsourced or otherwise moved to developing countries like China. One can predict that these emerging economies, built on relatively low-cost provision, will themselves develop as the cycles of wealth creation and increased opportunity begin to take their course.

We should also look to other societies in order to have 'early warnings' of trends and practices which might impact on us in future and also, of course, affect us directly if we conduct business with organisations in the other country. Over and above this, it is also useful to adopt an outward-facing approach so we can learn lessons from abroad. In 2015, for example, we saw an emerging pattern in Sweden, whereby some (although very much still a minority) of organisations were introducing a six-hour work day (Davidson 2015). There were several reasons behind this trend, including desire for flexible working. However, there were other potential benefits cited too, including greater employee focus at work coupled with less procrastination. Efforts to reduce time spent 'in the office' by reducing meetings and clamping down on use of work time for conducting personal tasks, resulted in higher energy levels which translated to improved performance, such as national productivity, which one should acknowledge is influenced by many factors. In short, an appreciation of trends and events elsewhere in the world is highly recommended.

13.4 SUMMARY: THEMES AND FUTURE TRENDS

13.4.1 KNOWLEDGE WORKERS

What are the implications of such trends for the HR manager? French (2015) notes that one consequence of globalisation has been the concentration of clusters of world-class expertise in particular sectors, grouped by location. Thus we find high-technology clusters in Silicon Valley in northern California, parts of Japan and Cambridge in the UK. Much of the net inflow of workers to London (170,000 in 2006 alone), can be attributed to the status of London as a magnet for talent and world-class cities continue to welcome in talented workers. In 2013, the then London Mayor, Boris Johnson, stressed the need for London to attract 'the brightest entrepreneurial minds', noting that a new development in Canary Wharf was well placed to 'foster just the talent we need to futureproof the capital's technology and financial sectors' (Wood 2013). Who would take the lead in fostering such talent and what is HR's role?

In Chapter 8 we recorded the view that an upskilling of the UK's workforce could be accompanied by a workforce desiring greater autonomy and control in their jobs; this notion was supported by a CIPD report (2015e), *Productivity: Getting the best out of people*. The conclusions of this report will be summarised later in the chapter.

The term 'knowledge workers' has come to denote people engaged in non-repetitive results-oriented work, who require continuous learning and the exercise of creativity (see

Bratton and Gold 2012). It is argued that the demands of such high-level employees can be dealt with more effectively by those organisations which lead and manage workers in imaginative ways and develop them to a very high level of competence.

REFLECTIVE ACTIVITY 13.1

Traditionally, financial indicators have been the only measure of performance that really mattered. Profitability, earnings-per-share and return-on-capital-employed, among others, were considered to be the best barometers of business performance.

Some businesses, especially knowledge-based firms, are now recognising that short-term financial metrics provide a poor indication of organisational health. Current profitability provides no clue to future performance, financial or otherwise. If customer satisfaction, in terms of quality and delivery, is low, for example, then consumers will search for alternatives.

The primacy of financial measures has given way to a basket of performance indicators – including quality, customer satisfaction and employee satisfaction – as organisations grapple with the ever-changing environment in which they operate.

It is no longer good enough to manage tangible assets efficiently; the effectiveness of intangible assets must also be added to the equation. The bulk of intangible assets are knowledge-based, including the competence of staff and feedback from customers.

Importantly, and unlike conventional tangible assets, knowledge grows when it is shared. The growth of predominantly knowledge-based organisations – that is, businesses whose activities are based principally on the expertise, skills and creativity of their staff rather than on the physical production of goods – has raised the importance of measuring the so-called invisible factors that determine corporate success or otherwise.

As Margareta Barchan, chief executive of Celemi, the Swedish-owned global consultancy specialising in corporate learning tools, has explained: 'As a knowledge-based business, we at Celemi realised early on that our financial statement did not represent the true value of our firm. Where was it reflected that we were a team of highly skilled professionals who provided effective service to our clients? Where would a stakeholder be able to assess the value of the unique learning processes that we were creating for our clients? Where did we account for the value of our loyal and growing customer base?'

1   To what extent have Celemi added value to their business?

As we saw in Chapter 9, the concepts involved in recruiting, retaining and retraining knowledge workers have changed considerably in recent years. Less emphasis is placed on recruiting and training knowledge workers for specific jobs because jobs are changing so quickly. Instead, employees are recruited and developed who can contribute in a flexible way to an organisation's future. If HR adopts more of a fit-the-job-to-the-person (FJP) approach, as opposed taking an FPJ (fit-the-person-to-the-job) stance, there may be additional benefits in terms of performance and future performance.

Perhaps HR needs to be more innovative in terms of capturing talent, and then nurturing it. The extent to which HR adopts a risk-averse approach by following standardised processes and not 'thinking beyond the box' could result in the loss of talent.

Emphasis needs to be placed upon seeking talent, with contribution to performance – a key criteria for recruitment and selection, not just in the job/role being filled following a prescriptive process, including possible avoidance of legislative malpractice and concerns over potential discriminatory practice.

Getting the best from knowledge workers is dependent on their having the autonomy and discretion to contribute to their maximum ability. Clearly, this can be risky for the organisation and requires a certain level of trust and more subtle (and probably informal) forms of performance management. A full system thus comprises hired, empowered and bright, well-managed knowledge workers with managers who have commensurate skills and abilities. If the whole system does not work from a process point of view, however, sustainability and the high-performance working ideal is lost.

Whilst there are many challenges facing HR, as we have seen throughout the book, there has been a recent preoccupation with managing 'high-end', multiskilled, highly qualified, high-contributing talent. However, not all jobs are prescribed as high end, and inevitably, many workers and managers will occupy 'standard' jobs, and in some cases, what could be deemed 'dirty' jobs.

Concepts such as knowledge management, knowledge workers, talent, talent pipeline and talent management may be commonplace in many organisations. To what extent these terminologies are rhetoric rather than reality may come down to definition.

13.4.2 MANAGING ROUTINE WORK AND THE 'STANDARDISED' WORKER

Much HR literature – for example, Harrison and Kessels (2003) and Holbeche (2008a and 2014) – focuses on achieving the best from knowledge workers. As the authors of several chapters have pointed out, in so doing we can be in danger of ignoring the less glamorous, often worse-paid staff who occupy more routine functions. Some would argue, especially from a total quality view, that all jobs can be treated as holding knowledge and all staff should be seen as knowledge workers, and this is probably true. For the most part, however, our rhetoric fails to meet that reality, and in many instances standardised jobs are, potentially, just that.

Beardwell and Collin (2014) indicate that the term 'talent' has typically been used to identify individuals who make a difference to organisational performance. As such, this could, and arguably should, refer to all employees, in addition to the more specific connotation of key positions that are important to fill for an organisation. In summary, talent management is a broad term referring to all important workers and roles which are pivotally important to organisational success.

Certain tasks (such as serving at a food counter) have been through the mill of cost-cutting. Sections of employment have very often been deskilled, to the point where workers feel alienated from their tasks (see Chapter 8). These workers experience pressures different from those of the uncertainties connected to knowledge workers, which include the pressure from high-volume repetitive work with little control and the associated dangers of work intensification.

Managing standardised workers is usually more straightforward because the tangible outputs are measurable (Chapter 12). In reality, one is often looking to neutralise or minimise the damage that can be caused by staff not bothering (consciously or unconsciously) to undertake routine tasks effectively. In such instances a person–job fit approach (Chapter 8) is appropriate in order to align expectations on both sides of the employment relationship. Clearly, this strategy has consequences for the psychological contract, which was discussed in Chapter 7.

While performance management of standardised workers might be straightforward (because their tasks are straightforward), reward is not. In Chapter 12 Rees and Tymon concluded that wages were unsurprisingly an important aspect of reward, although important up to a point. For many standardised workers, wages are of high importance. However, an organisation must ensure that it does not create an escalating cost-drain from year-on-year wage increases at high levels because these are difficult to correct at a later stage.

Traditionally, HR is mainly associated with FPJ, where a standardised procedure includes a job description, person specification and a set of guiding rules and principles around matching the 'best' candidate to a job. To recruit and retain standardised staff, the 'cocktail' of benefits has to be thought through carefully to match the needs of a targeted set of available staff. Simple financial rewards can be used in an uncomplicated contract that has supervisors who are strong in 'management' using conventional performance management processes.

Alternatively, one might try to cut the wage bill and offer other types of inducements, such as prospects of internal development and promotion (used commonly by media companies), a strong sense of positive-value culture, or promote positive aspects of the work – as is commonly seen in parts of the voluntary sector, where the nature of a job-holder's contribution makes a difference to vulnerable people. The 'leadership' aspect of our text would be more important if such non-wage angles were adopted in order to provide proximal reinforcement of the offer.

Regarding leadership in such contexts (Chapter 5), it is likely that selection of managers who deal mainly with standardised workers will depend on strength in management with leadership (at a high level) being less crucial. However, managers who are in this situation really do need to have skills in leading, managing and developing people. The importance of focusing effort on business objectives and the need for a clear direction and purpose is crucial in order to ensure that the managing and leading of staff has a clear aim, and thus provides the basis for performance management. Staff will detect any absence of a clear direction, and its lack will undermine efforts of leading (nowhere?) and managing (for what purpose?). This presents a fundamentally important but difficult task.

13.4.3 MANAGING MORE WITH LESS: THE CASE OF THE UK PUBLIC SECTOR

The previous two editions of this book, published in 2010 and 2013, looked at the heightened challenges faced by HR during an economic recession. As such they had a somewhat different tone to earlier editions which reflected sunnier economic times. From 2007 a prolonged economic downturn, initially fuelled by a crisis in sub-prime mortgage lending in the USA (itself demonstrating the interconnectedness of national economies) led to a rapidly developing crisis in diverse parts of the planet. For HR there were documented job cuts in many sectors, with many businesses failing in the course of the recession. We reflected a widely held view that many progressive HR policies and practices were swept away in the economic and financial maelstrom. However, there was evidence that many organisations re-emphasised the key role of effective HR policies during the downturn, while attempting to maintain their overall strategic focus. The CIPD (2009a, p2) thus quoted a corporate HR leader from a financial services group:

> Our talent management initiatives are robust and believed to add value to the organisation. We therefore believe that the attraction and retention of talent is even more important in the current economic environment than it has been at any time in the past.

A CIPD (2009a) report presented findings from a research study carried out among a sample of 705 members who held senior roles across the private, public and third (not-for-profit) sectors. Some findings resulting from reduced budgets were perhaps predictable with concerns regarding employee development initiatives, coupled with the macro-level economic situation (recession) impacting on pay and recruitment and selection – with many respondents reporting a shift of focus from recruitment to employee retention.

The impact of economic recession also though, and interestingly, was seen to have resulted in some more innovative strategic refocusing according to this report. Findings included:

- organisations focusing more of their time on engaging, motivating, retaining and fully using the skills of existing employees
- recognition of increasing opportunities to recruit talent discarded by competitors
- as noted earlier, renewed scrutiny on talent management systems and processes
- more honest and frequent communications between managers and other employees, with greater individual understanding of the situation faced by the business
- reconsideration of pay and reward, with more creative thinking about non-financial rewards
- greater emphasis on ethical leaders who are able to lead and motivate in both bad and good times.

By 2015 while many sectors of the UK economy had recovered, there was still evidence that times remained tough for others and once again this harsh environment offered both a series of difficulties for HR professionals and, at the same time, opportunities for more radical thinking in areas like recruitment, training and HR delivery more broadly. Chynoweth (2015) in providing an overview of HR in the UK public sector from 2010 to 2015, illustrates this seemingly paradoxical finding. She firstly identifies major cuts to public spending over that period (the biggest among the major developed economies). A further challenge has been a pay freeze across much of the sector, coupled with significant job losses.

We saw in Chapter 3 that while differences in HR between the private and public sectors may not be great in many instances, the high proportion of staff costs in many public sector institutions meant that HR had a fundamental role in determining expenditure levels. In 2015 all the main political parties in the UK set out policies intended to reduce costs, at the very least by asking the same staff to do more. Few expected the years following 2015 to be anything other than tough and this has been borne out by measures introduced by the new UK government, including a financial squeeze on their own departments.

In 1992 a leading HR academic, John Storey, published a scheme which differentiated between traditional personnel management/industrial relations (IR) and the emerging term HRM. Storey provided 27 points of difference which would locate the characteristics of personnel/IR and HRM in relation to each other. Such differences included beliefs and assumptions, strategic aspects and key levers exhibited by both traditions. Storey's scheme identified the following points. While in the personnel/IR model the manager would be preoccupied with developing and enforcing contractual obligations, in HR there was a move to get employees to go beyond contract. The HR role was seen as transformational as opposed to transactional (see Chapter 5 for a summary of these terms). There was also a difference in that HRM was concerned to foster a greater link between performance and reward in contrast to highly regulated pay. It can be argued that the personnel/IR tradition as outlined here is strongly reminiscent of the way in which people were managed in the public sector. The flagging up of the HRM alternative opened the way to a reconsideration of how people were to be led, managed and developed in the sector.

In the same period (from roughly 1990), a revolution occurred within UK local government and public service providers – see also Chynoweth (2015). Political agendas comprising reduction in taxes (local and national) together with advances in transparency and public audit resulted in generational change in the sector. UK governments of all political persuasions have consistently rewarded those organisations which do well and public service providers are now used to a variety of league tables. Such processes increase expectation to perform in ever-spiralling demands. The more recent downturns in global and local economies have, as indicated earlier, squeezed the public sector still further as governments seek to balance expenditure.

Such pressures have changed the nature of leadership and management in the sector. Hospitals and universities now attract a different type of chief executive from what was expected 20 years ago. The same is true of most of the public sector and the expanding voluntary sector. Top leaders now need to 'drive' the organisation in more senses than one: steering has always been a function, but chief executives are pressing the accelerator for change and achievement as never before.

One can conclude that linked developments in the academic and political spheres led to a situation whereby the nature of people management in the UK public sector was reviewed and in many cases took on a new direction emphasising a performance focus combined with an attempt to engage workers and to derive added value from employees.

The HR function itself came under pressure with new roles evolving and a need to demonstrate relevance in terms of performance, together with cost savings and efficiencies.

13.5 KEY THEMES

Having outlined some of the key external factors confronting those who manage people in organisations, we now turn to identify some of the important themes contained within this book which, we have argued, underpin people management in contemporary workplaces.

13.5.1 MANAGING DIVERSITY

How organisations approach and manage diversity – introduced in Chapter 4, and explored in greater depth in Chapter 11 – will be a 'differentiator' for the future. It is much easier, and tempting, to hire similar people who get on easily. A homogeneous workforce might be thought to be an easy means of avoiding the 'diversity issue'. However, there is much evidence suggesting that enhancing diversity within groups and teams has a potential pay-off in terms of performance; see Belbin (1993). Notwithstanding this classic finding from the field of social psychology, it is also true that a diverse workforce needs careful managing if the benefits of diversity are to be secured. In examining the specific case of cultural diversity, French (2015) recorded the consensus view of research in this area – namely, that multicultural work teams will either perform much better than monocultural groups or much worse. So the key to securing performance is good management. Surowiecki (2004) made a similar point in highlighting the potential wisdom of crowds. He noted, for example, that if one wanted to guess the weight of an ox, the average of a crowd's guesses would always give the best estimate. The more diverse the crowd, the more accurate they would be.

Surowiecki also recognised, however, that if a high-performing team were left to their own devices, they may come to feel invincible and hence vulnerable to making blatant mistakes. This is an important finding reminiscent of the notion of 'groupthink' (Janis 1982). A seemingly excellent work team, or trouble-free work environment more generally, should never be taken for granted, therefore, and both their outcomes and processes should be monitored with a view to swift intervention if problems are signalled.

So we see that managing diversity is a challenging activity offering both the promise of enhanced worker performance while at the same time containing in-built dangers. More generally, the recent findings outlined above point to another key theme within this book: namely, the need to review evidence and to be open to new research insights.

In view of persistent global economic and social trends, it remains unlikely that any sector can survive without embracing diversity, depending on the level of supply of specific workers. Where there are staff shortages, finding homogeneous workers will require either specialised recruitment and selection (Chapter 9), selective internal promotion through learning, training and development (Chapter 10), or increasing rewards (Chapter 12).

We have also suggested that diversity can be a source of competitive advantage despite the caveats in the last but one paragraph. It is hard to see how an organisation can only partially adopt the changes needed to cope with a diverse organisation and still remain effective. For example, if current trends continue, the UK and other markets with high employment levels will continue to be net importers of skilled workers, with most entrants having a diverse range of backgrounds. Organisations which learn how to take advantage of new pools of talent – wherever they come from – have potential for differentiation.

13.5.2 MANAGING DIFFICULTY

We conclude this section by highlighting several further areas which can prove problematic for those engaged in HR, together with some suggestions for overcoming problems.

Hand-in-hand with diversity come the effort and challenge involved in managing the inevitable conflicting interests that difference produces – which can lead to actual conflict. The effective manager will ensure that any ensuing problems are limited to constructive and task-related conflicts (see Chapter 11) and do not degenerate into damaging interpersonal disputes. As we have suggested, diverse groups can produce innovative and smart solutions that provide (differentiated) competitive advantage. To be successful such staff will need context- or contingency-based leadership styles (Chapter 5) rather than one-best-way. Managers who can cope with such demands will have to be recruited or developed.

CASE STUDY 13.1

SOCIAL MEDIA AT NOKIA

In February 2011, it looked like things couldn't get any worse for Nokia, the Finnish mobile phone company. The now famous 'burning platform' blog post by CEO Stephen Elop (which many at first thought to be a leaked internal memo) rapidly went viral, with millions of people reading his painfully frank thoughts on where the company was going wrong, how it had missed out on market share and that it had to decide whether to 'plunge into icy waters' or perish.

Matthew Hanwell, Nokia's community and social media HR director, remembers it well: 'I was angry,' he says. 'It's a great metaphor for where we are, but we actually knew all of this already. That said, it was a wake-up call for the company in terms of saying, "We have some very difficult decisions to make now, which way are we going to go?"'

What Nokia's detractors at the time probably didn't know was that Hanwell, alongside teams from IT and other parts of the business, had already started work some months before on encouraging employees to have a more open and honest dialogue. A project known as 'Reconnecting Nokia' had commenced six months prior to Elop joining the company in September 2010. Central to this was the use of social media. This encapsulated a portfolio of internal social networking platforms, including a Facebook-type tool known as SocialCast, whereby people can post questions, 'follow' each other, rate videos and share ideas.

The idea was to lower the barriers to participation in the wider company dialogue and improve employee engagement at a time when the company's fortunes seemed to be uncertain. 'If you invite participation, rather than broadcasting everything to employees, you lower the threshold to people providing ideas,' explains Hanwell. 'Those who are able to participate and interact are generally more engaged in what they are doing.'

Openness and honesty

Social media is also central to the new leadership values of openness and honesty at the company. On his first day at Nokia, new CEO Elop posted in one of the social media forums, saying: 'Imagine we're having a cup of coffee together. What would you say that we need to change, what must we keep and what do you think that I might miss?' The response was immense, with some threads on the discussion attracting hundreds of posts.

But where some executives might treat this feedback as a box-ticking exercise, Elop started a dialogue about some of the things that had been said. 'We knew that he was listening because he was responding to some of the comments in that social media thread. And, better than that, he would at every opportunity stand up at a "town hall" meeting and reference these conversations that he had been having online. It was very powerful,' says Hanwell.

Using social media to bring employees together was not new at Nokia, however. It had introduced an employee forum known as 'Jazz Cafe' in 2001, but, over time, a raft of new forums, wikis and blogs had been introduced without any of them becoming truly effective. Ensuring that employees know where to go to access intelligence has been crucial in how social media has helped to turn Nokia's fortunes around. 'We decided that if we were going to create a social media culture in Nokia we should have a portfolio,' explains Hanwell. 'We wanted something where, in the same way you don't have to think before you send an email or start a PowerPoint presentation, people would not have to think where to go to interact in a certain way.' SocialCast now has approaching 30,000 users across the organisation.

Role of technology

Having had 'a foot in both camps', as Hanwell describes his career, helps him understand the role of technology in improving employee collaboration. His background is in technology, having worked in HR and enterprise resource planning systems implementation before joining Nokia in 1999 to roll out its global HR software system. He 'officially' joined the HR function in 2000, but admits that he is 'fascinated by the balance between technology and people'. 'How do you get people to use technology really well; how do you get the most out of that investment?' he asks.

His job title is a highly unusual one for an HR professional, but one he believes to be forward-thinking. 'I had this responsibility for creating a community way of working and working out how we get communities to come together in Nokia. Social media would enable all of that to happen, so I was given this title,' says Hanwell. The sponsor for social media at Nokia is its head of HR, Juha Akras.

Fear around social media

'In my opinion, HR needs to be much more involved in [social media] and take a much stronger role in it going forward,' he adds. 'It affects the way people collaborate and the extent to which they come together. That's an HR issue.' However, he recognises that there is considerable fear around embracing social media (on the *Personnel Today* website) in the HR community. 'The analogy I always use is swimming – if you can't swim, if you've never learnt to swim, being confronted with a piece of deep water is pretty frightening,' he explains. 'The digital natives will dive straight in, but some people are afraid to even dip their toe in the water. If you don't actually try it, you'll never understand the benefits of it.'

But while social media is helping Nokia to overcome the issues that have hampered its success in the past few years – silo working, a failure to innovate quickly enough and not recognising how the market for mobile phones had changed – Hanwell appreciates that it is not a 'silver bullet' that is going to make everything right. 'But it does give you a sense of openness and participation so you can understand and debate what's wrong,' he says. 'The discussion we had about how Nokia should change told us what we already knew as a company, but perhaps before we had not been able to utilise that intelligence, because we had no way of accessing those conversations. If every individual had sent an email, nobody else would have been able to know what was being said.'

New strategy

When the company announced its new strategy, days after the 'burning platform' post made headlines in February 2011, Hanwell and his team precreated a number of groups within SocialCast so conversations about the new strategy

could take place. Every opportunity is taken to embed openness and discussion into employees' working lives. Social media is also being used to help employees affected by the changes at the company, for example by redundancy, to discuss those changes with colleagues and share the burden.

It might seem counterintuitive to place social media at the heart of Nokia's future strategy when there is so much it needs to achieve to claw back a share of this fast-changing market, but Hanwell and the other leaders at the company do not doubt its role. 'We find people get more done, and better things done, as a result of being better connected,' he says. It is difficult to argue with that.

Questions

1   What went wrong at Nokia, and why?

2   What actions should Hanwell have taken to have ensured a better outcome for social media usage at Nokia?

There is evidence that an increasing number of organisations have outsourced activities, for example to subcontractors in order to concentrate on their own core capabilities (Child 2005). In an important sense outsourcing has become normal and accepted practice within the notion of flexibility and its associated benefits; see Chapter 7.

Subcontractors, offering a better price than can be generated internally, might be using legitimate means (such as economies of scale) in their cost-cutting, but they might not. How far the contracting organisation should (and does) investigate the terms and conditions of subcontracted workers is an area ripe for investigation as the structure of our economy changes. HR is likely to be at the forefront when such investigations do become routine. They will have to be well placed in terms of their investigating skills and extend their understanding of all aspects of managing and leading people beyond the legal issues into the ethical dimensions of employment; see Chapter 4.

13.6 ENDURING THEORIES AND MODELS FOR LEADING, MANAGING AND DEVELOPING PEOPLE

13.6.1 CONTINGENCY APPROACHES

Which concepts and models are especially relevant when leading, managing and developing people? One important insight is that there are few universally applicable principles and prescriptions. Throughout this book we find numerous examples of policy measures which can work very well – but only in particular situations. The guiding philosophy of a contingency perspective is that the best way to organise and manage is dependent on the circumstances faced by the manager or work organisation. This insight is itself not new as several British and American studies, which concluded that organisations should be designed and structured according to their size or technology employed or the turbulence they encountered in their market, are now five decades old; see Burns and Stalker (1961) and Lawrence and Lorsch (1967). So a contingency approach to business and management is part of mainstream thought.

Returning to the area of leading, managing and developing people in the early twenty-first century, we find examples of the continuing value of the essential contingency insight in this book.

In Chapter 3 we saw how HR practices and their delivery could themselves vary according to the organisational context. Charlotte Rayner and Liza Howe-Walsh note, for example, that the recruitment and retention of volunteer workers in the third sector (charitable and voluntary organisations) was especially tough, together with funding and reward of employees. Meanwhile the particular circumstances surrounding small and medium-sized enterprises (SMEs) led to much HR work being outsourced. Growing organisations also faced specific issues with Greiner's (1972) model of crises in such organisations pointing to possible variances in how people were managed. We saw, finally, how the field of international HRM was associated with specific strategic decisions, for example whether to adopt an ethnocentric or global approach to managing people and the use of particular methods, such as mentoring for expatriate managers.

In Chapter 5 on leadership, we again saw how many academics found that particular leadership styles would be more appropriate in some situations than others; very much the core idea underpinning the contingency approach to the topic. Wenjin Dai and Alex Tymon suggest in their chapter that contingency perspectives remain highly relevant for the exercise of leadership in modern organisations.

These contributors conclude in Chapter 5, that the contingency perspective should inform training of leadership and management skills and that leadership might change hands in response to changed circumstances.

Contingency perspectives form the main thrust of the conclusions to Chapters 8 and 9, with the implication that principles of, and actual practices in, job design and recruitment and selection respectively could and should alter according to the situation. In Chapter 10, Alex Tymon and Margaret Mackay find value in applying the contingency principle to the area of developing employees. They indicate that the choice of learning and development techniques is strongly influenced by contingent factors such as prevailing organisational culture, resources available and learner-related factors. In Chapter 12 Gary Rees and Alex Tymon conclude that what an organisation chooses to measure within its performance management policies (an important underpinning factor) will depend on the organisational context; for example, what, deep down, it really values in its employees. In this chapter we also encounter expectancy theories of motivation which show how individual workers evaluate the link between effort, performance and reward, thereby suggesting that workers might vary considerably in terms of what motivates them and how.

13.6.2 ENDURING PRINCIPLES

While contingency theory is undoubtedly alive and kicking in the field of people management, we do not wish to suggest that effective leadership, management and development of people can be attained by adopting a pure 'pick and mix' of those strategies and practices which we diagnose as fitting a situation at any one time. To do so would be both simplistic and misleading, since there are undoubtedly core principles and insights which should inform managers no matter what situation they find themselves in.

We set out below some of these enduring principles which have been associated with successful management over a long period.

There is a need first to ensure that all people management initiatives are seen to add value to an organisation. In Chapter 3 we presented findings of research by Truss and Gill (2009), who noted that HR was perceived as adding value if it delivered services reliably and on time. Stronger performance was correlated with a strong sense of identity and purpose amongst HR practitioners. A CIPD report (2010a) found that high-achieving HR departments were embedded in the core business of their organisations. So, in summary, the success of any policy initiative, as applied to leading, managing and developing people, will be dependent on other key managers' perceptions of how it adds value and also their pre-formed views on the credibility of the people who put forward that initiative. It is also important to employ measures and techniques which are valid – see our discussion of recruitment and selection techniques in Chapter 9 – and also relevant, as shown by the necessity of transferring learning to the workplace in Chapter 10.

Further support for the need for HR to establish a credible role in order to bring about change is found in the CIPD (2015d) research report *Landing Transformational Change: Closing the gap between theory and practice*, written by academics from the University of Bath School of Management. We referred to this report earlier in the chapter. To reiterate, drawing on findings from a series of case study organisations based in the UK, including the BBC and Her Majesty's Revenue and Customs, the authors note the critical importance of HR carving out a recognisable niche within the change process. In three of the organisations studied senior HR managers were critical in directing the change but not leading it. As we saw earlier, they were seen as 'expert facilitators'; not centre stage but acting more as stage directors. Were the HR managers visible and even recognised? Although the HR managers did not seek to be recognised as leading actors, they did want real recognition of their substantial contribution in directing the changes. One might liken their role to directors of stage or film productions whose names would appear in final credits, even though some of the audience might have left the venue by the time these appear! At any rate, whatever we call their role, as we saw in Chapter 3, a credible power base is a prerequisite for implementing progressive HR policies.

In Chapters 4 and 11 we saw how the management of people was influenced by employment law, so there is a need always to ensure that existing and new measures are compliant with both national and supra-national (for example, EU) legal frameworks. The effective management of the employment relationship, as set out in the first part of Chapter 11, underpins the work of all those involved in managing people. Managers' perception of this relationship should ideally go beyond ensuring minimum legal compliance. If the relationship is characterised by a proactive investment orientation towards employees, we saw that it is more likely to result in employee engagement and organisational success.

This long-standing conclusion continues to be reinforced – see for example MacLeod and Clark (2009) and Alfes et al (2010).

Workers' perceptions of how they are treated continue to influence their sense of identity with the employing organisation and motivation to their work. In Chapter 12 we saw how performance management must be carried out in a fair and equitable way; for example, in an appraisal process. Performance management and reward policies should be transparent and understandable. Equity theory dates from the work of Adams (1965) and continues to receive support; see Hollyforde and Whiddett (2002). If workers perceive an injustice when they compare their own inputs and outputs – for example, effort and reward – with those of others, the resultant unpleasant feeling will motivate them to take action. In Chapter 7 we reviewed the concept of the psychological contract, which again indicates that we all make a mental comparison between inputs and outcomes at work and that a balanced state is desirable in this regard. In Chapter 4, Matthew Anderson and Charlotte Rayner began their discussion of ethics and professionalism by emphasising that human beings are special and can reasonably demand to be treated in certain ways by employers. They go on to conclude that managers have an important role to play in terms of acting with integrity, going beyond that which is required by the law. There is no more enduringly important and relevant principle in leading, managing and developing people than that of fair treatment.

13.7 THE FUTURE OF HR?

HR remains under threat from forces that may intend to reduce or possibly eradicate it in the near future. There will continue to be the need for an HR function, but in what guise it exists and how it operates has scope to change dramatically. The nature of communication around the globe will continue to change the ways that organisations operate. Both internal and external communication patterns will change, but what is more significant is the speed at which communication now travels. This was witnessed in March 2012 in the UK when Francis Maude, then a government minister, suggested that people should top up their spare petrol cans in preparation for a potential strike by petroleum distribution companies. The result was catastrophic in terms of petrol stations running out of fuel due to panic-buying by motorists. Closely allied to this is the use of social media at work. A CIPD report (2013d, p3) found that 'Social media has profound implications when applied to organisations, because it is changing the way that people interact at work and even the nature of the employment relationship.'

In a CIPD (2012k, p21) research report it is argued that 'within organisations, openness and transparency will be the vital business characteristics that will make all the difference in the coming years'. The question remains as to whether this proposition is sustainable. With transparency comes trust, and perhaps an assessment of the openness of the line manager role, as well as the HR role. In future years, employment contracts may change by adopting a shorter, more transient type of arrangement. The concept of trust may become a higher-level priority for both organisations and employees, as may the constant renegotiation of the employment relationship (CIPD 2012k).

A great deal of work in HR has been undertaken under the guise of 'employee engagement' (see Chapter 11), often referred to as the 'new motivation'. Another angle on this concept is that engagement may be the new 'retention', whereby employers seek to retain their valued employees. Whilst trust may be an important element here, remaining employed may be reward itself during times of economic recession.

In a recent CIPD survey (CIPD 2012b), 60% of higher-earning HR professionals prioritise business issues over what matters to HR compared to one-third for lower earning HR professionals. Perhaps the concept of the HR business partner is finally taking root, but whether this is beneficial is still to be seen. Aligned with the concept of trust is visibility, where senior managers in particular need to be more visible (face-to-face and virtually), and adopt a collaborative (two-way communication) approach (CIPD 2012k).

In 2009, Sullivan et al from the Work Foundation argued that the employment relationship, together with the employer–employee relationship, trust and employer branding and segmentation are critical areas for the future of HR. All of these areas remain critical in the near future. The ultimate office for corporate social responsibility should not only lie within the HR function, but should be part of the DNA of HR (CIPD 2013a).

Ultimately, HR holding high office may not be sufficient to maintain its standing in organisations. The point of reference may change from the organisation and from the manager to the employee. 'The future of work will be influenced by more networked ways of operating. Firms are more likely to manage people whom they don't employ directly. This fundamentally challenges how we define an "employee" and has massive impact upon our profession – we need to rethink how we view what an employee is' (Kinnie et al 2012, p3). It is vital that HR embraces and relishes its leadership role in organisations.

13.8 CONCLUSION

We began this book by stating that leading, managing and developing people is a tough topic. It is not possible to manage people effectively by adhering to a checklist. One size definitely does not fit all. Managing people is hard work, which requires thought, care and considerable attention to detail in every interaction and decision made. The sheer breadth of sub-topics covered by the chapters in this book is impressive, and expertise is developing in all areas. The ideas presented in this book provide the reader with a wide set of options to take into their own work environment. The basics are needed to survive, but with changes to people's psychological contracts and changes in employee expectations, the 'basics' are likely to become more complex and demanding.

This text is being written at a time when it is widely acknowledged that change is a constant feature of our work context and all sectors are under pressure to produce results within a negative economic environment. The resource-based view of organisations, summarised by Pilbeam and Corbridge (2010), has helped in placing people centre-stage in the achievement of competitive advantage. Mobilising this potential should be a fundamental task in leading, managing and developing people. More recent concepts such as engagement, openness, visibility and honesty may take a higher profile within organisations, permeating through HR, line managers and employees.

Solutions are increasingly geared to process (how we do things) rather than content (what we do). This trend is reflected in all chapters, and provides a considerably more sophisticated challenge than previously.

Leading, managing and developing people is demanding due to the inherently problematic nature of people as resources, taken together with a challenging external context. The other side of the coin is that it is also rewarding on a whole range of levels for practising or aspiring HR managers. Leading, managing and developing people can be a source of fulfilment even when it involves taking tough decisions. Helping employees to fulfil their potential can be the most rewarding task within any workplace.

EXPLORE FURTHER

Throughout this book we have stressed the importance of keeping abreast of current research. Indeed, this is one important theme within the CIPD Leading, Managing and Developing People unit. You are recommended to search appropriate websites in order to be aware of emerging reports and data surveys. Suitable websites include those listed below:

- Chartered Institute of Personnel and Development: **cipd.co.uk**
- CIPD magazine: **www.peoplemanagement.co.uk**
- Institute for Employment Studies: **www.employment-studies.co.uk**
- International Labour Organization: **www.ilo.org**
- Department of Business, Innovation and Skills: **www.bis.gov.uk**
- Office of National Statistics: **www.ons.gov.uk**
- European Union Employment and Social Affairs: **ec.europa.eu/social/home.jsp**
- Chartered Institute of Management: **www.managers.org.uk**
- Trades Union Congress: **www.tuc.org.uk**
- *Independent* newspaper: **www.independent.co.uk**
- *Daily Telegraph* newspaper: **www.telegraph.co.uk**
- The BBC: **www.bbc.co.uk/news**
- CNN business news: **www.cnn.com/business**

Bibliography

ACAS (2010) How to Manage Change: ACAS Guidelines. January 2010. Available at: www.acas.org.uk [Accessed 12 April 2013].

ACAS (2015a) *Code of Practice on Disciplinary and Grievance Procedures, Code of Practice 1*. London: The Stationery Office.

ACAS (2015b) *Discipline and Grievances at Work: The ACAS Guide*. London, ACAS.

ACCENTURE (2014) *Career capital 2014 global research results [online]*. London: Accenture. Available at: www.accenture.com/IWD2014 [Accessed 4 January 2016].

ADAIR, J. (1983) *Effective Leadership*. London: Pan Books.

ADAIR, J. (2003) *The Inspirational Leader: How to motivate, encourage and achieve success*. London: Kogan Page.

ADAMS, J.S. (1965) Inequality in social exchange. In: BERKOWITZ, L. (ed.) *Advances in Experimental Social Psychology*. New York: Academic Press.

ADLER, P.S. (1999) The emancipatory significance of Taylorism. In: CUNHA, M.P.F. and MARQUES, C.A. (eds) *Readings in Organisation Science – Organisational Change in a Changing Context*. Lisbon: Instituto Superior de Psicologia Aplicada.

AGUILAR, F.J. (1967) *Scanning the Business Environment*. New York: Macmillan.

AGUINIS, H. (2009) *Performance Management*. 2nd ed. New Jersey: Pearson Prentice Hall.

AHMED, S. (2007) The language of diversity. *Ethnic and Racial Studies*. Vol 30, No 2. pp235–56.

ALFES, K., TRUSS, C., SOANE, E.C., REES, C. and GATENBY, M. (2010) *Creating an Engaged Workforce: Findings from the Kingston Employee Engagement Consortium Project*. London: CIPD.

ALIMO-METCALFE, B. (1995) An investigation of female and male constructs of leadership and empowerment. *Women in Management Review*. Vol 10, No 2. pp3–8.

ALLEN, M.R. and WRIGHT, P. (2007) Strategic management and HRM in BOXALL, P., PURCELL, J. AND WRIGHT, P. (eds) *The Oxford Handbook of Human Resource Management*. Oxford: Oxford University Press.

ALLEN, W.C. and SWANSON, R.A. (2006) Systematic training – straightforward and effective. *Advances in Developing Human Resources*. Vol 8, No 4. pp427–429.

ALLIO, R.J. (2008) C.K. Prahalad heralds a new era of innovation. *Strategy and Leadership*. Vol 36, No 6. pp11–14.

ALVAD, S. and BANG, S. (2015) *A change in FIFA requires a change of organisation structure [online]*. Available at: http://playthegame.org/news-articles/2015/0042 [Accessed 6 July 2015].

ALVESSON, M. and WILLMOTT, H. (2000) Identity regulation as organizational control: producing the appropriate individual. [Electronic version.] *Journal of Management Studies*, Vol 39, No 5. pp619–644.

ALVESSON, M. and WILLMOTT, H. (2002) Identity regulation as organizational control: producing the appropriate individual. *Journal of Management Studies*. Vol 39, No 5. pp619–644.

ANDERSEN, M., BIEMANN, T. and PATTIE, M.W. (2015) What makes them move abroad? Reviewing and exploring differences between self-initiated and assigned expatriation. *The International Journal of Human Resource Management*. Vol 26, No 7. pp 932–947.

ANDERSON, M. (2015) *A History of Fair Trade in Contemporary Britain: From civil society campaigns to corporate compliance*. Basingstoke: Palgrave Macmillan

ANDERSON, N., BORN, M. and CUNNINGHAM-SNELL, D. (2001) Recruitment and selection: applicant perspectives and outcomes. In: ANDERSON, N., ONES, D. and SINANGIL, H.K. (eds) *Handbook of Industrial Work and Organizational Psychology*. Vol 1. London/New York: Sage.

ANDERSON, V. (2007) *The Value of Learning: From return on investment to return on expectation*. London: CIPD.

ANDERSON, V. and BOOCOCK, G. (2002) Small firms and internationalisation: learning to manage and managing to learn. *Human Resource Management Journal*. Vol 12, No 3. pp5–24.

ANDERSON, V. and SKINNER, D. (1999) Organisational learning in practice: how do SMEs learn to operate internationally? *Human Resource Development International*. Vol 2, No 3. pp235–258.

ANELL, B. and WILSON, T. (2000) The flexible firm and the flexible co-worker. *Journal of Workplace Learning: Employee Counselling Today*. Vol 12, No 4. pp165–170.

ANKIL, E. and PALLIAM, R. (2012) Enabling a motivated workforce: exploring the sources of motivation. *Development and Learning in Organizations*. Vol 26, No 2. pp7–10.

ARGYRIS, C. (1960) *Understanding Organizational Behaviour*. London: Tavistock.

ARKIN, A. (2005a) Power play. *People Management*. Vol 11, No 5. pp40–42.

ARKIN, A. (2005b) Mr Bright Side. *People Management*. 5 May. pp28–30. Available at: http://www.cipd.co.uk/pm/peoplemanagement/b/weblog/archive/2013/01/29/mrbrightside-2005–05.aspx [Accessed 7 January 2016].

ARMSTRONG, M. (2000) *Performance Management Practice: Key practices and practical guidelines*. London: Kogan Page.

ARMSTRONG, M. and BARON, A. (2005) *Managing Performance: Performance management in action*. London: CIPD.

ARNOLD, J. (1996) The psychological contract: a concept in need of close scrutiny? *European Journal of Work and Organisational Psychology*. Vol 5, No 4. pp511–520.

ARNOLD, J., COOPER, C.L. and ROBERTSON, I.T. (2005) *Work Psychology: Understanding human behaviour in the workplace*. 4th ed. Harlow: FT/Prentice Hall.

ARNOLD, J., COOPER, C.L. and ROBERTSON, I.T. (2010) *Work Psychology: Understanding human behaviour in the workplace.* 5th ed. Harlow: FT/Prentice Hall.

ARRATA, P., DESPIERRE, A. and KUMRA, G. (2007) Building an effective change team. *McKinsey Quarterly.* No 4. pp1–4.

ARSTEIN, V. (2015) Number of workers relying on zero hours contracts rises to 700,000. *People Management.* 26 February. Available at: http://www.cipd.co.uk/pm/peoplemanagement/b/weblog/archive/2015/02/26/number-of-workers-relying-on-zero-hours-contracts-rises-to-700–000.aspx [Accessed 7 January 2016].

ARTHUR, M. (2008) Examining contemporary careers: a call for interdisciplinary enquiry. *Human Relations.* Vol 61, No 2. pp163–186.

ASHFORD, S. and DERUE, S. (2012) Developing as a leader: the power of mindful engagement. *Organizational Dynamics.* Vol 41, No 2. pp146–154.

ASTON, L. (2013) Time to address the engagement deficit. *People Management.* 7 January. Available at: http://www.cipd.co.uk/pm/peoplemanagement/b/weblog/archive/2013/01/07/timeto-address-the-engagement-deficit.aspx [Accessed 18 June 2013].

ATKINSON, C. (2002) Career management and the changing psychological contract. *Career Development International.* Vol 7, No 1. pp14–23.

ATKINSON, J. (1984) Manpower strategies for flexible organisations. *Personnel Management.* Vol 16 No 8. pp28–31.

AVOLIO, B.J., KAHAI, S. and DODGE, G.E. (2000) E-leadership: implications for theory, research and practice. *The Leadership Quarterly.* Vol 11, No 4. pp615–668.

AVOLIO, B., WALUMBWA, F. and WEBER, T. (2009) Leadership: current theories, research and future directions. *Annual Review of Psychology.* Vol 60. pp421–449.

BACKHAUS, K. (2003) Importance of person–organisation fit to job-seekers. *Career Development International.* Vol 8, No 1. pp221–226.

BAKAN, I., SUSENO, Y., PINNINGTON, A. and MONEY, A. (2004) The influence of financial participation and participation in decision-making on employee job attitudes. *International Journal of Human Resource Management.* Vol 15, No 3. pp587–596.

BAKER, K. (2009) Whitehall HR business partners get skills refresher to deal with cuts. *Personnel Today.* 17 November. Accessed through XpertHR, 27 April 2010.

BALLANTYNE, I. (2009) Recruiting and selecting staff in organizations. In: GILMORE, S. and WILLIAMS, S. (eds) *Human Resource Management.* Oxford: Oxford University Press.

BALOGUN, J., GLEADLE, P., HOPE HAILEY, V. and WILLMOTT, H. (2005) Managing change across boundaries: boundary-shaking practices. *British Journal of Management.* Vol 16, No 4. pp261–278.

BANDURA, A. (1977) Self-efficacy: toward a unifying theory of behavioural change. *Psychological Review.* Vol 84, No 2. pp91–215.

BANDURA, A. (1993) Perceived self-efficacy in cognitive development and functioning. *Educational Psychologist.* Vol 28, No 2. pp117–148.

BARBER, A. and BRETZ, R. (2000) Compensation, attraction and retention. In: RYNES, S.L. and GERHART, B. (eds) *Compensation in Organisations*. San Francisco, CA: Jossey-Bass.

BARNEY, J.B. and HESTERLY, W.S. (2008) *Strategic Management and Competitive Advantage*. 2nd ed. Harlow: Pearson/Prentice Hall.

BARUCH, Y. (2004) The desert generation. *Personnel Review*. Vol 33, No 2. pp241–256.

BARUCH, Y. (2004a) Transforming career: from linear to multidimensional career paths. Organizational and individual perspectives. *Career Development International*. Vol 9, No 1. pp58–73.

BARUCH, Y. (2006) Career development in organisations and beyond: balancing traditional and contemporary viewpoints. *Human Resource Management Review*. Vol 16, No 2. pp125–128.

BARUCH, Y. and ROSENSTEIN, E. (1992) Career planning and managing in high tech organisations. *International Journal of Human Resource Management*. Vol 3, No 3. pp477–496.

BASS, B.M. (1985) *Leadership and Performance Beyond Expectations*. New York: Free Press.

BAWDEN, T. (2009) BT returns call-centre jobs to Britain from India. *The Times*. 16 July.

BBC (2015) *FIFA Corruption Crisis: Key questions answered [online]* Available at: http://www.bbc.co.uk/news/world-europe-32897066 [Accessed 7 January 2016].

BBC RADIO 4 (2008) Interview with Professor Joseph Nye. *Today Programme*. 23 April.

BEARD, C.M. and WILSON, J.P. (2006) *Experiential Learning: A best practice guide for trainers and educators*. London: Kogan Page.

BEARDWELL, J. and CLAYDON, T. (2010) *Human Resource Management: A contemporary approach*. 6th ed. Harlow: FT/Prentice Hall.

BEARDWELL, J. and COLLIN, A. (2014) Talent management. In: BEARDWELL, J. and THOMPSON, A. (eds) *Human Resource Management: A contemporary approach*. 7th ed. Harlow: Pearson.

BEARDWELL, J. and THOMPSON, A. (2014) *Human Resource Management: A contemporary approach*. Harlow: Pearson.

BEAUMONT, P. and HARRIS, R. (2002) Examining white-collar downsizing as a cause of change in the psychological contract: some UK evidence. *Employee Relations*. Vol 24, No 4. pp378–388.

BECKER, B. and HUSELID, M.A. (2006) Strategic human resource management: where do we go from here? *Journal of Management*. Vol 32, No 6. pp898–925.

BECKETT, J. (1999) Agency, entrepreneurs and institutional change. The role of strategic choice and institutional practices in organisations. *Organisation Studies*. Vol 20, No 5. pp777–799.

BEECROFT, A. (2011) Report on Employment Law. Available at: https://www.gov.uk/government/publications/employment-law-review-report-beecroft [Accessed 10 January 2016].

BEER, M. and SPECTOR, B. (1989) Corporate-wide transformations in human resource management. In: WALTON, R.E. and LAWRENCE, P.R. (eds) *Human Resource Management, Trends and Challenges*. Boston, MA: Harvard University School Press.

BEER, M., SPECTOR, B., LAWRENCE, P.R., MILLS, D.Q. and WALTON, R.R. (1984) *Managing Human Assets*. New York: Simon & Schuster, Free Press.

BELBIN, M.R. (1990) *Team Roles at Work*. Oxford: Butterworth-Heinemann.

BELBIN, M.R. (1991) *Management Teams – Why They Succeed or Fail*. Oxford: Butterworth.

BELBIN, M.R. (1993) *Team Roles at Work*. Oxford: Butterworth-Heinemann.

BENNETT, N., WISE, C., WOODS, P. and HARVEY, J. (2003) *Distributed Leadership*. Nottingham: National College for School Leadership.

BENTLEY, R. (2008) Where did the business partner model go wrong? *Personnel Today*. 31 March. Accessed through XpertHR, 27 April 2010.

BERGMAN, S. (2012) Open thread: what are the best methods to recruit staff? *Guardian*. 22 November.

BERNADIN, H.K., KANE, J.S. and ROSS, S. (1995) Performance appraisal design, development and implementation. In: FERRIS, G.R., ROSEN, S.D. and BARNUM, D.J. (eds) *Handbook of Human Resource Management*. Cambridge, MA: Blackwell.

BERNHARD, F. and O'DRISCOLL, M.P. (2011) Psychological ownership in small family-owned businesses: leadership style and nonfamily-employees' work attitudes and behaviors. *Group & Organization Management*. Vol 36, No 3. pp345–384.

BERRY, M. (2007) Cadbury-Schweppes launches UK graduate recruitment campaign with a new online chatroom. *Personnel Today*. 7 November. Available at: http://www.personneltoday.com [Accessed 16 May 2008].

BERSIN AND ASSOCIATES (2011) *UK Talent Acquisition Factbook 2011: Benchmarks and trends in spending, staffing and key recruiting metrics*. Report.

BIGGS, D. and SWAILES, S. (2006) Relations, commitment and satisfaction in agency workers and permanent workers. *Employee Relations*. Vol 28, No 2. pp130–143.

BIRON, M., FARNDALE, E. and PAUUWE, J. (2011) Performance management effectiveness: lessons from world leading firms. *International Journal of Human Resource Management*. Vol 22, No 6. pp1294–1311.

BJORKMAN, I. and YUAN, L. (1999) The management of human resources in Chinese–Western joint ventures. *Journal of World Business*. Vol 34, No 2. pp1–19.

BLAKE, R.R. and MCCANSE, A.A. (1991) *Leadership Dilemmas – Grid Solutions*. Houston: Gulf Publishing.

BLAKE, R.R. and MOUTON J.S. (1964) *The Managerial Grid*. London: Gulf Publications.

BLANCHARD, P.N. and THACKER, J.W. (2004) *Effective Training: Systems, strategies and practices*. New Jersey: Pearson/Prentice Hall.

BLIGH, C. and SCHYNS, B. (2007) The romance lives on: contemporary issues surrounding the romance of leadership. *Leadership*. Vol 3, No 3. pp343–360.

BLOISI, W., COOK, C.W. and HUNSAKER, P.I. (2003) *Management and Organisational Behaviour*. London: McGraw-Hill.

BLOISI, W., COOK, C.W. and HUNSAKER, P.I. (2007) *Management and Organisational Behaviour*. 2nd ed. London: McGraw-Hill.

BLONK, R.W.B., BRENNINKMEIER, V., LAGERVELD, S.E. and HOUTMAN, I.L.D. (2006) Treatment of workrelated psychological complaints: a randomised field experiment among self-employed. *Work and Stress*. Vol 20, pp129–144.

BLOOM, B.S. (ed.) (1956) *Taxonomy of Educational Objectives Handbook 1: Cognitive domain*. New York: Longman.

BLYTON, P. and MORRIS, J. (1992) HRM and the limits of flexibility. In: BLYTON, P. and MORRIS, J. (eds) *Reassessing Human Resource Management*. London: Sage.

BOATMAN, J., WELLINS, R. and SELKOVITZ, A. (2011) *Global leadership forecast 2011 [online]* Available at: http://www.ddiworld.com/DDI/media/trend-research/globalleadershipforecast2011_globalreport_ddi.pdf [Accesssed 11 January 2016].

BOATRIGHT, J.R. (2000) *Ethics and the Conduct of Business*. 3rd ed. London: Prentice Hall.

BOLDEN, R. (2011) Distributed leadership in organizations: a review of theory and research. *International Journal of Management Reviews*. Vol 13, No 3. pp251–269.

BOLLAERT, H. and PETIT, V. (2010) Beyond the dark side of executive psychology: current research and new directions. *European Management Journal*. Vol 28, No 5. pp362–376.

BOND, R. (2004) Call centre is 'my dream job'. *BBC News website*. 14 April.

BOSELIE, P., BREWSTER, C. and PAAUWE, J. (2009) In search of balance – managing the dualities of HRM. *Personnel Review*. Vol 38, No 5. pp461–471.

BOUSKILA-YAM, O. and KLUGER, A. (2011) Strength-based performance appraisal and goal setting. *Human Resource Management Review*. Vol 21, No 2. pp137–147.

BOWLES, M.L. and COATES, G. (1993) Image and substance: the management of performance as rhetoric or reality? *Personnel Review*. Vol 22, No 2. pp3–21.

BOXALL, P. (1996) The strategic HRM debate and the resource-based view of the firm. *Human Resource Management Journal*. Vol 6, No 3. pp59–75.

BOXALL, P. and PURCELL, J. (2000) Strategic human resource management: where have we come from and where should we be going? *International Journal of Management Review*. Vol 2, No 2. pp183–203.

BOXALL, P. and PURCELL, J. (2003) *Strategy and Human Resource Management*. Basingstoke: Palgrave Macmillan.

BOXALL, P. and PURCELL, J. (2008) *Strategy and Human Resource Management.* 2nd ed. Basingstoke: Palgrave Macmillan.

BOXALL, P. and PURCELL, J. (2011) *Strategy and Human Resource Management.* 3rd ed. Basingstoke: Palgrave Macmillan.

BOXALL, P. and PURCELL, J. (2015) *Strategy and Human Resource Management.* 4th ed. Basingstoke: Palgrave Macmillan.

BOYLE, M. (2001) Performance reviews: perilous curves ahead. *Fortune Europe.* Vol 143, No 11. p187.

BRADSHAW, D. (1985) Transferable intellectual and personal skills. *Oxford Review of Education.* Vol 11, No 2. pp201–216.

BRAMLEY, P. (1996) *Evaluating Training Effectiveness.* Maidenhead: McGraw-Hill.

BRATTON, J. (2015) *Introduction to Work and Organizational Behaviour.* 3rd ed. London: Palgrave.

BRATTON, J. and GOLD, J. (2007) *Human Resource Management Theory and Practice.* 4th ed. Basingstoke: Palgrave Macmillan.

BRATTON, J. and GOLD, J. (2012) *Human Resource Management Theory and Practice.* 5th ed. Basingstoke: Palgrave Macmillan.

BRAVERMAN, H. (1974) *Labour and Monopoly Capital: The degradation of work in the twentieth century.* New York: Monthly Review Press.

BRECH, E.F.L. (1975) *Principles and Practice of Management.* 3rd ed. Harlow: Longman.

BRIDGE, S. (2007) What's the future of HR? *Times Online.* 7 February.

BRISCOE, J. and HALL, D. (2006) The interplay of boundaryless and protean careers: combinations and implications. *Journal of Vocational Behaviour.* Vol 69. pp4–18.

BROCKETT, J. (2010) See HR as a professional services firm, says Ulrich. *People Management.* No 14. 25 March. p11.

BROEWAYS, M.-J. and PRICE, R. (2011) *Understanding Cross-cultural Management.* 2nd ed. Harlow: FT Prentice Hall.

BROWN, A.D. (2015) Identities and identity work in organizations. *International Journal of Management Reviews.* Vol 17, No 1. pp20–40.

BROWN, M. (2012) George Entwistle deserves his £450,000 BBC payoff. *Guardian.* 29 November. Available at: www.guardian.co.uk [Accessed 18 December 2012].

BRUMBACH, G.B. (1988) Some ideas, issues and predictions about performance management. *Public Personnel Management.* Winter. pp387–402.

BRYCE, V. (2007) Give me strength. *People Management.* 8 February, p7. Available at: http://www.cipd.co.uk/pm/peoplemanagement/b/weblog/archive/2013/01/29/givemestrength-2007–02.aspx [Accessed 10 January 2016].

BUCHANAN, D. and BADHAM, R. (1999) *Power, Politics and Organizational Change: Winning the turf war game.* London: Sage.

BUCHANAN, D. and BODDY, D. (1992) *The Expertise of the Change Agent*. London: Prentice Hall.

BUCHANAN, D. and HUCZYNSKI, A. (2007) *Organizational Behaviour*. 6th ed. London: FT/Prentice Hall.

BUCHANAN, D. and HUCZYNSKI, A. (2010) *Organizational Behaviour*. 7th ed. London: FT/Prentice Hall.

BUCHANAN, D.A. and WILSON, B. (1996) Next patient please: the operating theatres problem at Leicester General Hospital NHS Trust. In: STOREY, J. (ed.) *Cases in Human Resource and Change Management*. Oxford: Blackwell Business.

BUCHNER, T.W. (2007) Performance management theory: a look from the performer's perspective with implications for HRD. *Human Resource Development International*. Vol 10, No 1. pp59–73.

BUCKLEY, R. and CAPLE, J. (2009) *The Theory and Practice of Training*. London: Kogan Page.

BUDRIA, S. (2012) The shadow value of employer-provided training. *Journal of Economic Psychology*. Vol 33, No 3. pp494–514.

BUDWORTH, M. and MANN, S. (2011) Performance management: where do we go from here? *Human Resource Management Review*. Vol 21, No 2. pp81–84.

BULLER, P.F., and MCEVOY, G.M. (2012) Strategy, human resource management and performance: sharpening line of sight. *Human Resource Management Review*. Vol 22, No 1. pp43–56.

BURNES, B. (2004) *Managing Change*. 4th ed. Harlow: FT/Prentice Hall.

BURNS, J. (2008) Informal learning and transfer of learning: how new trade and industrial teachers perceive their professional growth and development. *Career and Technical Education Research*. Vol 33. pp3–24.

BURNS, J.M. (1978) *Leadership*. New York: Harper & Row.

BURNS, T. and STALKER, G.M. (1961) *The Management of Innovation*. London: Tavistock.

BURNS, T. and STALKER, G.M. (1994) *The Management of Innovation*. 3rd ed. Oxford: Oxford University Press.

BUTLER, M.G. and CALLAHAN, C.M. (2014) Human resource outsourcing: market and operating performance effects of administrative HR functions. *Journal of Business Research*. Vol 67, No 2. pp 218–224.

CALDWELL, R. (2003) Models of change agency: a fourfold classification. *British Journal of Management*. Vol 14, No 2. pp131–142.

CALDWELL, R. (2008) HR business partner competency models: re-contextualising effectiveness. *Human Resource Management Journal*. Vol 18, No 3. pp275–293.

CALDWELL, S.D. (2013) Are change readiness strategies overrated? A commentary on boundary conditions. *Journal of Change Management*. Vol 13, No 1. pp 19–35.

CALIGIURI, P. and TARIQUE, I. (2012) Dynamic cross-cultural competencies and global leadership effectiveness. *Journal of World Business*. Vol 47, No 4. pp612–622.

CALIGIURI, P., LEPAK, D. and BONACHE, J. (2010) *Managing the Global Workforce*. Chichester: Wiley.

CAMERON, J., BANKO, K.M. and PIERCE, W.D. (2001) Pervasive negative effects of rewards in intrinsic motivation: the myth continues. *The Behaviour Analyst*. Vol 24. pp1–44.

CANTRELL, S. and BENTON, J.M. (2007) The five essential practices of a talent multiplier. *Business Strategy Series*. Vol 8, No 5. pp358–364.

CARNALL, C. (2003) *Managing Change in Organizations*. 4th ed. Harlow: FT/(Prentice Hall).

CARVER, C., SUTTON, S. and SCHEIER, F. (2000) Action, emotion and personality: emerging conceptual integration. *Personality and Social Psychology Bulletin*. Vol 26. pp741–751.

CASSELL, C., NADIN, S. and GRAY, M. (2002) Exploring human resource management practices in small and medium-sized enterprises. *Personnel Review*. Vol 31, No 6. pp671–692.

CAULKIN, S. (2003) How to catch a rising star. *The Observer*. 9 November.

CBI (2009) *Education and Skills Survey*. Available at: www.cbi.org.uk/ndbs/content.nsf/b80e12d0cd1cd37c802567bb00491cbf/e83f616f81370ce880256dc60047ede9 [Accessed 29 April 2010].

CBI (2015) Inspiring Growth: CBI/Pearson Education and Skills Survey 2014. Available at: http://news.cbi.org.uk/reports/education-and-skills-survey-2015/education-and-skills-survey-2015 [Accessed 4 January 2016].

CERVERO, R. (2001) Continuing professional education in transition 1981–2000. *International Journal of Lifelong Education*. Vol 20, No 1/2. pp16–30.

CHALOFSKY, N. and KRISHNA, V. (2009) Meaningfulness, commitment and engagement: the intersection of a deeper level of intrinsic motivation. *Advances in Developing Human Resources*. Vol 11, No 2. pp189–203.

CHAUDHRY, A., COYLE-SHAPIRO, J. and WAYNE, S. (2011a) A longitudinal study of the impact of organizational change on transactional, relational, and balanced psychological contracts. *Journal of Leadership and Organizational Studies*. Vol 18, No 2. pp247–259.

CHAUDHRY, A., WAYNE, S. and SCHALK, R. (2011b) A sensemaking model of employee evaluation of psychological change fulfilment: how and when do employees respond to change? *The Journal of Applied Behavioural Science*. Vol 45, No 4. pp498–520.

CHAUDHURI, S. and GHOSH, R. (2012) Reverse mentoring: a social exchange tool for keeping the Boomers engaged and Millennials committed. *Human Resource Development Review*. Vol 11, No 1. pp55–76.

CHAVAN, M. (2009) The balanced scorecard: a new challenge. *Journal of Management Development*. Vol 28, No 5. pp393–406.

CHEESE, P. (2015) *Putting the human into HR [online]*. Available at: http://www.cipd.co.uk/community/blogs/b/peter_cheese/archive/2015/08/26/headline-putting-the-human-into-hr [Accessed 10 January 2016].

CHEETHAM, G. and CHIVERS, G. (2001) How professionals learn in practice: an investigation of informal learning amongst people working in professions. *Journal of European Industrial Training*. Vol 25. pp250–288.

CHHOKAR, J.S., BRODBECK, F.C. and HOUSE, R.J. (eds) (2007) *Culture and Leadership Across the World*. New Jersey: Lawrence Erlbaum Associates.

CHILD, J. (1972) Organizational structure, environment and performance: the role of strategic choice. *Sociology*. Vol 6. pp1–22.

CHILD, J. (2005) *Organization: contemporary principles and practice*. Oxford: Blackwell.

CHILD, J. (2015) *Organisation: Contemporary Principles and Practice*. 2nd ed. Chichester: John Wiley & Sons.

CHO, Y., CHO, E. and MCLEAN, G.N. (2009) HRD's role in knowledge management, advances in developing human resources. *OnlineFirst*. 14 July. doi: 10.1177/1523422309337719.

CHRYSSIDES, G. and KALER, J. (1996) *Essentials of Business Ethics*. Maidenhead: McGraw-Hill.

CHURCHARD, C. (2015) Zero hours contract workers 'as happy as permanent staff'. *People Management [online]* Available at: http://www.cipd.co.uk/pm/peoplemanagement/b/weblog/archive/2015/12/04/zero-hours-contract-workers-as-happy-as-permanent-staff.aspx [Accessed 7 January 2016].

CHYNOWETH, C. (2015) The public sector faces terrifying challenges. *People Management [online]* Available at: http://www.cipd.co.uk/pm/peoplemanagement/b/weblog/archive/2015/09/23/the-public-sector-faces-terrifying-challenges.aspx [Accessed 7 January 2016].

CIPD (2004a) *Human Capital Reporting: An internal perspective*. London: CIPD.

CIPD (2004b) *Graphology*. Factsheet. London: CIPD.

CIPD (2005a) *Training to learning*. Change agenda. London: CIPD.

CIPD (2005b) *Managing Diversity: People make the difference at work – but everyone is different*. London: CIPD.

CIPD (2006) *Diversity: An overview*. Factsheet. Available at: www.cipd.co.uk/subjects/dvsequl/general/divover.htm?Issrchres=1 [Accessed 8 May 2008].

CIPD (2007a) *Leadership and Management Standards*. Available at: www.cipd.co.uk [Accessed 21 April 2008].

CIPD (2007b) *Diversity in Business: A focus for progress*. Survey report. London: CIPD.

CIPD (2008a) *Smart Working: The impact of work organisation and job design*. Research Insight. London: CIPD.

CIPD (2008b) *Annual Survey Report: Recruitment, retention and turnover*. London: CIPD.

CIPD (2009a) *Employee Outlook*. Quarterly survey report. London: CIPD. Available at: www.cipd.co.uk/surveys [accessed 20 March 2010].

CIPD (2009b) *Organisation Development*. Factsheet. London: CIPD.

CIPD (2010a) *HR Business Partnering*. Factsheet. London: CIPD.

CIPD (2010b) *Diversity: An overview*. Factsheet. London: CIPD.

CIPD (2010c) *Learning and Talent Development*. Report. London: CIPD.

CIPD (2011) *Managing Careers for Organisational Capability*. Research Insight. Available at: http://www.cipd.co.uk/binaries/managing-careers-for-organisational-capability_2011. pdf [Accessed 4 January 2016].

CIPD (2012a) *HR and its role in innovation, Part 1 – November 2012: Innovative forms of organising: Networked working*. London: CIPD. Available at: https://www.cipd.co.uk/ binaries/hr-and-its-role-in-innovation_2014-part-1-networked-working.pdf [Accessed 25 January 2016].

CIPD (2012b) *HR Outlook: Views of our profession 2012–13*. Available at: www.cipd.co.uk/ hroutlook [Accessed 12 February 2016].

CIPD (2012c) *Code of Professional Conduct*. Available at: http://www.cipd.co.uk/cipd-hr-profession/about-us/code-professional-conduct.aspx [Accessed 12 February 2016].

CIPD (2012d) *CIPD unveils evidence highlighting the solid business case supporting an extension of rights to request flexible working*. Available at: http://www.cipd.co.uk/ pressoffice/press-releases/cipd-unveils-business-case-flexible-working-080512.aspx [Accessed 12 February 2016].

CIPD (2012e) *The Psychological Contract*. Factsheet. July 2012. London: CIPD.

CIPD (2012f) *Managing for Sustainable Employee Engagement: Developing a behavioural framework*. Policy report. London: CIPD. Available at: http://www.cipd.co.uk/binaries/ managing-for-sustainable-employee-engagement-developing-a-behavioural-framework_2012.pdf [Accessed 25 January 2016].

CIPD (2012g) *Competence and Competency Frameworks*. Factsheet. Available at: www. cipd.co.uk/hr-resources/factsheet/competency-frameworks [Accessed 20 December 2012].

CIPD (2012h) *Game on! How to keep diversity progress on track*. Policy report. London: CIPD. Available at: http://www.cipd.co.uk/binaries/game-on-how-to-keep-diversity-progress-on-track_2012.pdf [Accessed 25 January 2016].

CIPD (2012i) *Performance Management: An overview*. Factsheet. London: CIPD.

CIPD (2012j) *Reward Management*. Annual survey report. London: CIPD. Available at: http://www.cipd.co.uk/binaries/reward-management_2012.pdf [Accessed 25 January 2016].

CIPD (2012k) *Where has all the Trust Gone?* Research Report. London: CIPD. Available at: http://www.cipd.co.uk/binaries/where-has-all-the-trust-gone_2012-sop.pdf [Accessed 25 January 2016].

CIPD (2012l) *Continuing Professional Development Policy*. Available at: https://www.cipd. co.uk/cpd/policy.aspx[accessed 11 January 2016].

CIPD (2013a) *The Role of HR in Corporate Responsibility.* Research report. February 2013. London: CIPD. Available at: http://www.cipd.co.uk/binaries/the-role-of-hr-in-corporate-responsibility_2013-sop.pdf [Accessed 25 January]

CIPD (2013b) *HR Outsourcing.* Factsheet. London: CIPD.

CIPD (2013c) *Learning and Talent Development.* Survey report. London: CIPD. Available at: http://www.cipd.co.uk/hr-resources/survey-reports/learning-talent-development-2013.aspx [Accessed 25 January 2016].

CIPD (2013d) *Social Media and Employee Voice – The Current Landscape.* Research report. London: CIPD. Available at http://www.cipd.co.uk/binaries/social-media-and-employee-voice_2013-current-landscape-sop.pdf [Accessed 25 January 2016].

CIPD (2013e) *Employers are from Mars, Young People are from Venus.* Research report. London: CIPD. Available at http://www.cipd.co.uk/binaries/MarsVenus%20FINAL%2030%2004%2013.pdf [Accessed 8 January 2016].

CIPD (2014a) *HR: Getting Smart about Agile Working.* Research Report. Available at: http://www.cipd.co.uk/binaries/hr-getting-smart-agile-working_2014.pdf [Accessed 25 January 2016].

CIPD (2014b) *Neuroscience in Action. Applying Insight to L&D Practice.* Research report. Available at: http://www.cipd.co.uk/binaries/neuroscience-action_2014-applying-insight-LD-practice.pdf [Accessed 25 January 2016].

CIPD (2015a) *HR Outlook: Winter 2014–15.* Survey report. London: CIPD. Available at: http://www.cipd.co.uk/binaries/hr-outlook_2015-winter-2014–15-views-of-our-profession.pdf [Accessed 25 January 2016].

CIPD (2015b) *Absence Management Survey 2015.* Survey report. London: CIPD. Available at: https://www.cipd.co.uk/hr-resources/survey-reports/absence-management-2015.aspx [Accessed 13 November 2015].

CIPD (2015c) *Over-qualification and Skills Mismatch in the Graduate Labour Market.* Policy report. London: CIPD. Available at: http://www.cipd.co.uk/binaries/over-qualification-and-skills-mismatch-graduate-labour-market.pdf [Accessed 7 January 2016].

CIPD (2015d) *Landing Transformational Change: Closing the Gap between Theory and Practice.* Research Report. London: CIPD. Available at: https://www.cipd.co.uk/hr-resources/research/landing-transformational-change-gap-theory-practice.aspx [Accessed 17 November 2015].

CIPD (2015e) *Productivity: Getting the Best out of People.* Policy report. London: CIPD. Available at: https://www.cipd.co.uk/publicpolicy/policy-reports/productivity-getting-best-out-of-people.aspx [Accessed 7 January 2016].

CIPD (2015f) *Resourcing and Talent Planning 2015.* Survey report. London: CIPD. Available at: https://www.cipd.co.uk/hr-resources/survey-reports/resourcing-talent-planning-2015.aspx [Accessed 25 January 2016].

CIPD (2015g) *Learning and development survey 2015.* Survey report. London: CIPD. Available at http://www.cipd.co.uk/hr-resources/survey-reports/learning-development-2015.aspx [Accessed 17 November 2015].

CLARK, J. (1993) Full flexibility and self-supervision in an automated factory. In CLARK, J. (ed.) *Human Resource Management and Technical Change.* London: Sage.

CLARKE, C. and PRATT, S. (1985) Leadership's four-part progress. *Management Today.* March. pp84–86.

CLEGG, S., KORNBERGER, M. and PITSIS, T. (2008) *Managing and Organisations.* London: Sage.

CLEGG, S., KORNBERGER, M. and PITSIS, T. (2011) *Managing and Organisations.* 3rd ed. London: Sage.

CLEGG, S., KORNBERGER, M. and PITSIS, T. (2015) *Managing and Organisations.* 4th ed. London: Sage.

COGIN, J. (2012) Are generational differences in work values fact or fiction? *International Journal of Human Resource Management.* Vol 23, No 11. pp 2268–2294.

COHEN, A., FETTER, M. and FLEISCHMANN, F. (2005) Major change at Babson College: curricular and administrative, planned and otherwise. *Advances in Developing Human Resources.* Vol 7, No 3. pp324–337.

COHEN, T.R., PANTER, A.T. and TURAN, N. (2012) Guilt proneness and moral character. *Current Directions in Psychological Science.* Vol 21, No 5. pp355–359.

COLLINGS, D.G., SCULLION, H. and DOWLING, P.J. (2006) Global staffing: a review and thematic research agenda. *International Journal of Human Resource Management.* Vol 20, No 6. pp1253–1272.

COLLINS, H., EWING, K. and MCCOLGAN, A. (2012) *Labour Law.* Cambridge: Cambridge University Press.

COLLINSON, D. (2006) Rethinking followership: a post-structuralist analysis of follower identities. *Leadership Quarterly.* Vol 17, No 2. pp179–189.

CONFESSORE, S.J. and KOPS, W.J. (1998) Self-directed learning and the learning organisation: examining the connection between the individual and the learning environment. *Human Resource Development Quarterly.* Vol 9. pp365–375.

CONGER, J. (1999) Charisma and how to grow it. *Management Today.* December. pp78–81.

CONGER, J. (2002) Danger of delusion. *Financial Times.* 29 November.

CONGER, J. (2004) Developing leadership capability: what's inside the black box? *Academy of Management Executive.* Vol 18, No 3. pp136–139.

COOMBS, J., LIU, Y., HALL, A. and KETCHEN, D. (2006) How much do high-performance work practices matter? A meta-analysis of their effects on organizational performance. *Personnel Psychology.* Vol 59, No 3. pp501–528.

COOPER, C. (2005) The future of work: careers, stress and wellbeing. *Career Development International.* Vol 10, No 5. pp396–399.

COWELL, C., HOPKINS, P.C., MCWHORTER, R. and JORDEN, D.L. (2006) Alternative training models. *Advances in Developing Human Resources.* Vol 8, No 4. pp460–475.

COYLE-SHAPIRO, J. and KESSLER, I. (2000) Consequences of the psychological contract for the employment relationship: a large-scale survey. *Journal of Management Studies.* Vol 37, No 7. p903.

CRAIL, M. (2007) Online recruitment delivers more applicants and wins vote of most employers. *Personnel Today*. 20 November. Available at: http://www.personneltoday.com/hr/online-recruitment-delivers-more-applicants-and-wins-vote-of-most-employers [Accessed 16 May 2008].

CRANE, A. and MATTEN, D. (2010) *Business Ethics*. 3rd ed. Oxford: Oxford University Press.

CRANE, A. and MATTEN, D. (2016) *Business Ethics: Managing corporate citizenship and sustainability in the age of globalization*. 4th ed. Oxford: Oxford University Press.

CRANET (2011) *Cranet survey on comparative human resource management: International executive report 2011*. Cranfield: Cranfield University.

CROOK, C. (2005) The good company. *The Economist*. 22 January. pp3–4.

CRUSH, P. (2013) Parental leave mums v dads. *People Management*. 8 January. p20.

CRUSH, P. (2015) Government backs 'name-blind CVs' to end discrimination. *People Management*. 26 October. Available at: http://www.cipd.co.uk/pm/peoplemanagement/b/weblog/archive/2015/10/26/government-backs-name-blind-cvs-to-end-discrimination.aspx [Accessed 8 January 2016].

CSIKSZENTMIHALYI, M. (1990) *Flow: The psychology of optimal experience*. New York: Harper Perennial.

CULLY, M., WOODLAND, S. and O'REILLY, A. (1999) *Britain at Work, as Depicted by the 1998 Workplace Employee Relations Survey*. London: Routledge.

CUNNINGHAM, I. (2008) A race to the bottom? Exploring variations in employment conditions in the voluntary sector. *Public Administration*. Vol 86, No 4. pp1033–1053.

CUNNINGHAM, I. (2010) Leadership development in crisis: leadership development hasn't made much difference to organizations. *Development and Learning in Organizations*. Vol 24, No 5. pp5–7.

DAFT, R.L., MURPHY, J. and WILLMOTT, H. (2010) *Organization Theory and Design*. Andover: Cengage.

DAFT, R.L., MURPHY, J. and WILLMOTT, H. (2016) *Organization Theory and Design*. 2nd ed. Andover: Cengage.

DALAKOURA, A. (2010) Differentiating leader and leadership development. *Journal of Management Development*. Vol 17, No 5. pp432–441.

DANY, F., GUEDRI, Z. and HATT, F. (2008) New insights into the link between HRM integration and organizational performance: the moderating role of influence distribution between HRM specialists and line managers. *International Journal of Human Resource Management*. Vol 19, No 11. pp2095–2112.

D'ARCY, C. and GARDINER, L. (2014) *Just the job – or a working compromise? The changing nature of self-employment in the UK [online]*. The Resolution Foundation. May. Available at: http://www.resolutionfoundation.org/wp-content/uploads/2014/05/Just-the-job-or-a-working-compromise-FINAL.pdf [Accessed 4 January 2016].

DAVENPORT, T.H. (1993) *Process Innovation: Re-engineering work through information technology*. Boston, MA: Harvard Business School Press.

DAVENPORT, T., HARRIS, J. and SHAPIRO, J.(2010) Competing on talent analytics. *Harvard Business Review.* Vol 88, No 10. pp 52–58. Available at: https://hbr.org/2010/10/competing-on-talent-analytics [Accessed 4 January 2016].

DAVIDSON, L (2015) Why the UK should adopt Sweden's six-hour workday. *The Telegraph.* 1 October.

DAVIES, M.E. (2013) *Women on Boards.* Cranfield, Bedford: Cranfield School of Management.

DAY, D. and SIN, H.P. (2011) Longitudinal tests of an integrative model of leader development: charting and understanding development trajectories. *The Leadership Quarterly.* Vol 22, No 3. pp545–560.

DAY, D.V. (2001) Leadership development: a review in context. *Leadership Quarterly.* Vol 11, No 4. pp581–613.

DAY, D.V. and HARRISON, M.M. (2007) A multilevel, identity-based approach to leadership development. *Human Resource Management Review.* Vol 17, No 4. pp360–373.

DCSF (2009a) *14–19 Briefing: Making change happen.* Available at: www.dcsf.gov.uk/14–19 [Accessed 4 January 2016].

DCSF (2009b) *Quality, Choice and Aspiration.* Report. Available at: http://webarchive.nationalarchives.gov.uk/20130401151715/http://www.education.gov.uk/publications/eOrderingDownload/IAG-Report-v2.pdf [Accessed 10 January 2016].

DECI, E.L., RYAN, M. and KOESTNER, R. (2001) The pervasive negative effects of rewards on intrinsic motivation: response to Cameron. *Review of Educational Research.* Vol 71. pp43–51.

DE GAMA, N., MCKENNA, S. and PETTICA-HARRIS, A. (2012) Ethics and HRM: theoretical and conceptual analysis. *Journal of Business Ethics.* Vol 111, No 1. pp97–108.

DELOITTE (2009) *Shaping Up: Evolving the HR function for the 21st century.* New York/London: Deloitte MCS Limited.

DELOITTE (2014) *Global Outsourcing and Insourcing Survey [online]* Available at: https://www2.deloitte.com/content/dam/Deloitte/us/Documents/strategy/us-2014-global-outsourcing-insourcing-survey-report-123114.pdf [Accessed 11 January 2016].

DELOITTE and BERSIN (2014) *Global Human Capital Trends 2014: Engaging the 21st-century workforce.* Available at: http://dupress.com/wp-content/uploads/2014/04/GlobalHumanCapitalTrends_2014.pdf [Accessed 17 November 2015].

DE MENEZES, L. and KELLIHER, C. (2011) Flexible working and performance: a systematic review of the evidence for a business case. *International Journal of Management Reviews.* Vol 13, No 4. pp452–474.

DENCKER, J.C., JOSHI, A. and MARTOCCHIO, J.J. (2008) Towards a theoretical framework linking generational memories to workplace attitudes and behaviours, *Human Resource Management Review.* Vol 18, No 3. pp 180–187.

DEPARTMENT FOR BUSINESS, INNOVATION AND SKILLS (2013) *The Business Case for Equality and Diversity: A survey of academic studies.* BIS Occasional Paper No 4. London: Department for Business Innovation and Skills.

DEPARTMENT FOR BUSINESS, INNOVATION AND SKILLS (2015) *Trade Union Membership 2014: Statistical bulletin.* London: Department for Business Innovation and Skills.

DEVANNA, M.A., FOMBRUN, C.J. and TICHY, N.M. (1984) A framework for strategic human resource management. In: FOMBRUN, C.J., TICHY, M.M. and DEVANNA, M.A. (eds) *Strategic Human Resource Management.* New York: John Wiley.

DE VOS, A. and MEGANCK, A. (2009) What HR managers do versus what employees value. *Personnel Review.* Vol 38, No 1. pp45–60.

DE WIT, B. and MEYER, R. (2004) *Strategy: Process, content and theory.* 3rd ed. London: Thomson Publishing.

DIMBLEBY, D. (2012) The BBC has throttled itself with its own bureaucracy. *Daily Telegraph.* 12 November. Available at: www.telegraph.co.uk [Accessed 18 December 2012].

DINH, J.E., LORD, R.G., GARDNER, W.L., MEUSER, J.D., LIDEN, R.C. and HU, J. (2014) Leadership theory and research in the new millennium: current theoretical trends and changing perspectives. *Leadership Quarterly.* Vol 25, No 1. pp36–62.

DOBSON, J. (2007) Applying virtue ethics to business: the agent-based approach. *Journal of Business Ethics and Organization Studies.* Vol 12, No 2. p1.

DOHERTY, N. (2013) Understanding the self-initiated expatriate: a review and directions for future research. *International Journal of Management Reviews.* Vol 15, No 4. pp447–469.

DOHERTY, N.T. and DICKMANN, N. (2012) Measuring the return in investment in international assignments: an action research approach. *International Journal of Human Resource Management.* Vol 23, No 16. pp3434–3454.

DONALDSON, T. and PRESTON, L. (1995) The stakeholder theory of the corporation: concepts, evidence and implications. *Academy of Management Review.* Vol 5. pp265–269.

DOWLING, P.J., FESTING, M. and ENGLE, A.D. (2008) *International Human Resource Management.* 5th ed. London: Thomson.

DOZ, Y.L. and PRAHALAD, C.K. (1988) A process model of strategic redirection in large complex firms: the case of multinational corporations. In: PETTIGREW, A.M. (ed.) *The Management of Strategic Change.* Oxford: Blackwell.

DRATH, W. (2001) *The Deep Blue Sea: Rethinking the source of leadership.* San Francisco: Jossey Bass.

DRIES, N. and PEPERMANS, R. (2008) Real high-potential careers. *Personnel Review.* Vol 37, No 1. pp85–108.

DRUCKER, P.F. (1989) *The Practice of Management.* Heinemann Professional.

DRUCKER, P.F. (1993) *Post-Capitalist Society.* Oxford: Butterworth-Heinemann.

DRUCKER, P.F. (2005) Managing oneself. *Harvard Business Review.* Vol 8, No 1. pp100–109.

DTI (2001) *Diversity Best Practice in the Corporate World: A guide for business.* London: Department of Trade and Industry, Women and Equality Unit.

DTI (2005) *High Performance Work Practices: Linking strategy and skills to performance outcomes*. London: DTI in association with the CIPD.

DYER, L. and SHAFER, R. (1999) Creating organizational agility: implications for strategic human resource management. In WRIGHT, P., DYER, L. and BOUDREAU, J. (eds) *Research in Personnel and Human Resource Management* (Supplement 4: Strategic human resources management in the twenty-first century). Stamford, CT: JAI Press.

ECONOMIST, THE (2009) Talent on tap: the fashion for hiring temps has reached the executive suite. 10 December.

EDEN, D. and LEVIATHAN, U. (1975) Implicit leadership theory as a determinant of the factor structure underlying supervisory behavior scales. *Journal of Applied Psychology*. Vol 60. pp736–741.

EDUCATION AND TRAINING (2006) Vol 48, No 8/9.

EDWARDS, P. (2003) The employment relationship and the field of industrial relations. In: EDWARDS, P. (ed.) *Industrial Relations*. 4th ed. Oxford: Blackwell.

EGAN, J. (2009) HR roles and responsibilities. *IRS Employment Review Survey* (2nd ed. January). Available at: www.xperthr.co.uk/searchresults.aspx?s=egan [Accessed 8 June 2010].

EGLIN, R. (2004) Cash is not king in holding on to staff. *Sunday Times* Appointments. 15 February. p7.

EHNERT, I. (2014) Paradox as a lens for theorizing sustainable HRM. In EHNERT, I., HARRY, W. and ZINK, K.J. (eds) *Sustainability and Human Resource Management*. Berlin Heidelberg: Springer.

EIKHOF, D.R., WARHURST, C. and HAUNSCHILD, A. (2007) Introduction: what work? What life? What balance? Critical reflections on the work-life balance debate. *Employee Relations*. Vol 29, No 4. pp325–333.

ELLESWORTH, R.E. (2002) *Leading with Purpose: The new corporate realities*. Palo Alto, CA: Stanford University Press.

ELLINGER, A. (2004) The concept of self-directed learning and its implications for human resource. *Advances in Developing Human Resources*. Vol 6. p158.

ELLIOTT, L. (2004) Job flexibility can tie you up in knots. *Guardian Weekly*. 25–31 March, p16.

ELY, K., BOYCE, L., NELSON, J., ZACCARO, S., HERNEZ-BROOME, G. and WHYMAN, W. (2010) Evaluating leadership coaching: a review and integrated framework. *The Leadership Quarterly*. Vol 21. pp585–599.

EMERY, Y. (2004) Rewarding civil service performance through team bonuses: findings, analysis and recommendations. *International Review of Administrative Sciences*. Vol 70, No 1. pp157–168.

EMERY, Y. (2008) Lecture presentation at Portsmouth University, based upon three research articles by Emery, Y. and Glauque, D. (2005) *Paradoxes de la gestion publique*. Paris: L'Harmattan.

EMERY, Y. and GONIN, F. (2007) *Dynamiser la gestion des resources humaines.* Lausanne: Presses polytechniques et universitaires romandes.

ENGLE, A.D., DOWLING, P.J. and FESTING, M. (2008) Globalisation of SMEs and implications for international human resource management research and practice. *European Journal of International Management.* Vol 2, No 2. pp153–169.

ENTWISTLE, N. (2001) Styles of learning and approaches to studying in higher education. *Kybernete*s. Vol 30, No 5. pp593–603.

EUROPEAN FOUNDATION FOR THE IMPROVEMENT OF LIVING AND WORKING CONDITIONS (2013a) *Work organisation and innovation in Ireland. Case study: Medtronic Galway [online].* Available at: www.eurofound.europa.eu/sites/default/files/ef_publication/field_ef_document/ef1348en2.pdf [Accessed 4 January 2016].

EUROPEAN FOUNDATION FOR THE IMPROVEMENT OF LIVING AND WORKING CONDITIONS (2013b) *United Kingdom: GlassEco, case study [online]* Available at: www.eurofound.europa.eu/observatories/emcc/case-studies/the-greening-of-industries-in-the-eu/united-kingdom-glasseco-case-study [Accessed 4 January 2016].

EVANS, J. (2008) Leaders need to be humble, not heroes. *People Management.* 17 April. Available at: www.peoplemanagement.co.uk [Accessed 5 December 2012].

EVANS, P., PUCIK, V. and BJORKMAN, I. (2012) *The Global Challenge: International human resource management.* 2nd ed. London: McGraw-Hill.

EVETTS, J. (2013) Professionalism: value and etiology. *Current Sociology Review.* Vol 61, No 5–6. pp778–796.

EXPRESS & ECHO (2014) *Britain's smallest cop still looks up to new Met rival.* 27 January.

FANG, M. and GERHART, B. (2012) Does pay for performance diminish intrinsic interest? *The International Journal of Human Resource Management.* Vol 23, No 6. pp1176–1196.

FARNDALE, E. and BREWSTER, C. (2005) In search of legitimacy: personnel, management associations worldwide. *Human Resource Management Journal.* Vol 15, No 3. pp33–48.

FARNDALE, E., PAUUWE, J., MORRIS, S.S., STAHL, G., STILES, P., TREVOR, J. and WRIGHT, P. (2010a) Context-bound configurations of corporate HR functions across the globe. *Human Resource Management.* Vol 49, No 1. pp45–66.

FARNDALE, E., SCULLION H. and SALLOW, P. (2010b). The role of the corporate HR function in global talent management. *Journal of World Business.* Vol 45, No.2. pp161–168.

FARNHAM, D. and PIMLOTT, J. (1995) *Understanding Industrial Relations.* 4th ed. London: Cassell.

FARNHAM, D. and STEVENS, A. (2000) Developing and implementing competence-based recruitment and selection in a social services department. *International Journal of Public Sector Management.* Vol 13, No 4. pp369–382.

FAYOL, H. (1949) *General and Industrial Management.* London: Pitman.

FESTING, M., SCHÄFER, L. and SCULLION, H. (2013) Talent management in medium-sized German companies: an explorative study and agenda for future research. *The International Journal of Human Resource Management.* Vol 24, No 9. pp1872–1893.

FINCHAM, R. and RHODES, P. (2005) *Principles of Organizational Behaviour.* Oxford: Oxford University Press.

FITZGERALD, C. and HOWE-WALSH, L. (2008) Self-initiated expatriates: an interpretative phenomenological analysis of professional female expatriates. *International Journal of Business and Management.* Vol 21, No 3. pp156–175.

FLEMING, P. (2015), There's nothing good about zero-hours contracts – ban them now. *The Guardian.* 7 September.

FLETCHER, C. (2007) *Appraisal, Feedback and Development: Making performance review work.* 4th ed. London: Taylor & Francis.

FLETCHER, C. and WILLIAMS, R. (1996) Performance management, job satisfaction and organisational commitment. *British Journal of Management.* Vol 7. pp169–179.

FOMBRUN, C.J., TICHY, M.M. and DEVANNA, M.A. (eds) (1984) *Strategic Human Resource Management.* New York: John Wiley.

FOOT, M. and HOOK, C. (2005) *Introducing Human Resource Management.* 4th ed. Harlow: FT/Prentice Hall.

FOOT, M. and HOOK, C. (2011) *Introducing Human Resource Management.* 6th ed. Harlow: FT/Prentice Hall.

FOOTE, D. (2001) The question of ethical hypocrisy in human resource management in the UK and Irish charity sectors. *Journal of Business Ethics.* Vol 34. pp25–38.

FORTUNE MAGAZINE (2013) *Marissa Mayer and Marc Benioff on changing company culture [video].* Available at: http://fortune.com/video/2015/11/03/marissa-mayer-marc-benioff-company-culture/ [Accessed 13 January 2016].

FOSTER, C. and HARRIS, L. (2005) Easy to say, difficult to do: diversity management in retail. *Human Resource Management Journal.* Vol 15, No 3. pp4–17.

FOSTER, D. and WILLIAMS, L. (2011) The past, present and future of workplace equality agendas. In: BLYTON, P., HEERY, E. AND TURNBULL, P. (eds) *Reassessing the Employment Relationship.* Basingstoke: Palgrave Macmillan. pp318–341.

FOURNIER, V. (1999) The appeal to 'professionalism' as a disciplinary mechanism. *Sociological Review.* Vol 47, No 2. pp280–307.

FOX, A. (1966) *Industrial Sociology and Industrial Relations.* Research Paper No 3. Royal Commission on Trade Unions and Employers' Associations. London: HMSO.

FOX, A. (1974) *Beyond Contract: Work, power and trust relations.* London: Faber & Faber.

FOX, M. (1994) *The Reinvention of Work: A new vision of livelihood for our time.* New York: HarperCollins.

FRAHM, J. and BROWN, K. (2005) First steps: linking change communication to change receptivity. *Journal of Organisational Change Management.* Vol 20, No 3. pp370–387.

FRANCIS, H. and KEEGAN, A. (2006) The changing face of HRM: in search of balance. *Human Resource Management Journal.* Vol 16, No 3. pp231–249.

FRANK, E. (1991) The UK's Management Charter Initiative: the first three years. *Journal of European Industrial Training.* Vol 17, No 1. pp9–11.

FREDMAN, S. (2001) Equality: a new generation? *Industrial Law Journal.* Vol 30, No 2. pp145–168.

FREEMAN, R.E. (1984) *Strategic Management: A stakeholder approach.* Boston MA: Pitman.

FREEMAN, R.E., HARRISON, J.S., WICKS, A.C., PARMAR, B.L. and DE COLLE, S. (2010) *Stakeholder Theory: The state of the art.* Cambridge: Cambridge University Press.

FREER, T. (2011) Social media gaming – a recipe for employer brand success. *Strategic HR Review.* Vol 11, No 1. pp13–17.

FREIFELD, L. (2009) Brain sells. *Training.* Vol 46, No 6. p9.

FRENCH, J. and RAVEN, B. (1968) The bases of social power. In: CARTWRIGHT, D. and ZANDER, A. (eds) *Group Dynamics: Research and theory.* London: Harper & Row.

FRENCH, R. (2010) *Cross-Cultural Management in Work Organisations.* 2nd ed. London: CIPD.

FRENCH, R. (2015) *Cross-Cultural Management in Work Organisations.* 3rd ed. London: CIPD.

FRENCH, R., RAYNER, C., REES, G. and RUMBLES, S. (2011) *Organizational Behaviour.* 2nd ed. Chichester: John Wiley & Sons.

FRENCH, R., RAYNER, C., REES, G. and RUMBLES, S. (2015) *Organizational Behaviour.* 3rd ed. Chichester: John Wiley & Sons.

FRENCH, W.L. and BELL, C.H. (1999) *Organizational Development: Behavioural science interventions for organizational improvement.* 6th ed. Upper Saddle River, NJ: Prentice Hall.

FRENCH, W.L., KAST, F.E. and ROSENZWEIG, J.E. (1985) *Understanding Human Behaviour in Organizations.* London: Harper & Row.

FRIEDMAN, M. (1970) The social responsibility of business is to increase its profits. *New York Times Magazine.* 13 September. p32ff.

FURNHAM, A. (1997) *The Psychology of Behaviour at Work.* Hove: Psychology Press, Taylor & Francis.

FURNHAM, A. (2004) Performance management systems. *European Business Journal.* Vol 16, No 2. pp83–94.

FURNHAM, A. (2005) Where egos dare. *People Management.* Vol 11, No 3. pp40–42.

GARAVAN, T., WATSON, S., CARBERY, R. and O'BRIEN, F. (2015) The antecedents of leadership development practices in SMEs: the influence of HRM strategy and practice. *International Small Business Journal.* January. pp1–21.

GARCIA, M.F., POSTH GARAVAN, T., WATSON, S., CARBERY, R. and O'BRIEN, F. (2015) The antecedents of leadership development practices in SMEs: the influence of HRM strategy and practice. *International Small Business Journal.* doi: 0266242615594215.

GARCIA, M.F., POSTHUMA, R.A. and COLELLA, A. (2008) Fit perceptions and the employment interview: the role of similarity, liking and expectations. *Journal of Occupational and Organizational Psychology.* Vol 81, No 2. pp173–189.

GEAL, M. and JOHNSON, B. (2002) Management performance: a glimpse of the blindingly obvious. *Training Journal.* October. pp24–27.

GERSHON EFFICIENCY REVIEW (2004) Available at: www.hm-treasury.gov.uk/spend_sr04_index.htm [Accessed 29 April 2010].

GHOSHAL, S., BARTLETT, C. and MORAN, P. (1999) A new manifesto for management. *Sloan Management Review.* Vol 40, No 3. pp9–22.

GILES, C., GUHA, K. and ATKINS, R. (2010) At the sharp end – the failings of flexibility. *Financial Times.* 22 January. Available at: www.ft.com [Accessed 1 February 2010].

GILLILAND, S.W. (1993) The perceived fairness of selection systems: an organizational justice perspective. *Academy of Management Review.* Vol 18. pp694–734.

GILMORE, S. (2009) Conclusions. In: GILMORE, S. and WILLIAMS, S. (eds) *Human Resource Management.* Oxford: Oxford University Press.

GILMORE, S. (2013) Introducing human resource management. In GILMORE, S and WILLIAMS, S. *Human Resource Management.* 2nd ed. Oxford: Oxford University Press.

GILMORE, S.E. and WILLIAMS, S. (2003) Constructing the HR professional: a critical analysis of the Chartered Institute of Personnel and Development's professional project. *Third International Critical Management Studies Conference.* Lancaster University Management School.

GILMORE, S. and WILLIAMS, S. (2007) Conceptualising the 'personnel professional': a critical analysis of the Chartered Institute of Personnel and Development's professional qualification scheme. *Personnel Review.* Vol 36, No 3. pp398–414.

GILMORE, S. and WILLIAMS, S. (eds) (2009) *Human Resource Management.* Oxford: Oxford University Press.

GILMORE, S. and WILLIAMS, S. (2013) *Human Resource Management.* 2nd ed. Oxford: Oxford University Press.

GIOIA, D.A. and THOMAS, J.B. (1996) Identity, image and issue interpretation: sense making during strategic change in academia. *Administrative Science Quarterly.* Vol 41. pp370–403.

GLAISTER, A.J. (2014) HR outsourcing: the impact on HR role, competency development and relationships. *Human Resource Management Journal.* Vol 24. pp211–226.

GLOVER, L. and BUTLER, P. (2012) High-performance work systems, partnerships and the working lives of HR professionals. *Human Resource Management.* Vol 22, No 2. pp199–215.

GMAC (2008) *Global Relocation Trends – 2008 Survey Report*. Available at: http://www1.expatica.com/hr/story/Reporting-on-global-relocation-trends-in-2008.html [Accessed 18 January 2016].

GOLD, J., THORPE, R. and MUMFORD, A. (2010) *Leadership and Management Development*. 5th ed. London: CIPD.

GOLD, J., HOLDEN, R., ILES, P., STEWART, J. and BEARDWELL, J. (2013) *Human Resource Development: Theory and Practice*. 3rd ed. Basingstoke: Palgrave Macmillan.

GOLDTHORPE, J.H., LOCKWOOD, D., BECHHOFER, F. and PLATT, J. (1968) *The Affluent Worker: Attitudes and behaviour*. Cambridge: Cambridge University Press.

GOLEMAN, D. (1995) *Emotional Intelligence. Why it can matter more than IQ*. New York: Bantam.

GOSLING, J. and MINTZBERG, H. (2003) The five minds of a manager. *Harvard Business Review*. Vol 81, No 11. pp54–63.

GOULD-WILLIAMS, J. (2003) The importance of HR practices and workplace trust in achieving superior performance: a study of public sector organizations. *International Journal of Human Resource Management*. Vol 14, No 1. pp28–54.

GRATTON, L. (2000) *Living Strategy: Putting people at the heart of corporate purpose*. Harlow: FT/Prentice Hall.

GREENLEAF, R. (1977) *Servant Leadership: A journey into the nature of legitimate power and greatness*. New York: Paulist Press.

GREENWOOD, M. and FREEMAN, R.E. (2011) *Ethics and HRM. Business and professional ethics journal*. Vol 30, No 3/4. pp269–292.

GREINER, L. (1972) Evolution and revolution as organizations grow. *Harvard Business Review*. July–August. Available at: https://hbr.org/1998/05/evolution-and-revolution-as-organizations-grow [Accessed 10 January 2016].

GRELLER, M. (2006) Hours invested in professional development during late career as a function of career motivation and satisfaction. *Career Development International*. Vol 11, No 6. pp544–559.

GREY, C. (2009) *A Very Short, Fairly Interesting and Reasonably Cheap Book about Studying Organizations*. 2nd ed. London: Sage.

GREY, C. (2013) *A Very Short, Fairly Interesting and Reasonably Cheap Book about Studying Organizations*. 3rd ed. London: Sage.

GRINT, K. (1997) *Fuzzy Management*. Oxford: Oxford University Press.

GRINT, K. (2005) Problems, problems, problems: the social construction of leadership. *Human Relations*. Vol 58, No 11. pp1467–1494.

GRINT, K. (2010) *Leadership: A very short introduction*. New York: Oxford University Press.

GRONN, P. (2000) Distributed properties a new architecture for leadership. *Educational Management Administration and Leadership*. Vol 28, No 3. pp317–338.

GRONN, P. (2002) Distributed leadership as a unit of analysis. *The Leadership Quarterly.* Vol 13, No 4. pp423–451.

GRUMAN, J. and SAKS, A. (2011) Performance management and employee engagement. *Human Resource Management Review.* Vol 21. pp123–136.

GRUNDY, T. (1993) *Managing Strategic Change.* London: Kogan Page.

GUARDIAN (2013) *CPS manager and taxi driver jailed over £1m fraud.* 30 August. Available at: www.theguardian.com/uk-news/2013/aug/30/cps-manager-taxi-driver-jailed-fraud [Accessed 4 January 2016].

GUBBINS, C. and GARAVAN, T.N. (2009) Understanding the HRD role in MNCs: the imperatives of social capital and networking. *Human Resource Development Review.* Vol 8. pp245–275.

GUEST, D. (1997) Human resource management and performance: a review of the research agenda. *International Journal of Human Resource Management.* Vol 8, No 3. pp263–276.

GUEST, D. (1998) Is the psychological contract worth taking seriously? *Journal of Organizational Behaviour.* Vol 19. pp649–664.

GUEST, D. (2004) Flexible employment contracts, the psychological contract and employee outcomes: an analysis and review of the evidence. *International Journal of Management Reviews.* Vol 5/6, No 1. pp1–19.

GUEST, D.E. and CONWAY, N. (2002) *Pressure at Work and the Psychological Contract.* London: CIPD.

GUEST, D.E. AND WOODROW, C. (2012) Exploring the boundaries of human resource managers' responsibilities. *Journal of Business Ethics.* Vol 111, No 1. pp109–119.

GUO, C., BROWN, W.A., ASHCRAFT, R.F., YOKISHIOKA C.F and DONG, H.K.C. (2011) Strategic human resource management in non-profit organizations. *Review of Public Personnel Administration.* Vol 31, No 3. pp248–269.

GURDJIAN, P. HALBEISEN, T. and LANE, K. (2014) Why leadership-development programs fail. *Mckinsey Quarterly.* January.

HACKMAN, J.R. and OLDHAM, G.R. (1980) *Work Redesign.* New York: Addison-Wesley.

HAINES III, V. and ST-ONGE, S. (2012) Performance management effectiveness: practices or context? *The International Journal of Human Resources Management.* Vol 26, No 6. pp1158–1175.

HAKIM, C. (2011) *Feminist Myths and Magic Medicine: The flawed thinking behind calls for further equality legislation.* Centre For Policy Studies. Available at: eprints.lse.ac.uk/36488/1/Feminist_myths_and_magic_medicine_the_flawed_thinking_behind_calls_for_further_equality_legislation_(lsero).pdf [Accessed 5 June 2013].

HALL, D. (1996) *The Career Is Dead, Long Live the Career.* San Francisco, CA: Jossey-Bass.

HALL, D. (2004) The protean career: a quarter-century journey. *Journal of Vocational Behaviour.* Vol 65, No 1. pp1–13.

HALL, D. (2009) How smart are targets? *HR Bulletin: Research and Practice*. Vol 4. pp8–10.

HALL, D., JAMES, D. and MARSDEN, N. (2012) Marginal gains: Olympic lessons in high performance for organisations. *Human Resource Bulletin: Research and Practice*. Vol 7, No 2. pp9–13.

HAMMER, M. and CHAMPY, J. (1993) *Re-engineering the Corporation: A manifesto for business revolution*. London: Nicholas Brealey.

HANDY, C. (1976) *Understanding Organisations*. London: Penguin Books.

HANDY, C. (1989) *The Age of Unreason*. London: Business Books.

HANLON, G. (1998) Professionalism as enterprise: service class politics and the redefinition of professionalism. [Electronic version.] *Sociology*. Vol 32, No 43.

HARDY, C. (1994) *Managing Strategic Action: Mobilizing change – concepts, readings and cases*. London: Sage.

HARDY, C. (1996) Understanding power: bringing about strategic change. *British Journal of Management*. Vol 7 (special issue). ppS3–S16.

HARRINGTON, S., RAYNER, C. and WARREN, S. (2012) Too hot to handle? trust and human resource practitioners' implementation of anti-bullying policies. *Human Resource Management Journal*. Vol 22, No 4. pp392–408.

HARRIS, L. (2005) Employment law and human resourcing strategies. In: LEOPALD, J., HARRIS, L. and WATSON, T.J. (eds) *The Strategic Managing of Human Resources*. Harlow: Pearson Education.

HARRISON, R. (2005) *Learning and Development*. 3rd ed. London: CIPD.

HARRISON, R. (2009) *Learning and Development*. 5th ed. London: CIPD.

HARRISON, R. and KESSELS, J. (2003) *Human Resource Development in a Knowledge Economy*. Basingstoke: Palgrave Macmillan.

HARRISON, T. and AULUCK, R. (2014) Establishing learning needs. In: STEWART, J. and CURETON, P. (eds) *Designing, Developing and Evaluating L & D: Essentials for practice*. London: CIPD.

HARRY, W. and COLLINGS, D. (2012) Localisation, societies, organisations and employees. In: STAHL, G.K, MENDENHALL, M.E. and ODDOU, G.R. (2012) *Readings and Cases in International Human Resource Management and Organisational Behaviour*. 5th ed. London: Routledge.

HASSON, J. (2007) Blogging for talent. *HR Magazine*. Vol 52, No 10. pp65–68.

HAYS-THOMAS, R. (2004) Why now? The contemporary focus on managing diversity. In: STOCKDALE, M.S. and CROSBY, F.J. (eds) *The Psychology and Management of Workplace Diversity*. Oxford: Blackwell.

HAZARD, P. (2004) Tackling performance management barriers. *Strategic HR Review*. Vol 3. pp3–7.

HEENAN, D. and PERLMUTTER, H. (1979) *Multinational Organizational Development: A social architecture perspective*. Reading, MA: Addison-Wesley.

HEIETZ, R., GRASHAW, A. and LINSKY, M. (2009) Leadership in a (permanent) crisis. *Harvard Business Review*. July–August.

HENDERSON, S. (1997) Black swans don't fly double loops: the limits of the learning organisation. *The Learning Organisation*. Vol 4, No 3. pp99–105.

HENDRICK, H. (1983) Pilot performance under reversed control stick conditions. *Journal of Applied Psychology*. Vol 56, No 4. pp297–301.

HENDRY, C. (1995) *Human Resource Management*. Oxford: Butterworth-Heinemann.

HENEMAN, R.L. (1992) *Merit Pay: Linking pay increases to performance ratings*. Reading, MA: Addison-Wesley.

HERSEY, P., BLANCHARD, K. and JOHNSON, D. (2001*) Management of Organisational Behaviour: Leading human resources*. 8th ed. London: Prentice Hall.

HERZBERG, F. (1968) One more time: how do you motivate your employees? *Harvard Business Review*. January–February. pp109–120.

HILTROP, J.-M. (1996) Managing the changing psychological contract. *Employee Relations*. Vol 18, No 1. pp36–49.

HIRSCHI, A. (2012) The career resources model: an integrative framework for career counselors. *British Journal of Guidance and Counselling*. Vol 40, No 4. pp369–383.

HOBSON, J. (2009) Bullying in the workplace. *Personnel Today*. 5 March.

HOCHSCHILD, A.R. (2012) *The Managed Heart: Commercialization of human feeling*. Berkeley: University of California Press.

HOFSTEDE, G. (1991) *Cultures and Organizations*. Maidenhead: McGraw-Hill.

HOFSTEDE, G. (2001) *Culture's Consequences: Comparing values, behaviours, institutions and organizations across nations*. London: Sage.

HOLBECHE, L. (2008a) *Aligning Human Resources and Business Strategy*. Oxford: Butterworth-Heinemann.

HOLBECHE, L. (2008b) Where is leadership going? *Impact*. Issue 22, February. pp16–17.

HOLBECHE, L. (2013) The future of HR. In REES, G. and SMITH, P.E. (eds) *Strategic Human Resource Management: An International Perspective*. London: Sage.

HOLBECHE, L. (2014) *The Future of Engagement: Thought Piece Collection. Is it right to expect employees to be permanently engaged?* Engage for Success leadership paper. Available at: http://www.cipd.co.uk/binaries/the-future-of-engagement_2014-thought-piece-permanently-engaged-linda-holbeche.pdf [Accessed 7 January 2016].

HOLBECHE, L. and MATTHEWS, G. (2012) *Engaged: Unleashing your organisation's potential through employee engagement*. Chichester: Wiley/Josey Bass.

HOLDEN, N. (2002) *Cross-Cultural Management: A knowledge management perspective*. Harlow: Pearson.

HOLLYFORDE, S. and WHIDDETT, S. (2002) *The Motivation Handbook*. London: CIPD.

HOLST, J.D. (2009) Conceptualizing training in the radical adult education tradition. *Adult Education Quarterly*. Vol 59, No 4. pp318–334.

HONEY, P. (1998) *101 Ways to Develop Your People Without Really Trying: A manager's guide to work-based learning*. Maidenhead: Peter Honey Publications.

HOWELL, W.S. (1982) *The Empathetic Communicator*. University of Minnesota: Wadsworth Publishing.

HOWE-WALSH, L.J. and SCHYNS, B. (2010) Self-initiated expatriates: implications for HRM. *International Journal of Human Resource Management*. Vol 21, No 2. pp260–273.

HR-INFORM (2012) *Does an organisation have to hold a Christmas party for its staff?* Available at: www.cipd.co.uk/pm/peoplemanagement/p/paymentgateway.aspx?returnURL=/pm/peoplemanagement/b/weblog/archive/2012/11/06/does-anorganisation-have-to-hold-an-annual-christmas-party-for-itsstaff-2012-11.aspx&blogid=2&postid=96710 [Accessed 5 June 2013].

HR OUTLOOK (2015) *Views of our profession, Winter 2014–5*. London: CIPD. Available at: http://www.cipd.co.uk/hr-resources/survey-reports/hr-outlook-winter-2014–15-views-profession.aspx [Accessed 13 November 2015].

HUCZYNSKI, A. and BUCHANAN, D. (2007) *Organisational Behaviour: An introductory text*. 6th ed. Harlow: Pearson Education.

HUCZYNSKI, A. and BUCHANAN, D. (2010) *Organisational Behaviour: An introductory text*. 7th ed. Harlow: Pearson Education.

HUCZYNSKI, A. and BUCHANAN, D. (2013) *Organisational Behaviour*. 8th ed. Harlow: Pearson Education.

HUGHES, M. (2006) *Change Management: A critical perspective*. London: CIPD.

HUMBLE, J. (1972) *Management by Objectives*. London: Management Publications.

HUNT, B. (2007) Managing equality and cultural diversity in the health workforce. *Journal of Clinical Nursing*. Vol 16. pp2252–2259.

HUSELID, M.A. (1995) The impact of human resource management practices on turnover, productivity and corporate financial performance. *Academy of Management Journal*. Vol 38. pp635–672.

HUTCHINSON, S. and PURCELL, J. (2003) *Bringing Policies to Life: The vital role of front-line managers in people management*. London: CIPD.

HUTTON, W. (2004) Got those old blue-collar blues. *Observer*. 22 August.

HUWS, U. (2013) Capitalism's zero hour. *Times Higher Education*. 15 August.

HUWS, U. and O'KEEFE, B. (2008) *EMCC company network – Managing change in EU cross-border mergers and acquisitions – Case example: Impress: Meeting company goals through strategic acquisitions [online]*. Available at: www.eurofound.europa.eu/publications/htmlfiles/ef08043.htm [Accessed 11 July 2013].

IBARRA, H. (2004) *Working Identity: Unconventional strategies for reinventing your career*. Boston, MA: Harvard Business School Press.

IBE (2014) Collaboration between the ethics function and HR. *Business Ethics Briefing*. Issue 40. April. Available: http://www.ibe.org.uk/userassets/briefings/b40_hr.pdf [Accessed 4 January 2016].

IBE (2016) Frequently Asked Questions. Available: ibe.org.uk/frequently-asked-questions/3~faq273 [Accessed 12 February 2016].

IBM (2013) *IBM Graduate Scheme*. Available at: www-05.ibm.com/employment/uk/graduate-programmes/index.shtml [Accessed January 2013].

IDS (2006) *Online Recruitment*. IDS study 819. April. London: Incomes Data Services.

ILES, P., FORSTER, A. and TINLINE, G. (1996) The changing relationships between work commitment, personal flexibility and employability: an evaluation of a field experiment in executive development. *Journal of Managerial Psychology*. Vol 11, No 8. pp18–34.

INKSON, K. and ARTHUR, M. (2001) How to be a successful career capitalist. *Organisational Dynamics*. Vol 30, No 1. pp48–61.

IQBAL, M. and KHAN, R. (2011) The growing concept and uses of training needs assessment. *Journal of European Industrial Training*. Vol 35, No 5. pp439–466.

IRS (2000) Measuring intangible assets. *IRS Management Review*. Issue 19. Available at: www.xperthr.co.uk/article/6106/measuring-span-span-classhighlightintangible-spanspan-classhighlightassets.aspx [Accessed 4 June 2013].

IRS (2008) Line managers' role in people management. *IRS Employment Review*. Issue 894. Available at: www.xperthr.co.uk/article/84008/survey–line-managers-role-in-peoplemanagement.aspx [Accessed 11 July 2013].

IRS (2009) IRS flexible working survey 2009: availability, take-up and impact. *IRS Employment Review*. Issue 92. Available at: www.xperthr.co.uk/article/93627/irs-flexibleworking-survey-2009–availability,-take-up-and-impact.aspx [Accessed 11 July 2013].

IRS (2010) *Evaluation of training: the 2010 IRS survey*. IRS Employment Review. Available at: www.xperthr.co.uk/article/100298/evaluation-span-of-spanclasshighlighttraining–the-2010-irs-survey.aspx [Accessed 11 July 2013].

J. SAINSBURY'S (2014) *Our 20 sustainability commitments to help us all Live Well For Less: An update on our progress so far – 2014 [online]* Available at: www.j-sainsbury.co.uk/media/2383702/20x20_sustainability_plan_2013–14.pdf [Accessed 4 January 2016].

JACKSON, B. and PARRY, K. (2008) *A Very Short Fairly Interesting and Reasonably Cheap Book about Studying Leadership*. London: Sage.

JACKSON, B. and PARRY, K. (2011) *A Very Short Fairly Interesting and Reasonably Cheap Book about Studying Leadership*. 2nd ed. London: Sage.

JAMALI, D.R., EL DIRANI, A.M. and HARWOOD, I.A. (2015) Exploring human resource management roles in corporate social responsibility: the CSR–HRM co-creation model. *Business Ethics: A European Review*. Vol 24, No 2. pp125–143.

JAMROG, J.J., VICKERS, M., OVERHOLT, M.H. and MORRISON, C.L. (2008) High-performance organizations: finding the elements of excellence. *People and Strategy, The Human Resource Planning Society Journal*. Vol 31, No 1. pp29–38.

JANIS, I.L. (1972) *Victims of Groupthink*. Boston, MA: Houghton Mifflin.

JANIS, I.L. (1982) *Groupthink: Psychological studies on policy decisions and fiascos*. New York: Free Press.

JARRETT, T. (2011) *The Equality Act 2010 and Positive Action*. Standard Note SN/BT/ 6093. London: House of Commons Library.

JEHN, K. (1994) Enhancing effectiveness: an investigation of advantages and disadvantages of value-based intragroup conflict optimising performance by conflict stimulation. *International Journal of Conflict Management*. Vol 5, No 3. pp223–238.

JENNER, S. and TAYLOR, S. (2007) *Employer Branding – Fad or the Future for HR?* Research Insight Paper. London: CIPD.

JENNINGS, C. and WARGNIER, J. (2010) Experiential learning – a way to develop agile minds in the knowledge economy? *Development and Learning in Organizations*. Vol 24, No 3. pp14–16.

JOHNSON, G. and SCHOLES, K. (2002) *Exploring Corporate Strategy*. 6th ed. London: FT/Pitman.

JOHNSON, G., SCHOLES, K. and WHITTINGTON, R. (2007) *Exploring Corporate Strategy: Texts and cases*. 7th ed. London: FT/Pitman.

JOHNSON, G., SCHOLES, K. and WHITTINGTON, R. (2011) *Exploring Corporate Strategy*. 8th ed. London: FT/Pitman.

JONES, T.W. (1995) Performance management in a changing context. *Human Resource Management*. Fall. pp425–442.

JUDGE, T.A. and CABLE, D.M. (1997) Applicant personality, organisational culture and organisation attraction. *Personnel Psychology*. Vol 50, No 2. pp359–394.

JUDGE, W.Q., NAOUMOVA, I. and DOUGLAS, T. (2009) Organizational capacity for change and firm performance in a transitional economy. *International Journal of Human Resource Management*. Vol 20, No 8. pp1737–1752.

KAHN, W.A. (1990) Psychological conditions of personal engagement and disengagement at work. *The Academy of Management Journal*. Vol 33, No 4. pp692–724.

KAKABADSE, A., MYERS, A., MCMAHON, T. and SPONY, G. (1997) Top management styles in Europe: implications for business and cross-national teams. In: GRINT, T. (ed.) *Leadership: Classical, contemporary and critical approaches*. Oxford: Oxford University Press.

KANDOLA, R. and FULLERTON, J. (1998) *Diversity in Action: Managing the mosaic*. 2nd ed. London: CIPD.

KANG, D. and STEWART, J. (2007) Leader-member exchange (LMX) theory of leadership and HRD. *Leadership and Organization Development Journal*. Vol 28, No 6. pp531–551.

KATOU, A.A. and BUDHWAR, P.S. (2009) Causal relationship between HRM policies and performance: evidence from the Greek manufacturing sector. *European Management Journal*. Vol 28. pp25–39.

KATZENBACH, J.R. and SMITH, D.K. (2005) *The Wisdom of Teams: Creating the high performance organisations.* New York: McGraw-Hill Professional.

KEARNS, P. (2005) *Evaluating the ROI from Learning: How to develop value-based training.* London: CIPD.

KELLIHER, C. and ANDERSON, D. (2010) Doing more with less? Flexible working practices and the intensification of work. *Human Relations.* Vol 63, No 1. pp83–106.

KESSLER, I. and PURCELL, J. (1992) Performance-related pay: objectives and application. *Human Resource Management Journal.* Vol 2, No 3. pp6–33.

KHAPOVA, S. and ARTHUR, M. (2011) Interdisciplinary approaches to contemporary career studies. *Human Relations.* Vol 64, No 1. pp3–17.

KING, Z. (2004) *Guide to Career Management.* London: CIPD.

KINNIE, N., SWART, J., HOPE-HAILEY, V. and VAN ROSSENBERG, Y. (2012) *Innovative forms of Organizing: Networked working in HR and its role in innovation, Part 1.* Report. November. London: CIPD.

KINNIE, N., SWART, J., KUND, M., MORRIS, S., SNELL, S. and KANG, S.C. (2006) *Managing People and Knowledge Development in Professional Service Firms.* London: CIPD.

KISSLER, G. (1994) The new employment contract. *Human Resource Management.* Vol 33, No 3. pp335–352.

KNIES, E., BOSELIE, P., GOULD-WILLIAMS, J. and VANDENABEELE, W. (2015) *Special Issue of International Journal of Human Resource Management:* Strategic Human Resource Management and Public Sector Performance. Vol 26, No. 3. pp421–424.

KNOWLES, M. (1990) *The Adult Learner: A neglected species.* London: Gulf Publications.

KOSTER, F. (2011) Able, willing, and knowing: the effects of HR practices on commitment and effort in 26 European countries. *The International Journal of Human Resource Management.* Vol 22, No 14. pp2835–2851.

KOTTER, J.P. (1990) What leaders really do. *Harvard Business Review.* Volume 90. pp103–111.

KOTTER, J.P. (1996) *Leading Change.* Boston, MA: Harvard Business School Press.

KOTTER, J.P. (1999) *What Leaders Really Do.* Boston, MA: Harvard Business School Press.

KRAMAR, R. (2014) Beyond strategic human resource management: is sustainable human resource management the next approach? *The International Journal of Human Resource Management.* Vol 25, No 8. pp1069–1089.

KREITNER, R. (2001) *Management.* 6th ed. Boston, MA: Houghton Mifflin.

KREITNER, R. and KINICKI, A. (2001) *Organisational Behaviour.* 5th ed. New York: McGraw-Hill.

KREITNER, R., KINICKI, A. and BUELENS, M. (2002) *Organizational Behaviour.* 2nd ed. New York: McGraw-Hill.

KREMER, W. (2012) Why feeling guilty may make you a better boss. *BBC News Magazine.* Available at: www.bbc.co.uk/news/magazine-20257373 [Accessed 13 December 2012].

KULIK, C.T., RYAN, S., HARPER, S. and GEORGE, G. (2014) Aging populations and management. *Academy of Management Journal.* Vol 57, No 4. pp929–935.

KUVAAS, B. (2006) Performance appraisal satisfaction and employee outcomes: mediating and moderating roles of work motivation. *International Journal of Human Resource Management.* Vol 17, No 3. pp504–522.

LADKIN, D. (2008) Leading beautifully: how mastery, congruence and purpose create the aesthetic of embodied leadership practice. *The Leadership Quarterly.* Vol 19, No 1. pp31–41.

LADKIN, D. and TAYLOR, S. (2009) Enacting the true self: towards a theory of embodied authentic leadership. *The Leadership Quarterly.* Vol 21, No 1, pp64–74.

LAGERVELD et al (2012) Work-focused treatment of common mental disorders and return to work: a comparative outcome study. *Journal of Occupational Health Psychology.* Vol 17, No 2. pp220–234.

LASHLEY, C. (1995) Towards an understanding of employee empowerment in hospitality services. *International Journal of Contemporary Hospitality Management.* Vol 7, No1. pp27–32.

LATHAM, G. (2007) *Work Motivation: History, theory, research and practice.* London: Sage.

LAWLER, E. (2005) Creating high-performance organisations. *Asia Pacific Journal of Human Resources.* Vol 43, No 1, pp10–17.

LAWLER, E. (2009) The knowing–doing gap. *Conference Board Review.* Vol 46, No 3, May/June. p29.

LAWRENCE, P. and LORSCH, J. (1967) *Organisation and Environment.* Boston, MA: Harvard Business School Press.

LEACH, D. and WALL, T. (2004) *What is Job Design?* Sheffield: Institute of Work Psychology.

LEANNA, C. and BARRY, B. (2000) Stability and change as simultaneous experiences in organizational life. *Academy of Management Review.* Vol 25, No 4. pp75–79.

LEGGE, K. (2000) HRM in a critical analysis. In: STOREY, J. (ed.) *Human Resource Management: A critical text.* London: Thomson.

LEGGE, K. (2005) *Human Resource Management: Rhetorics and realities.* 2nd ed. Basingstoke: Palgrave Macmillan.

LEITCH, S. (2006) *Review of Skills: Prosperity for all in the global economy – world-class skills.* Final Report. Norwich: HMSO. Available at: www.hm-treasury.gov.uk/leitch [Accessed November 2009].

LESSEM, R. (1989) *Global Management Principles.* Harlow: Prentice Hall.

LEVINSON, H. (1970) Management by whose objectives? *Harvard Business Review*. July–August. pp125–134.

LEVINSON, H. (1976) Appraisal of what performance? *Harvard Business Review*. July–August. pp30–46.

LEWIN, D. (2001) IR and HR perspectives on workplace conflict: what can each learn from the other? *Human Resource Management Review*. Vol 11, No 4. pp453–485.

LEWIN, K. (1947) Frontiers in group dynamics. *Human Relations*. Vol 1. pp5–42.

LEWIN, K. (1951) *Field Theory in Social Science*. New York/London: Harper & Row.

LEWIS, G. (2015) *Obsessive email checking damaging productivity and family life* *[online]* Available at: http://www.cipd.co.uk/pm/peoplemanagement/b/weblog/archive/2015/05/08/obsessive-email-checking-damaging-productivity-and-family-life.aspx [Accessed 11 January 2016].

LINSTEAD, S., FULLOP, L. and LILLEY, S. (2009) *Management and Organisation: A critical text*. 2nd ed. Basingstoke: Palgrave Macmillan.

LLOYD, M. and MAGUIRE, S. (2002) The possibility horizon. *Journal of Change Management*. Vol 3, No 2. pp149–157.

LOCKE, E.A. (1968) Towards a theory of motivation and incentives. *Organizational Behaviour and Human Performance*. Vol 3, No 2. pp157–189.

LOCKE, E.A. (1976) The nature and causes of job satisfaction. In: DUNNETTE, M.D. (ed.) *Handbook of Industrial and Organizational Psychology*. Chicago: Rand McNally.

LOCKE, E.A. and LATHAM, G.P. (1990) *A Theory of Goal-Setting and Task Performance*. Englewood Cliffs, NJ: Prentice Hall.

LOCKWOOD, N.R. (2007) *Leveraging Employee Engagement for Competitive Advantage: HR's strategic role*. Alexandria, VA: Society for Human Resource Management.

LOWRY, C. (2006) HR managers as ethical decision makers: mapping the terrain. *Asia Pacific Journal of Human Resource Management*. Vol 44, No 20. pp211–221.

LUPTON, T. (1991) Organisational change: top-down or bottom-up management? *Personnel Review*. Vol 20, No 3. pp4–10.

MABEY, C. and MAYON-WHITE, B. (eds) (1998) *Managing Change*. 2nd ed. Buckingham: Open University/Paul Chapman Publishing.

MACDONALD, D.J. and MAKIN, P.J. (2000) The psychological contract, organisational commitment and job satisfaction of temporary staff. *Leadership and Organization Development Journal*. Vol 21, No 2. pp84–91.

MACKAY, M. (2015a) Professional development seen as employment capital. *Professional Development in Education*. Vol 42, No 1. pp1–18.

MACKAY, M. (2015b) Identity formation: professional development in practice strengthens a sense of self. *Studies in Higher Education*. Vol 40, No 8. pp1–18.

MACKAY, M. and TYMON, A. (2014) Taking a risk to develop reflective skills in business practitioners. *Journal of Education and Work*. Vol 18, No 6. pp643–655.

MACKIE, J.L. (1977) *Ethics – Inventing Right and Wrong.* Harmondsworth: Penguin.

MACLEOD, D. and CLARK, N. (2009) *Engaging for Success: Enhancing performance through employee engagement.* London: Office of Public Sector Management.

MAGUIRE, H. (2002) Psychological contracts: are they still relevant? *Career Development International.* Vol 7, No 3. pp167–180.

MAHONEY, J. (1994) How to be ethical: ethics resource management. In: HARVEY, B. (ed.) *Business Ethics – A European Approach.* Hemel Hempstead: Prentice Hall.

MAMMAM, A., AKURATIYAGAMAGE, V.W. and REES, C.J. (2006) Managerial perceptions of the role of the human resource function in Sri Lanka: a comparative study of local, foreign-owned and joint venture companies. *International Journal of Human Resource Management.* Vol 17. pp2009–2020.

MARCHINGTON, M. (2015) Human resource management (HRM): too busy looking up to see where it is going longer term? *Human Resource Management Review.* Vol 25, No 2. pp176–187.

MARCHINGTON, M., CARROLL, M., GRIMSHAW, D. and PASS, S. (2009) *Managing People in Networked Organizations.* London: CIPD.

MARCHINGTON, M., GRIMSHAW, D., RUBERY, J. and WILLMOTT, H. (2005b) *Fragmenting Work: Blurring organizational boundaries and disordering hierarchies.* Oxford: Oxford University Press.

MARCHINGTON, M., RUBERY, J. and GRIMSHAW, D. (2011) *Alignment, Integration and Consistency in HRM across Multi-employer Networks.* London: CIPD.

MARCHINGTON, M., VINCENT, S. and COOKE, F.L. (2005a) The role of boundary-spanning agents in inter-organizational contracting. In: MARCHINGTON, M., GRIMSHAW, D., RUBERY, J. and WILLMOTT, H. (eds) *Fragmenting Work: Blurring organizational boundaries and disordering hierarchies.* Oxford: Oxford University Press.

MARKS, A. (2001) Developing a multiple foci conceptualization of the psychological contract. *Employee Relations.* Vol 23, No 5. pp454–469.

MARKS & SPENCER (2008) *About Plan A.* Available at: plana.marksandspencer.com [Accessed 18 April 2008].

MARRIS, P. (1986) *Loss and Change.* 2nd ed. London: Routledge & Kegan Paul.

MARSDEN, D. and FRENCH, S. (1998) *What a Performance: Performance-related pay in the public services.* London: Centre for Economic Performance.

MARTIN, G. (2012) *Lens on Talent, a Collection of Next Generation HR Thought Pieces. Part 2, August.* London: CIPD.

MASLOW, A.H. (1943) A theory of human motivation. *Psychological Review.* Vol 50, No 4. pp370–396.

MAURER, T. and CHAPMAN, E. (2013) Ten years of career success in relation to individual and situational variables from the employee development literature. *Journal of Vocational Behaviour.* Vol 83, No 3. pp450–465.

MAYFIELD, M. and MAYFIELD, J. (2012) Logo leadership: breathing life into loyalty and putting meaning back into work. *Development and Learning in Organizations*. Vol 26, No 2. pp11–15.

MAYON-WHITE, B. (1993) Problem-solving in small groups: team members as agents of change. In: MABEY, C. and MAYON-WHITE, B. (eds) *Managing Change*. 2nd ed. Buckingham: Open University/Paul Chapman Publishing.

MCCALL, M. (2010) Peeling the onion: getting inside experience-based leadership development. *Industrial and Organizational Psychology*. Vol 3,No 1. pp61–68.

MCCALMAN, J. and PATON, R.A. (1992) *Change Management*. London: Paul Chapman Publishing.

MCCLEAN, E. and COLLINS, C. (2011) High-commitment HR practices, employee effort, and firm performance: investigating the effects of HR practices across employee groups within professional services firms. *Human Resource Management*. Vol 50, No 3. pp341–363.

MCCLERNON, T. (2006) Rivals to systematic training. *Advances in Developing Human Resources*. Vol 8, No 4. pp442–459.

MCCRACKEN, M. and WALLACE, M. (2000) Towards a redefinition of strategic HRD. *Journal of European Industrial Training*. Vol 24, No 5. pp281–290.

MCDONALD, P., BROWN, K. and BRADLEY, L. (2005) Have traditional career paths given way to protean ones? Evidence from senior managers in the Australian public sector. *Career Development International*. Vol 10, No 2. pp109–129.

MCDOWALL, A. and SAUNDERS, M. (2010) UK managers'' conceptions of employee training and development. *Journal of European Industrial Training*. Vol 34, No 7. pp609–630.

MCGUIRE, D. and GUBBINS, C. (2010) The slow death of formal learning: a polemic. *Human Resources Development Review*. Vol 9, No 30. pp249–265.

MCLELLAN, D. (ed.) (2000) *Karl Marx: Selected writings*. Oxford: Oxford University Press.

MCNAIR, S. (2012) *Older People's Learning in 2012: A survey*. London: National Institute of Adult Continuing Education.

MEGGINSON, D. and WHITAKER, V. (2007) *Continuing Professional Development*. 2nd ed. London: CIPD.

MERCER SURVEY (2008/9) Available at:http://www.cos-mag.com/human-resources/hr-stories/2009-pay-increases-vary-greatly-by-industry-mercer-survey-finds.html [Accessed 10 January 2016].

MESSERSMITH, J.G., PATEL, P.C., LEPAK, D.P. and GOULD-WILLIAMS, J. (2011) Unlocking the black box: exploring the link between high-performance work systems and performance. *Journal of Applied Psychology*. Vol 96, No 6. pp1105–1118.

MEYER, J.P. and ALLEN, N.J. (1991) A three-component conceptualization or organizational commitment. *Human Resource Management Review*. Vol 1. pp61–89.

MEYER, J.P. and HERSCOVITCH, L. (2001) Commitment in the workplace: towards a general model. *Human Resources Management Review*. Vol 11. pp299–326.

MEYER, J.P and HERSCOVITCH, L. (2002) Commitment to organizational change: extension of a three-component model. *Journal of Applied Psychology*. Vol 87, No 3. pp474–487.

MILLER, D. (2004) Building sustainable change capability. *Industrial and Commercial Training*. Vol 36, No 1. pp9–12.

MILLS, C. (2010) HMRC running out of time to regain its sense of purpose. *The Times*. 14 January.

MILLWARD, N., BRYSON, A. and FORTH, J. (2000) All change at work: British employment relations 1980–1998 as portrayed by the Workplace Industrial Relations Series. In: BLYTON, P. and TURNBULL, P. (eds) *The Dynamics of Employee Relations*. 3rd ed. Basingstoke: Palgrave Macmillan.

MITCHELL, L. (2009) David Fairhurst interview. *Managing People*. 30 July. Available at: www.hrzone.co.uk. [Accessed 25 December 2009].

MOERSCHELL, L. (2009) Resistance to technological change in aacademia. *Current Issues in Education* Vol 11, No 6. pp1 –10.

MOHRMAN, A.M. and MOHRMAN, S.A. (1995) Performance management is 'running the business'. *Compensation and Benefits Review*. July–August. pp69–75.

MOLLEMAN, E. and TIMMERMAN, H. (2003) Performance management when innovation and learning become critical performance indicators. *Personnel Review*. Vol 32, No 1. pp93–113.

MORGAN, R. (2006) Making the most of performance management systems. *Compensation and Benefits Review*. Vol 38. pp22–27.

MORRISON, J. (2015) *Business Ethics: New challenges in a globalised world*. Basingstoke: Palgrave Macmillan.

M'PELE (2015) P.M. Flexible working: A win–win situation or a recipe for disaster? *People Management*. Available at: https://www.linkedin.com/grp/post/4004145–65045126590180917 [Accessed 21 September 2015].

MULLINS, L.J. (2007) *Management and Organisational Behaviour*. 8th ed. Harlow: FT/Prentice Hall.

MULLINS, L. (2010) *Management and Organisational Behaviour*. 9th ed. Harlow: FT/Prentice Hall.

MULLINS, L.J. (2013) *Management and Organisational Behaviour*. 10th ed. Harlow: Prentice Hall.

MUMFORD, E. (1995) Contracts, complexity and contradictions: the changing employment relationship. *Personnel Review*. Vol 24, No 8. pp54–70.

MURPHY, N. (2008a) Line manager's role in people management. *IRS Employment Review Survey*. Issue 894, 3 April. Available at: www.xperthr.co.uk/article/84008/survey-linespan-span-classhighlightmanagers-span-span-classhighlightrole-span-in-peoplespanclasshighlightmanagement.aspx?searchwords=murphy_2008_line_managers_role [Accessed 8 June 2010].

MURPHY, N. (2008b) HR roles and responsibilities. *IRS Employment Review Survey*. Available at: www.xperthr.co.uk/searchresults.aspx?s=murphy_2010 [Accessed 8 June 2010].

MURPHY, N. (2008c) Trends in recruitment methods in 2006 and 2007. *IRS Employment Review*. Issue 893. Available at: www.xperthr.co.uk [Accessed 16 May 2008].

MURRAY-WEST, R. (2002) Sunderland car workers are Europe's most productive. *Daily Telegraph*. 9 July.

NEEDLE, D. (2004) *Business in Context*. 4th ed. London: Thomson Learning.

NEEDLE, D. (2010) *Business in Context*. 5th ed. Andover: Cengage.

NEEDLE, D. (2015) *Business in Context*. 6th ed. Andover: Cengage

NELSON, D. and BERGMAN, D. (2013) Bangladesh dispatch: the miracle of Rana Plaza gives way to grief as body count rises. *Daily Telegraph*. 25 April.

NELSON, L. (2003) A case study in organisational change: implications for theory. *The Learning Organization*. Vol 10, No 1. pp18–30.

NEWBERY, C. (2015) *Case study: John Lewis Partnership [online]*. People Management [online] Available at: http://www.cipd.co.uk/pm/peoplemanagement/b/weblog/archive/2015/05/20/case-study-john-lewis-partnership.aspx [Accessed 3 February 2016].

NIELSEN, R. (2006) Introduction to the special issue. In search of organizational virtue: moral agency in organizations. *Organization Studies*. Vol 27, No 3. pp379–404.

NIJSSEN, M. and PAAUWE, J. (2012) HRM in Turbulent times: how to achieve agility. *International Journal of Human Resource Management*. Vol 23, No 16. pp3315–3335.

NOHRIA, N., GROYSBERG, B. and LEE, L. (2008) Employee motivation. *Harvard Business Review*. Vol 86, No 7/8. pp78–84.

NONAKA, I. and TAKEUCHI, H. (1995) *The Knowledge-Creating Company*. Oxford: Oxford University Press.

NOON, M. and BLYTON, P. (2002) *The Realities of Work*. 2nd ed. Basingstoke: Palgrave Macmillan.

NYE, J. (2008) *The Powers to Lead: Soft, hard, and smart*. Oxford: Oxford University Press.

OLSON, M. (2014) *The Business Partner Balancing Act: An Analysis of Alternative Employee Advocacy Practices in the Modern HR Function [online]* Available at: http://digitalcommons.ilr.cornell.edu/chrr/73 [Accessed 26 August 2015].

ONS (2010) Office for National Statistics. Available at: www.statistics.gov.uk [Accessed 24 March 2010].

ONS (2014) *An Analysis of Employee Contracts That do not Guarantee a Minimum Number of Hours*. Report. London: ONS.

OPEN UNIVERSITY (1985) Block 1. Managing and Messy Problems. Course T244. *Managing in Organizations*. Milton Keynes: Open University.

OUCHI, W. (1981) *Theory Z: How American business can meet the Japanese challenge*. Reading, MA: Addison-Wesley.

PAAUWE, J. (2009) HRM and performance: achievements, methodological issues and prospects. *Journal of Management Studies*. Vol 46, No 1. pp129–142.

PAAUWE, J. and BOSELIE, P. (2005) HRM and performance: what next? *Human Resource Management Journal*. Vol 15. pp68–83.

PAPAVASILEIOU, E.F and LYONS, S.T. (2015) A comparative analysis of the work values of Greece's 'Millenial' generation. *The International Journal of Human Resource Management*. Vol 26, No 17. pp 2166–2186.

PARKES, C. and DAVIS, A.J. (2013) Ethics and social responsibility – do HR professionals have the 'courage to challenge' or are they set to be permanent 'bystanders?' *The International Journal of Human Resource Management*. Vol 4, No 12. pp2411–2434.

PARRY, K. and SINHA, P. (2005) Researching the trainability of transformational organisational leadership. *Human Resource Development International*. Vol 8, No 2. pp165–183.

PATON, G. (2010) Exploited work experience students forced to make tea. *Daily Telegraph*. 11 January.

PATON, R.A. and MCCALMAN, J. (2000) *Change Management: Guide to effective implementation*. 2nd ed. London: Sage.

PATTERSON, M., WEST, M., LAWTHORN, R. and NICKELL, S. (1997) *Impact of People Management Practices on Business Performance*. London: Institute for Personnel and Development.

PEACOCK, L. (2010) Abercrombie & Fitch adverts run risk of discrimination claims. *Personnel Today*. Available at: www.personneltoday.com/articles/11/02/2010/54093/abercrombie.htm [Accessed 24 May 2013].

PERKIN, H. (1989) *The Rise of Professional Society – England since 1880*. London: Routledge.

PERKINS, S.J. and SHORTLAND, S.M. (2006) *Strategic International Human Resource Management*. 2nd ed. London: Kogan Page.

PERKINS, S.J. and WHITE. G. (2011) *Reward Management: Alternatives, consequences and context*. London: CIPD.

PERLMUTTER, H.V. (1969) The tortuous evolutions of the multinational corporation. *Columbia Journal of World Business*. January–February. pp9–18.

PERRY, M. (2001) Flexibility pays. Accountancy Age. In: (2002) *Human Resource Management International Digest*. Vol 10, No 4. pp13–15.

PERSONNEL TODAY (2008) *Survey reports continued growth in CPD importance [online]*. Available at: www.personneltoday.com/articles/04/09/2008/47385/survey-reports-continuedgrowth-in-cpd-importance.htm [Accessed 25 July 2013].

PERSONNEL TODAY (2012) *HR needs to invest in its own development, says report [online]*. Available at: www.personneltoday.com/articles/13/07/2012/58663/hr-needs-toinvest-in-its-own-development-says-report.htm [Accessed 24 May 2013].

PERSONNEL TODAY (2014) *Four areas to grow your HR career in 2014 [online]* Available at: http://www.personneltoday.com/hr/four-areas-grow-hr-career-2014 [Accessed 12 January 2016].

PESTON, R. (2007) Rose goes green in pursuit of profit. *BBC News website.* 15 January. Available at: news.bbc.co.uk [Accessed 18 April 2008].

PETERS, T.J. (1999) *The Brand You 50; Or: Fifty ways to transform yourself from an 'employee' into a brand that shouts distinction, commitment, and passion!* New York: Knopf Publishing.

PETTIGREW, A. (1985) *The Awakening Giant: Continuity and change at ICI.* Oxford: Blackwell.

PETTIGREW, A. and WHIPP, R. (1993) Understanding the environment. In: MABEY, C. and MAYON-WHITE, B. (eds) *Managing Change.* 2nd ed. London: Paul Chapman Publishing.

PIELKE, R. (2015) Keeping score at FIFA. *Transparency International [online]* Available at: http://blog.transparency.org/2015/08/10/keeping-score-at-fifa [Accessed 8 January 2016].

PILBEAM, S. and CORBRIDGE, M. (2006) *People Resourcing: Contemporary HRM in Practice.* 3rd ed. Harlow: FT/Prentice Hall.

PILBEAM, S. and CORBRIDGE, M. (2010) *People Resourcing and Talent Planning: HRM in Practice.* 4th ed. Harlow: FT/Prentice Hall.

PITCHER, G. (2008) Backlash against HR business partner model. *Personnel Today.* 29 January.

PLUMMER, K. (2010) *Sociology: The basics.* Abingdon: Routledge.

POLLERT, A. (1991) The orthodoxy of flexibility. In: POLLERT, A. (ed.) *Farewell to Flexibility?* Oxford: Blackwell.

POLLITT, D. (2003) Shift-pattern switch improves staff turnover and recruitment at Seeboard. *Human Resource Management International Digest.* Vol 11, No 1. pp12–14.

PORTER, M. (1985) *Competitive Advantage: Creating and sustaining superior performance.* New York: Free Press.

PORTER, M. (1998) *Competitive Strategy: Techniques for analyzing industries and competitors.* New York: Free Press.

PORTER, M.E. and KRAMER, M.R. (2006) Strategy and society: the link between competitive advantage and corporate social responsibility. *Harvard Business Review.* Vol 84, No 12. pp78–92.

POVAH, L. and SOBCZAK, K. (2010) A context-oriented approach to leader selection: a strategy for uncertain times. *People Strategy.* Vol 33, No 4. pp40–47.

PREECE, D. (2012) HRM in an organizational context. In GILMORE, S. and WILLIAMS, S. (eds) *Human Resource Management*. 2nd ed. Oxford: Oxford University Press.

PRICE, A. (2004) *Human Resource Management in a Business Context*. 2nd ed. London: Thomson.

PRICE, D. (ed.) (2009) *Principles and Practice of Change*. Basingstoke: Palgrave Macmillan.

PRICEWATERHOUSECOOPERS (2014) *Number of employees working overseas set to surge, but organisations struggle to recoup investment*. Report. Available at: http://pwc.blogs.com/press_room/2014/11/number-of-employees-working-overseas-set-to-surge-but-organisations-struggle-to-recoup-investment-pwc-report.html [Accessed 4 January 2016].

PRITCHARD, K. and SYMON, G. (2011) Identity on the line: constructing professional identity in a HR call centre. *Work, Employment and Society*. Vol 25, No. 3. pp434–450.

PUGH, D.S. and HICKSON, D.J. (1976) *Organizational Structure in Its Context*. Farnborough: Saxon House.

PULAKOS, E. (2009) *Performance Management: A new approach for driving business results*. Malden, MA: Wiley-Blackwell.

PURCELL, J. and AHLSTRAND, B. (1994) *Human Resource Management in the Multi-Divisional Company*. Oxford: Oxford University Press.

PURCELL, J. and HUTCHINSON, S. (2007) Front-line managers as agents in the HRM performance causal chain: theory, analysis and evidence. *Human Resource Management Journal*. Vol 17, No 1. pp3–20.

PURCELL, J., KINNIE, N., HUTCHINSON, S., RAYTON, B. and SWART, J. (2003) *Understanding the People and Performance Link: Understanding the black box*. London: CIPD.

QUATRO, S., WALDMAN, B. and GALVIN, D. (2007) Developing holistic leaders: four domains for leadership development and practice. *Human Resource Management Review*. Vol 17. pp427–441.

RAELIN, J. (2004) Don't bother putting leadership into people. *Academy of Management Executive*. Vol 18, No 3. pp131–135.

RAELIN, J. (2011) Work-based learning: how it changes leadership. *Development and Learning in Organizations*. Vol 25, No 5. pp17–20.

RAJAN, A. (2002) Meaning of leadership in 2002. *Professional Manager*. March. p33.

RAO, T.V. and VARGHESE, S. (2008) Trends and challenges of developing human capital in India. *Human Resource Development International*. Vol 12, No 1. pp15–34.

RAYNER, C. and ADAM-SMITH, D. (eds) (2009) *Managing and Leading People*. London: CIPD.

RAYNER, C., DJURKOVIC, N. and MCCORMACK, D. (2014) Who are you calling 'dirty'? Actors' and observers' perceptions of dirty work and implications for taint management. *International Journal of Work Organisation and Emotion*. Vol 6, No 2. pp209–222.

RAYNER, G. and SWINFORD, S. (2013) Chaos and faffing at BBC as Jimmy Savile scandal detonated. *Daily Telegraph*. 22 February. Available at: www.telegraph.co.uk [Accessed 22 April 2013].

REED CONSULTING SURVEY (2004) Available at: www.reedpressoffice.co.uk/docs/Employee%20Attrition.pdf [Accessed 4 June 2013].

REES, C., ALFES, K. and GATENBY, M. (2013) Employee voice and engagement: connections and consequences. *The International Journal Of Human Resource Management*. Vol 24, No 14. pp2780–2798.

REES, D. and MCBAIN, R. (2004) *People Management*. Basingstoke: Palgrave Macmillan.

REES, G. and SMITH, P.E. (eds) (2014) *Strategic Human Resource Management: An international perspective*. London: Sage.

REEVES, N. (2012) JT (formerly Jersey Telecom), Leadership Development Initiative. *People Management*. Available at: www.peoplemanagement.co.uk/pm/articles/2012/09/jtformerly-jersey-telecom-leadership-development-initiative.htm [Accessed 19 December 2012].

REEVES, R. (2008) The trouble with targets. *Management Today*. 8 January. Available at: www.managementtoday.co.uk/news/774435/the-trouble-with-targets [Accessed 5 June 2013].

REICHEL, A. and LAZAROVA, M. (2013) The effects of outsourcing and devolvement on the strategic position of HR departments. *Human Resource Management*. Vol 52, No 6. pp923–946.

REID, M., BARRINGTON, H. and BROWN, M. (2007) *Human Resource Development*. 7th ed. London: CIPD.

REVANS, R.W. (1982) What is action learning? *Journal of Management development*. Vol 1, No 3. pp64–75.

RICHARDSON, J. and MCKENNA, S. (2014) Towards an understanding of social networks among organizational self-initiated expatriates: a qualitative case study of a professional services firm. *International Journal of Human Resource Management*. Vol 25, No 19. pp2627–2643.

RIDDER, H.G., PIENING, E.P. and BALUCH, A.M. (2012) The third way reconfigured: how and why non-profit organizations are shifting their human resources management. *Voluntas*. Vol 23, No 3. pp605–625.

ROBBINS, S. (1993) *Organisational Behaviour: Concepts, controversies and applications*. 6th ed. Englewood Cliffs, NJ: Prentice Hall.

ROBERTS, P. (2006) Analysis: the defining phase of systematic training. *Advances in Human Resource Development*. Vol 8, No 4. pp476–491.

ROCHE, W.K. and TEAGUE, P. (2012) Do recessions transform work and and employment? Evidence from Ireland. *British Journal of Industrial Relations*. Vol 52, No 2. pp261–285.

RODRIGUES, C.A. (1988) Identifying the right leader for the right situation. *Personnel Today*. September. pp43–46.

RODWELL, J.J., NOBLET, A.J., STEAN, P., OSBORNE, S. and ALLISEY, A.F. (2008) Investigating people management issues in a third sector health care organisation – an inductive approach. *Australian Journal of Advanced Nursing.* Vol 27, No 2. pp55–62.

ROLLINSON, D. (2008) *Organisational Behaviour and Analysis: An integrated approach.* 4th ed. Harlow: FT/Prentice Hall.

ROPER, J. (2015) The war on modern slavery. *HR Magazine [online]* Available at: http://www.hrmagazine.co.uk/article-details/the-war-on-modern-slavery [Accessed 25 January 2016].

ROSE, S. (2007) Back in fashion: how we're reviving a British icon. *Harvard Business Review.* May. pp51–58.

ROSEN, M., BEDWELL, W., WILDMAN, J., FRITZSCHE, B., SALAS, E. and BURKE, C. (2011) Managing adaptive performance in teams: guiding principles and behavioral markers for measurement. *Human Resource Management Review.* Vol 21, No 2. pp107–122.

ROSENER, J. (1990) Ways women lead. *Harvard Business Review.* November–December. pp119–125.

ROSENFELD, R. and WILSON, D. (1999) *Managing Organisations: Texts, readings and cases.* 2nd ed. London: McGraw-Hill.

ROTHWELL, A. (2005) How HR professionals rate 'continuing professional development'. *Human Resource Management Journal.* Vol 15, No 3. pp18–32.

ROUSSEAU, D. (1995) *Psychological Contracts in Organizations: Understanding written and unwritten agreements.* London: Sage.

SABBAGH, D. (2012) George Entwistle: 23 years getting to the top of the BBC. Gone in 54 days. *The Observer.* 10 November. Available at: http://www.theguardian.com/media/2012/nov/10/george-entwistle-bbc-resigns-profile [Accessed 18 December 2012].

SADLER-SMITH, E., ALLINSON, C. and HAYES, J. (2000) Learning preferences and cognitive style: some implications for continuing professional development. *Management Learning.* Vol 31, No 2. pp239–256.

SALIMAKI, A., HAKONEN, A. and HENEMAN, R. (2009) Managers generate meaning for pay. *Journal of Managerial Psychology.* Vol 24, No 2. pp161–177.

SANTOS, J., CAETANO, A. and TAVARES, S. (2015) Is training leaders in functional leadership a useful tool for improving the performance of leadership functions and team effectiveness. *The Leadership Quarterly.* Vol 26. pp470–484.

SARGEANT, M. and LEWIS, D. (2014) *Employment Law.* 7th ed. Harlow: Pearson.

SAUNDERS, M.N.K. and THORNHILL, A. (2006) Forced employment contract change and the psychological contract. *Employee Relations.* Vol 28, No 5. pp449–467.

SCHAUMBERG, R. and FLYNN, F. (2012) Uneasy lies the head that wears the crown: the link between guilt proneness and leadership. *Journal of Personality and Social Psychology.* Vol 103, No 2. pp327–342.

SCHEIN, E. (1978) *Career Dynamics: Matching the individual and organisational needs.* Reading, MA: Addison-Wesley.

SCHEIN, E. (1984) Coming to a new awareness of organizational culture. *Sloan Management Review.* Vol 25, No 2. pp3–16.

SCHULER, R.S., DOWLING, P.E. and DE CIERI, H. (1993) An integrative framework of strategic international human resource management. *Journal of Management.* Vol 19, No 2. pp419–59.

SCHYNS, B. and HANSBROUGH, T. (2010) *When leadership goes wrong: Destructive leadership, mistakes, and ethical failures.* Charlotte, NC.: IAP.

SCHYNS, B. and HANSBROUGH, T. (2012) The romance of leadership scale and causal attribution. *Journal of Applied Social Psychology.* Vol 42, No 8. pp1870–1886.

SCHYNS, B., KIEFER, T., KERSCHREITER, R. and TYMON, A. (2011) Teaching implicit leadership theories to develop leaders and leadership: how and why it can make a difference. *Academy of Management Learning and Education.* Vol 10, No 3. pp397–408.

SCHYNS, B., TYMON, A., KIEFER, T. and KERSCHREITER, R. (2013) New ways to leadership development: a picture paints a thousand words. *Management Learning.* Vol 44, No 1. pp11–24.

SEARLE, R. (2003) *Selection and Recruitment: A critical text.* Milton Keynes: Palgrave Macmillan in association with the Open University.

SEARLE, R.H. and SKINNER, D. (2011) New agendas and perspectives. In: SEARLE, R.H. and SKINNER, D. (eds) *Trust and Human Resource Management.* Cheltenham: Edward Elgar Publishing.

SEARS, L. (2010) *Next Generation HR: Time for change – towards a next generation HR.* London: CIPD.

SEGAL, J. (2010) Performance management blunders. *HR Magazine.* November. pp75–78.

SEIBERT, S., KRAIMER, M. and LINDEN, R. (2001) A social capital theory of career success. *Academy of Management Journal.* Vol 44, No 2. pp219–237.

SELDEN, S.C. and SOWA, J.E. (2015) Voluntary turnover in non-profit human service organizations: the impact of high performance work practices. *Human Service Organizations Management Leadership and Governance.* Vol 39, No 3. pp182–207.

SELIGMAN, M. (1998) *Learned Optimism.* New York: Simon & Schuster.

SEMLER, R. (1993) *Maverick: The success story behind the world's most unusual workplace.* London: Arrow Books.

SENGE, P. (1993) *The Fifth Discipline: The art and practice of the learning organisation.* New York: Random House.

SENIOR, B. and SWAILES, S. (2010) *Organisational Change.* 4th ed. Harlow: FT/Prentice Hall.

SENNETT, R. (1998) *The Corrosion of Character: The personal consequences of work in the new capitalism.* London: Norton.

SHARP, R. (2009) Total reward at Arup. *IRS Employment Review.* Issue 916. 19 February.

SHARP, R. (2015) *Public-sector pay 2014/15: pay restraint continues [online]* Available at: http://www.xperthr.co.uk/survey-analysis/public-sector-pay-201415-pay-restraint-continues/154029 [Accessed 4 January 2016].

SHEN, J., CHANDRA, A., D'NETTO, B. and MONGA, M. (2009) Managing diversity through human resource management: an international perspective and conceptual framework. *International Journal of Human Resource Management.* Vol 20, No 2. pp235–251.

SIMPSON, S. (2010) Volcano update: seven things employers should be doing. *Personnel Today.* 22 April. Available at: www.personneltoday.com [Accessed 23 April 2010].

SINCLAIR, A. (2007) *Leadership for the disillusioned.* Crowsnest, NSW: Allen and Unwin.

SIRKIN, H.L, KEENAN, P. and JACKSON, A. (2005) The hard side of change management. *Harvard Business Review.* Vol 83, No 10. pp108–118.

SLATER, M. (2012) *Olympic Cycling: Marginal gains underpin Team GB dominance [online]* Available at: http://www.bbc.co.uk/sport/0/olympics/19174302 [Accessed 4 January 2016].

SLOMAN, M. (2007) *The Changing World of the Trainer.* London: Routledge.

SOUTHWICK, S.M., VYTHILINGAM, M. and CHARNEY, D.S. (2005) The psychobiology of depression and resilience to stress: implications for prevention and treatment. *Annual Review of Clinical Psychology.* Vol.1. pp255–291.

SPARROW, P.R. (2005) Global human resource management. In: SHAMS, M. and JACKSON, P. (eds) *Developments in Work and Organizational Psychology: Implications for international business.* London, New York and Amsterdam: Elsevier.

SPARROW, P.R. (2012) Globalising the international mobility function: the role of emerging markets, flexibility and strategic delivery models. *International Journal of Human Resource Management.* Vol 23, No 12. pp2404–2427.

SPRINGETT, N. (2002) The impact of corporate purpose on strategy, organisations and financial performance. *Human Resources and Employment Review.* Vol 2, No 2. pp117–124.

SPRINGETT, N. (2004) Corporate purpose as the basis of moral leadership of the firm. *Strategic Change.* Vol 13, No 6. pp297–307.

STAHL, G.K., BJORKMAN, I., FARNDALE, E., MORRIS, S.S., PAAUWE, J., STILES, P., TREVOR, J. and WRIGHT, P. (2012) Six principles of effective global talent management. *MIT Sloan Management Review.* Vol 53, No 2. pp25–32.

STERNBERG, E. (2000) *Just Business.* 2nd ed. Oxford: Oxford University Press.

STEVENS, M. (2013) Employers are from Mars, young people are from Venus. *People Management.* Available at: www.cipd.co.uk/pm/peoplemanagement/b/weblog/archive/2013/04/25/employers-are-from-mars-young-people-are-from-venus.aspx [Accessed 25 April 2013].

STEWART, J. and CURETON, P. (2014) *Designing, Delivering and Evaluating L & D.* London, CIPD.

STEWART, J. and MCGOLDRICK, J. (eds) (1996) *Human Resource Development: Perspectives, strategies and practice*. London: Pitman.

STOGDILL, R. (1948) Personal factors associated with leadership: a survey of the literature. *Journal of Psychology*. Vol 25. pp35–71.

STOREY, J. (1983) *Managerial Prerogatives and the Question of Control*. London: Routledge.

STOREY, J. (1989) From personnel management to human resource management. In: STOREY, J. (ed.) *New Perspectives on Human Resource Management*. London: Routledge.

STOREY, J. (1992) *Developments in the Management of Human Resources*. Oxford: Blackwell.

STOREY, J. (1995) *Human Resource Management: A critical text*. London: Routledge.

STOUT, L. (2012) *The Shareholder Value Myth*. San Francisco: Berrett-Koehler.

SUBRAMONY, M. (2009) A Meta-analytic investigation of the relationship between HRM bundles and firm performance. *Human Resource Management*. Vol 48, No 5. pp745–768.

SUFF, R. (2008) Business partnering at the AA. *IRS Employment Review*. Issue 908.

SUFF, R. (2012a) Recruiting and selecting graduates: 2012 XpertHR survey. *IRS Employment Review*. Available at: www.xperthr.co.uk/article/114836/recruiting-span-andspan-classhighlightselecting-span-span-classhighlightgraduates–2012-xperthrsurvey. aspx?searchwords=recruiting+and+selecting+graduates [Accessed 28 November 2012].

SUFF, R. (2012b) XpertHR recruitment trends survey 2012: activity picks up. *IRS Employment Review*. Available at: www.xperthr.co.uk/article/112441/xperthrrecruitment-span-span-classhighlighttrends-span-span-classhighlightsurvey-2012–activity-picks-p. aspx?searchwords=recruitment+trends+survey [Accessed 21 March 2012].

SUFF, R. (2013a) Using corporate websites for recruitment: 2013 XpertHR survey. Available at: http://www.xperthr.co.uk/survey-analysis/using-corporate-websites-for-recruitment-2013-xperthr-survey/115260/ [Accessed 12 January 2016].

SUFF, R. (2013b) Using job boards for recruitment: 2013 XpertHR survey. Available at: www.xpertHR.co.uk/articleusingjobboardsforrecruitment [Accessed 30 January 2013].

SULLIVAN, J., WONG, W., ADUSUMILLI, D., ALDER, A., BLAZEY, L., HUGGETT, M. and PARKIN, J. (2009) *Deal or No Deal? An exploration of the modern employment relationship*. The Future of HR Working Paper. London: The Work Foundation.

SULLIVAN, S. (1999) The changing nature of careers: a review and research agenda. *Journal of Management*. Vol 25, No 3. pp457–484.

SULLIVAN, S. and BARUCH, Y. (2009) Advances in career theory and research: a critical review and agenda for future exploration. *Journal of Management*. Vol 35, No 6. p1542.

SUROWIECKI, J. (2004) *The Wisdom of Crowds*. New York: Doubleday.

SUTHERLAND, J. (2009) WERS Report. Training and employee use of skills in Scotland: some evidence. *Fraser Economic Commentary*. Vol 33, No 1. pp60–64.

SUUTARI, V. and BREWSTER, C. (2000) Making their own way: international experience through self-initiated foreign assignments. *Journal of World Business*. Vol 35, No 4. pp417–436.

SWART, J., KINNIE, N., RABINOWITZ, J., LUND, M., SNELL, S., MORRIS, S. and KANG, S.C. (2007) *Managing across boundaries: human resource management beyond the firm*. London: CIPD.

TAKEUCHI, R., LEPAK, D. and SWART, J. (2011) How organizations evaluate and maintain fit of human capital with their needs. In: BURTON-JONES, A. and SPENCER, J. C. (eds) *Oxford Handbook of Human Capital*. Oxford: Oxford University Press.

TAMKIN, P., BARBER, L. and HIRSH, W. (1995) *Personal Development Plans: Case studies of practice*. Brighton: Institute for Employment Studies.

TAMS, S. and ARTHUR, M. (2010) New directions for boundaryless careers: agency and interdependence in a changing world. *Journal of Organizational Behaviour*. Vol 31, No 5. pp629–646.

TAN, V. and TIONG, T.N. (2005) Change management in times of economic uncertainty. *Singapore Management Review*. Vol 27, No 1. pp49–68.

TANNENBAUM, R. and SCHMIDT, W.H. (1973) How to choose a leadership pattern. *Harvard Business Review*. May–June. pp162–180.

TAYLOR, F.W. (1911) *Principles of Scientific Management*. New York: Harper.

TAYLOR, R. (2002) The future of work–life balance. *Human Resource Management International Digest*. Vol 10, No 4. pp13–15.

TESCO (2008) Tesco.com website [Accessed 13 September 2004; 16 February 2005; 4 May 2008].

THE NEXT GENERATION OF MARCOMS EUROPEAN REPORT (2013) European Communications School.

THE UK LEARNING TRENDS INDEX (2015) *Good Practice*. Available at: www.goodpractice.com [Accessed 4 January 2016].

THOMAS, R.M. (2001) *Recent Theories of Human Development*. Thousand Oaks, CA: Sage.

THOMAS, R. (2009) The business environment of human resource management. In GILMORE, S. and WILLIAMS, S. (eds) *Human Resource Management*. Oxford: Oxford University Press.

THOMPSON, P. and MCHUGH, D. (2009) *Work Organisations: A critical approach*. 4th ed. Basingstoke: Palgrave Macmillan.

THOMSON, P. (2008) The business benefits of flexible working. *Strategic HR Review*. Vol 7, No 2. pp17–22.

THUNNISSEN, M., BOSELIE, P. and FRUTYIER, B. (2013) A review of talent management: 'infancy or adolescence?' *The International Journal of Human Resource Management*. Vol 24, No 9. pp1744–1761.

TOMLINSON, F. and SCHWABENLAND, C. (2010) Reconciling competing discourses of diversity? The UK non-profit sector between social justice and the business case. *Organisation*. Vol 17. pp101–121.

TOMPROU, M., ROUSSEAU, D.M. and HANSEN, S.D. (2015) The psychological contracts of violation victims: a post-violation model. *Journal of Organizational Behavior*. Vol 36, No 1. pp561–581.

TORRINGTON, D., HALL, L. and TAYLOR, S. (2002) *Human Resource Management*. 5th ed. Harlow: FT/Prentice Hall.

TORRINGTON, D., HALL, L. and TAYLOR, S. (2008) *Human Resource Management*. 7th ed. Harlow: FT/Prentice Hall.

TORRINGTON, D., HALL, L., TAYLOR, S. and ATKINSON, C. (2014) *Human Resource Management*. 9th ed. Harlow: FT/Prentice Hall.

TOWNSEND, R. (1981) *Up the Organisation*. Greenwich, CT: Fawcett.

TOYNBEE, P. (2008) MPs must fulfil Labour's pledge to low paid and temporary workers. *The Guardian*. 23 February. p33.

TRAINING MAGAZINE (2012) *Training Magazine Ranks 2012 Top 125 Organizations [online]*. Available at: www.trainingmag.com [Accessed 17 January 2013].

TRAINING MAGAZINE (2015) *Training Magazine Ranks 2015 Top 125 Organizations [online]*. Available at: http://www.trainingmag.com/training-magazine-ranks-2015-top-125-organizations [Accessed 4 January 2016].

TREVINO, L.K. and NELSON, K.A. (2014) *Managing Business Ethics: Straight Talk about How to Do It Right*. 6th ed. John Wiley & Sons.

TRUSS, C. and GILL, J. (2009) Managing the HR function: the role of social capital. *Personnel Review*. Vol 38, No 6. pp674–695.

TRUSS, C., SOANE, E. and EDWARDS, C. (2006) *Working Life: Employee attitudes and engagement 2006*. Research report. London: CIPD.

UKCES (2009) *National Employer Skills Survey 2009. Key Findings Report*. March. London: UK Commission for Employment and Skills.

UKCES (2012) *National Employers Skills Survey 2011*. Available at: www.ukces.org.uk/publications/er46-employer-skills-survey-2011-england-results [Accessed 2 May 2013].

ULRICH, D. (1997) *Human Resource Champions: The next agenda for adding value and delivering results*. Boston, MA: Harvard Business School Press.

ULRICH, D. and BROCKBANK, W. (2005) *The HR Value Proposition*. Boston, MA: Harvard Business School Press.

ULRICH, D. and SMALLWOOD, N. (2004) Capitalizing on capabilities. *Harvard Business Review*. Vol 82, No 6. pp119–127.

ULRICH, D., YOUNGER, J. and BROCKBANK, W. (2008) The twenty-first-century HR organization. *Human Resource Management*. Vol 47, No 4. pp829–850.

VAIMAN, V., HASLBERGER, A. and VANCE, C. M. (2015) Recognizing the important role of self-initiated expatriates in effective global talent management. *Human Resource Management Review*. Vol 25, No 3. pp280–286.

VAN BUREN, H.J., GREENWOOD, M. and SHEEHEN, C. (2011) Strategic human resource management and the decline of employee focus. *Human Resource Management Review*. Vol 21, No 30. pp209–219.

VAN DIERENDONCK, D. (2010) Servant leadership: a review and synthesis. *Journal of Management*. Vol 37, No 4. pp1228–1261.

VAN WANROOY, B., BEWLEY, H., BRYSON, A. FORTH, J., FREETH, S., STOKES, L. and WOOD, S. (2013) *Employment Relations in the Shadow of the Recession*. Basingstoke: Palgrave Macmillan.

VERBRIGGHE, J. and BUYENS, D. (2015) Adding value and HRM practice: evidence-based HR. In: ANDRESEN, M. and NOWAK, C. (eds), *Human resource management practices: assessing added value*. pp15–30.

VILANOVA, M., LOZANO, M. and ARENAS, D. (2009) Exploring the nature of the relationship between CSR and competitiveness. *Journal of Business Ethics*. Vol 87. pp57–69.

VISSER, W. (2012) *The Quest for Sustainable Business: An epic journey in search of corporate responsibility*. Sheffield: Greenleaf Publishing.

VOEGTLIN, C. and GREENWOOD, M. (2013) CSR and HRM: A review and conceptual analysis. *Academy of Management Proceedings*. Issue 1.

VON BERGEN, C.W., SOPER, B. and PARNELL, J.A. (2005) Workplace diversity and organisational performance. *Equal Opportunities International*. Vol 24, No 3/4. pp1–16.

VROOM, V. (1964) *Work and Motivation*. New York: John Wiley.

WAHRENBURG, M., HACKETHAL, A., FRIEDRICH, L. and GELLRICH, T. (2006) Strategic decisions regarding the vertical integration of human resource organizations: evidence for an integrated HR model for the financial services and non-financial services industry in Germany, Austria and Switzerland. *International Journal of Human Resource Management*. Vol 17, No 10. pp1726–1771.

WAIN, D. (2009) Command performance. *People Management*. Vol 15, No 23. p17.

WAINWRIGHT, S., CLARK, J. AND GRIFFITH, M. (2006) *The UK Voluntary Sector Almanac*. London: NVCVO Publications.

WALUMBWA, F., AVOLIO, B.J., GARDNER, W.L, WERNSING, T. and PETERSON, S. (2008) Authentic leadership: development and validation of a theory-based measure. *Journal of Management*. Vol 34, No 1. pp89–126.

WANG, C., INDRIDASON, T. and SAUNDERS, M. (2010) Affective and continuance commitment in public private partnership. *Employee Relations*. Vol 32, No 4. pp396–417.

WANG, D. and SHYU, C. (2008) Will the strategic fit between business and HRM strategy influence HRM effectiveness and organizational performance? *International Journal of Manpower*. Vol 29, No 2. pp92–110.

WANG, G.G. and SUN, J.Y. (2009) Clarifying the boundaries of human resource development. *Human Resource Development International.* Vol 12, No 1. pp93–103.

WARECH, M. and TRACEY, J.B. (2004) Evaluating the impact of human resources: identifying what matters. *Cornell Hotel and Restaurant Administration Quarterly.* Vol 45. pp76–87.

WARREN, C. (2009) HR and OD 'should be one and the same'. *People Management.* 20 November.

WARING, J. (2002) The link between the management of employees and patient mortality in acute hospitals. *International Journal of Human Resource Management.* Vol 13, No 8. pp1299–1310.

WATERMAN, R., WATERMAN, J. and COLLARD, B. (1994) Toward a career resilient workforce. *Harvard Business Review.* July–August. pp87–95.

WATSON, T.J. (2006) *Organising and Managing Work.* 2nd ed. Harlow: FT/PrenticeHall.

WATSON, T.J. (2012) *Sociology Work and Organisation.* 6th ed. Abingdon: Routledge.

WEBER, M. (1947) *The Theory of Social and Economic Organization.* Oxford: Oxford University Press.

WEST, M., BORRIL, C., DAWSON, J., SCULLY, J., CARTER, M., ANELAY, S., PATTERSON, M., MALCOLM, G. and WARING, J. (2002) The link between the management of employees and patient mortality in acute hospitals. *International Journal of Human Resource Management.* Vol 13, No 8. pp1299–1310.

WHITE PAPER (1999) Available at: archive.cabinetoffice.gov.uk/moderngov/download/modgov.pdf [Accessed 27 January 2010].

WHITFORD, A. (2003) *Why You Can't Ignore Internet Recruitment: One-stop guide [online]* Available at: http://www.xperthr.co.uk/commentary-and-analysis/online-recruitment-why-you-cant-ignore-internet-recruitment/38314/ [Accessed 16 May 2008].

WIGHT, G. (2007) Bending the rules: Surrey County Council embraces flexible working. *Development and Learning in Organizations.* Vol 21, No 4. pp20–21.

WIGNALL, A. (2004) Work in progress. *The Guardian.* 21 September.

WILEY, C. (2000) Ethical standards for human resource management professionals: a comparative analysis of five major codes. *Journal of Business Ethics.* Vol 25. pp93–114.

WILKINSON, T., BOOHAN, M. and STEVENSON, M. (2014) Does learning style influence academic performance in different forms of assessment? *Journal of Anatomy.* Vol 224. pp304–308.

WILLIAM, N. (2008) Competency-based interviews and online psychometric tests are best for choosing candidates. *Personnel Today.* 10 March. [Accessed 7 May 2008].

WILLIAMS, R.S. (1998) *Performance Management: Perspectives on employee performance.* London: International Thomson Business Press.

WILLIAMS, S. (2014) *Introducing Employment Relations: a critical approach.* 3rd ed. Oxford: Oxford University Press.

WILSON, E. and ILES, P. (1999) Managing diversity – an employment and service delivery challenge. *International Journal of Public Sector Management*. Vol 12, No 1. pp27–48.

WILSON, F.L. (2006) *Organizational Behaviour and Work: A critical introduction*. 2nd ed. Oxford: Oxford University Press.

WOLFF, C. (2008) Wychavon District Council: staff engagement proved vital to success. *IRS Employment Review*. Issue 909. 17 November.

WOMACK, J.P. and JONES, D.T. (1996) *Lean Thinking: Banish waste and create wealth in your corporation*. Simon & Schuster: London.

WOOD, A. (2013) *Boris Johnson Opens Level 39 at Canary Wharf [online]*. Available at: http://techcitynews.com/2013/03/19/canary-wharf-launches-level39/ [Accessed 3 May 2013].

WOOD, J., ZEFFANE, R., FROMHOLTZ, M., WIESNER, R. and CREED, A. (2010) *Organisational Behaviour*. 2nd ed (Australasia). Milton, Queensland: John Wiley & Sons.

WOODALL, J. and GOURLAY, S. (2004) The relationship between professional learning and continuing professional development in the United Kingdom. In WOODALL, J., LEE, M. and STEWART, J. (eds) *New Frontiers in HRD*. London: Routledge.

WOODALL, J., SCOTT-JACKSON, W., NEWHAM, T. and GURNEY, M. (2009) Managing the decision to outsource human resources. *Personnel Review*. Vol 38, No 3. pp236–52.

WOODS, D. (2011) UK talent acquisition costs rise to £5,311 per hire, compared to £2,226 in US. *HR Magazine*. Available at: www.hrmagazine.co.uk [Accessed 30 January 2013].

WOODWARD, J. (1965) *Organisation and Technology*. Oxford: Oxford University Press.

WORKFORCE MANAGEMENT (2004) Available at: www.workforce.com/section/09/feature/23/85/39/index.html [Accessed 30 April 2010].

WORK FOUNDATION (2003) *The Missing Link: From productivity to performance*. Work and Enterprise Panel of Inquiry. London: The Work Foundation.

WORK FOUNDATION (2009) *Quality People Management for Quality Outcomes: The future of HR review on evidence on people management*. Report. July. London: The Work Foundation.

WORK FOUNDATION (2010) *Employability and Skills in the UK: Redefining the debate. A report prepared for the London Chamber of Commerce and Industry Commercial Education Trust [online]* Available at: http://www.theworkfoundation.com/assets/docs/lcci-cet%20future%20skills%20policy%20final%2001%2011%2010.pdf [Accessed 11 January 2016].

WRIGHT, C. (2008) Reinventing human resource management: business partners, internal consultants and the limits of professionalization. *Human Relations*. Vol 61, No 8. pp1063–1086.

WRIGHT, P.M. and HAGGERTY, J.J. (2005) Missing variables in theories of strategic human resource management: time, cause and individuals. *Management Review*. Vol 16. pp164–173.

WRIGHT, P.M. and MCMAHAN, G. (1992) Theoretical perspectives for strategic human resources management. *Journal of Management*. Vol 18, No 2. pp295–320.

XPERT HR (2008) International HR: the people agenda. *Personnel Today*. 24 November.

XPERT HR (2012a) How employers align HR with the business: 2012 XpertHR survey. *Employment Review*. 30 July

XPERT HR (2012b) *Do you have a behaviour policy for the work Christmas party? [online]*. Available at: http://www.xperthr.co.uk/hr-benchmarking/question/160088/do-you-have-a-behaviour-policy-for-the-work-christmas-party.aspx [Accessed 11 January 2016].

XPERT HR (2014a) *WorkGuru: an online solution to employee resilience [online]*. Available at: http://www.xperthr.co.uk/commentary-and-analysis/workguru-an-online-solution-to-employee-resilience/152463/? [Accessed 9 January 2014].

XPERT HR (2014b) *HR Careers [online]*. Available at: http://www.xperthr.co.uk/survey-analysis/hr-roles-and-responsibilities-2014-xperthr-survey/152858 [Accessed 11 January 2016].

YORKS, L., LAMM, S. and O'NEIL, J. (1999) Transfer of learning from action learning programs to the organizational setting. *Advances in Developing Human Resources*. Vol 1. p56.

YUKL, G. (2006) *Leadership in Organisations*. 6th ed. London: Prentice Hall.

YUKL, G. (2009) *Leadership in Organisations*. 7th ed. Harlow: Pearson International.

YUKL, G. (2012) *Leadership in Organisations*. 8th ed. Harlow: Pearson

ZALEZNIK, A. (1977) Managers and leaders: are they different? *Harvard Business Review*. Vol 55 (May–June). pp67–78.

ZALEZNIK, A. (1992) Managers and leaders: are they different? *Harvard Business Review*. Vol 72, No 2. pp126–135.

ZHELTOUKHOVA, K. (2015) Are business ethics HR's business? Blog. Available at: http://www.cipd.co.uk/community/blogs/b/research-blog/archive/2015/09/30/are-business-ethics-hr-s-business [Accessed 30 September 2015].

ZIGURS, I. (2003) Leadership in virtual teams: oxymoron or opportunity? *Organizational Dynamics*. Vol 31, No 4. pp339–351.

Index